HISTORY

OF

ENGLAND.

VOL. V

HISTORY

OF

ENGLAND

FROM THE PEACE OF UTRECHT

TO THE PEACE OF VERSAILLES.

1713—1783.

BY LORD MAHON.

IN SEVEN VOLUMES.—VOL. V.

1763—1774.

THIRD EDITION, REVISED.

BOSTON:
LITTLE, BROWN, AND COMPANY.
1853.

CONTENTS

OF

THE FIFTH VOLUME.

CHAPTER XLI.

CHAPTER XLII.

CHAPTER XLIII.

CHAPTER XLIV.

CHAPTER XLV.

CHAPTER XLVI.

CHAPTER XLVII.

CHAPTER XLVIII.

CHAPTER XLIX.

CHAPTER L.

THE

HISTORY OF ENGLAND

FROM

THE PEACE OF UTRECHT.

CHAPTER XLI.

THE first ten years of the reign of George the Third are marked by frequent change of ministers, and intricate evolution of parties. To thread the maze which these afford is not always a pleasant, nor always a profitable, task. The want both of great men and of great objects is too often painfully apparent. Chatham, but Chatham only at this time, like some lofty pine tree in the forest, soars high above the under-growth of Rockinghams and Hillsboroughs, while the creeping parasite plants—the Rigbys and the Dodingtons—trail along the ground.

A knowledge of the party changes during these ten years is indeed essential to the study of English politics. But before we again embark upon them it may be instructive to reflect how far less important they were to the well-being of the country, than some other not so striking events which History does not always deign to record. What are they to the gradual extension of our manufacturing and commercial greatness? What are they to the growth of such cities as Manchester and Glasgow? What are they to that system of agricultural improvement under which so many a barren down has teemed with luxuriant harvests,—that system unknown to Virgil, which, leaving no fallow to the soil, loses no profit to the husbandman? How little thought does the mere annalist bestow upon these things in parallel with White Staves or Gold Sticks, or at least with the exact succession of Prime Ministers! Yet when no man of real genius succeeds to the helm,—when the spectacle is only of a crowd of mediocrities, distinguished from each other by nothing but their party badges, who throng and jostle for places, and shove off each other in turn,—can the philosopher doubt to which of these classes of events the greater weight is due? Or will posterity always lend a willing ear to the contests between the Noble Earl in the green riband and the Noble Marquis in the blue?

The very year of which I now resume the narrative was distinguished by an event of more real importance than the rise or the resignation of Lord Bute. In 1763 an artisan of Staffordshire, Mr. Josiah Wedgwood, produced a new kind of cream-coloured earthenware, superior both in fineness and in durability to the French and Dutch. The tide of public taste immediately turned in its favour, the foreign earthenwares were neglected, and the home-made preferred. In the following years Mr. Wedgwood introduced many new kinds of porcelain of various colours and sizes. Until then the district called "the Potteries" had been of slight significance. But so much did this branch of industry grow and thrive that, according to Mr. Wedgwood's evidence before the House of Commons in 1785, there were then employed upon it in that district only from fifteen to twenty thousand persons. "And thus," says the annalist of trade, "thus "are the meanest materials, the clay and flint stones "under our feet, converted into objects of the greatest "utility and beauty." *

Still far more essential was the progress which the same period beheld in Lancashire and Yorkshire. At the beginning of the century the yearly exports of cotton goods did not much exceed in value 20,000*l.*, while the yearly exports of woollen goods, now so inferior by comparison, amounted to 2,000,000*l.* In 1750 the cotton

* Macpherson's History of Commerce, vol. iii. p. 381—383.

exports had risen to no more than 45,000*l.* Towards 1766 Mr. Postlethwayte, in his "Universal Dictionary "of Trade," estimates the annual value manufactured of what were termed Manchester wares (made however at many other places beside Manchester) at 600,000*l.*, of which one third went to foreign countries. These, he tells us, were sent on pack-horses to London, Bristol, Liverpool, and other ports for shipment. Up to that time it has been observed that the machines used in the cotton trade of England were nearly as simple as those of India. It was only that the loom was better constructed, and that cards for combing the cotton had been adopted from the woollen trade.* With woollens indeed the old form of the shuttle and lathe may still be noticed in Hogarth's first picture of "Industry and Idleness," where the two apprentices are seen at their looms. But an era of great discoveries was now at hand. It came, as few discoveries have done, not from men of leisure and learning, but from the poor, the illiterate, the lowly. Sir Richard Arkwright had no advantages of birth or study. He was the thirteenth child of humble parents; he was by trade a barber. Happily for his country and for his descendants (now the heirs of millions of pounds sterling) he turned his strong clear mind to mechanical invention. He discovered, or at least he perfected, a machine for spinning by rollers. His first patent, for which funds were not obtained without much difficulty and solicitation, bears the date of 1769. The greatest improvements in that machine were afterwards effected by himself. In the ensuing year, namely 1770, another patent was granted to James Hargreaves, a poor weaver, the inventor of the Spinning Jinny. A further stride in advance was made by the discovery of the Mule; this also is due to a weaver of the common rank,—to Samuel Crompton. It was first completed in 1779, having cost its inventor nearly five years of experiment and toil, "wherein"—these are his own words in a letter to a friend—"every moment of time and power of mind, as

* All these facts are derived from the seventh and part of the eighth chapters of Mr. Baines's History of the Cotton Trade, p. 84—115.

"well as expense, which my other employment would "permit, were devoted to this one end." *

No human sagacity could have foreseen, none at least did foresee, how strong the impulse, how wide the extension, which this era of discovery imparted to the cotton trade. Such words as twentyfold, thirtyfold, an hundredfold scarcely convey an adequate representation of the real fact. From Manchester as from their capital or centre, and along whole lines of country, mills were built and factories were formed; hamlets have swelled to villages, villages to towns, and towns to cities; and gathering strength with each successive year that gigantic system has still rolled onwards, until, as at present, we behold it give bread to many hundreds of thousands of our people, and clothing to the world.

This new manufacturing system, so honourable for its skill and enterprise, and so mighty in its commercial aspects, but far indeed from unmingled good, — in which the most deplorable poverty and ignorance have grown up side by side with enormous wealth, — might most aptly perhaps be reviewed in treating of these years when it received its last and greatest developments by the discovery and application of the steam engine. The early years of George the Third, however, may claim as more especially their own those new facilities for the transport of goods and raw materials, which nothing but steam could supersede, — that network of canals which, contributing in the highest degree to our commercial progress, formed in fact the transition state between the old high road and the modern railway.

Of the British internal navigation Francis, the third and last Duke of Bridgewater, has been surnamed the Father. He was born in 1736, and succeeded as a boy to his title and estates. For that very reason, perhaps, his education was very much neglected. To the last he appears to have known nothing of politics or books. No higher sayings are recorded of him, even in his later years, than that he preferred brown meats to white, and that the day which brought him no letters might be called a DIES NON. At the age of twenty-two he was deeply

* Extract in Mr. Baines's History, p. 199.

smitten with the charms of one of the two Gunning sisters — those far-famed beauties of their day. But this suit did not prosper. The lady preferred to him a more accomplished rival, Colonel Campbell, afterwards Duke of Argyle.* This early disappointment appears to have sunk deep into the mind of the shy and proud young man. All his relish for society was gone. He retired to his domain of Worsley, about seven miles from Manchester There stood an antique manor house, black and white timbered, near the same spot on which more lately almost a palace has been reared. There the state of the property had already engaged the Duke's attention. The soil was rich in coal mines, but the coal lay useless within the earth from the difficulty and expense of the land carriage. A canal nearly straight to Manchester had been projected, but on further inquiry and reflection, with the ground before him, the Duke's idea was much extended; he engaged with ardour in a larger scheme, and to this and the like undertakings henceforth devoted his entire fortune and his whole remaining life.

Happily for the Duke at this juncture he did not fall into the hands of knaves or false pretenders. He found at once in James Brindley a most able instrument to carry out his ends. Brindley was thirty years older than his patron. Born at the opposite extremity of the social scale, he was equally, or more than equally, neglected in his training. It has been said of him, probably with some exaggeration, that at least for many years he could not write, having only learnt how to sign his own name. Be this as it may, he had an inborn and intuitive genius for mechanical skill. When the canal from Worsley on its extended scheme was intrusted to his making, he determined that it should be perfect of its kind, and wholly

* In the Quarterly Review (No. cxlvi. p. 301—318.) is contained a graceful and pleasing sketch of the Duke of Bridgewater's life, ascribed to the heir of his name and fortune, the present Earl of Ellesmere. The reviewer relies on a family tradition, that the Duke was not rejected, and himself broke off the match; a tradition supported by some MS. letters of later date which I have seen, but opposed to the contemporary evidence. (Walpole to Conway, January 28., and Lord Chesterfield to his son, February 2. 1759.)

free from the usual obstruction of locks. For this purpose it was necessary to raise stupendous mounds of earth, and, maintaining an uniform level, convey the water straight across the valleys. With no great difficulty he completed his works as far as Barton, where the Irwell is navigable for large vessels. Here Brindley proposed to carry the canal over that river by an aqueduct of thirty-nine feet above the surface of the stream. To most men this appeared a wild and fantastic design. "Let the Duke," said Brindley, "before he decides, consult another engineer." Accordingly a gentleman eminent in the profession was brought to the spot. Brindley pointed out, high above, the place of his intended aqueduct, upon which the other gentleman drily said, "I have often heard "of castles in the air, but I never before was shown where "any of them were to be erected!" It is greatly to the Duke of Bridgewater's credit that he stood firm against this sneer. The aqueduct was immediately begun, and was carried on with so much speed and so much success as to astonish all those who had so recently turned it into ridicule.

It should be noted that, besides this line of open navigation, Brindley was constructing other lines of subterranean canals, by which the main produce of the Worsley coal fields was brought out in boats. These most singular and skilful works have been gradually augmented as new pits were opened and old ones became exhausted. Their vast amount at present may justly excite surprise. In 1843 the total length of these navigable tunnels on the Duke's estate was upwards of forty-two miles, of which, however, only one third was in actual use.*

The Duke, perceiving more and more the importance of inland navigation, extended his ideas to Liverpool. In 1762 he obtained another Act of Parliament for branching his canal to the tideway in the Mersey. This part of the canal is carried across both the Mersey and the Bollan and over deep and wide valleys. In the execution of every part Brindley displayed the utmost skill and ingenuity. Yet the progress of prosperity was by no means uniform, nor yet immediate. Monied men —

* Quarterly Review, No. cxlvi. p. 317.

the prudent and the steady as they called themselves — shook their heads and kept their purses closed. Large as was the Duke's estate, it proved unequal to the strain upon it. So low did his credit sink that at one time his bill for 500*l.* could scarcely be cashed in Liverpool. He found it necessary to send his agent, John Gilbert, to ride round the neighbouring districts of Cheshire, and to borrow small sums from the farmers. On one occasion the enterprising agent, greatly to his own dismay, found himself mistaken for a highwayman. But under every difficulty the Duke showed a resolute energy of purpose. He diminished his establishment at Worsley, brought his personal expenses within the narrow limits of 400*l.* a year, and bade his engineer proceed.

Brighter days soon came. In 1766 was begun the canal from the Trent to the Mersey, which Brindley emphatically named "the Grand Trunk Navigation." Not long before his death in 1772 he drew the plans for and directed the Oxfordshire Canal, connected through Coventry with the Trent on one side and with the Thames upon the other. Thus in the course of only a few years was opened an inland water communication across the island from Liverpool to London.

During this period other men of wealth had trod in the footsteps of the Duke of Bridgewater; other men of genius in Brindley's. High among the latter stood Smeaton and Watt. Smeaton, already famous for that lighthouse of Eddystone, which has now well nigh for a century breasted the Atlantic waves, laid out in 1767 the line of the great canal connecting the Forth and Clyde. Watt, who, as the principal improver of the steam engine, may deserve to be ranked among the foremost benefactors of mankind, was employed at the same time in planning and executing other works of Scottish navigation, — a canal, for instance, to convey the produce of the Monkland collieries to Glasgow.

It is worthy of note that scarce any of the great improvements which I have here commemorated were free at first from the obstructions of prejudice and ignorance. In 1768 a mob broke into the house of Hargreaves and destroyed his jinnies. Hargreaves found it necessary to escape as might a felon from his native town of Blackburn, and seek shelter at Nottingham. Eleven years later, his machinery having been perfected by others, there ensued fresh riots against it. By that time the jinnies which had only twenty spindles were admitted to be beneficial, and these accordingly the rioters spared, but those with a greater number being pronounced mischievous were either torn to pieces or cut down to the prescribed dimensions.* A large mill built by Arkwright near Chorley was wholly destroyed. Mr. Peel, grandfather of the celebrated statesman, saw his machinery at Altham flung into the river, and was in personal danger from the fury of the people. Thus again in 1769, when there was pending in Parliament the Bill for the canal between Coventry and Oxford, I find that several petitions were presented against it as prejudicial to one most important service,—the seamen employed in the coal trade.† From popular errors of this kind the more remote districts or distant dependencies were of course still less exempt. As late as the year 1769 a law was passed in Virginia prohibiting inoculation for the small-pox, and imposing on it as on a crime a penalty of 1,000*l*.‡ Thus incompetent judges are the multitude of their own true interest! So ill could any Government, depending solely on their pleasure, promote in truth the greatest happiness of the greatest number!

The great works and the great discoveries of this period — discoveries of which it may be said that in their final results they are destined to overspread and civilise the globe — were yet all but overlooked by their contemporaries amidst the stir and strife of their party politics. To these I must now return.

Lord Bute had succeeded in concluding the war. He had succeeded in obtaining for his Peace the approval of large majorities in Parliament. Yet he found that his success in both these objects had by no means lessened his remaining difficulties. Several statesmen, Pitt especially, had till then, however sorely tried by libels and

* Baines's History of the Cotton Trade, p. 158. and 159.

† See the Cavendish Debates, vol. i. p. 337.

‡ Note of Mr. Jared Sparks to Washington's Writings, vol. v. p. 22, and Hening's Statutes at Large, vol. viii. p. 371.

lampoons, maintained a lofty moderation, and descanted on the need of harmony and concord to carry on the war. Thus, for instance, in the debate on the declaration of hostilities from Spain, Pitt had eloquently exclaimed: "This is no season for altercation and recrimination. "A moment is come when every Englishman should stand "forth for his country. Arm the whole! Be one people! "Forget every thing but the public. I set you the ex- "ample. Harassed by slanderers, sinking under pain "and disease, for the public I forget both my wrongs and "my infirmities." *

When once, however, the Preliminaries had been signed, and Parliament was called on to express an opinion in their favour, we have seen elsewhere how fiercely Pitt had darted forth even from his sick bed to oppose them. No consideration of public danger any longer stood in his way; no necessity of warlike armaments remained to curb his tongue. Since my description of that memorable scene of the 9th of December 1762 some further details have been supplied by the publication of Horace Walpole's contemporary Memoirs. We there find how eager was the expectation of his coming; how prevalent the doubt whether his illness might not keep him away. At length a shout from the thronged streets was heard by the assembled Members; the doors were thrown open; and in the midst of a large acclaiming concourse was seen Mr. Pitt borne along in the arms of his servants. He was set down at the Bar from whence, by the aid of a crutch and of several friends, he crawled to his seat on the front Opposition bench. His countenance appeared emaciated and ghastly; his dress was of black velvet, but both hands and feet were swathed in flannel. His speech, which, as I have elsewhere said, extended to three hours and a half, he delivered sitting down at in-

* Edinburgh Review, No. clxii. p. 546., a passage in which Mr. Macaulay, by judicious condensation, has in all probability brought much nearer to the original the words reported in Lord Orford's Memoirs of the Reign of George III., vol. i. p. 134. This, the second series, of the Memoirs from the pen of Horace Walpole, is comprised in four volumes, extending from 1760 to 1771. They were first published from the MS. in 1845, and edited with much ability and candour by Sir Denis Le Marchant.

tervals by the hitherto unprecedented indulgence of the House; his voice was faint and low, and he was more than once compelled to take a cordial before he could proceed. At the conclusion his agony of pain was such as to compel him to leave the House without taking part in the division. When he passed out the huzzas which had greeted his coming redoubled, and the multitude catching at the length of his speech as a topic of praise shouted again and again: "Three hours and a half! Three hours "and a half!"

From the length of this speech, and from the state of languor in which it was spoken, it could not be ranked amongst the highest oratorical achievements of Pitt.* Yet it comprised several passages of great beauty, and the slightness of its effect on the division which followed may perhaps be explained by the corrupt traffic which is said to have preceded it. We are assured that Fox, on accepting the lead of the House of Commons, had undertaken to purchase a majority in favour of the Peace. A kind of mart for Members of Parliament was opened by him at his own, the Paymaster's, office. It is alleged that the lowest bribe for a vote upon the Peace was a bank note of 200*l.*, and that Mr. Martin, the Secretary of the Treasury, afterwards acknowledged 25,000*l.* to have been thus expended in a single morning.† Charges of that nature, which it is easy to make and impossible to disprove, are always to be received with much reserve. For my own part I am inclined wholly to reject them. Yet I must acknowledge that in this case they derive some indirect corroboration, first, from the character of Henry Fox as the least scrupulous of all Sir Robert Walpole's pupils, and, secondly, because the immense majority obtained by the Government on this single point of the Preliminaries, was held as in no degree a token of its permanent strength, or of the general support which

* "It is impossible for a human creature to speak well for three "hours and a half." (Lord Chesterfield to his son. Dec. 13. 1762.) Several speeches of Sir Robert Peel, one of Mr. Brougham on Feb. 7. 1828, and another of Lord Stanley on May 25. 1846, occur to me as strong proofs of the contrary.

† Lord Orford's Memoirs of George III. vol. i. p. 199.

the House of Commons might hereafter be willing to bestow.

On the re-assembling of Parliament after the Christmas holidays it became apparent how shifting and uncertain was the ground on which the Government depended. Thus, for example, when Beckford, seconded by Pitt, moved an Address to the King to prefer officers on half pay to those whose commissions were more recent, Fox, as the Ministerial leader, opposed it, but in vain. Another day, on a Committee of Accounts, Beckford having desired Fox to save appearances, Fox replied, that he never minded appearances, but — he was going to say realities, when a loud burst of laughter from the whole House interrupted him. On sitting down he exclaimed to Onslow, son of the late Speaker: "Did you ever see "a man in my situation so treated?" Another day besides, when Fox presented a petition from the sufferers by the late war in Newfoundland, he found himself faintly supported by one colleague, Sir Francis Dashwood, and directly withstood by another, Mr. George Grenville; and at last on a point of informality in the signatures he was obliged to ask pardon and withdraw the paper. It is clear from our wholesome system of yearly estimates and public accounts, and from the scanty amount either of Secret Service Money or of Ministerial contributions, that such corruption, as is alleged on the Preliminaries, could, if indeed at all, take place only on few and rare occasions. It is clear also that such corruption, when not supported by any eminent public services, did not add to, but rather took away from, the subsequent weight and popularity of those who practised it. For, as a great historian has observed, the tempters to evil deeds bear ever afterwards a reproving and hateful aspect, even in the eyes of those with whom they had unhappily prevailed.*

While Fox was thus browbeat in the Commons, he was, on the other hand, by no means smiled upon at Court. Lord Bute and the Princess Dowager had only raised him to power at their utmost need, and as their

* Malorum facinorum ministri quasi exprobrantes aspiciuntur. (Tacit. Annal., lib. xiv. c. 62.)

best instrument to carry through the Peace, but that object once achieved, they — and still more their dependents — treated him with ill-disguised aversion. To explain the cause of that aversion we must notice some secret rumours of the day. It was known that the King about the time of his accession had conceived a romantic passion for one of the most lovely of his subjects, — the young and blooming Lady Sarah Lennox, sister of the Duke of Richmond, and sister-in-law of Fox. It was whispered that His Majesty had even formed the scheme or the wish to make her the partner of his throne. Such a thought might be properly and justly resisted to the uttermost by the Princess Dowager and, at her instigation, by Lord Bute. Such a thought might as naturally rouse and kindle the ambitious hopes of Fox. It was observed in the spring of 1761 that the King used almost every morning to ride along the Kensington road, while Lady Sarah, fancifully attired as a shepherdess, used to stand close by, on the lawn of Holland House, making hay.* Finally, however, His Majesty, feeling the manifold objections that might attend his marriage with one of his own subjects, generously sacrificed his inclinations to the remonstrances of his mother and to the good of his people. Lady Sarah on her part with a high spirit suppressed whatever chagrin she may have felt. On the King's nuptials with the Princess of Mecklenburg, which shortly followed, she appeared as one of the bridesmaids, — ten young ladies of the highest rank and beauty who had been appointed at the ceremony to bear the train of their new Sovereign. In the ensuing year Lady Sarah became the wife of Sir Charles Bunbury. Yet although the whole transaction had thus terminated with high honour to the King, and without scandal or discredit to any other of the parties concerned, the remembrance of it still rankled, as a ground of hatred against Fox, in the mind of the Princess Dowager.

With such sources of mortification both below and above him, it is not strange that Fox became weary of his invidious elevation in the House of Commons, and de-

* Lord Orford's Memoirs of George III., vol. i. p. 64.

sired to quit it for his promised reward, — the ease and dignity of the peerage.

Apart from such cabals, and looking to the immediate conduct of affairs, the main difficulty of the Government seemed to lie in the finances. During the war the yearly excess of expenditure had been provided for by yearly loans, but such a system could not of course be permanent, and it was found that after all reductions, and for the first year of peace, the estimates would still, though slightly, outrun the supplies. The funded debt had grown to above a hundred millions, the floating debt, or the deficit on former estimates, to three and a half.* For this last sum, as well as for the future equalization of income and expenditure, it became urgent to provide, by two measures, a new loan and a new tax, — strange followers in the train of the Peace so lately concluded!

To cope with these difficulties became the task of the newly appointed Chancellor of the Exchequer, Sir Francis Dashwood. He had travelled in Italy, and had acquired taste and skill in the fine arts, as even now the frescoes at his house of West Wycombe, though mouldering with damp and neglect, remain to show. But his profligate morals are no less denoted by another painting also still preserved. In this he allowed himself to be delineated with the habit of a Franciscan friar, and upon his knees, but with the Venus de Medici before him as the object of his adoration.† He was in truth and almost professedly what is termed a man of pleasure; an associate of Wilkes and Lord Sandwich; a partaker in the orgies of Medmenham Abbey. In public life he had hitherto shown no knowledge of finance, but only plain good sense, and he had been chiefly remarkable for his high Tory politics, which the public said must have been his sole recommendation with Lord Bute.

With such a Chancellor, — "my Chancellor," as Lord Bute was accused of calling him too much in the Regal

* See the Abstract of the Supplies in the Annual Register, 1763, p. 175—190.

† A full description of this picture is given in the "New Found- "ling Hospital for Wit," vol. iii. p. 78. ed. 1784. It is still, I believe, in the possession of the Society of *Dilettanti* at the Thatched House.

style *, — there was little likelihood of the Exchequer thriving. The loan was disposed of without publicity or open competition, and the shares rose almost immediately to eleven per cent. of premium. Thus was afforded a reason for alleging that the bargain had been most improvident, and a pretext for the calumny that the Favourite and his friends had secured the shares for themselves to their own enormous emolument, and to the public loss.† Nor was the reputation of Sir Francis Dashwood retrieved by the Budget which he brought forward at nearly the same time. Overwhelmed by the magnitude of the occasion, his usual plain good sense appeared to have forsaken him; his speech was conveyed in mean and common language, and yet was wanting in perspicuity and clearness. His good sense, however, made him afterwards conscious — which fools are seldom — of his failure. "What shall I do?" he exclaimed to some friends. "People will point at me and cry: 'There 'goes the worst Chancellor of the Exchequer that ever 'lived!'"‡

The matter of the new Budget pleased as little as its oratory. Sir Francis proposed, besides some additional duties on wines, a new tax on cyder and perry, amounting to ten shillings on the hogshead, and to be paid by the first buyer. The City of London, which had lately chosen Pitt's friend, Alderman Beckford, against his own wishes, as Lord Mayor, and which was well prepared to take part against anything or everything emanating from Lord Bute, forthwith raised an angry cry, and sent petitions against the scheme, not only to the House of Commons, but to the Lords and to the King. On more obvious grounds of interest the western counties, as Worcestershire and Devonshire, were eager and loud in their complaints. The ancient loyalty of these districts — "the "Cyderland," as they were termed, — was not forgotten. It had been proved in King Charles's battles. It had

* North Briton, No. 42. See also vol. iv. p. 278. of the Collection relative to Mr. Wilkes, published in 1772.

† "History of the Minority," p. 100. Parl. Hist. vol. xv. p. 1305.

‡ Lord Orford's Memoirs of George III., vol. i. p. 250.

been chaunted in the Cyder-poet's verse.* How grievous the enormity to lay a special and peculiar tax upon such well affected counties! In the eyes of some exasperated country gentlemen and orchard gardeners it seemed little short of a tax upon loyalty itself.

So loud indeed were the complaints, and so many the cavils, that Bute and Dashwood speedily agreed to some modification of their scheme. They proposed a duty no longer of ten shillings, but only of four shillings, the hogshead, to be paid not by the first buyer but by the grower. The produce of the tax was then estimated at only 75,000*l.* Even thus there remained the hardship that there being various kinds of cyder varying in price from five to fifty shillings on the hogshead, the same duty was laid indiscriminately upon all. This change, moreover, involved the necessity that the grower should be made liable to the regulations of excise and to the visits of excisemen. And the mere name of extending the excise immediately opened a more formidable class of objections. The old weapons which had been brandished against Sir Robert Walpole in 1733 were again unsheathed. A petition from the City of London prayed "that the meritorious subjects of this country may not feel an extension of excise laws among the first fruits of peace."† In the House of Commons Pitt thundered against the intrusion of hired officers into private dwellings, and quoted the proud old maxim that every Englishman's house was, or should be, his castle.

* "Oh Charles! Oh best of Kings!

. . . .

"Yet was the Cyder-land unstained with guilt;
"The Cyder-land, obsequious still to thrones,
"Abhorred such base, disloyal deeds, and all
"Her pruning-hooks extended into swords!"

John Philips, CYDER, book ii.

In France likewise the Bretons are celebrated both for loyalty and cyder. A late traveller observes, between Lorient and Rennes: "La route est parsemée de petites auberges; il en sortait une femme qui nous demandait en Breton si nous voulions un verre de cidre. Je faisais signe que oui; et réellement ce cidre n'était point désagréable. Cette soirée a été charmante." (Mém. d'un Touriste (M. Beyle), vol. ii. p. 127. ed. Bruxelles, 1838.)

† Parl. Hist. vol. xv. p. 1309.

George Grenville, who had hitherto stood sullenly aloof because he thought himself neglected, rose on this occasion, unfortunately for himself, to support his wavering colleagues, and to answer his eloquent kinsman. He bid the House remember the profusion with which the late war had been carried on, — a profusion which alone, he said, had made new taxes necessary. If the Right Honourable Gentleman objected to this particular tax, he was bound to tell them where else he would have taxes laid. "Let him tell me where!" he repeated. "I say, Sir, "let him tell me where!" While dwelling for some time on this phrase in a peevish and monotonous voice, Pitt, who sat opposite, and who had been provoked by Grenville's reflections on the profusion of the war, quoted from his seat, and in nearly the same tone as Grenville's, a line from a well known song — "Gentle Shepherd, tell "me where!" And then starting up he added some sentences of bitter ridicule. The laughter of the House may be imagined, nor probably did it diminish when Grenville resumed his speech in a transport of rage: "If," he cried, "gentlemen are to be treated with this contempt —." Pitt had already left his seat, and was deliberately and in the most public manner walking out of the House, — a common practice with him when desiring to manifest that he thought the subject or the speaker unworthy of attention, — but at the word "contempt" he turned round, and made a marked and sarcastic bow to his foaming kinsman, — "the most contemptuous look and manner that I "ever saw," says Mr. Rigby, who was present.* This scene fixed on Grenville during several years "the Gentle "Shepherd" as a nick-name, which in the opinion of those who used it had the more point and pungency from the contrast between the pastoral character in poetry and his own starched and ungainly mien.

During the progress of the Cyder Bill in the House of Commons there were many divisions taken against it, but in spite of all the clamour out of doors, the Opposition could never muster so many as 120 votes. In the Upper House it drew forth keen attacks from Lords Hardwicke, Lyttleton, and Temple; and thirty-nine Peers recorded

* Bedford Correspondence, vol. iii. p. 219.

their votes against it; the first time it is said when that branch of the Legislature ever divided on a money-Bill. At the beginning of April the tax on cyder had become the law of the land; the other business of the Session was also well-nigh completed, and a prorogation without any further political event was speedily expected.

Meanwhile, from several other quarters, and on many other grounds, the clamours against Lord Bute rose higher and higher. A swarm of libellers had closed upon him, ready with their buzz and sting, and each no sooner flapped away than thirsting to come back. Foremost among these stood John Wilkes, a name which, partly from his own skill and boldness, but much more from the ill-judged resentment which he provoked, will often re-occur in the course of this History as the object of popular admiration and applause. He was born in 1727, the son of a rich distiller. Early in life he set up a brewery for himself, but soon relinquished the wearisome business. Early in life also he improved his fortune by his marriage with the daughter and heiress of Mr. William Mead, a rich drysalter.* But this lady, being of maturer age than himself, and of slight personal attractions, was speedily slighted, and he left her with as much disgust as he had his brewery. In 1757 he was elected Member of Parliament for Aylesbury, but never obtained any success as an orator, his speeches being, though flippant, yet feeble. In truth he had no great ability of any kind, but dauntless courage and high animal spirits. Nor should we deny him another much rarer praise, — a vein of good humour and kindliness which did not forsake him through all his long career, amidst the riot of debauchery or the rancour of faction. So agreeable and insinuating was his conversation that more than one fair dame as she listened found herself forget his sinister squint and his ill-favoured countenance. He used to say of himself in a laughing strain, that though he was the ugliest man in England, he wanted nothing to

* In the sketch of Wilkes's Life, to be found in the Ann. Register 1797, p. 370., this lady is erroneously called the daughter of the celebrated Dr. Mead, the author of the Treatise on Poisons. Dr. Mead had only two daughters; the one married to Dr. Wilmot, and the other to Dr. Nicholls. (1853.)

make him even with the handsomest but half an hour at starting.

Politics indeed seemed at first wholly alien from Wilkes's sphere; gaiety and gallantry were his peculiar objects. For some time he reigned the oracle of green rooms and the delight of taverns. In conjunction with other kindred spirits, as Paul Whitehead and Sir Francis Dashwood, amounting in all to twelve, he rented Medmenham Abbey, near Marlow. It is a secluded and beautiful spot on the banks of the Thames, with hanging woods that slope down to the crystal stream, a grove of venerable elms, and meadows of the softest green. In days of old it had been a convent of Cistertian monks, but the new brotherhood took the title of Franciscans in compliment to Sir Francis Dashwood, whom they called their Father Abbot. On the portal, now again in ruins, and once more resigned to its former solitude and silence, I could still a few years since read the inscription placed there by Wilkes and his friends: FAY CE QUE VOUDRAS.* Other French and Latin inscriptions, now with good reason effaced, then appeared in other parts of the grounds, some of them remarkable for wit, but all for either profaneness or obscenity, and many the more highly applauded as combining both.† In this retreat the new Franciscans used often to meet for summer pastimes, and varied the round of their debauchery by a mock celebration of the principal Roman Catholic rites.

The pleasures of Wilkes combined with his election contests in 1757 and 1761 to embarrass his affairs. As Member for Aylesbury he had formed a political connection with the Lord Lieutenant of the county, Earl Temple, and had received from him the appointment of Lieutenant-Colonel in the Buckinghamshire regiment of Militia. Through the same patronage he looked forward to some

* Copied from the Abbey of Theleme in Rabelais. See Book i. ch. 57.

† These are transcribed and described (from the pen, as is alleged, of Wilkes himself,) in the "Foundling Hospital for Wit," vol. iii. p. 104—108. In like manner Sir Francis Dashwood had set up in his garden at West Wycombe two urns, sacred to the Ephesian widow and to Potiphar's wife, with the inscriptions: MATRONÆ EPHESIÆ CINERES. DOMINÆ POTIPHAR CINERES.

more lucrative post,—the embassy of Constantinople perhaps, or the government of Canada. But he found his applications slighted by the influence, as he believed, of Lord Bute, and in October 1761 the secession of Pitt and Temple from the Government annihilated the source of his hopes. Seeing that he could not be a placeman, he resolved to be a patriot. His first performance was a tract on the recent negotiations with Spain, and in June 1762 he began conjointly with Churchill the publication of the celebrated periodical paper—the "North Briton." In this, as I have elsewhere shown*, he manifested a fierce and persevering hostility, not only against Lord Bute, but against the whole Scottish people. He had to compete with two rival papers on the opposite side,—the "Briton" conducted by Smollett, and the "Auditor" conducted by Murphy,—but Wilkes, being by far the more vituperative and unreasonable, speedily obtained the larger share of the popular favour.

On this subject, as on many others, the demeanour of Pitt was in striking contrast to that of Lord Temple. Seldom have two such near kinsmen, and for the most part friends, differed so essentially in temper and feeling. Of Lord Temple it was currently believed, if not as yet certainly known, that he continued in secret his amicable connection with Wilkes, viewed him as an excellent instrument of Opposition, and connived at, nay even prompted and encouraged, the most rancorous productions of his pen. Pitt, on the other hand, lofty and unbending as ever, publicly denounced as false and calumnious these insults on the Scots, asserted their merits even at the height of their unpopularity in England, and prided himself on having been the means, by the Highland regiments which he had raised, of reclaiming so many brave and loyal spirits to the service of the Crown.

Up to this time it had been usual for pamphleteers and satirists in England to carry on their warfare against the initials only of the great men whom they assailed. The North Briton first departed from this practice, and ven-

* Vol. iv. of this History, p. 259. On Wilkes's general character see the sketch in the Annual Register, 1797, p. 369., and the article by M. Dezos de la Roquette in the *Biographie Universelle*.

tured to print at full length even the redoubted names of Lord Bute and his Royal Master. Slight as this change may be deemed, there was in it an appearance of boldness such as will always attract attention and often win support. Nor did Wilkes's political opponents find their former friendship with him afford any immunity from his attacks. Thus the Abbot of Medmenham was most unsparingly lashed as soon as he became Chancellor of the Exchequer. With some others, as with Lord Talbot, Wilkes embroiled himself needlessly and wantonly. Lord Talbot was son of the late Chancellor, and had been recently promoted to an Earldom; a man of no mean ability in public life, but, like Wilkes himself, of licentious morals in private. Twenty years before, when already married, he had borne off from her husband the beautiful Duchess of Beaufort.* He was now held up to ridicule by Wilkes for inordinate flattery, on the ground that when officiating at the late Coronation as Lord High Constable, and having to appear on horseback in Westminster Hall, he had backed his horse to the gate that he might not turn his own back upon the King. The fiery Peer sent a challenge to the careless libeller, and there ensued a duel between them by moonlight on Bagshot Heath. Neither fire took effect, and the conflict ended in compotation. According to Wilkes's own account, drawn up the next day: "His Lordship "desired that we might now be good friends and retire "to the inn to drink a bottle of claret together, which "we did with great humour and much laugh."

It was part of Wilkes's character to be animated by the notoriety of such collisions rather than deterred by their danger. Through all the debates on the Cyder Bill, through all the negotiations for the definitive treaty of peace, he continued to rail in the bitterest terms against the Favourite. "The great cry against Lord "Bute," writes Chesterfield, "was upon account of his "being a Scotchman, the only fault which he could not "possibly correct."† But besides this original crime,

* H. Walpole to Sir H. Mann, June 10. 1742. This Duchess was the daughter and heiress of the last Lord Scudamore.

† Characters, as printed in Correspond., vol. ii. p. 473. ed. 1845.

there was urged against him the further fault of undue preference and partiality to his countrymen. Thus Ramsay, a Scotchman, had been named the Court painter, in preference to Reynolds. Thus Adam, another Scotchman, had been named the Court architect, and was accused of bringing several hungry kinsmen in his train.* Why, it was asked, should we show so much partiality to Scotchmen while Scotchmen show so little to us,—while since the Union there can be named only one gentleman of English birth who has been elected Member for any place in Scotland? †

On impartial examination, however, it will be found that the cases of national partiality in Lord Bute were by no means numerous, nor yet extending to the higher offices of state. Even his own private secretary — in which beyond all others a national or personal bias may be fairly indulged — was born south of Tweed. This was Mr. Charles Jenkinson, a man of slender patrimony, or, perhaps to speak more truly, of none at all, but who by his application and aptitude for state affairs gave lustre to his name. He did not fill any important post until the close of 1778, when he succeeded Lord Barrington as Secretary-at-War, and when the cry of secret influence, which had died away as regarded Lord Bute, was with little reason revived against him. But he rose at last to be Earl of Liverpool, and his son to be Prime Minister of England.

The patronage of literature which Lord Bute had at his outset too ostentatiously professed was also in its exercise much inveighed against. The cavils indeed which at the time were numerous against Dr. Johnson's pension only recoil on those who uttered them. Never was any stipend more richly earned by literary merit, or more

* " 'Four Scotchmen, by the name of Adam,
" 'Who keep their coaches and their Madam,'
" Quoth John in sulky mood to Thomas,
" 'Have stole the very river from us.' "

See the "Foundling Hospital for Wit," vol. iv. p. 189. Robert Adam had planned the Adelphi Buildings, which were thought to encroach upon the Thames.

† Annual Register, 1770, p. 114. This single exception was Mr. Chauncy Townshend.

nobly employed in charitable deeds. But Lord Bute can scarcely be defended for having granted a similar pension to Shebbeare, or for having refused a professorship to Gray. Dr. Shebbeare was a hackney pamphleteer, who had once stood in the pillory for a libel on George the First, and had more recently been concerned in some fraudulent practices at Oxford when employed to arrange the Clarendon papers. Gray, who was not only a great poet but a most accomplished scholar, wished to be appointed Professor of Modern Languages at Cambridge, notwithstanding his avowed dislike of his academical associates.* But he found preferred to him an obscure tutor of Sir James Lowther, for no better reason apparently than because Sir James had lately married the eldest daughter of the Favourite.

From several such appointments and selections, nearly all on the Tory side, not merely a Tory but even a Jacobite bias came to be imputed to Lord Bute. See, said his opponents in further proof, how graciously and warmly was received at Court the Address from the University of Oxford,—that University so notorious for its attachment to the exiled race of Stuart,—that University against which General Stanhope had to send a troop of horse! † Even Dr. King, well known as the Pretender's correspondent, has been admitted to kiss hands! ‡ But then, asked the friends of Lord Bute with better reason, should no effort be made in a new reign to put an end to the unhappy divisions of the former? Ought not loyalty, however late, to be welcomed, nay invited? And why should cordiality to the lately Jacobite University of Oxford be held to imply coldness to the ever Hanoverian University of Cambridge?

But far harder was the task of vindication when Lord Bute's friends heard him arraigned for wide stretches of

* "Cambridge is a delight of a place now there is nobody in it! "I do believe you would like it if you knew what it was without inhabitants." Gray to Dr. Clarke, August 12. 1760. The account of his disappointment in the affair of the professorship is given by himself, with great temper and good humour, in his letter to Dr. Warton of December 4. 1762.

† See vol. i. p. 158.

‡ Dr. King's Anecdotes of his own Time, p. 190.

prerogative and reckless arrogance of power. Thus, when three great Peers, the Dukes of Newcastle and Grafton and the Marquis of Rockingham, presumed to censure the terms of the Peace, they were dismissed from the Lords Lieutenancies of their several counties, — a most arbitrary proceeding, to which certain other dismissals after the Excise Bill of 1733 afforded neither a sufficient nor yet a successful precedent. It had been intended to put the same affront, and for the same cause, upon the Duke of Devonshire, "the Prince of the Whigs," as the Princess Dowager sarcastically called him, but Fox, as an early and warm friend of his Grace, interposed. The Duke, however, who had been, it was said, personally disobliged by the King *, and who had already resigned his Lord Chamberlain's key, threw up his Lord Lieutenancy also, to share in the fate of his friends. It would have been well had Lord Bute waged this arbitrary warfare only against the great and powerful. But even the poor and lowly felt the full weight of his resentment. Inoffensive clerks in the public offices were dismissed from their employment merely because they had been, in the first instance, recommended to it by some statesmen adverse to the Peace. Several old servants of the Duke of Newcastle, who had retired and been preferred to small places, were rigorously hunted out and deprived of their bread. A yeoman in Sussex, who had been rewarded with an office for his gallantry in a fight with some smugglers, was now treated as harshly as the smugglers themselves might have been, — discarded with compensation as an adherent of the Grafton family. The widow of an Admiral, who had enjoyed for many years in lieu of a pension the appointment of housekeeper at one of the public offices, now received notice to quit for no better reason than that she bore the name of Cavendish.

In all these acts of harshness Fox, to the surprise of his friends, was more eager and forward than any other of his colleagues. "Fox has grossly deceived me,"

* See in my Appendix the statement of the scene of October 28. 1762, as given by Lord John Cavendish. It is derived from the MS. Memoirs of the Duke of Grafton, — a curious and valuable document, which has been most kindly placed in my hands by his grandson, the present Duke.

said His Royal Highness of Cumberland to Lord Waldegrave. " I do not mean by giving me up, but I thought " him good-natured, and yet in all these transactions he " has shown the bitterest revenge and inhumanity." Nay more, had Fox's wish prevailed the proscription would have been carried further still. He observed that some of the great patent places — as the Auditorships and the Justices of Eyre — were held by men at that time in Opposition, and he caused a question to be put to Lord Chancellor Henley, whether the King could not cancel the patents granted in the last reign, and whether a case to that effect might not be laid before the twelve Judges. The Chancellor, who was bold and blunt, and was also, perhaps, as Horace Walpole intimates, " prophetically " affectionate to grants for life, so heaped upon him after- " wards," answered roughly: " Aye, they may lay the " idea before the Judges, and refer Magna Charta to " them afterwards to decide on that too!" * On this caustic reply the design was dropped.

Unpopular as Fox became by his share in such severities, Lord Bute was more unpopular still. Fox was considered as at least a statesman, but Lord Bute as only a Favourite, and amongst us the very name of Favourite has ever been a by-word of reproach. We were determined not to resemble certain contemporary nations that quietly allowed themselves to be ruled by any minion to whom the Sultan might trust his signet-ring, or the Czarina toss her handkerchief. So strong was this feeling in England that it rendered the nation unjust to several good and estimable qualities which, mingled with his faults, Lord Bute in truth possessed. He durst not, or fancied that he durst not, any longer appear in the public streets without being attended at a small distance by a hired gang of bruisers to protect him. " Thus," adds Lord Chesterfield, " he who had been deemed a pre- " sumptuous, now appeared to be a very timorous, Minis- " ter, — characters by no means inconsistent." † In many

* Memoirs of George III., vol. i. p. 240. The Duke of Grafton adds in his MS. Memoirs: " When we came into office in 1765 we " stipulated in the very first instance that every person who was dis- " missed at this juncture should be restored to his place."

† Corresp., vol. ii. p. 477. ed. 1845.

country districts, and, above all, in the Cyder counties, his Lordship was burned in effigy under the emblem of a jack-boot, — a poor pun upon his name and title as John, Earl of Bute. To the jack-boot in these burnings it was not unusual to add a petticoat, — a further compliment to the Princess Dowager of Wales. Such bonfires of the jack-boot were renewed during several years, both in England and America, as tokens of hostility to the Court, and whilst the secret influence of Lord Bute was still supposed, however untruly, to prevail.

By some very few and very keen observers Lord Bute was deemed not unlikely to quail before the storm. It is remarkable that the forty-fourth number of the North Briton, published on the 2d of April, contains these words: "The Minister himself seems conscious of his "decline; his fears appear in spite of his pride." But the great mass of politicians of all parties, seeing how large in this Session his majorities had been, and how near at hand was now the prorogation, and knowing also his unabated favour with the King, considered as absolutely certain, and as admitting of no doubt, the prolongation of his power. Thus, with rare exceptions, the public amazement knew no bounds when on the 7th of April it was suddenly announced that Lord Bute's health had become unequal to the fatigues of business, and that on the following day he would resign all his employments — which his Lordship did accordingly.

This sudden step, it is said, took the King by surprise nearly as much as the people. After the first pause for wonder, men began to inquire Lord Bute's motive, and according to their own prejudices or partialities assigned the most various, — from a philosophic love of retirement down to a craven fear. According to some friends he had always declared that as soon as he had signed the Peace, and carried through the Budget, he should consider his objects as attained and his official life as ended. Others thought that his nerves had been shaken by the libels and clamours against him. Others again observed that the emoluments of office were no longer of importance to Lord Bute, since he had secured for his son the reversion of a rich sinecure, and on the death of his father-in-law, Mr. Wortley Montagu, had inherited a large estate.

Lord Bute himself in public pleaded ill-health, — a plea which imposed on no one. In private he wrote to one of his friends as follows: "Single in a Cabinet of my own "forming; no aid in the House of Lords to support me, "except two Peers (Denbigh and Pomfret), both the "Secretaries of State (Lords Egremont and Halifax) "silent, and the Lord Chief Justice (Mansfield), whom I "myself brought into office, voting for me and yet speak-"ing against me *, — the ground I tread upon is so hol-"low that I am afraid not only of falling myself, but of "involving my Royal Master in my ruin. It is time for "me to retire." †

On calmly reviewing the whole of this transaction there seems no reason to doubt that, according to Lord Bute's own statement of his motives, his coolness with his colleagues and his sense of duty to his Sovereign might weigh with him no less than the violence of his opponents. It is certain, however, that he did not then, nor for some time afterwards, lose his back-stairs influence, nor lay aside his ambitious hopes. It is probable that he expected to allay the popular displeasure by a temporary retirement, and meanwhile, in merchants' phrase, to carry on the same firm with other clerks.

With Lord Bute retired both Dashwood and Fox. For the former an ancient Barony, to which he was one of the co-heirs, was called out of abeyance, and thus he became Lord Le Despencer. Fox was likewise raised to the Upper House as Lord Holland—the same title which had been already bestowed upon his wife. But an un-

* This alludes to the debate on the Cyder Tax, when, as Horace Walpole says, nearly to the same effect: "Lord Mansfield made a "bad trimming speech, but voted for the Bill." (Memoirs, vol. i. p. 253.) He had been Chief Justice since 1756, but Lord Bute had first placed him in the Cabinet.

† Mr. Adolphus has inserted this letter in his History (vol. i. p. 117. ed. 1840) as derived "from private information," but even in that recent edition does not state to whom the letter was addressed. Another letter from Lord Bute to the Duke of Bedford, dated April 2. 1763, has since been published in the Bedford Correspondence. From this last it now appears certain (as indeed other circumstances always seemed to me to prove) that neither Pitt as Mr. Adolphus supposes, nor yet Fox as Horace Walpole asserts, were at this period offered the lead of affairs before it devolved upon George Grenville.

seemly altercation arose in private between him and Lord Bute as to his retirement, which was now expected, from his office of Paymaster. Lord Bute had understood that he would quit the Pay-Office for a peerage. Fox had only stipulated to carry through the Peace for that reward. Both parties now appealed to Lord Shelburne, who in the preceding autumn had been the negotiator between them. Lord Shelburne, much embarrassed, was obliged to own that he had in some degree extenuated or exaggerated the terms to each, from his anxiety to secure at all events the support of Fox, which he thought at that period essential to the Government. These misrepresentations Lord Bute, now forgiving, called, "a "pious fraud." "I can see the fraud plain enough," cried Fox, "but where is the piety?" * At last, however, the new-made Peer prevailed, and was allowed still to be Paymaster so long as power remained with Lord Bute's successor.

But although Lord Holland thus, during two more years, continued a placeman, it may be said of him that he had ceased to be a politician. Henceforth, until his death in 1774, he took little or no further part in public affairs. He turned moodily aside from the ill opinion which he had irretrievably raised. In his retirement his principal pleasure was the construction of a fantastic villa at Kingsgate, on the coast of Thanet. It was this building which drew forth that most bitter and stinging lampoon of Gray, a lampoon omitted in the earlier edition of his works, but perhaps only the better known on that account. That lampoon is a signal proof how strong was the aversion which the once gay, the warm-hearted, the buoyant Fox had ended by exciting. The shore where "cormorants dwell," and where "mariners though shipwrecked dread to land," is represented as to him the most "congenial spot." Worse still, the poet makes him bewail that the cowardice of Lord Bute withheld him from punishing the free spirit of London by fire and sword, when amidst the city's ruins owls might have

* See Lord Orford's Memoirs of George III., vol. i. p. 258. Some clearer and fuller details (including Fox's exclamation) were given in conversation by Fox's grandson, the late Lord Holland.

hooted in Westminster Abbey, and foxes made their burrows in St. Paul's!

The successor to Lord Bute proved to be George Grenville, who on the very day that the Favourite resigned kissed hands on his appointment as both First Lord of the Treasury and Chancellor of the Exchequer. No one doubted that this choice had been made under the influence of Lord Bute, and was designed for the preservation of that influence. At the same time it was intimated to the Foreign Ministers that the King had now intrusted the principal direction of his affairs to three persons, namely, to Mr. Grenville and the Secretaries of State, Lords Egremont and Halifax. Thus it happened that the chiefs of the new administration received from the public the name of "the Triumvirate," although, says Lord Chesterfield, "the public looked still at Lord Bute "through the curtain, which indeed was a very trans- "parent one." According to the same calm and close by-stander, writing within a year of the event, "Lord "Halifax had parts, application, and personal disinte- "restedness; Lord Egremont was proud, self-sufficient, "but incapable." * I may observe, however, that Lord Egremont's speeches in Parliament, though few in number, have been praised for their force and clearness †, and that, besides his high rank and his princely possessions, he had the advantage of a considerable following in the Tory party as the son of their late champion Sir William Wyndham. He was at the same time nearly allied to Mr. Grenville, who had married his sister.

Several smaller changes followed. The Duke of Bedford returned from his embassy to France, but did not resume the Privy Seal; thus the former post was left to be bestowed upon the Earl of Hertford, and the latter upon the Duke of Marlborough. The place of First Lord of the Admiralty, left vacant by George Grenville, was intended for Charles Townshend, who was already First Lord of the Board of Trade. "After his usual "fluctuation," as Horace Walpole says ‡, he accepted it;

* Account of Lord Bute's Administration. Corresp., vol. ii. p. 478. ed. 1845.

† Memoirs by Bishop Newton; Works, vol. i. p. 88. ed. 1787.

‡ Memoirs of George III., vol. i. p. 264.

nay, even went to St. James's to kiss hands for it. But rashly presuming that the seats of his colleagues at the Board must be in his own nomination (which had never yet been admitted or allowed), he, without asking it, without even naming it to any Minister, carried to Court with him Mr. Burrell, one of his followers, intending that this gentleman should kiss hands along with himself as another Lord of the Admiralty. He thought his honour engaged to carry through this most unusual pretension, and said he would not go in to kiss the King's hand unless Mr. Burrell was admitted also. This was flatly refused, and Townshend was told that the King had no further occasion for his services in any department. The Earl of Sandwich was appointed to the head of the Admiralty, and the Earl of Shelburne to the head of the Board of Trade.

Another change at this period was in favour of Lord Granby, named Master of the Ordnance. From that post a deserving veteran, old Marshal Ligonier, was removed, not without great reluctance on his part, and much comment on the public's *; the removal, however, being softened both by a pension and by an English peerage.

At this period also retired from office James Oswald of Dunnikier, who, among the Lords of the Treasury, had grown a veteran junior. He showed himself as a speaker clear, acute, and well informed; and he possessed considerable weight, especially among his countrymen—the Scotch. But he was now declining in years and health, and at the next dissolution withdrew altogether from public life. Oswald's colleagues at the Treasury, during several years of the late reign, had been no mere cyphers, but men of note,—Lord North and Robert Nugent. Lord North already took an active part in the House of Commons, and enjoyed some reputation there, although his future mastery over it was not yet foreseen by others, nor probably anticipated by himself. Nugent, a native of the

* "The mean subterfuge,—the indignity upon so brave an officer,' &c. &c. "That step was taken to give the whole power of the army "to the Crown, that is, to the Minister!" (North Briton, No. 45.) At a later period Lord Chesterfield quietly observes: "It was cruel to "put such a boy as Lord Granby over the head of old Ligonier." (To his son, Sept. 12. 1766.)

sister island, became three years afterwards Viscount Clare, and, later still, Earl Nugent, in its peerage. His wit and humour, combined with shrewd sense, may still be traced in that fine full-length portrait by Gainsborough which lately adorned the walls of his descendant at Stowe.* Sometimes he spoke in the House of Commons with considerable success and applause, but was still more frequently drawn from it by his love of letters and of ease. Perhaps he will be best known to posterity, not as the politician or the Peer, but rather as Goldsmith's patron and friend.

Only eleven days after the resignation of Lord Bute the King in person closed the Session of Parliament. His Majesty's Speech on this occasion referred with natural complacency to the recent conclusion of peace, " on terms," it was added, " so honourable to my Crown, and so bene- " ficial to my people." Such an eulogy from such a quarter roused the ire of the writers in the North Briton; and on the 23d of April came forth the last and most renowned of their lampoons, NUMBER FORTY-FIVE.

Of this celebrated Number, of which Wilkes was the author, and from the first almost the avowed one, it may be observed that bitter and scurrilous as were its comments on the Royal expressions, it referred throughout to those expressions in a proper Constitutional tone, not as any emanation of the Royal Mind, but as merely " the " Minister's Speech." We may also remark, that celebrated as it became from the proceedings adopted against it, yet in wit, or point, or pungency it was inferior to almost any of its predecessors, even without rating these predecessors very high. A few years afterwards, in the House of Commons, Burke described this Number Forty-five as " a spiritless, though virulent, performance,—a " mere mixture of vinegar and water, at once vapid and " sour!"†

A more timid statesman than Grenville might have shrunk from any conflict with the Press. A wiser would

* No. 347. in the Catalogue of Pictures, 1848.

† Debate of November 27. 1770. Mr. Adolphus, in referring to this passage, changes the " vinegar and water " into " milk and " water," which entirely alters the meaning (perhaps I should rather say the *flavour*) intended by Mr. Burke.

probably have left the cure of this libel to its own dullness and defects. But the new Prime Minister was eager to signalize his accession by a vigorous defence of the Prerogative, and thus, after a few days' deliberation, on the 30th of April Wilkes was arrested in his own apartment by the authority of a "General Warrant," that is, a Warrant not specifying the names of any person, but directed against the "authors, printers, and publishers," whoever they might be, of the paper complained of. Under this Warrant, which, as will presently be seen, was at least of doubtful legality, Wilkes was carried to the house of Lord Halifax, by whom the Warrant had been signed. Here he was examined by Halifax and his brother Secretary Egremont, and then committed a prisoner to the Tower. At the same time his papers were seized and examined by Mr. Wood, the Under Secretary of State, and Mr. Carteret Webb, the Solicitor of the Treasury. His two printers, Balfe and Kearsley, being also taken into custody, acknowledged him to be the author of Number Forty-five. Wilkes in his confinement was at first denied the use of pen and paper, or the privilege of receiving visits, but these restraints were almost immediately afterwards removed. His high spirits and powers of wit did not for a moment forsake him. When brought to the Tower he asked in derision to be allowed the same room in which Lord Egremont's father had been confined on a charge of treason.* A few days afterwards he wrote a letter to his daughter, his only child, whom he had placed for her education at a convent in France, and this letter he sent open for previous perusal to Lord Halifax. It was found to wish her joy of living in a free country!

No sooner was the prison-rule relaxed than Lord Temple, who had once already called in vain, hastened ostentatiously to pay a visit to Wilkes. The same compliment was shown him by the Duke of Grafton; but in general men of character and station shrunk from any intercourse with this profligate adventurer. Wilkes had lost no time in applying for a writ of Habeas Corpus to the Court of Common Pleas, then presided over by Sir Charles Pratt, lately Attorney General, and afterwards

* See vol. i. p. 157.

Lord Chancellor Camden. Being carried before this eminent magistrate on the 3d of May, he (after a speech from his learned counsel, Serjeant Glynn,) spoke himself for an hour with no slight degree of flippancy, declaring that he had been " worse treated than any rebel Scot." At these words, so consonant to the popular humour of the moment, the crowd in Westminster Hall raised a great shout until the Lord Chief Justice with much dignity reproved them. Wilkes proceeded to say, that the Ministry adopted this mode of persecution because they had failed in their earlier attempts to corrupt him. The effrontery of this assertion cannot be fully appreciated without remembering that in fact Wilkes himself had been a disappointed suitor for place, and that from such disappointment had all his libels sprung.

The Court took time to consider the arguments, and Wilkes was led back to the Tower amidst the acclamations of the mob. Three days afterwards he again appeared in Westminster to hear the judgment which the Lord Chief Justice delivered in the name of his brethren. Waiving the question as to the legality of General Warrants, which the Crown lawyers by a technical contrivance had avoided, Sir Charles Pratt pronounced Wilkes entitled to his discharge, from his privilege as a Member of Parliament, since that privilege holds good in all cases, except treason, felony, and an actual breach of the peace. " We are all of opinion," he said, " that a libel is not a " breach of the peace; it tends to a breach of the peace, " and that is the utmost. But that which only tends to a " breach of the peace cannot be an actual breach of it. In " the case of the Seven Bishops, Judge Powell, the only " honest man of the four Judges, dissented, and I am " bound to be of his opinion, and to say that case is not " law,—but it shows the miserable condition to which " the law was then reduced. Let Mr. Wilkes be dis" charged from his imprisonment." *

Much elated at this victory, and determined to pursue

* Lord Campbell's Lives of the Chancellors, vol. v. p. 247. In referring for the first time to these most agreeable volumes I am anxious to bear my testimony to their merit, and to state how much new and valuable information I have derived from them.

it to the utmost, Wilkes erected a printing press in his own house, pretended that his goods had been stolen by the messengers, set on foot an action for damages against them, and threatened Lord Egremont with a challenge as soon as these proceedings should be over. During the continued recess of Parliament he proceeded on a visit to his daughter at Paris, where he was himself challenged by Captain Forbes, a Scottish exile in the French service; the duel, however, being prevented by the interposition of the Lieutenant de Police. Meanwhile in England the Court could only show its chagrin by depriving him of his commission in the Buckinghamshire Militia. Earl Temple being looked upon, and not unreasonably, as his patron and his instigator, was dismissed from the Lord Lieutenancy of the same county, and likewise struck off the list of Privy Councillors, the former post being now bestowed on Lord Le Despencer.

Such was the first campaign of that memorable Seven Years' War which the Government of England thought fit to wage against John Wilkes. Little blame beyond that of imprudence seems to rest on the first proceedings, but far heavier the fault of those that followed, when, as will be seen, the powers of the House of Commons being brought into play, notwithstanding the popular voice, and against an Electoral body, were unconstitutionally wielded, and at last disgracefully foiled. So great were the acclamations and rejoicings at Wilkes's present release from the Tower, that they might well have warned any prudent statesman against the policy of a further prosecution. Nor were these confined to London alone. In the Cyder counties, still exasperated by the new tax laid upon them, the triumph over the administration was celebrated in a mode not extremely consistent with their boasted loyalty. Besides the usual emblems of the jack-boot and petticoat, a figure was carried round, dressed in Scotch plaid and with a blue riband, to denote Lord Bute, and this figure was made to lead by the nose an ass Royally crowned! *

* Lord Orford's Memoirs of George III., vol. i. p. 280.

CHAPTER XLII.

Mr. George Grenville, the new Prime Minister, was (to sum up his character in three words) an excellent Speaker spoiled. All his first training, all his earlier inclinations, had qualified him to fill the Chair of the House of Commons with dignity, firmness, and learning. His whole mind, as I have elsewhere noticed, was cast in the mould of precedents and order. Of even his most familiar letters I should have guessed that they must have been grave and solemn; and I have been surprised to find that they do not all begin exactly like an Act of Parliament with the word "Whereas —."

It is worthy of note that whenever any man who has been most respectable and most respected in the Speaker's Chair is called on to assume the office of Prime Minister, — as Sir Spencer Compton in 1727, Mr. Addington in 1801, and Sir Charles Manners Sutton during a few days of negotiation in 1832, — the result in each instance has been far from satisfactory. Mr. George Grenville's might properly be added to this class of cases, since, although he was never in fact raised to the Chair, he had been designated for it by the Ministry in 1761, with the general concurrence of the House and of the public, until the retirement of Pitt brought before him, unhappily for himself, the allurements of political office. As a Minister his two principal measures were the Parliamentary expulsion of Wilkes and the Parliamentary taxation of America. Both have long since been acknowledged not only as disastrous, but as in the highest degree unwise. But both, it may be added, took their rise from one and the same feeling in his mind, — the most lofty notion, namely, of the rights and privileges of the House of Commons, — a feeling which, had he been only Speaker, would have been natural, praiseworthy, and harmless, nay even beneficial.

But few weeks had elapsed since Mr. Grenville had been placed at the head of the Treasury before a coolness was observed to arise between him and Lord Bute. Nor is the reason hard to be assigned. Lord Bute regarded the choice of Grenville as an act of grace and favour on his part, to be followed by corresponding marks of gratitude and deference. Grenville, on the other hand, could see no other cause for his elevation beyond his own genius and merit.

Concurrently with this coolness in Lord Bute, "The "Triumvirate" found that they were far from enjoying, as they had hoped, the full confidence of the King. Each of the Three, at various times, but especially Grenville, remonstrated, argued, and complained. At last, in the first week of August, when Grenville, intending to go out of town, was renewing his representations, the King said that he would take ten days or a fortnight to consider the whole case fully, and decide whether he would dismiss or only seek to strengthen his administration.*

The Ministerial crisis, however, took a different and wholly unexpected turn. Lord Egremont, who was of a plethoric habit of body, was seized with apoplexy and expired on the 20th of August. "He was observed," says Bishop Newton, "to be remarkably cheerful several "days before, and the very morning of his death; and it "was while he was sitting at breakfast with his lady and "reading a letter that the fatal stroke was struck. He "called for a glass of water, but before it could be given "him he was insensible, and so continued till he died." †

Lord Bute considering the administration as dissolved by this sudden event, and weighing all his animosities, past and present, against each other, advised His Majesty as the least evil to apply to Mr. Pitt. In his letter to the Duke of Bedford of the 2nd of April, in which he announced his own impending resignation, he had referred to the great Commoner as follows: "One thing the King

* The confidential letters on this subject between Mr. Grenville and Lord Egremont are among the Grenville Papers. (Aug. 3. and 4. 1763.)

† Memoirs, in Newton's Works, vol. i. p. 89. ed. 1787. See also Mr. Grenville's MS. Diary now on the point of publication; a most curious and valuable document, though sometimes warped by the prejudices or passions of the writer. It exhibits him on the whole as very jealous of power, and ever fretting with his brother Ministers.

"is determined to abide by . . . . . never upon any account to suffer those Ministers of the late reign who have "attempted to fetter and enslave him ever to come into "his service while he lives to hold the sceptre." * Now, not yet five months having fully elapsed, we find Lord Bute who wrote that letter advise that Pitt should be called to the head of affairs; we find the Duke of Bedford who received that letter hasten up to town from Blenheim on a separate impulse, and give the same counsel to the King; we find His Majesty whose fixed determination had been (though perhaps it may be said without adequate authority) announced in that letter yield to the twofold suggestion which he now received! Was not that statesman in the right who exclaimed that there is no such word in party politics as "Never!"

Having thus obtained the Royal consent Lord Bute immediately proceeded to open the desired negotiation by a message to Mr. Pitt at Hayes, through Beckford, then Lord Mayor. An interview ensued between the Earl and the Great Commoner at the house of the latter in Jermyn Street. On this occasion Pitt expressed his sentiments on public affairs with the utmost freedom, but refused to ask an audience of the King, or to thrust himself unsolicited into the Royal presence. "But suppose "His Majesty should order you?" asked Bute. "The "King's command," said Pitt, "would make it my duty, "and I should certainly obey it."

On the day ensuing Pitt did receive the King's command, although in an unusual form, namely, an open note unsealed, requiring him to attend His Majesty at noon of Saturday the 27th of August at Buckingham House, then called the Queen's Palace, in the Park. At the hour appointed Pitt accordingly proceeded through the Mall in his chair, the boot of which being constructed for the accommodation of his gouty foot made it, according to his own phrase, as much known as if his name were written upon it. Some time afterwards Mr. Grenville arriving at Buckingham House for the usual transaction of business beheld in the Court the unwelcome apparition of this well-remembered chair. The public,

* Bedford Correspondence, vol. iii. p. 224.

and amongst the rest Horace Walpole, believed that this was the first notice which the Prime Minister received of the negotiation then already in progress. In truth, however, the King had apprised Mr. Grenville of his purpose the day before, and both Grenville and Halifax had remonstrated against it, but in vain.*

The audience of Pitt with His Majesty lasted three hours. A full and in most respects trustworthy account of it may be found in a letter from Lord Hardwicke to his son,—an account taken from Pitt's own mouth only six days afterwards.† The Sovereign, it seems, was very gracious, and the statesman very explicit. He, Pitt, went through the defects of the Peace; the things needed and hitherto neglected to improve and preserve it; the claims of the great Whig noblemen, those steady friends of the House of Hanover, who had been driven from His Majesty's council and service, and whom it would be for his interest to restore. The King still said he liked to hear him, and bade him go on, but now and then let fall the words, that his honour must be consulted. To a young and high-spirited Prince there seemed, not mere inconsistency, but even ignominy, in the thought that he must summon back with smiles and favours the same men so lately sent away with anger. Such, however, is the lesson which all Constitutional Monarchs have to learn.

At this interview of Saturday the 27th of August no final decision was arrived at, and His Majesty desired Pitt to come again on Monday. Nevertheless, Pitt felt sanguine of a favourable issue. He sent expresses summoning to town the Duke of Devonshire and the Marquis of Rockingham, and on the intervening Sunday went

* Lord Orford's Memoirs (vol. i. p. 288.) must be compared with and corrected by Mr. Grenville's own statement, both in the Diary and in his letter of Sept. 2. 1763. On the 27th he was admitted after Pitt had gone, and writes the same evening to Lord Halifax: "My "interview was very short, and no notice was taken of the long "audience that preceded mine."

† Letter to Lord Royston, Sept. 4. 1763. Parl. Hist., vol. xv. p. 1327., and notes to Chatham Correspondence, vol. ii. p. 236—242. The correspondence itself supplies some further hints, while on the other hand the Grenville Diary contains several points of contradiction or counter-statement.

himself to Claremont to see the Duke of Newcastle. On that Sunday evening, however, it appears from Mr. Grenville's Diary that a secret interview took place between himself and the King, when His Majesty expressed a strong repugnance to Pitt's conditions as too hard, and when Grenville did his best to confirm him in these feelings.

Next morning, as appointed, there ensued another audience of Pitt at Buckingham House of nearly two hours' duration, but of far less satisfactory tenor. The effect of Grenville's last representations was now apparent. The King, after a few words of gracious welcome, began that he had considered fully what had been said. He spoke strongly of supporting his honour; and he then proceeded to suggest the Earl of Northumberland as head of the Treasury. It was understood throughout that Pitt should resume his former post as Secretary of State. The Earl of Northumberland, lately Sir Hugh Smithson, had been ennobled from his marriage with the heiress of the Percys; an honourable nobleman, but without abilities or reputation in public affairs. But he was an intimate friend of Lord Bute, and his son a few months afterwards became the husband of one of Lord Bute's daughters,—a claim no doubt to the highest honours of the realm! Pitt, much surprised, hesitated an objection that certainly Lord Northumberland might be considered for some office, but that he should not have thought of him for the head of the Treasury. His Majesty then mentioned Lord Halifax for that high office. Pitt said: "Suppose Your Majesty should think "fit to give his Lordship the Paymaster's place?" "But, "Mr. Pitt," rejoined the King, "I had designed that for "poor George Grenville; he is your near relation, and "you once loved him!"—To this the only answer made was a low but by no means an assenting bow.

Pitt, on the whole matter, stated to the King that he was a poor infirm man, declining in years as well as in health, unable to go through a constant Parliamentary attendance,—that such little strength as he could bring to His Majesty was derived from the good opinion of his friends and of such people as attributed part of the former successes to his poor endeavours,—but that if

His Majesty thought fit to make use of such a little knife he must not blunt the edge, — that he and his friends could never come into government but as a party, — that with such views of his party-ties he must now be empowered to offer the headship of the Treasury to Lord Temple, although he was by no means sure that his Lordship would take that or any other office. The name of Temple might well cause His Majesty to start and pause, considering that only a few weeks since that Noble Lord as the declared partisan of Wilkes had been visited with the severest marks of Royal displeasure, — had been struck from the list of Privy Councillors, and dismissed from the Lord Lieutenancy of Bucks.*

Beside Lord Temple's, it appears that Pitt brought forward several other of his intended nominations. Among these was Lord Hardwicke for the Presidency of the Council, and Chief Justice Pratt for a Peerage, with a future view of the Great Seal. Lord Rockingham was designed as First Lord of the Admiralty, Charles Townshend as Secretary of State, the Duke of Newcastle as Privy Seal, and the Duke of Devonshire as Lord Chamberlain. This last appointment, like Lord Temple's, and for nearly the same reason, must have been personally most distasteful to His Majesty. "Well, Mr. Pitt," such it is said were the concluding words of George the Third, "I see (or I fear) this will not do. My honour "is concerned, and I must support it."

Thus ended this remarkable interview. "Mr. Pitt," continues Lord Hardwicke in his letter, "professes him-"self firmly persuaded that my Lord Bute was sincere "at first, and that the King was in earnest the first day,

* The letter of Lord Hardwicke and the Diary of Mr. Grenville stand here in point-blank contradiction to each other. The letter states that the King proposed Lord Temple to Pitt, and the Diary states that Pitt proposed Lord Temple to the King. The authority of each may be taken as equal, since Lord Hardwicke derived his information directly from Pitt, and Mr. Grenville directly from His Majesty. My main reasons for preferring the latter are as follows: — 1. The proposal here ascribed to Pitt in 1763 exactly agrees with that which we know him to have made on two similar occasions in 1765 and 1766; 2. It seems most improbable that the King should himself propose Lord Temple, whom he had so recently with the highest resentment dismissed his service.

" but that on the intermediate day, Sunday, some strong " effort was made which produced the alteration. He " likewise affirms that if he was examined upon oath he " could not tell upon what this negotiation broke off, " whether upon any particular point or upon the general " complexion of the whole."

At the time, however, every detail of these negotiations was left by the parties to them clouded with doubt and mystery, and the concealment of the truth gave birth as usual to a thousand fictions. Lord Chesterfield, writing to his son, drily remarks that all the newsmongers and coffee-houses, as they asserted, knew the facts minutely, but that he did not. Upon the whole, however, it was rightly felt and urged that this sudden re-appearance of Lord Bute in the character of go-between entirely belied all the assertions made since his resignation of his having ceased to advise the King, or to take any part in public affairs. The statesmen whom he had tried to supplant were, as may be supposed, most open-mouthed against him. "He has attempted to sacrifice us to his own " fears and timidity;"—"he has carried us to market in " his pocket;"—such were some of their expressions. Thus when, after parting with Pitt, the King found it necessary to press Grenville to remain Prime Minister, Grenville, though nothing loth, seized the occasion to lecture His Majesty at great length and in no courtly terms against the now no longer secret ascendency of the Scottish Favourite.

Grenville, feeling the need of new strength, or at least new names, in his Cabinet, now invited to his aid the Bedford party. The Duke was made to believe (which was not the fact) that Pitt had proscribed him by name as the author of a disgraceful Peace, and he was consequently filled with indignation. His Grace was by no means eager for office, and pleaded against it the indolence of his temper*, but his dependants, such as Rigby, for their own sakes urged him onwards. Thus he con-

* Bedford Papers, vol. iii. p. 245. On the 6th of September, the very day on which Bedford from Woburn Abbey accepted office, the " proscribing " expressions imputed to Pitt were on his part, it seems, fully and distinctly denied. See the letter of Mr. Robert Wood in the Chatham Papers, vol. ii. p. 249.

sented to become President of the Council (an office left vacant since the death of Lord Granville in the January preceding), and Lord Sandwich Secretary of State, being succeeded at the Admiralty by Lord Egmont. Lord Shelburne, who had been in close correspondence with Pitt during the late negotiation, resigned the Board of Trade, and was replaced by Lord Hillsborough. On the general complexion of the Government thus altered Lord Chesterfield writes: "In my opinion they cannot as they "are meet the Parliament. The only and all the efficient "people they have are in the House of Lords, for since "Mr. Pitt has firmly engaged Charles Townshend to "him there is not a man of the Court side in the House "of Commons who has either abilities or words enough "to call a coach."* I have observed, however, that such predictions, common though they be, of oratorical feebleness and failure in any administration, are scarcely ever borne out by the event, since high office in some cases calls forth latent powers of eloquence, and, still oftener, by its weight and authority supplies to a great extent the want of them.

The recent negotiation with Pitt had been so rapid in its progress, and so secret in its circumstances, that it afforded the people at large no opportunity to express their feelings upon it. But their indifference at least towards the Ministry was shown throughout the summer by their slackness to subscribe Addresses of Congratulation on the Peace. Such Addresses had been eagerly solicited by letters from men in office to the friendly Mayors of towns and Lord Lieutenants of counties; nevertheless, with every exertion but few could be obtained. One such there came from each English University, but the Duke of Newcastle as Chancellor, and Lord Hardwicke as High Steward, of Cambridge, refused to go to St. James's with the Address of that learned body. The same course was adopted by Pitt with regard to an Address from his constituents—the Corporation of Bath,—and he carried his resentment further still on finding that they had applied the term "adequate" to the Peace, which he deemed a reflection on himself, who

* To his son, Sept. 30. 1763.

had repeatedly called it "inadequate." It afterwards appeared that the term had been inserted hastily, and without any offensive view, by Mr. Ralph Allen of Prior Park, the leading member of the Bath Corporation. This gentleman, whose kind heart endeared him to his contemporaries, has become known to posterity from the direct praise of Pope and the implied praise of Fielding. For the "humble Allen" of the Satires* was also, it is said, the original of Allworthy in Tom Jones. To him, Pitt now addressed a letter declaring that he would never stand again for Bath. "Give me leave, my dear "good Sir, plainly to confess that I perceive I am but "ill-qualified to form pretensions to the future favour of "gentlemen who are come to think so differently from "me on matters of the highest importance." Mr. Allen, much mortified and grieved, answered Pitt by special express, imploring him to forego his resolution. Pitt, however, persevered, and the letters which had passed on this occasion were, as he desired, made public.† So great was Mr. Allen's concern, that he not only resigned his seat in the Corporation, but withdrew from any further part in public affairs until his death which happened in the ensuing year.

It was supposed at the time, though without foundation, that in the Address which Mr. Allen framed he had been instigated by Dr. Warburton, who some years since, on Pitt's recommendation, had become the Bishop of Gloucester. Warburton had certainly promoted a similar Address from his own Chapter, and finding Pitt displeased he wrote him a letter of explanation and apology.‡ The reply of Pitt is couched in his usual

* "Let humble Allen, with an awkward shame,
"Do good by stealth, and blush to find it fame."

Pope had at first written "low-born," but afterwards changed the epithet to "humble,"—a proof that in some quarter pride was lurking. See Bowles's ed., vol. iv. p. 330.

† Annual Register, 1763, part i. p. 206. These letters, which bear date the beginning of June, are reprinted in the Chatham Correspondence.

‡ To Mr. Pitt, Sept. 4. 1763. The Bishop grievously complains of a popular caricature at Bath, in which "your humble servant is brought "in, in his Episcopal habit, prompted by the Devil, to whisper in

epistolary style of humility, bordering on obsequiousness, which affords so strange a contrast to the proud and lofty tenor of his life. He first declares that he should be guilty of temerity were he to presume to exercise his own judgment in such a case, but he then proceeds to lay—as the Bishop himself afterwards confessed—his finger on the weak point of this transaction. "I will "only venture to observe, my Lord, that the Cathedral "of Gloucester, which certainly does not stand alone "in true duty and wise zeal towards His Majesty, has, "however, the fate not to be imitated by any other "Episcopal See in the kingdom in this unaccustomed "effusion of fervent gratulations on the Peace."

At nearly the same period we find Pitt in his private correspondence refer to the Government as "a rash and "odious Ministry," and express his hope for "some solid "union on Revolution principles."* He was reckoning on the future co-operation of Charles Yorke, the second son of Lord Hardwicke, and at this time Attorney General, who it was thought differed from his colleagues in the case of the North Briton. But this expectation was not fulfilled. For, although Yorke did resign his office before the meeting of Parliament, he put it on family reasons, and professed himself ready to concur in the violent measures against Wilkes.

Under such circumstances did the Session of Parliament commence on the 15th of November; and the very first day was marked in both Houses by a vehement prosecution—or rather, as the public deemed it, persecution—of Wilkes. In the Upper House Lord Sandwich started up, even before the King's Speech could be considered, and sprung a wholly unexpected mine upon his former associate, denouncing him as the author of a

Mr. Allen's ear the word '*adequate!*'" His Lordship adds, not very consistently, the usual phrase on such occasions: "I for my part, "am callous to these things."

* To the Duke of Newcastle, Oct. 13. 1763. See also the Duke's answer the next day. It is curious to contrast Newcastle's letters in the autumn of 1761 with those in the autumn of 1763; the former in the Bedford Collection, and the latter in the Chatham; the former all fire and flame against Pitt, the latter all humility and devotion towards him.

scandalous, obscene, and impious libel, called "the Essay "on Woman." It appears that Wilkes had, several years before, and in some of his looser hours, composed a parody of Pope's "Essay on Man." In this undertaking which, according to his own account, cost him a great deal of pains and time *, he was, it is said, assisted by Thomas Potter, second son of the late Archbishop of Canterbury, who had been Secretary of Frederick Prince of Wales, and had since shown ability and gained office in the House of Commons, but was (as well became one of Wilkes's friends) of lax morals in his private life.† The result of their joint authorship, however, has little wit or talent to make any amends for the blasphemy and lewdness with which it abounds. As the original had been inscribed by Pope to Lord Bolingbroke, so was the parody by Wilkes to Lord Sandwich; thus it began, "Awake my Sandwich!" instead of "Awake my St. "John!" Thus also, in ridicule of Warburton's well-known commentary, some burlesque notes were appended in the name of the Right Reverend the Bishop of Gloucester.

This worthless poem had remained in manuscript, and lain in Wilkes's desk, until in the previous spring he had occasion to set up a press at his own house, and was tempted to print fourteen copies only as presents to his boon companions. Of one of these copies the Government obtained possession, through a subordinate agent, and by not very creditable means, and Lord Sandwich holding it forth in his hand with the air of injured innocence denounced it as not only scandalous and impious, but also as a breach of Privilege against the Bishop as a Peer of Parliament. He likewise complained of another profane parody, written by the same hand, and printed on the same occasion; this last was entitled, "The VENI "CREATOR paraphrased."—The most offensive passages of

* Examination of Michael Curry, printer, at the Bar of the House of Lords, Nov. 15. 1763.

† Potter had died in 1759 as Vice-Treasurer of Ireland. See a note to Lord Orford's Memoirs of George III., vol. i. p. 310. In the last year of his life, according to his own account, he had become "a useless load to others, and a wretched being to himself." (Letter to Pitt, Oct. 25. 1758, Chatham Correspondence.)

both were now by Lord Sandwich's order read aloud to the House, until Lord Lyttleton with a groan entreated that they might hear no more.

In the discussion which ensued Bishop Warburton, forgetting that such ribaldries could not really tarnish his character, showed a heat which little became it. He exclaimed that the blackest fiends in Hell would disdain to keep company with Wilkes,—and then asked pardon of Satan for comparing them together! Both the Earl and Bishop in their passion would have readily over-leaped the common forms of justice. The former, after producing evidence at the Bar as to the authorship of Wilkes, wished the House to take measures for his prosecution without the least delay. But the Peers, although readily agreeing to vote the two parodies blasphemous and breaches of Privilege, resolved, on the motion of Lord Mansfield, to adjourn all further questions until the day after the next, so as to give Wilkes the opportunity, if he desired it, of alleging any matter in denial or defence.

While these things were transacting in the Lords, Horace Walpole, as a Member of the House of Commons, happened to hear of them, and going up to Pitt, with whom he was dividing in the lobby, told him what had passed,—how, as it seemed, the Government had been ransacking Wilkes's desk in search of libels. Pitt replied with just indignation: "Why do they not search "the Bishop of Gloucester's study for heresy?" *

The Commons had, however, on that day sufficient business of their own. Grenville delivered a message from the Crown acquainting the House with the imprisonment of one of their Members during the recess. Wilkes stood up in his place to complain of that imprisonment as a breach of Privilege. Lord North, still one of the Board of Treasury, who had undertaken the management of this business conjointly with the new Attorney General, Sir Fletcher Norton, caused the depositions of the two printers to be read confessing Wilkes the author of the famous Number 45; and after such preliminaries Lord North and the Attorney pressed for vigorous measures against it and him. Several debates

* Lord Orford's Memoirs of George III., vol. i. p. 312.

and divisions ensued, but at length it was carried by large majorities that the Paper entitled the North Briton, Number 45, was a false, scandalous, and seditious libel, tending to traitorous insurrections, and that it should be burned by the hands of the common hangman,—an order in which the other House afterwards concurred. Pitt spoke several times with great spirit and effect. He moved to omit the epithet "traitorous," fully acknowledging, however, the guilt of the libel and of the libeller, but always distinguishing between the criminal act and the illegal prosecution. "For my part," he added, "I "never could learn exactly what is a libel."—Alas, could any lawyer tell him now?

It was not till the next day that Pitt found occasion in another speech to refer to the late negotiation with His Majesty, which he did in obscure and doubtful terms. One of his political opponents owns in a private letter to a friend that "he spoke civilly and not unfairly of the "Ministers, but of the King said everything which duty "and affection could inspire." *

Among the speeches on the first evening of the Session was one from Mr. Samuel Martin, who had been Secretary of the Treasury under both the Duke of Newcastle and Lord Bute. In an earlier Number of the North Briton Wilkes had mentioned him with some contempt as a low fellow and dirty tool of power. Mr. Martin mindful of the affront took this opportunity of referring to it, and said that he did not know its author, but that, be he who he might, he was a cowardly, malignant, and infamous scoundrel; and these words he repeated twice over trembling with anger. Wilkes took no notice at the time, but next morning addressed to Mr. Martin a letter, concluding as follows: "To cut off every pretence "of ignorance as to the author, I whisper in your ear, "that every passage of the North Briton in which you "have been named or even alluded to was written by "your humble servant, JOHN WILKES." A duel ensued

* Lord Barrington to Mr. Mitchell, Nov. 1763. Note to Chatham Papers, vol. ii. p. 263. Lord Barrington adds (a little too much in the style of Sir Robert Walpole): "I think if fifty thousand pounds "had been given for that speech it would have been well expended. "It secures us a quiet Session."

between them that very day, when Wilkes was dangerously wounded with a bullet in the body. His wound produced some delay but no mitigation in the measures against him. The House of Lords carried an Address to the Crown praying for a prosecution of the author of the "Essay on Woman." The House of Commons manifested at least equal rigour against the author of the North Briton, Number 45. Wilkes himself, dauntless as he seemed on most occasions, quailed before this formidable combination of King, Lords, and Commons, and when only half recovered of his wound withdrew for safety to France. He sent certificates of his continued illness from Paris, and sued for further time, but nevertheless the House of Commons proceeded with his case. A whole night was spent in stormy debates and divisions on collateral points, but at last at four in the morning, Wilkes's friends having then mostly withdrawn, he was by an unanimous vote expelled.

Meanwhile, however, there arose among the people an idea that Wilkes was a persecuted man, and that as a persecuted man he ought to be upheld. This is a feeling which prevails in England more perhaps than in any other country, and which should never be referred to without high respect and praise, often as it has led, or may lead, to the support of unworthy objects. In the case of the "Essay on Woman" a most acute bystander observes that the public mind was instantly diverted from indignation at the piece itself to indignation at the means by which it was obtained.* The conduct of Lord Sandwich, above all, was loudly reprobated. His private life was known to be full as irregular as Wilkes's, and it was asserted that only a fortnight before Wilkes and he had been supping with other loose revellers at a London tavern, and singing lewd catches together. A few days after the opening scene in the House of Lords a strong proof of the popular sentiment was given at Covent Garden Theatre as the Beggar's Opera was acting. When Macheath came to the words, "That Jemmy Twitcher "should peach I own surprises me,"—the whole audience with one unanimous shout of applause marked the ap-

* H. Walpole to Sir H. Mann, Jan. 8. 1764.

plication. It was an age of nicknames, and from that night forward the by-word of Jemmy Twitcher was applied to Lord Sandwich as often and more gladly than his title.*

Nor should I neglect to note on this occasion the caustic irony of Chesterfield: "It is a great mercy that Mr. "Wilkes, the intrepid defender of our rights and liberties, "is out of danger, and may live to fight and write again "in support of them; and it is no less a mercy that God "has raised up the Earl of Sandwich to vindicate and "promote true religion and morality! These two bless- "ings will justly make an epoch in the annals of this "country!"†

With such feelings amongst both low and high, we need scarcely wonder at the scene which the Royal Exchange presented on the 3d of December, when the attempt to burn the North Briton, Number 45, by the hands of the common hangman, and according to the order of both Houses, was disturbed, and well-nigh prevented by a riot. Before the order could be fully executed the proper officers were thrust aside, and a jack-boot with a petticoat was committed to the flames amidst loud acclamation and applause. The cry of the multitude on this occasion was "Wilkes and liberty for ever;" and the Sheriffs declared that the tumult was encouraged by gentlemen from windows and balconies. — Only three days afterwards came on for trial Wilkes's action for damages against the Under Secretary of State, when Lord Chief Justice Pratt delivered a charge on the popular side, and the jury by their verdict awarded to Wilkes one thousand pounds.

Some months afterwards, however, Wilkes being still abroad, and not appearing to answer to the indictments against him, he was outlawed by the Courts, as he had already been expelled by the Commons. "And this," says a contemporary with pity, as it proved a little premature, "this completed the ruin of that unfortunate "gentleman."‡

* Lord Orford's Memoirs of George III., vol. i. p. 313.
† Letter to his son, Dec. 3. 1763.
‡ Annual Register, 1764, part i. p. 25.

Other incidental proceedings arising from his case took up nearly the whole remainder of this Session. — Complaint was made against a person named Dun — a madman as he was afterwards clearly shown to be — who had attempted, or more accurately speaking threatened, the life of Wilkes. — In contradiction to the judgment of the Court of Common Pleas in the previous spring the Ministry proposed and carried through both Houses a Resolution: "That Privilege of Parliament does not extend "to the case of writing and publishing seditious Libels." Pitt, though at that time ill of the gout, came down in flannels and on crutches to speak against this surrender of Privilege. He took occasion in the course of his remarks to express both his reprobation of Wilkes and his tender friendship for Temple. "I condemn," he cried, "the whole series of North Britons; they are illiberal, "unmanly, detestable. I abhor all national reflections. "The King's subjects are one people; whoever divides "them is guilty of sedition. His Majesty's complaint "was well-founded; it was just, it was necessary. The "author of these Essays does not deserve to be ranked "among the human species; he is the blasphemer of his "God, and the libeller of his King. I have no connec-"tion with him; none with any such writer. I neither "associate nor communicate with any such men. It is "true I have friendships and warm ones; I have obliga-"tions and great ones; but no friendships, no obligations, "could induce me to approve what my conscience con-"demns. It may be supposed that I allude to my Noble "Relative Lord Temple. I know nothing of any connec-"tion between him and the writer of the libel. If there "exists any I am totally unacquainted with it. I am "proud to call him my Relative; he is my friend, my "bosom friend, whose fidelity is as unshaken as his "virtue. We went into office together, and we went out "of office together; we have lived together and we will "die together!"* — These words were not forgotten

* Parl. Hist., vol. xv. p. 1363. Wilkes afterwards accused the great orator of having expressed warm admiration for the "Essay "on Woman" when shown to him in manuscript. But this charge, besides being utterly repugnant to the tenor of Pitt's acknowledged

some time afterwards, but were quoted with a kind of malignant pleasure when the friendship thus vaunted as eternal came to be dissolved.

It was noticed that in some of these divisions the only two Scots Members of Parliament who were then in Opposition forsook their party and voted with the Minister for the most stringent measures against Wilkes, — so much had their national wrath been kindled by the jests of the North Briton!

It was also observed, and condemned as a shallow artifice, that the House of Lords, to counterbalance their condemnation of Wilkes's violent democracy, took similar measures against a book of exactly opposite principles. This was a treatise or collection of precedents lately published under the title of DROIT LE ROI, to uphold the prerogative of the Crown against the rights of the people. The Peers, on the motion of Lord Lyttleton, seconded by the Duke of Grafton, voted this book "a false, malicious, "and traitorous libel, inconsistent with the principles of "the Revolution to which we owe the present happy "establishment;" they ordered that it should be burned by the hands of the common hangman, and that the author should be taken into custody. The latter part of the sentence, however, no one took any pains to execute. The author was one Timothy Brecknock, a hack scribbler, who twenty years afterwards was hanged for being accessory to an atrocious murder in Ireland.

Another question of far greater importance, but springing from the same fertile source of discord — Wilkes's case, — arose on the legality of General Warrants, such as that by which Wilkes had been arrested. There had been many precedents of that kind in former years, and two even under Pitt's administration, the one for apprehending a suspected foreigner, who proved to be the Count de St. Germain, the other for seizing a number of persons on board a ship that was outward bound; both, however, in a time of war with France. Such former in-

moral character, does not well accord with Wilkes's own previous statement that "he never read it but to two persons, Lord Sandwich "and Lord Le Despencer." (See Horace Walpole's letter to Mann, Nov. 17. 1763.)

stances had passed by unquestioned and almost unnoticed, but the case of Wilkes stirred up inquiry, and then it appeared that the most eminent lawyers of the day, headed by Chief Justice Pratt, on consideration, held this form of warrant to be utterly illegal. It was argued that a Warrant to apprehend all persons guilty of a crime therein specified is in truth no warrant at all, since the point upon which its authority rests, — namely, whether the person apprehended thereupon be really guilty or not, — is a fact to be decided on a subsequent trial.* Several warm debates upon the subject took place in the course of the Session. Once the House of Commons sat for above seventeen hours, that is, until past seven in the morning, without intermission, the longest sitting yet on record. The eloquence of Charles Townshend and the readiness of Colonel Barré were justly admired on the side of Opposition.† Pitt, as usual the foremost, spoke with great spirit on the same side, avowing the precedents in his own administration, but vindicating them on the ground of national necessity in time of war. Several of the most honest and steady friends of Government found themselves unable to support it here, and thus on one occasion when the House was fullest the Ministerial majority dwindled to fourteen. Still, however, that majority remained, and enabled Grenville to postpone indefinitely the Resolution which was sought to be carried, declaring General Warrants illegal.

In this debate Charles Yorke, though a party to the use of General Warrants in the case of Wilkes, argued strongly against the course of postponing a decision upon them, as not consistent with either the dignity of the House,

* See Blackstone's Commentaries, vol. iv. p. 291. ed. 1825.

† A most spirited sketch of the debates on General Warrants is given by Horace Walpole in his letter to the Earl of Hertford, February 15. 1764. Colonel Barré had just before, on account of his votes in Parliament, been dismissed from his military posts, and thus when he rose to speak, says Walpole, "Sir Edward Dering, one of "our noisy fools, called out '*Mr.* Barré!' The latter seized the "thought with admirable quickness, and said to the Speaker, who in "pointing to him had called him '*Colonel*,' 'I beg your pardon, Sir, "'you have pointed to me by a title I have no right to;'—and then "made a very artful and pathetic speech on his own services and dis-"mission."

or the importance of the subject. Pitt, as usual, adopted a most lofty tone: "I am no Judge," he cried, "but sit "here to judge Judges! There has not been a violation "of the Constitution but has been sanctified by the "greatest Judges." Sir Fletcher Norton, stung, per-"haps, by this attack, declared, on the other hand, that were he a Judge he should regard a Resolution of the House of Commons no more than the oaths of so many drunken porters in Covent Garden! For these words Norton was often afterwards taunted and reviled. Yet, though the words might be rough and coarse, the sentiment was in its substance just and true. It expressed the immense Constitutional interval between an enactment concurred in by both branches of the Legislature and a Resolution voted by only one,—an interval which the House of Commons in later years has been far too prone to overlook and overleap.

On reviewing in its present aspect the whole question of General Warrants, it must, I think, be acknowledged that the precedents for them are so numerous as fully to vindicate the Government for having had recourse to them. No Ministry, no Minister, is bound to make discoveries in Constitutional law. But after public attention had been called to the subject, and when the illegal nature of these Warrants had been established, both on argument and authority,—then Mr. Grenville may be justly blamed for persevering in their palliation or defence. He appears, however, to have acted in perfect good faith. His mind, though well cultivated, had no extensive range, and was ever swayed by form and precedent far more than by argument and reasoning. In his point of view no error could possibly attach to what as yet no House of Commons had condemned.

At the close of the Session in April 1764 the Ministers, after all the attacks levelled against them, were not subverted, scarcely shaken. They proceeded to give a proof both of their power and their resentment by turning out General Henry Seymour Conway, only brother of the Earl of Hertford, and connected either in blood or friendship with many of the first houses in the kingdom. He was by confession of all a brave soldier and honourable politician, and had no otherwise offended than by a conscientious vote against the Government on the question of General Warrants. For this crime he was now deprived, not only of his post in the Royal Bedchamber, but also of his regiment. A similar course, and for a similar reason, had a few weeks previously been pursued with respect to another respectable officer, General Acourt, then Member of Parliament for Heytesbury. These arbitrary steps, however, kindled little patriot fury in return. In like manner the flame which had arisen in Wilkes's case, far from becoming strong enough to consume his adversaries, rather languished and declined, now that Wilkes was no longer on the spot to fan it. Thus the Opposition could only descant with slighter effect on their more general topics, — the illegality of the arrest, — the danger to the Constitution, — and, above all, the continued influence and undiminished ascendency, as they proclaimed it, of the Northern Favourite.

There is no doubt that the King at this period continued to look upon Lord Bute in the light of a personal friend. But he was no longer, as the public continued to suppose, wholly or even mainly guided by Lord Bute's counsels. At the outset of his reign, as is owned by himself in one of his letters to Lord North, he had been quite ignorant of public business.* Day by day, however, his steadfast attention to his Royal duties, — the interviews with statesmen, and the reading of state papers, — made him more and more conversant with state affairs, and better able to transact them. He had therefore begun to rely less on any advice, or any adviser, than on his own careful and conscientious deliberation.†

The fixed popular belief in the unbounded favour of the Scottish Earl tended more than any other cause, perhaps, to injure His Majesty in the popular esteem. It must, I fear, be acknowledged, that during the first years of his reign George the Third was not beloved. Yet when we seek the cause, how slight, how trifling, are the reasons assigned! How little beyond his continued adherence to his early friend could be laid to his charge!

* To Lord North, May 19. 1778.

† A remarkable instance of this, *anno* 1764, appears in the Bedford Papers, vol. iii. p. 264.

Thus we find as a serious complaint urged by no mean authority,—from the son of a Prime Minister, and himself both a man of letters and a Member of Parliament,—that when the King left his palaces to enjoy a brief summer retirement, and dwell in the shades of Richmond with his youthful Queen, he was guilty of "such an "excess of privacy and economy" that Her Majesty's hairdresser waited on them at dinner, and that they allowed only four pounds of beef daily for their soup.* None but a hired flatterer, I presume, could, on the contrary, discover any topic of praise in this dislike of lavish waste, this preference for simple pleasures and homely fare.

More seriously speaking, however, we may well lament that imputations such as these should even for a time have marred and dimmed that popularity which the upright and worthy character of George the Third so well deserved. In every transaction, great or small, public or private, there was found in him the same unostentatious desire to judge wisely and do right. Franklin, no flatterer surely, no courtier at any period of his life, writes in 1769 as follows to a private friend: "I can "scarcely conceive a King of better dispositions, of more "exemplary virtues, or more truly desirous of promoting "the welfare of his subjects." † But besides this general character from a most competent witness, let me be allowed to cite one single instance of the conduct of George the Third in contrast to his grandfather's. When George the Second had to receive the Holy Eucharist, his main anxiety seems to have been that the sermon on that day might be a short one, since otherwise he was, to use his own words, "in danger of falling asleep and catching "cold." ‡ On the contrary how devout appears the

* H. Walpole to the Earl of Hertford, September 9. 1764. "This," he adds, "disgusts all sorts of people."

† Franklin's Correspondence, vol. vii p. 440. ed. 1840.

‡ Bishop Newton's Memoirs. (Works, vol. i. p. 76. ed. 1787.) The caution as to brevity was addressed to Newton himself when Sub-Almoner, and he adds: "The Doctor (himself) had before taken "care in his sermons at Court to come within the compass of twenty "minutes; but after this, especially on the great festivals, he never "exceeded fifteen, so that the King sometimes said to the Clerk of the "Closet, 'A short good sermon!'"

demeanour of George the Third partaking of that most solemn rite on a most solemn occasion,—on the very day when he was crowned. — When the young King approached the Communion Table for that object, he inquired of the Archbishop whether he should not lay aside his Crown? The Archbishop asked the Bishop of Rochester, but neither of them knew or could say what had been the usual form. Thus they left the point to His Majesty's own judgment: "Humility," thus he immediately determined, "best becomes such an act of "devotion;" and taking off his Crown laid it aside during his reverent reception of the holy rite.*

His Majesty's mother, the Princess Dowager, was at this time leading a wholly secluded life, and afforded little scope for the imputations still levelled against her.—But the most important member of the Royal Family, next to the King himself, was his uncle William, Duke of Cumberland. He too had been living for several years in retirement, and that retirement, as often happens to the great, had gone far to retrieve his previous unpopularity. Besides, one main cause of the disfavour under which he had suffered was his cruelty to the Scots after Culloden; and the change of feeling in England as regarded the Scots produced of course a corresponding change as regarded himself. All the countrymen of Lord Bute had most unjustly and most unhappily become included in the widely-spread aversion to that Minister. There was not one of his kinsfolk or retainers, — not a high-Tory Elliot from the Lowlands †, — not a Jacobite Macpherson from the Spey, — appointed to a place, but provoked a bitter national sneer. Thus it gradually grew to be thought that His Royal Highness of Cumberland had in 1746 exercised only a needful severity, and

* Bishop Newton's Memoirs. (Works, vol. i. p. 84.)

† Sir Gilbert Elliot, Member for the county of Selkirk, and father of the first Earl of Minto, stood high in the confidence and favour of Lord Bute, who in 1762 made him Treasurer of the Chamber. He was an able politician, and no contemptible poet; the author of "that beautiful pastoral song," as Sir Walter Scott calls it,

"My sheep I neglected, I broke my sheep-hook,
And all the gay haunts of my youth I forsook," &c. &c.

See Note xix. to Canto I. of the Lay of the Last Minstrel.

had not dealt with our northern countrymen (though our countrymen at that time they were seldom called!) more harshly than he ought.

It was certainly felt, even by those who could least excuse the barbarities which followed Culloden, that the Duke — "the Butcher," as he had been not unaptly termed — on that occasion deserved nevertheless the fullest praise of courage, honour, and sincerity. His hard stern sense of political duty, founded as it was on military discipline, though seldom winning affection, at last inspired confidence. Even the King, though trained up by the Princess Dowager to view him as a personal enemy, came ere long, as we shall find, to trust and to employ him. At this time, however, he was closely leagued with the Opposition. He had been much disappointed at the failure of the negotiation with Mr. Pitt in August 1763, and had ever since professed openly his admiration of that great statesman, though not apparently receiving any confidence in return. But his weight in the scale of politics was lessened by the ill state of his health. During the year 1764 his face was distorted by a stroke of apoplexy; while other painful maladies, and still more painful incisions to relieve them, racked his frame without ever depressing his courage. To the last, undaunted and serene, he was as little appalled by the scalpel of the surgeon as he had been by the sword of the enemy.

Another Member of the Royal Family, the Princess Augusta, one of the King's sisters, contracted in this year a marriage with the Hereditary Prince of Brunswick. For her portion she received the sum of 80,000*l*., which was cheerfully voted by the House of Commons. The Hereditary Prince, who was the favourite nephew and pupil of Frederick the Second, gave some offence at St. James's during his stay in this country by the veneration which he expressed for Mr. Pitt and a visit which he paid at Hayes. — As Duke of Brunswick in after life he commanded the Prussian armies against the French without any of the success of his Royal teacher, and died in 1806 from a wound received at the battle of Jena. The Duchess, his wife, who never ceased to be an Englishwoman in her feelings and habits *, was always highly esteemed for her private virtues. One of their daughters to her own and others, misfortune became Queen Caroline of England.

The profound peace which happily prevailed at this period rendered of slight concern to us the transactions of other Powers. But we found ourselves baffled by Spain in our demands for the Manilla ransom. It has been already related that when that city surrendered, the Archbishop Governor purchased an exemption from plunder by two millions of dollars in money and two more in bills upon the Spanish treasury.† When, however, these Bills came to be presented the Spanish Ministers were loud and angry in rejecting them. "As well," cried Grimaldi, "might the Archbishop have drawn on the King for the "province of Granada, or agreed to deliver up the city of "Madrid. I myself will rather be cut in pieces than lay "so disgraceful a proposal before the King my master." Squilaci, another of their Ministers, assumed a tone of irony: "Give us the two millions of dollars which you "have already received, and in return we will yield you "Manilla and all its dependencies!"—The objections of these gentlemen when calmly stated and reduced to writing resolved themselves to two; first, that the capitulation had been extorted by force, and, secondly, that Colonel Draper had broken it by permitting the city to be plundered. Of these grounds the second was false, and the first wholly frivolous, for, as Sir William Draper argues: "The ob-"jection and pretence of force and violence may be made "use of to evade any military agreements whatsoever, "where the two parties do not treat upon an equality; "for who in war will submit to an inconvenient and pre-"judicial compact unless from force? But have the "Spaniards forgot their own histories? Or will they "not remember the just indignation expressed against "Francis the First, who pleaded the like subterfuge of

* Mirabeau writes of her in 1786: "A la verité elle est toute "Anglaise, par les goûts, par les principes, et par les manières; au "point que son independence presque cynique fait avec l'etiquette "des Cours Allemandes le contraste le plus singulier que je con-"naisse." (Histoire Secrète de la Cour de Berlin, vol. i. p. 240.)

† History, vol. iv. p. 267.

"force and violence to evade the treaty made after the "battle of Pavia and his captivity?"*

Plain, however, as our right appears, and frequently as it was urged at the Court of Madrid, it was always either rejected or eluded. In this case, as in many others, was felt the loss of Pitt's high reputation with foreign Powers. Grenville, though a most accurate and ready reckoner in finance, had little skill, little weight, in diplomacy. This view of his character was some years afterwards expressed by a great writer with much wit. In the pamphlet on the Falkland Islands in 1771 Dr. Johnson had in his first edition inserted, though he afterwards expunged, these words: "Let not Mr. George Grenville be depreciated "in his grave. He had powers not universally possessed; "could he have enforced payment of the Manilla ransom "he could have counted it!"†

In the autumn of this year the high price of provisions throughout England caused many complaints and some tumults. In Derbyshire especially the colliers, finding wheat one day in the market at eight shillings and four-pence the bushel, used violence, and insisted on purchasing the whole quantity at five shillings the bushel, which, they said, was the London price. In York the chief gentlemen associated to raise a fund for the importation of corn from other counties, so that the poor might be supplied at a reasonable rate. In London the principal merchants presented a petition to Lord Halifax as chief of the Board of Trade, which led forthwith to the calling of a Council, the examination of evidence, and finally the issue of a Royal proclamation allowing the free import of salt beef, salt pork, and butter from Ireland, and promising a reward of 100*l.* for discovering any unlawful combinations in the sale of provisions of any kind.‡

The hand of Death fell heavy this year on the chiefs of Opposition in England. In March expired that great magistrate the Earl of Hardwicke. In the summer he was

* The memorial of Sir William Draper is printed in the Annual Register, 1764, part i. p. 138. For the negotiations at Madrid, see Coxe's History of the Bourbon Kings of Spain, vol. iv. p. 330.

† Boswell's Life of Johnson, vol. iii. p. 152. ed. 1835.

‡ Annual Register, 1764, part i. p. 103.

followed by Henry Legge, who as Chancellor of the Exchequer had been the able colleague of Pitt, and who still adhered to Pitt in politics, though not bound to him in friendship. He was a practical useful man of business, and, as Sir Robert Walpole said of him, had "very little "rubbish in his head," but lowered himself in some degree by his excessive addiction to puns and jests. Even on the very day before he died, when an old friend came in to see him, Legge could not forbear exclaiming: "Brother sportsman, I used to laugh at your being too "heavy for a chase, but now you are come in at the "death!"—In reward of his services the extinct Barony of Stawell of 1682 had been revived and granted to his wife, a daughter of that house*, but on the death of their only son in 1820 the title again became extinct.

In the autumn the Opposition party sustained a still greater and, as Pitt called it at the time, an irreparable loss in the Duke of Devonshire, whom a renewed attack of palsy carried off at Spa. It is not easy to discriminate between his character and his father's, the friend of Sir Robert Walpole, whom he seemed to have succeeded in principles and disposition as much as in title and estates. Like his parent he was distinguished not indeed by any shining talents, but by probity and worth, by a strict love of justice, and a conscientious attention to business. He was but forty-four years of age, but had already come to be regarded as the chief of the Great Houses of what were then termed Revolution principles. Had his life been spared a few years or even months longer, there is no doubt that on Pitt's return to power he would have been called to fill one of the highest offices of Court or State.

His son the succeeding Duke was at this time only sixteen years of age, and at no time did he study state affairs. But the importance of the House of Cavendish was in great measure upheld by the late Duke's brothers. Lord John especially, the youngest of all, was well-read, held in just esteem for his truth and honour, and resolute in his views, though shy and bashful in his manner. "Under "the appearance of virgin modesty," says Horace Wal-

* Collins's Peerage, vol. vii. p. 281.

pole, "he had a confidence in himself that nothing could "equal."* In reality, however, his abilities were only moderate, nor yet did he bring to public life any very steady application. If indeed we were to judge of him only by the overflowing eulogies of Burke after his retirement we might rank him among the greatest luminaries and benefactors of mankind. But far different are the hints which during his lifetime are dropped by Burke in familiar letters. Thus in one place he wishes that his friend could be induced to "show a degree of regular at-"tendance on business." And he adds: "Lord John "ought to be allowed a certain decent and reasonable "portion of fox-hunting; but anything more is intoler-"able!"†

The decease of Lord Hardwicke left vacant his honorary office as High Steward of the University of Cambridge. No sooner was his dangerous illness known than two candidates declared themselves; the first was his son, Lord Royston; the second, Lord Sandwich. It grew to be in some measure a trial of strength between the Opposition and the Government. Gray writes from the spot in February: "This silly dirty place has had all its "thoughts taken up with choosing a new High Steward;" yet contemptuously as he spoke of the contest, he was soon, as usually happens in such cases, drawn into its whirl. He took an eager part against the Minister, and contributed on this occasion a bitter lampoon, in which his Lordship's recent nick-name of "Jemmy Twitcher" was not forgotten.‡ When at last the day of election came the votes appeared to be equal, though each party claimed a majority of one. Great altercations ensued at

* Memoirs of George III., vol. iii. p. 24.

† To the Marquis of Rockingham, December 5. 1774. Corresp., vol. i. p. 505.

‡ In this pasquinade, which is not published in the earlier editions of his works, Gray alludes with especial acrimony to the number of clergyman who supported Lord Sandwich. He makes *Divinity* address him thus:

"Never hang down your head you poor penitent elf;
Come kiss me, — I'll be Mrs. Twitcher myself!"

(Poems, p. 91. ed. Chiswick, 1822.)

the moment, and a lawsuit afterwards, when after several months a decision was pronounced in favour of Lord Hardwicke.

Two remarkable incidents in Pitt's career took place about this time; the first, his renewed and final estrangement from the Duke of Newcastle. The causes are not quite clear, but it is equally easy to suspect capricious anger on the part of Pitt, or double dealing on his Grace's. It appears, however, that Newcastle had in some debate failed to defend his former colleague, and that he now applied for the Great Commoner's advice and direction on some overtures from Sir George Young relative to the movements in the Cyder counties. The Duke himself speaks of the subject of these overtures as "a delicate "one, and requiring many explanations." But his letter only drew from Pitt such resentful expressions as the following: "Having seen the close of last Session, and "the system of that great war, in which my share of the "Ministry was so largely arraigned, given up by silence "in a full House, I have little thoughts of beginning the "world again upon a new centre of union. Your Grace "will not, I trust, wonder if, after so recent and so "strange a phenomenon in politics, I have no disposition "to quit the free condition of a man standing single, and "daring to appeal to his country at large upon the sound-"ness of his principles, and the rectitude of his conduct."* And from this time forward we never find Pitt allude to Claremont but in terms of distrust and disdain.†

The other event in Pitt's life was more pleasing and wholly unexpected. A rich Baronet in Somersetshire, Sir William Pynsent, had been a Member of the House of Commons in the last years of Queen Anne, but had retired from Parliament and from the world in disgust at the Peace of Utrecht. Thenceforth he had lived at his seat of Burton Pynsent in moody seclusion, eccentric in his manners, and in his morals not free from grievous imputations.‡ But after half a century the news of the

* Letter to the Duke of Newcastle, October, 1764.

† See especially in the Chatham Papers, vol. ii. p. 322. and 345.

‡ The rumour against him (though wholly vague and without proof) was the same as against the father of Catherine Fillol, first

Peace of Paris stirred up again in his mind the feelings of his youth, and seemed to him a parallel to the times which he remembered. Above all, he was struck with admiration of that lofty-minded statesman who had flung away office sooner than accept unworthy terms, or consent to compromise the dignity of England. Having no near kinsman that survived him, he resolved when making his last Will to name Pitt for his heir; and thus at his death, which ensued in January 1765, Pitt suddenly found himself possessed of an excellent country house and nearly three thousand pounds a year. The pleasure which he may have felt on this occasion was without the slightest alloy. There was no descendant of Sir William could call himself defrauded of his rights or reasonable expectations. There was no enemy of Pitt could whisper against him the name of legacy-hunter, since he had never once seen nor even written to Sir William. The voice of Faction itself must be mute, or must acknowledge that this was an unsought tribute most honourably paid to high public character and eminent public services.

On the other hand, as if to balance this favour of Fortune, Pitt's old enemy, the gout, returned upon him at this period with new and most constant force, confining him to his room, and almost to his bed, at Hayes, during the first months of 1765.

On the 10th of January the Parliament had met, but its proceedings were at first languid and listless, chiefly on account of Pitt's absence and the daily hopes of his return. At last, however, the question of General Warrants was brought forward by Sir William Meredith, but without success. Warm debates also were raised by General Conway and his friends on the dismission of military officers for political votes. But while such personal or party questions were exciting the keenest attention, — a twelvemonth afterwards to be utterly forgotten as though they had never been, — another measure was gliding through both Houses, with little stir or notice, — a measure whose effects were not to be con-

wife of the Protector Somerset; — "repudiata, quia pater ejus post "nuptias eam cognovit." (Note to Vincent's Baronage at the Heralds' College.)

fined to a single century or a single hemisphere,—a measure which contained within it the first germ of a mighty revolution. This (now to be carefully traced) was the celebrated STAMP ACT for taxing our North American colonies.

CHAPTER XLIII.

By the Peace of Paris in 1763 the power of the French in America was utterly extinguished. They had yielded to the English Canada, Cape Breton, and Louisiana to the east of the Mississippi, while the remainder of that province was acquired from them by Spain as an indemnity for Florida, which Spain gave up to England. Thus there were only the two Peninsular nations to divide with ourselves the dominion of that immense Continent. From the Gulf of Mexico to the Gulf of the St. Lawrence a long line of thriving Colonies acknowledged as their sovereign King George the Third. Happy had it been for England if the views of her Ministers at that period had expanded with her territory, and led them to treat these distant settlers, not as lowly dependants, but rather as fellow-subjects and as freemen! Happy had they refrained from measures of aggression which — rashly urged in council, but feebly supported in war, — have converted many once loyal and contented provinces into a rival empire!

It is remarkable that of all these Colonies, besides some of the newly settled ones, only those last acquired, and least bound to Great Britain in language, in religion, or in race, — namely, the two Canadas, — have remained subject to the British Crown.

A slight sketch for the general reader of the Thirteen British Colonies which lay between the new British conquests, — between Canada and Florida, — and which afterwards became the Thirteen United States of North America, may properly precede an account of the Revolution to which they gave rise. We will take them in geographical order, beginning at the north and proceeding southwards.

First then appear the four Colonies to which the common name of New England was applied. These were MASSACHUSETTS, then comprising Maine; NEW HAMPSHIRE, then comprising Vermont; CONNECTICUT, and RHODE ISLAND. In the midst of them, and already thriving as a seaport, rose, almost surrounded by the waves, the fair city of Boston, regarded not merely as its capital by Massachusetts, but as a centre and point of union by the rest. These New England Colonies owe their origin to the Puritans, who, hating the Established Church, and persecuted by her, forsook their native country. The first of these — the Pilgrim Fathers, as they have been termed, — came over in 1620 in a single ship, the Mayflower, of only 180 tons. Landing near Cape Cod, on the shores of Massachusetts, they gave to the place the name of Plymouth, in memory of the last at which they had touched in England. Great were the hardships against which they had at first to battle, but their fortitude and perseverance, and reliance upon God, were greater still. Nor did they fail to gain strength by fresh accessions from England, although desiring them from no communion besides their own. Their Colony Seal bore an Indian, erect, with an arrow in his right hand, and the motto: "Come over and help us." * At one time Cromwell himself, then a man of little note, had been on board ship to join them, when there came an order from Whitehall that he and the other intended emigrants should be disembarked,—an order, it has been aptly said, which in its final consequences destroyed both King and Commonwealth. †

Knowledge in these Colonies made early and rapid strides. The College which derived its name from John Harvard, one of its first benefactors, was founded in 1636. The press began its work so soon as 1639, although the first American newspaper — the Boston News-Letter — was not published till 1704. ‡ In 1647 it was

* Bancroft's History of the United States, vol. i. p. 346. ed. 1839.

† Lord Byron, Preface to *Marino Faliero*. It is curious how closely the list of instances there given is found repeated (so far as the dates allowed) by *Angiolina* in the tragedy itself. (Act 5. scene 1.)

‡ See a note by Mr. Jared Sparks to Franklin's Life and Writings, vol. i. p. 23. ed. 1840. "At present," says Mr. Bancroft in his Introduction, "there are more daily journals in the United States than "in the world besides."

enacted by law, "that every township, after the Lord "hath increased them to the number of fifty householders, "shall appoint one to teach all children to write and "read; and where any town shall increase to the number "of one hundred families, they shall set up a grammar-"school."*

At the accession of George the Third the New England Colonies had greatly advanced in wealth and luxury. This is manifest in several passages of the Private Diary, not long since made public, of Mr. John Adams, the second President of the United States. Dining with one gentleman at Boston he describes with admiration "the "Turkey carpets, the painted hangings, the marble "tables, the rich beds with crimson damask curtains "and counterpanes, the beautiful chimney-clock, the "spacious garden, — all," he says, "most magnificent. "A seat it is for a nobleman, a prince!"† Much, therefore, of the austerity and gloom of the first Puritans had departed from their children. They no longer preached against wigs and curls; they no longer thought that female fashions of attire — "hoods of silk and scarfs of "tiffany" — were essential points of legislation. Still, however, it may be said that in slight circumstances or expressions some signs of the old leaven remained. Thus, for instance, in 1774 I find some disturbers of the public peace in one of the towns of Massachusetts designated by a favourite phrase of the Puritans — "certain sons of "Belial." Thus again in 1775 I observe it stated by a British officer on an exploring expedition through the province, that "nobody is allowed to walk the streets "during Divine Service without being taken up and "examined."‡ But passing from mere forms or words, it may be said of the people of New England at this juncture that there still dwelt among them undiminished the stern religious principle and the steadfast resolution of their fathers. They were as determined to assert for themselves their lawful — and perhaps more than their

* Bancroft's History of the United States, vol. i. p. 458.

† Diary, January 16. 1766. Collected Works, vol. ii. p. 179. ed. 1850.

‡ American Archives, edited by Mr. Peter Force, and published by the authority of Congress in 1837, &c., vol. i. p. 732. and 1265.

lawful — freedom of thought and action. They were as prompt to feel and to resent — or even sometimes as we may think to imagine and exaggerate — any aggression on their liberties; they were as ready if the need arose (and this all parties must own to their praise) to encounter peril and hardship rather than tamely suffer wrong.

The State of NEW YORK was first colonised by the Dutch, and first called the New Netherlands. In 1609 a hardy seaman, Hendrick Hudson, discovered and sailed up the majestic river, which has since come to bear his name. He was the earliest of all Europeans to view the swelling range of the Kaatskill mountains, to wake the echoes of the Dunderberg, or invade the solitude of Sleepy Hollow, — scenes which even then he pronounced "the most beautiful country that the foot of man ever "trod," * and which the genius of Washington Irving, — the Goldsmith, nay even the Addison, of America, — has since made familiar to us all. Not many years had passed ere a small town, or rather a cluster of cottages, rose on the island of Mohattan, near the mouth of the Hudson, with the name of New Amsterdam, while higher up the stream another town, Fort Orange, was founded. But the wars between Holland and England under Charles the Second led to the conquest of these settlements by the latter. Even before their conquest was achieved they had been yielded by the King as a grant to his brother, the Duke of York. Then the country changed not only its masters, but its names; New Amsterdam became New York, and Fort Orange was called Albany, from the Scottish title of His Royal Highness. Under the British rule the colony continued to grow and thrive, assisted mainly by its own fruitful territory and favourable skies. "Probably," says a native writer, "few countries possess a greater range of soils, or are so "well adapted to a great variety of productions." † The

* *het schoonste land dat men met voeten betreden kon.* See a note to Mr. Bancroft's History, vol. ii. p. 266.

† Agriculture of New York, by Dr. Emmons, 1846, p. 2. I observe, however, in the next page that in this State "certain fruit "trees, as the apple and plum, though they may flourish for several "years, are yet liable to be destroyed by an unseasonable frost." The

town of New York, moreover, was well placed for all purposes of trade, and possessed, by its bar of Sandyhook, flanked by Long and Staten Islands, an excellent port secure from every wind. Few cities accordingly have grown more rapidly in numbers and in wealth. The population which was estimated in 1756 at 13,000, and in 1774 at 22,000, exceeded in 1840 300,000 souls.* Stately edifices, public and private, have arisen in due season; and thus at present the grandeur of Broadway never fails to be admired, even by those who have gazed on the most splendid capitals of Europe.

NEW JERSEY was in its origin a part of the New Netherlands, but was dismembered from them on their acquisition by the Duke of York. His Royal Highness immediately made over to Lord Berkeley and Sir George Carteret the tract of land between the Hudson and the Delaware for "a competent sum of money," as the deed of assignment assures us. The province thus formed received from the Duke the name of New Jersey, in compliment to Carteret, who had defended the Isle of Jersey against the Long Parliament in the Civil Wars. It was the first care of the new Proprietaries (for such was the term applied to those who obtained from the Crown, directly or indirectly, the grant of any of the American settlements) to invite the resort of further settlers by a Charter of liberal popular rights. Great numbers accordingly came over, above all from the bodies of Dissenters which were smarting under disqualifications or discouragements at home. It was not long before Lord Berkeley sold his share to an association of Quakers, and the province was then formally divided between them and Sir George Carteret under the names of West New Jersey and East New Jersey.

At the accession of Queen Anne, however, the heirs of Carteret had become convinced that there seignorial rights tended only to embroil them with the colonists, and to diminish their own profits as in part owners of the

volume from which I quote is one of a series on the Natural History of New York, prepared and published at the expense of the State; a most munificent and enlightened undertaking in the cause of science.

* Mac-Gregor's Tariffs: UNITED STATES, p. 316.

soil. They, therefore, hearkened willingly to an overture from the English Ministers for a surrender of their powers of Government to the Crown, and the two Jerseys were then re-united under the same Governor, the same Council, the same House of Assembly. Still, however, the plural name of "the Jerseys" remained, and will be found still most frequently applied to this province. Under Queen Anne the population might be estimated at twenty thousand, of whom a great majority were Quakers, Presbyterians, and Anabaptists. There were only two clergymen of the Church of England, and even these with no place of public worship provided.*

The inland tract beyond the Delaware was still, in great measure, a primæval forest in the latter days of Charles the Second. But a large party of Quakers in England cast their eyes in that direction as eager to put in practice unmolested their theories of life and government. West New Jersey, which they had purchased, seemed a sphere too narrow for them, and they possessed a zealous and active leader in William Penn. That remarkable man was the son of a gentleman, and the heir of an estate, in Buckinghamshire, where the range of Penn Woods, near Beaconsfield, still preserves the family name. He had been designed for the army, and it is singular that the only authentic portrait remaining of the Quaker chief represents him as clad in complete armour.† On his espousing the tenets of "the Friends" he had to suffer imprisonment and persecution for conscience sake. By the course of time, however, and the change of parties, he acquired some influence at Court, and was able in 1681 to obtain a Royal Charter assigning to himself and his heirs a large tract of the land beyond the Delaware. Thither accordingly he proceeded with a numerous Quaker train. The city which they began to build near the confluence of the Schuylkill and the Delaware was called Philadelphia, from the brotherly love which they trusted would there prevail, while the Colony itself com-

* Grahame's History of the United States, vol. ii. p. 302. ed. 1836. In Mr. Grahame's last volume he becomes *Americanis ipsis Americanior.*

† See a note to Franklin's Works, vol. vii. p. 191. ed. 1840.

bined the remembrance of its forest-state and of its founder in the name of PENNSYLVANIA. How vast the scope which at that period the New World opened to enterprising spirits in the Old! To become from a plain country gentleman, or the spokesman of a few enthusiasts, the "Proprietary" in title, but in truth the Prince, of an immense territory! To gain Pennsylvania in the place of Penn Woods!

Even during the lifetime of Penn the interests of the Proprietary were found to clash with those of the colonists, and also with those of the Crown. But these differences grew much greater when on his death his sons succeeded to his rights, though not to his popularity and influence. There were also other difficulties to perplex the rising Colony. Though many other sectarians had arrived as settlers, the Quakers still formed a majority in the House of Assembly, and found it hard to reconcile their principles of peace with the frequent demands of the Crown for military aid. Franklin, who resided so many years among them, observes that they used a variety of evasions to avoid complying, and a variety of modes of disguising the compliance when it became unavoidable. The common mode at last was to grant money under the phrase of its being "for the King's use," and never to inquire how it was applied.*

DELAWARE, both the river and the state which lies near its mouth, derive their name from Thomas Lord Delaware, who had been Captain-General of Virginia under James the First. This territory was originally occupied by the Swedes, who indeed had also helped to colonise New Jersey on the opposite bank of the stream. Next it

* Life by himself, ch. viii. p. 154. ed. 1840. Franklin adds that on one occasion when powder was wanted for the garrison at Louisburg, which was much urged on the House by Governor Thomas, "they would not grant money to buy powder, because that was an ingredient of war; but they voted an aid to New England of 3,000*l.* "to be put into the hands of the Governor, and appropriated it for the "purchase of bread, flour, wheat, or *other grain.* Some of the Council, "desirous of giving the House still further embarrassment, advised "the Governor not to accept provision as not being the thing he had "demanded; but he replied: 'I shall take the money, for I understand very well their meaning; *other grain* is gunpowder,' which "he accordingly bought, and they never objected to it!"

passed to the Dutch, and afterwards with the New Netherlands to the English. Still later it became under William Penn an appanage of Pennsylvania. So it continued in some measure until the Revolutionary War, while in other respects it might be termed a separate Colony. Thus it had an Assembly of its own, but that Assembly was in general convened by the Pennsylvanian Governor, and the province was often designated by the dubious phrase of "the Lower Counties."

The Colony next in order owes its foundation to an upright and honourable statesman, Sir George Calvert, who had served as one of the Secretaries of State under James the First, and who under Charles the First was created Lord Baltimore in the Irish Peerage. To himself and his heirs as Proprietaries the new settlement was granted by the Crown, and in honour of Queen Henrietta Maria he gave it the name of MARYLAND. The chief city, which has now become one of the most flourishing in North America, received his own title of Baltimore. While yet a Commoner he had embraced the Roman Catholic faith, and relinquished office for its sake, and thus his settlement became the favourite resort for emigrants of the same persuasion. Yet the Roman Catholics as such enjoyed no special privileges or immunities in Maryland; freedom of conscience and equality of civil rights were from the outset conceded to all, except only the Socinians. For the clause granting this religious liberty was clogged with a proviso that "whatsoever person shall deny or "reproach the Holy Trinity, or any of the Three Persons "thereof, shall be punished with death." *

The noble bay of Chesapeak, formed by the estuaries of the Susquehanna and Potomac rivers, is bounded on its western side by the shores of VIRGINIA. This, the earliest of all the chartered Colonies of England, was first planned by the chivalrous Raleigh, and named by and from the maiden Queen, Elizabeth. Raleigh's coadjutors or lieutenants, as Lane and Greenville, bold and gallant spirits, were, however, more successful as explorers than

* Bancroft's History of the United States, vol. i. p. 256. An attempt, far from candid, to conceal this proviso, appears to be made by Mr. Bacon in his *Laws of Maryland at Large*, 1649, c. i.

as colonists. No real progress in settlement was made until the succeeding reign. Successive Charters were granted by King James, mainly in favour of the London Company, or as they were called "Adventurers," — a term honourable then, though reproachful now. But that Company which might have risen to an eminence resembling the East Indian, greatly abused its trust; it dissatisfied the colonists, it became involved in dissensions with the Crown; the Judges gave sentence against it; and finally in 1624 the Company was dissolved, and the Crown succeeded to its rights. Already had the colonists won for themselves the rights of a popular assembly; and these rights, which had been wrested from the London Company, were confirmed, or at least not annulled, by Charles the First.

Virginia, as the firstborn of the Colonies, grew, it may be said, to man's estate sooner than the rest. The settlers were chiefly of the Established Church, and comprised some of the highest rank of gentry, as, for example, the Lords Fairfax. Their staple produce was tobacco, a large source of wealth to them, as protected by a monopoly in England; at one period indeed in our common speech we may observe the word Virginia used as a synonym for the plant.* On the whole then at the accession of George the Third there might be found in this Colony less, no doubt, of commercial enterprise than among its neighbours, but a larger population in proportion to its settled territory; and a greater degree of landed affluence, perhaps also of mental refinement. It is a striking fact that of the five first Presidents of the United States no less than four were natives of Virginia.

In the two CAROLINAS—NORTH and SOUTH, and in Charleston, the chief city of the latter,—the appellation was either conferred or retained in honour of Charles the Second.† A Charter of that territory was granted

* As in Pope's humorous imitation of Swift and enumeration of blessings, entitled *The Happy Life of a Country Parson*:

" A wife that makes conserves; a steed
" That carries double when there's need;
" October store, and *best Virginia*,
" Tithe-pig, and mortuary guinea!"

† The name of Carolina was probably first given in honour of

by that King in 1663 to a large number of persons as Proprietaries, including not only those who wished to go forth and colonise, as Lord Berkeley and Sir George Carteret, but also various statesmen in office or favour at that time, as the Duke of Albemarle, the Earl of Clarendon, and Lord Ashley. Settlements were made accordingly, first in North and afterwards in South Carolina, sometimes increased by the emigration of persecuted Protestants from France or Germany. But the yoke of the Proprietaries proved hard to bear; some were distant and careless, others on the spot but grasping and oppressive; there ensued great misrule and oppression, and then the usual consequences,—popular insurrection and the final grant of a representative assembly. Still, however, the bickerings on a lesser scale continued, and finally in 1729 the remaining Proprietaries, on receiving the moderate sum of 17,500*l.*, surrendered their rights to the Crown.—The staple commodities of the Carolinas were rice, tar, and afterwards indigo. Here, as in Virginia, the influence of a southern latitude becomes apparent; both the climate and the produce, and the modes of life resulting from them, more nearly, perhaps, approach those of Jamaica than those of Massachusetts.

The most southerly and the last founded of all these Colonies was GEORGIA. It owed its name to King George the Second, but its origin, establishment, and furtherance to James Oglethorpe, a Member of the British Parliament. This most worthy man had chosen arms for his profession at an early age, and ardent as he was then for military fame had served as a volunteer under Prince Eugene at the siege of Belgrade. In our own army he in after years, and by due course of seniority, attained the rank of General. But objects of benevolence

Charles IX. of France, and confirmed in honour of Charles II. of England. But "it is curious what variety of origin might plausibly "be found for the name of Carolina." Such is the observation of Mr. Henry Reed, the American editor of this History, whose great care and accuracy, as well as courtesy, I am glad to have the opportunity of thus publicly acknowledging. He has justly noticed the error of a hasty allusion to that name of Carolina which I had made in my twentieth Chapter, and had left uncorrected. (See note in the American ed. 1849, vol. i. p. 476.)

and practical humanity had meanwhile become paramount in his mind. On entering the House of Commons he zealously applied himself to alleviate the sufferings of his kind. It was to him that the investigation and reform of our Prisons in 1728 and the succeeding years, as already related in this History*, was mainly due. The same zeal for humanity led him to plan a colony, for the remoter districts, hitherto unpeopled, of South Carolina, which he intended as a resource and asylum for insolvent debtors in England, and for persecuted Protestants in Germany. He found associates — as the Earl of Shaftesbury, the author of the Characteristicks, — in his benevolent designs; and in 1732 they obtained a Royal Charter for their new province during twenty-one years, not as Proprietaries, — not with any collateral view of personal advantage, such as might be traced in even the most upright and highminded of all their predecessors, as in Baltimore and Penn, — but solely, as the deed expresses it, "in trust for the poor." At their own request they were expressly restrained from receiving any grant of land, or any emolument whatever, for themselves. Their Common Seal represented a group of silk-worms at work, with the motto NON SIBI SED ALIIS; thus alluding not only to their own disinterested views, but also, more clearly, to the expected produce of their settlement.

A few months after the grant of the Charter Oglethorpe himself embarked with the first band of emigrants, and sailing up the boundary river of his province laid the foundations of the present city of Savannah. Other accessions speedily joined him, including Moravians from Germany; and so much favour did the rising colony find in England that the House of Commons voted in its support various sums of money which in the course of two years amounted to 36,000*l.* It is a remarkable indication of the spirit of that age or of these persons that the land open to Jews was closed against "Papists." But, on the other hand, it deserves most honourable commemoration that the introduction or use of negro-slaves was expressly prohibited, — prohibited notwith-

* Vol. ii. p. 150.

standing the complaints of many of the colonists, and even the secession of some. "Slavery," said Oglethorpe himself, "is against the Gospel, as well as against the "fundamental law of England. We refused, as Trustees, "to make a law permitting such a horrid crime."* With the native Indians Oglethorpe had from the first cultivated friendly and frequent intercourse, and he trusted ere long to hail them as brother Christians. Many zealous clergymen, including, as we have seen elsewhere, the two Wesleys, had come forth from England to assist in their conversion.

Oglethorpe, however, though the Colony which he had founded continued to thrive and grow, was by no means always wise, nor always successful, in his conduct. Several of his favourite schemes, small and great, from the cultivation of silk to the conversion of the Indians, may be considered to have failed. Nor did his prohibition of slavery endure against strong temptation and neighbouring example, when once his personal influence had been withdrawn. Returning to England in 1743, after ten years' toil upon his object, he never again revisited the Colony. In his later years he had the honour of numbering Dr. Johnson among his friends, and he died in a green old age in 1785. But Oglethorpe might have died more happy had his days been more few. He had lived too long, since he, a loyal subject, and soldier of the British Crown, and proud of having been the means of giving it one province more, survived to see that province severed from its sway, and arrayed against its arms.

At the time when the troubles began the numbers of the people in these thirteen States might be estimated at two millions of European blood, and about half a million of others.† Substantial comfort had prevailed among them from an early period, though in some, refinements, which we have come to consider almost necessaries, were of much later growth. Thus, notwithstanding the im-

* Memoirs of Sharpe, vol. i. p. 234, as quoted by Mr. Bancroft.

† See Burke's Speech on Conciliation with the Colonies, March 22. 1775. He adds, "I have taken for some years a good deal of pains "on [ascertaining] that point."

portance which the city of Philadelphia had attained, no measures were taken towards either lighting or paving it until 1757.* As in all rising settlements, skilled labour commanded a high price; we find, for example, Washington, when only a stripling of sixteen, and employed in surveying among the Alleghany mountains, write as follows:—"A doubloon is my constant gain every day "that the weather will admit, and sometimes six pis-"toles."† In only one of the States, namely, in Virginia, had there been introduced the English system of entails for landed property.‡ Monarchical as was the form of government in these Colonies, as being part of the British dominions, it can hardly be alleged that there prevailed in them at that time any arrogant state or haughty barrier of rank. As one instance to the contrary, we may observe that Benjamin Franklin, while still a very young man, and a journeyman printer at Philadelphia, used to be freely admitted to the table of Sir William Keith, the Governor of the province, who, as Franklin states, was wont to converse with him "in a most affable, "familiar, and friendly manner."—But when the Revolutionary War had once begun, and the Monarchical distinctions been cast aside, we find another and more galling distinction—that of wealth and poverty—even in the same societies, most punctiliously observed. For example, in the year 1780, and at the same city of Philadelphia, a French officer, and warm partisan of the Americans, the Marquis de Chastellux, after describing a ball, proceeds to say: "When the time came to go into "the supper-room, our Minister offered his arm to Mrs. "Morris, and made her walk out the first; an honour "here commonly paid to her, because she is the wealthiest "lady in the city, and because, all ranks being now equal, "men are free to follow their natural bent, which is to "award the highest respect to riches."§

* Franklin's Life by himself, ch. ix.

† Writings, vol. ii. p. 419. ed. 1840. For this large gain, however, young men had to undergo many hardships: "We camped in "the woods . . . every one was his own cook . . . our plates were "large chips; as for dishes, we had none."

‡ Wirt's Life of Patrick Henry, p. 33. ed. 1818.

§ Voyages du Marquis de Chastellux, vol. i. p. 235.

At the first plantation or the legal settlement of each American Colony, its government had been framed upon the English model, so far as its circumstances would allow. There was in each, a House of Assembly elected by the people. There was a Council, sometimes derived from election, but more commonly from nomination, or sometimes with a right of Veto on the former. There was a Governor appointed by the Crown, or, in the case of Proprietary rights, by the Proprietaries and the Crown in conjunction. In one single Colony, namely, in Connecticut, the Governor owed his post to popular election. But besides this and a few other such exceptions of principle, the general outline was moulded into a great variety of forms, nor were the laws of any one province assimilated in all respects to the laws of any other. There also prevailed between them no small amount of rival pretensions, of jealousies and heartburnings. It may be asserted that such variations were fully equal to those between the Italian states at the present day; there were as many and as wide differences, legal, political, and social; and in the case of America there were religious superadded. Thus the difficulty of concert and union, which we so often hear alleged in Italy, must have been felt not less keenly in North America. It is a difficulty which should ever be borne in mind by every candid historian of the Revolutionary War, as tending to enhance the success of the Americans when they succeeded, and to excuse in some degree their failure when they failed.

In all these North American states, except only, as we have seen, at the foundation of Georgia, both the use and the importation of negro slaves prevailed. For this, however, no blame whatever can be ascribed to the colonists, since at that time slavery and the slave trade formed a part of the general colonial policy of England. In some cases we may even observe that the colonists, dreading an excessive cultivation, and consequent low price of their produce, endeavoured to restrain the practice within more narrow bounds; thus in 1727 "the vast importation of "negroes" was a subject of complaint in South Carolina. All the indigo and rice from Carolina, and nearly all the tobacco from Virginia and Maryland, were the fruit of slave-labour. Even in the northern states, where negroes were far less numerous, they were still employed in menial offices, and the culture of wheat and maize.

An accomplished American writer of our own day has well observed of the negro, at that period, among his countrymen, that "the early writers tell us little of his "history, except the crops which he raised." * Testimonies of the planter's cruelty, and, still oftener, indifference towards him, are, however, to be found. Thus in the reign of George the Second, Bishop Berkeley, in referring to these Colonies, found it needful to rebuke "the irrational contempt of the blacks," which regarded them "as creatures of another species, having no right to "be instructed, or admitted to the Sacraments." † At the very same period Charles Wesley writes as follows from South Carolina: "I had observed much and heard more "of the cruelty of masters towards their negroes; but now "I received an authentic account of some horrid instances "thereof. I saw myself that the giving a slave to a child "of its own age, to tyrannize over, to abuse and beat out "of sport, was a common practice; nor is it strange that "being thus trained up in cruelty they should arrive at "such perfection in it." ‡

Besides the negro slaves, there were also in these Colonies bond-servants — felons transported from England and assigned in service to the settlers. It was nearly the same system as recently prevailed in New South Wales and Van Diemen's Land, but here the convicts were so few in comparative numbers as to exercise little or no tainting influence on the mass of the population. There were, besides, other bond-servants, obtained through the villany of some captains of merchant ships, who used by flattering promises to entice the forlorn and unwary to embark for America, and then sold them into slavery on the plea of defraying their passage and entertainment. In 1686 it was found necessary to issue an Order in Council against this infamous practice. Again, in other cases, these

* Bancroft's History, vol. iii. p. 407.

† Sermon preached before the Society for the Propagation of the Gospel, February 18. 1731.

‡ Charles Wesley's MS. Journal, A.D. 1736, as quoted in Mr. Grahame's History, vol. iii. p. 422. Wesley adds, "Another much "applauded punishment is drawing the teeth of their slaves."

Colonies were deemed a fitting refuge for persons of slender intellect or broken fortune. Thus, for instance, in Johnson's Life of Waller, we are told that Benjamin, the eldest son of the poet, "was disinherited, and sent to New "Jersey, as wanting common understanding."

Along the frontier of these states, and often within it, ranged far and wide divers tribes of the Red Men, the native Indians. The character of these tribes has been most variously portrayed; sometimes invested with imaginary virtues from a vague admiration of savage life, sometimes, to justify oppression, loaded with as imaginary crimes. It will be found that in general they are painted all bright in poetry, and all black in state-papers. In truth they might often be admired for generous and lofty feelings, but were ever liable to be swayed to and fro by any sudden impulse, by their passions or their wants. They would endure bodily torment with the most heroic courage, and inflict it with the most unrelenting cruelty. Whenever they had neither warfare nor the chase in view they seemed indolent, dissolute, and listless, yet always with an inborn dignity of demeanor and a peculiar picturesqueness of language. In hostilities, on the contrary, they were found most formidable from their skilful and stealthy marches, their unforeseen attacks, and their ferocity in slaying and scalping their opponents. It is to be feared that nearly all the Europeans who came in contact with them, whether French or English, Republicans or Royalists, have been, when at peace among themselves, too ready to neglect or oppress these Indians, and when at war with each other too ready to employ them.

At the foundation, however, of the several Colonies, the rights of the native Indians to the soil had been in general to some extent acknowledged. Contracts had been concluded with them; and many of the proprietors in New England and the other states held their land by this tenure. But it was scarcely an exaggeration of one of the early Governors (Andros) to declare that any deed executed by an Indian was no better than "the scratch "of a bear's paw." Such contracts, indeed, have little moral weight when framed between the civilized man and the untutored savage, who knows not the value either of what he gives away or of what he accepts in return.

Attempts to bring over the North American Indians to the truths of Christianity were not unfrequently made, and sometimes with much earnestness and zeal, but seldom with any lasting effect. They displayed on some occasions a strange degree of perverted ingenuity in their doubts or objections. Thus, when the leading events of the Gospel were explained to them, several asked how Judas could deserve blame for promoting the accomplishment of the purpose of God?—On another occasion one of the chiefs sent for an Indian convert, and desired to know how many Gods the English had? When he heard they had but one, he replied scornfully "Is that all? I have thirty-"seven. Do they suppose I would exchange so many for "one?" *

It is the just though painful remark of an ecclesiastical historian, how seldom in the first instance the intercourse with a civilized people has been a blessing to barbarians.† While the Indians were thus heedless or untaught on the most important of all subjects, there was unhappily one practice of the educated Christian stranger—the use of ardent spirits—into which they rushed with the most frantic eagerness. It seemed a temptation which they were wholly unable to resist. So long as rum was supplied to them they would drink on, regardless of every other consideration, until in a state either of stupefaction or of fury. Franklin, in a striking passage of his Memoirs, has described a scene of the kind which he witnessed in 1750, and pointed out the baleful effects of this taste, or rather passion, amongst them,—how, worse than any other scourge, as pestilence, famine, or the sword, it had unpeopled whole districts and extinguished whole nations. "Rum," he adds, "has already annihilated all "the tribes which formerly inhabited the sea-coast."

At various periods there had arisen between the North American Colonies and the mother country differences touching the restrictions of trade which the latter had imposed. These differences were, no doubt, of considerable extent and bitterness; but, in my opinion, had no

* See Grahame's History of the United States, vol. i. p. 373. and 441.

† Gieseler, Kirchen-Geschichte, vol. i. part ii. p. 449. ed. 1845.

other and stronger cause of quarrel broken forth, they might have been to this day quietly debated before the Board of Trade at Whitehall.* Nor can it be denied that the view of these differences taken after the event by the later American writers is in many respects overcharged and one-sided. While they allege the commercial restrictions on America, they overlook her commercial privileges. Yet surely the one may in fairness be admitted as some counterpoise to the other. If the English were to be debarred from smoking any but Virginian-grown tobacco, there seems the less hardship in debarring the Virginians from wearing any but English-made cloth.

The cause of the first real estrangement and of the final separation was not in the main commercial hindrance, or the result of the British Navigation laws, but rather the attempt to tax America without her own consent. That ill-omened idea had been once suggested to Sir Robert Walpole, when the Excise Scheme had failed in England, and as some compensation for that failure. It had been laid before the Prime Minister by Sir William Keith, who had been lately Governor of Pennsylvania. But Sir Robert being asked soon after by Lord Chesterfield what he thought of Keith's project, replied with his usual good humour and good sense, "I have Old England set against "me, and do you think I will have New England like-"wise?"† Unhappily the decision on this subject was now to rest with a statesman of far less either good sense or good humour than Sir Robert Walpole.

It used to be said some sixty years since by one of the Under Secretaries of State, that "Mr. Grenville "lost America because he read the American despatches, "which none of his predecessors ever did.‡ As in many other pithy sayings this jest contains a leaven of truth. So long as the American Colonies were let alone they flourished. But no sooner were they pried into with the view of exacting money from them, than they became a

* The opposite opinion, however, was asserted by Mr. Huskisson in 1826, and also by Mr. Labouchere in his able speech on the Navigation Laws twenty-two years afterwards (May 15. 1848).

† Coxe's Life of Walpole, vol. i. p. 753.

‡ See a note by Sir Denis Le Marchant to Lord Orford's Memoirs (vol. ii. p. 69.).

darkening scene of anger and complaints, of tumults and alarms.

The leading idea of Grenville, and his favourite taunt against Pitt, was the large expense, or, as he termed it, the profusion, with which the last war had been carried on. He anxiously looked round for some new sources of supply to his Exchequer, and then in an evil hour the thought arose in his mind that as the late war had been undertaken in some measure for the defence of North America, it was just that North America should bear a portion of the burthens which that war had imposed. It never occurred to him to doubt that the right of the House of Commons to tax these Colonies without their own consent by the voice of their own representatives could be called in question. It never occurred to him to consider the spirit of the Statute-Book as well as its letter. It never occurred to him to weigh the danger of wide-spread and increasing alienation against the profit of a petty impost.

In justice to Grenville, it must, however, be acknowledged, that he did not proceed with headlong haste. In the Session of 1764 he, without finding any resistance, imposed duties on several articles of American trade. At the same time with these he proposed a Resolution, drawn in vague and general terms, that "it may be proper to charge certain Stamp Duties," in America *,— such as were already payable in England. But he did not take any further step towards them at that time. He desired the measure to be postponed for a year, that the sentiments of the Americans might be clearly ascertained. He called together the agents of the several North American Colonies in London, explained to them his project in detail, and bid them write to their respective Assemblies, that if any other duty equally productive would be more agreeable to them he would readily comply with their wish in that respect.

The news of this intended impost reached America at a most unfavourable juncture. The colonists had only just gained breathing-time from a fierce war with the bordering Indians. Hostilities had been commenced by

* Commons Journals, March 10. 1764.

these savage tribes, especially along the frontiers of Maryland, Pennsylvania, and Virginia, at about the very period when the peace with France was signed. Not only had they plundered and murdered many itinerant dealers and fired many single houses, but they had succeeded in reducing several out-posts, and without mercy put the garrisons to death. They had repulsed a party of our troops at Detroit, and had invested Fort Pitt; but a larger detachment from our army afterwards coming up under Colonel Bouquet, they were themselves defeated at Bushy-Run. Next year they were brought to terms of peace, and withdrew to their own wastes, but still they had left behind them no light expenses to defray, no small havoc to repair. Thus, as was remarked at the time, the Americans first heard of the British Resolutions for imposing Stamp Duties upon them while the yell of Indian carnage was yet in their ears, and the smoke of their ruined habitations yet before their eyes.

Another cause of irritation which unhappily combined with the former was the severity with which illicit traffic had been of late restrained. It had been found requisite soon after the conclusion of the Peace to put a check on the prevalence of smuggling both in the old Continent and in the new. With this object there were stationed at various points of the coast several armed cutters and other King's ships of war, whose officers were sworn and directed to act as revenue officers. Even on the shores of England such a system was not free from objection, but on America it pressed far more heavily. There, as in all newly-settled countries, the distinction between the fair merchant and the smuggler was not so strongly marked in their characters nor so clearly felt by the public. There the great practical grievance was the loss of the large and general though illicit gains which had for a considerable period accrued to North America both from our West Indies and from the Spanish settlements. But as this grievance could not be so plausibly pleaded, other lesser, though no doubt real and galling, grievances were actively put forward. It was exclaimed that His Majesty's naval officers were disgraced and degraded by their new employment. It was urged that, however brave and expert in their own profession, they were wholly unskilled in that of tide-waiters and excisemen. They must needs be bewildered by the long and intricate array of forms which our law-givers have so wisely devised—bonds, clearances, cockets, affidavits, stamps, certificates, registers, and manifests! From their inexperience in these it was alleged that they made many wrongful seizures and acted in many cases with illegal violence, while the American traders had no right of appeal except to the Lords of the Admiralty or Treasury in England,—a process so tedious and difficult as to leave them in fact with no means of redress at all.

The new duties also on their foreign trade, which had been not only announced but enacted during the Session of 1764, proved most galling to them. It is true that by the terms of the Act all the money arising from these duties was to be reserved to defray the charges of protecting the Colonies on which it was levied. It is true, moreover, that these duties were accompanied by several laws to increase and encourage their commercial intercourse with the mother country, such as a bill granting a bounty on the importation of their hemp and their rough and undressed flax into England. These, however, when weighed against the oppression of the new commercial duties, seemed but a feather in the scale. The Americans did not, indeed, deny the right of the mother country to impose such duties; they distinguished between foreign and home taxation, between the custom-house and the stamp-office or excise; the former they owned as of imperial, the latter they claimed as of local jurisdiction. But though they did not deny the right, they felt the burthen, and that burthen they determined by every Constitutional effort to remove. It was computed at the time, perhaps with some exaggeration, that these Colonies consumed British produce and manufactures to the value annually of 3,000,000*l.** The Americans now resolved, as a measure of retaliation, to buy no clothing nor other commodities of our manufacture that they could possibly dispense with; they began to form associations for that object, and they strove to promote as far as possible every manufacture of their own.

* Annual Register, 1764, part i. p. 24.

With so much loss inflicted, so much irritation rankling, the Americans were but little inclined to accept the overtures of Grenville. In none of the Colonies would they either agree to the Tax on Stamps, nor suggest any other. They took their stand on the broad principle that as men of British blood and with British rights they were not liable to be taxed by the House of Commons, unless they were represented in that body. They demanded that, as in former cases, a letter from the Secretary of State written in the King's name, and requiring them to contribute to His Majesty's service, should be laid before their respective Assemblies, in which case they declared that they would always, as heretofore, manifest their loyalty and zeal by liberal grants. These views, enforced by Resolutions in several of their Assemblies, they instructed their agents to lay before the Government of England. For this object also the ablest among them, well known to and justly esteemed by all men of science in Europe, Dr. Franklin, hastened back to his post in London, as agent for the important province of Pennsylvania.

Grenville took little heed of these representations, however strenuously or ably urged. Early in the Session of 1765 he brought in a Bill laying on America nearly the same Stamp Duties as were already established in England. The expected amount was but small; I find it estimated by a member of the government at less than one shilling a head on the North American people—less therefore than 100,000*l.* a year.* Dr. Franklin long afterwards observed: "Had Mr. Grenville instead of his Stamp Act "applied to the King in Council for requisitional letters, "I am sure he would have obtained more money from the "Colonies by their voluntary grants than he himself ex-"pected from his Stamps. But he chose compulsion "rather than persuasion." †—Grenville himself with great imprudence termed his measure only an experiment towards further aid from the Americans ‡—thus of course

* Mr. Nugent's Speech on the Address, January 14. 1766.

† Letter to Mr. William Alexander, dated Passy, March 12. 1778, and printed in Mr. Jared Sparks's Life.

‡ Lord Orford's Memoirs of George III., vol. ii. p. 71.

provoking full as much resistance from them as a heavier impost might have done.

Fifty-five Resolutions laying Stamp Duties on America were now brought into the House of Commons, and afterwards embodied in an Act of Parliament. The House, since they viewed it as a Money-Bill, refused to receive four Petitions against it from the agents of Connecticut, Rhode Island, Virginia, and Carolina, besides one from the merchants of Jamaica. Within doors the scheme was opposed with little vigour. Pitt was ill in bed at Hayes, and only a few of his friends, as Colonel Barré and Alderman Baker, spoke or voted against it. Nine years afterwards, and in the presence no doubt of many men who had witnessed these discussions, Mr. Burke described them in the following terms: " Far from anything inflam-" matory, I never heard a more languid debate in this " House. No more than two or three gentlemen as I re-" member spoke against the Act, and that with great re-" serve and remarkable temper. There was but one " division in the whole progress of the Bill and the mi-" nority did not reach to more than thirty-nine or forty. " In the House of Lords I do not recollect that there was " any debate or division at all." *

There is extant, nevertheless, an eloquent and well known burst of oratory, which is ascribed to Colonel Barré, on one of these occasions. Mr. Grenville having spoken of the Americans as children of our own, planted by our care and nourished by our indulgence, Colonel Barré exclaimed: " Children planted by your care! No, " your oppression planted them in America, they fled from " your tyranny into a then uncultivated land;"—and there follows a fine philippic against the misgovernment of the mother country. These words are not recorded in the contemporary Debates of Debrett, and at first sight

* Speech on American Taxation, April 19. 1774. It is very remarkable, and strongly in corroboration of Burke's statement, that Horace Walpole in his close correspondence at this time, both with the Earl of Hertford at Paris and with Sir Horace Mann, at Florence, giving minute and frequent accounts of the state of parties and the proceedings of Parliament, never even mentions the Stamp Act, and only once adverts to the preparatory Resolutions as " a slight day on " the American Taxes." (Feb. 12. 1765.)

there seemed to me, as to an earlier historian, the strongest reason to doubt whether they were really uttered at the time, or whether at a later period they might not be supplied by the pen of Barré. It now appears, however, that Mr. Jared Ingersoll, joint agent for Connecticut, was sitting in the gallery, heard the speech of Barré, and made a report of it, which report was transmitted to his friends, and within three months printed in one of the Connecticut papers.*

It is remarkable that when the Stamp Bill had passed both Houses, and received the Royal Assent, Dr. Franklin entertained no other idea concerning it but acquiescence, and alleviating its burthen by patient industry. There seemed to him no prospect that the Americans could or should any further oppose it. He consented at Grenville's request, as did also the other agents, each for his own province, to nominate a person, whom he thought most likely to be acceptable, as the Stamp Distributor in Pennsylvania. To one of his confidential friends he wrote that he had found it impossible to prevent the passing of this Act. "We might as well have hindered the sun's setting. "That we could not do. But since it is down, my friend, "and it may be long before it rises again, let us make as "good a night of it as we can. We may still light candles. "Frugality and industry will go a great way towards in-"demnifying us." †

The Americans were by no means inclined to follow these prudent — perhaps they may have termed them pusillanimous — counsels. They received the news of the Royal Assent to the Stamp Act with less of dejection than

* See Mr. Bancroft's History, second series, vol. ii. p. 275., as published in 1852. The doubts upon this point are judiciously stated by Mr. Adolphus even in the first edition of his History. Note to vol. i. p. 190. After all, besides the wholly irreconcilable statement of Burke, it is not easy to explain why the Parliamentary History names Grenville as the person to whom Barré was replying, while Jared Ingersoll names Charles Townshend. How could either be mistaken on this point? (1853.)

† Letter to Mr. Charles Thomson, July 11, 1765, as printed in Mr. Jared Sparks's Biography, p. 294. Mr. Thomson says in his answer, "I much fear, instead of the candles you mentioned being lighted, "you will hear of the works of darkness!"

of anger. It was reprinted with a death's head affixed, instead of the King's Arms, and was hawked in the streets of New York by the title of "The Folly of England and "the Ruin of America." * At Boston the colours of the shipping were hoisted half-mast high, while the church bells were muffled, and tolled a funeral knell. By the terms of the Act, it was not to come into operation until the 1st of November, before which time it was intended that stamped papers ready for distribution, and required for use, should be sent from England. But during the interval the provincial Assemblies did not remain inactive. Of all the Colonies, the first to stir was Virginia, and of all men in Virginia the first was Patrick Henry. It was mainly through his eloquence and energy that the House of Burgesses of his province was induced to pass a series of Resolutions, and a petition to the King denying in strong terms the right of the mother country to tax them without their own consent, and claiming a repeal of the obnoxious Statute. Startled at these bold proceedings, the Governor of the province dissolved the Assembly, but too late; the blow had been already struck, the example already set. The other Colonies looked to the remonstrance of Virginia as a noble and inspiriting precedent to follow, and in most of their Assemblies carried similar Resolutions of their own.

It was felt, however, by all reflecting men in America, that the Colonies would have little weight so long as they stood singly, and that their best prospect of prevailing lay in combination. Many pamphlets and articles in newspapers written in a clear and easy style were now published, especially at Boston, serving to render the advantages of union apparent even to the meanest capacity, while the same truth was further enforced in prints and caricatures. One of these, for example, which served as frontispiece to "The Constitutional Courant," represents a snake cut in pieces, with the initial letters of the several Colonies from New England to South Carolina affixed to each piece. Such an emblem might not have been deemed in all points complimentary, but amends were made by

* Holmes, American Annals, vol. ii. p. 137. ed. 1829.

the motto; it stood thus — JOIN OR DIE.* Under such impressions, and at the suggestion of the House of Representatives at Boston, several Assemblies appointed delegates (from two to five in number) for a General Congress, which was to meet at New York in the ensuing month of October, and to seek measures of redress from the grievance of the Stamp Act.

It will be necessary to revert in full detail to the proceedings in America as soon as the intervening events in England have been told. But I shall conclude this Chapter by attempting to sketch the characters of those two eminent men, who at this time took the foremost part in opposing the pretensions of the mother country on either side of the Atlantic — Patrick Henry in America — and Benjamin Franklin in England.

The Colony of Virginia was the place, and the year 1736 the time, of birth to Patrick Henry. His parents were in easy circumstances, but burthened with a numerous family; they resided at a country seat to which the ambitious name of Mount Brilliant had been given. In childhood Patrick Henry gave little promise of distinction. His person is represented as having been coarse, his manners extremely awkward, his dress slovenly, and his aversion to study invincible. No persuasion could bring him either to read or to work.† At sixteen his father gave him means to open a small shop, which failed, however, in less than one year. Then he tried a small farm, and married; then again he entered upon the life of a tradesman, but in a few years more was a bankrupt. It was at this period that he became acquainted with Mr. Jefferson, afterwards President of the United States. "Mr. Henry," says Jefferson, "had a little before broken "up his store (shop), or rather it had broken him up, but "his misfortunes were not to be traced either in his "countenance or conduct. His manners had something

* Annual Register, 1765, part i. p. 50. and Dr. Gordon's History of the American Revolution, vol. i. p. 189.—This emblem and motto had been invented by Franklin many years before with the design of uniting the Colonies against the French. See a note by Mr. Sparks to his Writings, vol. iii. p. 25. (1853.)

† Sketches of the Life of Patrick Henry by W. Wirt, p. 6. ed. 1818.

"of coarseness in them; his passion was music, dancing, "and pleasantry. He excelled in the last, and it attached "every one to him."

As a last resource, Patrick Henry now determined to make a trial of the law. It cannot be said that his preparatory studies were unduly arduous, since, as his biographer informs us, they were all comprised in the period of six weeks.* Under such unpromising circumstances, and in the year 1763, he obtained a brief in the long-contested cause then raging in Virginia between the clergy on the one side, and the legislature on the other, as regarding the stipends which the former claimed. On this occasion Henry, to the astonishment of all who knew him, poured forth a strain of such impassioned eloquence as not only carried the cause, contrary to all previous expectation, but placed him ever afterwards at the head of his profession in the Colony. To this very day, says Mr. Wirt, writing in 1818, the impression remains, and the old people of that district think that no higher compliment can be paid to any public speaker than to say of him in their homely phrase, "He is almost equal to Patrick "when he plead (pleaded) against the parsons."

The natural eloquence which on this occasion flashed forth from the coarse and unlettered Henry, as the spark of fire from the flint, continued to distinguish him both as a Member of the House of Burgesses at Williamsburg, and afterwards as a Member of Congress. He took from the first a bold and active part against the pretensions of the mother country; indeed Mr. Jefferson goes so far as to declare that "Mr. Henry certainly gave the earliest impulse "to the ball of revolution." His most celebrated burst of oratory, or rather turn of phrase, was in this very year 1765, when descanting in the House of Burgesses on the tyranny of the Stamp Act. "Cæsar —" he cried in a voice of thunder and with an eye of fire — "Cæsar had "his Brutus — Charles the First had his Cromwell — "and George the Third" — "Treason!" here exclaimed the Speaker, "Treason! Treason!" re-echoed from every part of the House. Henry did not for an instant falter, but fixing his eye firmly on the Speaker, he concluded

* Life by Wirt, p. 16.

his sentence thus "——may profit by their example. If this be treason, make the most of it!"

Indolence and aversion to reading seemed almost as natural to Henry's mind as powers of debate. To the last he never overcame them. Thus, at his death in 1799 his books were found to be extremely few, and these too consisting chiefly of odd volumes.* But his gift of speech was (for his hearers) sufficiently supported by his fiery energy, his practical shrewdness, and his ever keen glance into the feelings and characters of others. Nor were these his only claims to his country's favor. He retained the manners and customs of the common people, with what his friendly biographer terms "religious caution."—"He dressed as plainly as the plainest of them," continues Mr. Wirt, "ate only their homely fare, and drunk "their simple beverage, mixed with them on a footing "of the most entire and perfect equality, and conversed "with them even in their own vicious and depraved "pronunciation."† By such means he soon acquired and long retained a large measure of popularity, and he applied himself with zeal and success before any audience, and on every occasion which arose, to increase and perpetuate the estrangement between the North American Colonies and England.

Dr. Benjamin Franklin is one of those men who have made the task of succeeding biographers more difficult by having been in part their own. He was born at Boston in 1706, the youngest of ten sons. "My father," he says, "intended to devote me, as the tithe of his sons, to the "service of the Church;" but on further reflection, the charges of a College education were thought too burthensome, and young Benjamin became a journeyman printer. From a very early age he showed a passionate fondness for reading, and much ingenuity in argument, but, as he acknowledges, had at first contracted a disputatious and wrangling turn of conversation. "I have since observed," he says, "that persons of good sense seldom fall into "it, except lawyers, University-men, and generally men "of all sorts who have been bred at Edinburgh."

* Life by Wirt, p. 406.

† Life of Patrick Henry, p. 35.

Young Franklin was at first bound apprentice to one of his elder brothers, a printer at Boston; but some differences arising between them, he proceeded to Philadelphia, where he soon obtained employment, and ere long set up for himself. His success in life was secured by his great frugality, industry, and shrewdness. In his own words: "I spent no time in taverns, games, or "frolics of any kind; reading was the only amusement "I allowed myself." His knowledge and shrewdness,—great zeal in urging any improvements, and great ingenuity in promoting them,—speedily raised him high in the estimation of his fellow-townsmen, and enabled him to take a forward part in all the affairs of his province. In England, and indeed all Europe, he became celebrated by his experiments and discoveries in Electricity. These may deserve the greater credit, when we recollect both their practical utility and their unassisted progress,—how much the pointed rods which he introduced have tended to avert the dangers of lightning, and how far removed was Franklin at the time from all scientific society, libraries, or patronage.*

It has also been stated by no less an authority in science than Sir Humphrey Davy, that "the style and manner of "Dr. Franklin's publication on Electricity are almost as "worthy of admiration as the doctrine it contains." The same remark may indeed be applied to all his writings. All of them are justly celebrated for their clear, plain, and lively style, free from every appearance of art, but, in fact, carefully pointed and nicely poised. In public speaking, on the other hand, he was much less eminent. His last American biographer observes of him, that he never even pretended to the accomplishments of an orator or debater. He seldom spoke in a deliberative assembly, except for some special object, and then only for a few minutes at a time.

As a slight instance of Franklin's humour and shrewdness in all affairs of common life I may quote the following: "QUESTION. I am about courting a girl I have

* On the pointed *conductors* of Franklin as distinguished from the blunt ones, see Mr. Nairne's Essay in the Philos. Trans., vol. lxviii. part 2., and Lord Mahon's "Principles of Electricity," London, 1779.

"had but little acquaintance with. How shall I come to "a knowledge of her faults? ANSWER. Commend her "among her female acquaintance!"*

Whether in science and study, or in politics and action, the great aim of Franklin's mind was ever practical utility. Here again we may quote Sir Humphrey Davy as saying of Franklin that he sought rather to make Philosophy a useful inmate and servant in the common habitations of man, than to preserve her merely as an object of admiration in temples and palaces. Thus also in affairs he had a keen eye to his own interest, but likewise a benevolent concern for the public good. Nor was he ever indifferent to cases of individual grievance or hardship. In the pursuit of his objects, public or private, he was, beyond most other men, calm, sagacious, and wary; neither above business nor yet below it; never turned aside from it by flights of fancy nor yet by bursts of passion.

Among the good qualities which we may with just cause ascribe to Franklin we cannot number any firm reliance on the truths of Revelation. Only five weeks before his death we find him express a cold approbation of the "system of morals" bequeathed to us by "Jesus of "Nazareth." In his Memoirs he declares that he always believed in the existence of a Deity and a future state of rewards and punishments, but he adds that although he continued to adhere to his first — the Presbyterian — sect, some of its dogmas appeared to him unintelligible, and others doubtful. "I early absented myself from the "public assemblies of the sect; and I seldom attended "any public worship; Sunday being my studying day."†

Such being Franklin's own practice, and such his own description of it as to public worship, it seems worthy of note that it was he who in the American Convention brought forward a motion for daily prayers. "I have "lived, Sir," said he, "a long time, and the longer I live "the more convincing proofs I see of this truth, that "God governs in the affairs of men. And if a sparrow "cannot fall to the ground without his notice, is it pro-

* Works, vol. ii. p. 550. ed. 1840.

† Memoirs, ch. vi.

" bable that an empire can rise without his aid?" — But in spite of this most earnest appeal the motion was rejected, since, as we are told, "the Convention, except " three or four persons, thought prayers unnecessary." *

The accomplished American biographer, by whom this last incident is recorded, expresses in the same passage deep regret that Dr. Franklin did not bestow more attention than he seems to have done on the evidences of Christianity. And indeed there are several indications that he was less well acquainted with points of Christian faith and discipline than with almost any other subject. One of these indications, and surely a most strange one, occurs in the Private Diary which he kept at Passy during part of 1784. It appears that two young American gentlemen had come over to London with the view of entering Holy Orders, but that the Archbishop of Canterbury refused them Ordination unless they would take the Oath of Allegiance. In this dilemma Franklin actually applied to the Pope's Nuncio at Paris to ascertain whether a Roman Catholic Bishop in America might not perform the ceremony for them as Protestants, and he transcribes as remarkable the natural reply: "The " Nuncio says the thing is impossible unless the gentle- " men become Roman Catholics." †

The religious scepticism or indifference of Franklin, which his present biographers justly lament, was, however, in his own day, a recommendation and a merit with the French philosophists. On the other hand, his hostility to England endeared him to the French politicians. On both these grounds, as well as from his high scientific attainments, he found himself during his residence of several years at Paris in no common measure courted, flattered, and caressed. A fine verse, one of the noblest which modern Latinity can boast, describes him as having plucked the lightning from Heaven and the sceptre from tyrants.‡

Descending from such lofty flights to the regions of

* Life by Mr. Jared Sparks, p. 514.

† Franklin s Private Journal, July 16. and 17. 1784.

‡ " Eripuit cœlo fulmen, sceptrumque tyrannis."

It is stated in Mr. Sparks's Life of Franklin, that this line " was " first applied to him by Turgot." (p. 421, note.) The original hint, sober reality, we may observe that Franklin in his later years, and especially in France, adopted to a great extent the Quaker garb. He laid aside the huge wig which he used to wear in England, and allowed his long white hair to flow down nearly to his shoulders. His clothes were of the plainest cut and of the dunnest colour. The Parisians of that period, ever swayed by external impressions, were greatly struck with, and in their writings, frequently refer to, his venerable aspect, and they compared him by turns to all the sages of antiquity. It is also probable that his Quaker-like attire may have tended to invest him in their estimation with the other attributes which they assigned to the ideal Quaker character, as simplicity, guilelessness, inviolable truth.

Dr. Franklin married early, and had several children, but one only of his sons, born out of wedlock, grew up to man's estate. That son afterwards became Governor of New Jersey for the King, and continued steady throughout the war to the Royal cause. He died in London at the close of 1813, in the receipt of a pension from the British Government. His son, William Temple Franklin, expired without issue, but the posterity of Dr. Franklin continues, and is numerous, in the female line.

however, was probably derived from Manilius (Astron. lib. i. vers. 104.), where the poet says of Epicurus :

"Eripuitque Jovi fulmen, viresque tonandi."

CHAPTER XLIV.

At nearly the same period that the Stamp Act was passing into law, the monarch who had sanctioned it became dangerously ill. The immediate cause was an humour which had appeared on his face, and which being, as is thought, unskilfully repelled, settled on his breast. His illness was said to be cough and fever, and at first probably was so. But it is certain that there were also symptoms of that mental malady which, unhappily recurring on three subsequent occasions, clouded His Majesty's career.* At the time, however, this fact was not known to the public at large, nor even in any degree suspected or surmised, but was confined to the nearest and most intimate circle in attendance on the Royal Person.

No sooner had the King recovered than he gave a token of his usual good sense and right feeling by himself propounding to his Ministers the question of a Regency. His eldest son, the heir apparent, was not yet fully three years of age. His own illness might return, and might be fatal. Parliament ought not to postpone legislation until the necessity for it drew nigh, nor yet to rely implicitly upon the prospect of early reports of any Royal illness in the Gazettes or Court Circulars, of which it has been said that they never contain substantially more than three announcements touching the health of Kings: — His Majesty is a little indisposed. — His Majesty is better. — His Majesty is dead.

There is not the smallest reason to suppose that the King had in view any other Regent than the Queen. But his desire was that he might be authorized to name

* See the statement, alleging "the best authority," and ascribed to Mr. Croker (Quarterly Review, No. cxxxi. p. 240.), and the note of Mr. Adolphus in the recent, but not in the first, edition of his H' tory (vol. i. p. 175.).

from time to time by an instrument in writing any person that he pleased. Mr. Grenville, according to his own statement in his Private Diary, much disapproved of this discretionary power; nevertheless he agreed to forward it to the utmost of his strength in the House of Commons. Thus at a meeting with his principal colleagues it was agreed to propose to Parliament that the power of appointment should be vested in the King, but limited to "either the Queen or any other person of the "Royal Family usually residing in Great Britain." Such accordingly were the words in which on the 24th of April the King laid the suggestion before both Houses in a Speech from the Throne. Both Houses in reply sent him Addresses, full of fervent loyalty,—and perhaps something more than loyalty. "We contemplate with "admiration," say the Commons, "that magnanimity "which enables Your Majesty to look forward with a "cool composure of thought to an event which, when-"ever it shall please God to permit it, must overwhelm "your loyal subjects with the bitterest distraction of "grief!"

When, however, the Bill founded on the very words of the Royal recommendation was brought into the House of Lords, a doubt arose as to what was meant by the "Royal Family." It then appeared that the Ministers with most unpardonable negligence had failed to clear up this point among themselves. It was found that the Lord Chancellor and the Duke of Bedford differed in opinion as to whether that term did or did not include the Princess Dowager of Wales. The Duke, on being asked the question in the House of Lords, replied that he looked upon the Royal Family to be only those in the order of succession one after another,—a definition in which he was zealously supported by his colleague, Halifax. This strange technical quibble—to declare that the King's parent did not belong to the King's family—can only be matched from a work of fiction of the same period, Tristram Shandy, where the bantering author lays it down as the opinion of the gravest schoolmen that the mother is not of kin to her own child.*

* Tristram Shandy, vol. iii. p. 228. ed. 1775. He quotes a saying

Such a doctrine was not likely to pass without debate. Lord Mansfield said mysteriously that he had his own private thoughts who are and who are not of the Royal Family, but that he did not choose to declare them. The question being resumed next day, Lord Chancellor Henley, not long since created Earl of Northington, publicly avowed his opinion as directly opposite to the Duke of Bedford's.* Amidst so much of doubt and contradiction it became indispensable that the persons intended should be more clearly designated in the Bill. It was then that Lord Halifax, eager to put himself forward in this business, hurried to the King, and assured him on the part of the Cabinet that if the name of his mother should be inserted, the House of Commons would in all probability strike it out. Far better therefore, urged Halifax, with a view to save the honour of His Majesty and of Her Royal Highness, that the Ministers should anticipate the insult, and themselves in the first instance omit her name. The young monarch taken unawares, and struck with painful surprise, answered mildly: "I will consent if it will satisfy my people." Armed with the consent obtained under such pretences, Halifax hastened back to the House of Peers. There, alleging the King's permission, he proposed words to limit the persons who should be capable of the Regency to the Queen and to all the descendants of the late King usually resident in England. Thus did he exclude the Princess Dowager and the Princess Dowager alone! Thus did he seek to stigmatize by Act of Parliament the mother of his Sovereign!

With such alterations the Regency Bill went through the House of Lords. But not many hours elapsed ere the King felt in its full force the insult offered to his parent, and bitterly complained of Lord Halifax for

of the learned Baldus: "*Mater non numeratur inter consanguineos.*" But Sterne carries the argument one step further: "Since Mrs. "Shandy the mother is nothing at all akin to him, — and since the "mother's side is the surest, — Mr. Shandy of course is still less than "nothing!"

* H. Walpole to the Earl of Hertford, May 5. 1765. and Memoirs of George III., vol. ii. p. 118.; to be carefully compared with Mr. Grenville's Diary.

having surprised his acquiescence. In one interview with Lord Mansfield His Majesty was moved even to a burst of tears. He strongly urged Mr. Grenville to propose the reinstatement of the name in the House of Commons. Grenville, however, was deaf to the King's entreaties; the utmost he would promise was to give way if he should be pressed by others. Meanwhile the friends of the Princess Dowager, political and personal, were filled with indignation, and determined, though unbidden, to make a stand in her behalf. One of these, Mr. Morton, the Chief Justice of Chester, made a formal motion to replace in the Bill as before the House of Commons the name of Her Royal Highness. George Grenville in much perplexity looked to the members of the Opposition for rescue, well knowing how much they hated the Princess. But he forgot that they hated the Prime Minister still more. Enjoying his confusion, and determined to increase it, they either walked out of the House, or sat still acquiescing in Morton's motion. Thus Grenville was reduced to stammer forth that he had hoped the words inserted by Lord Halifax would be universally acceptable, — thought there had been authority for the omission, but found that there was not, — and now would readily concur in any mark of respect to the mother of his Sovereign. In his letter to the King the same evening he takes merit to himself for having, as he says, "followed as nearly as I could the idea which "your Majesty pointed out to me."* A small number of Members still continued to object, but on dividing could muster no more than thirty-seven. In the result, therefore, the name of Her Royal Highness, which the King had been assured could not fail, if retained, to be struck out, was, on the contrary, by an immense and overwhelming majority reinstated.

In the whole of this strange transaction — "the vertigo "of the Regency Bill," as it is aptly termed by Burke †, — the Ministers seem to have wholly neglected — it might almost be said that they betrayed — the dignity

* Letter, May 9. 1765. Grenville Papers.

† Observations on a late State of the Nation; Works, vol. ii. p. 156. ed. 1815.

and honour of the Crown. Their affront upon the Princess Dowager was as gross and public as it was undeserved. There were indeed rumours and whispers against her fame, but these, as probably false and certainly unproved, it behoved the King's Servants to disregard and to defy; and next to the Queen herself no member of the Royal House then living appeared so fit for the post of Regent as the person whom it was attempted to exclude from it,—the grandmother of the infant Prince. But throughout this business party grudges and resentments, and, above all, jealousy of Lord Bute, with whom Bedford and Halifax especially were now at variance, seemed to be the all-absorbing, the paramount considerations.

The King himself, most justly grieved and offended, a few days afterwards opened his heart to his uncle of Cumberland, and besought advice and aid to rid him of his Ministers. His early dreams of governing without party, or of moulding every party to his will,—his resentment against the pride of Pitt standing singly,—his aversion to the confederacy of the great Whig houses,—all these seemed by comparison to vanish into air. To every mind, unless to the very greatest, the present evil ever seems the most intolerable. Nor were other causes wanting to swell the Royal displeasure. His Majesty, though always willing and ready for business, disliked (as who does not?) long speeches out of season; and grievously lamented the well-informed, but verbose and ill-timed, eloquence of Grenville. "When,"—such were the King's own words to Lord Bute,—"he has wearied "me for two hours, he looks at his watch to see if he "may not tire one for an hour more."* Besides such ill-timed eloquence, he had also to complain of ill-judged economy. Grenville had refused His Majesty a grant of 20,000*l.* for the purchase of the ground behind the gardens which the King had made at Buckingham House; thus the ground remaining in other hands, a new row of houses speedily sprung up, the present Grosvenor Place, to overlook the Sovereign and his family in their daily walks.

* Lord Orford's Memoirs of George III., vol. ii. p. 160.

But besides these more personal considerations, and looking mainly as George the Third ever did, or meant to do, to the welfare of the country, His Majesty could not fail to observe an uneasy feeling, a sullen resentment, which had arisen, no doubt, under Lord Bute, but which had grown, if not by Grenville's fault, at least during Grenville's administration. At this time also there was another special cause of animosity. On the very day that the Regency Bill passed there came up for discussion in the Lords a measure which had been carried through the Commons with little notice; it was for imposing as high duties on Italian silks as were paid on the French. The ground alleged was that the French sent their silks to Genoa and Leghorn, and there entered them as Italian merchandize; but the real object seems to have been to obtain, so far as possible, a total prohibition of foreign silks. The Duke of Bedford made a speech against this Bill; no Peer rose to defend it; and it was thrown out. Its rejection, however, was keenly resented by the Spitalfields weavers, whose trade was at this period languishing, and of whom a large proportion were unemployed.* On the day ensuing about three or four thousand of these poor men went very quietly and unarmed to Richmond to petition the King for redress. Finding him gone to a review at Wimbledon they followed him there. His Majesty told them he would do all that was in his power to relieve them, and they returned home well pleased and quite peaceable. But on the afternoon of the next day they appeared at Whitehall in unruly numbers, carrying red and black flags, and shouting forth invectives against the Peers. They stopped several of their Lordships' coaches; amongst others, the Chancellor's, and asked him if he had been against the Bill. He stoutly told them, Yes. They were abashed at his firmness, and said, they hoped he would do justice. He replied: "Always and every-"where; and whoever does need fear nothing!" The

* We are told by a contemporary of their "pallid looks and "emaciated carcases." The Duke of Bedford's speech concerning them is accused of "uncommon harshness." (Annual Register, 1765, part i. p. 41.)

Duke of Bedford was however, as may be supposed, the principal object of their anger. When his coach appeared it was hissed and pelted, and a large stone which was flung into it, not only cut the Duke's hand which he had raised to protect himself, but bruised him on the temple.

But this was not all. The Duke received intelligence that on the evening of next Friday (May the 17th) his own dwelling (Bedford House on the north side of Bloomsbury Square) would be attacked by the rabble. Accordingly he provided an adequate garrison, friends and dependents in great numbers, and soldiers both horse and foot. The rioters did appear at the time expected, and began to pull down the wall of the court, but the great gates being thrown open, while the Riot Act was read, the party of cavalry sallied out and rode round Bloomsbury Square slashing and trampling on the mob and putting them to flight. Some wounds were inflicted, but no lives were lost. In the meantime another body of rioters had passed to the back of the house, and were forcing their way through the garden, when they also were dispersed by the fortunate arrival of a fresh detachment of fifty horse. Nevertheless the Duke and his company kept watch all night, while the neighbouring coffee-houses were thronged with idlers who with great indifference sent from time to time to hear how the siege went on. The baffled weavers vented their rage that night on the windows, which they demolished, of Carr, a fashionable mercer who dealt in French silks, but they refrained from any further outrage.

On the Sunday which followed, Horace Walpole — from whose vivid and minute description these particulars are mainly drawn — went to compliment their Graces of Bedford, as did most of their acquaintance, upon their escape. "I found," says he, "the square crowded, but "chiefly with persons led by curiosity. As my chariot "had no coronets I was received with huzzas, but when "the horses turned to enter the court dirt and stones were "thrown at it. When the gates opened I was surprised "with the most martial appearance. The horse-guards "were drawn up in the court, and many officers and "gentlemen were walking about as on the platform of a "regular citadel. The whole house was open, and knots "of the same kind were in every room. When I came to "the Duchess and lamented the insult they had suffered, "she replied with warmth and acrimony that the mob had "been set on by Lord Bute."* Other persons no less clear-sighted and impartial were quite sure that the real instigators were the friends of Wilkes. Others again — some men grown grey in faction and cabals — could not repress a sigh that so promising an instrument of mischief was not wielded by themselves. Thus did Lord Holland whisper to a friend: "What an artful man might do with "these mobs!" Finally, however, the resentment of the suffering weavers was appeased without further disturbance by a seasonable subscription for their present relief, and an association amongst the principal silk mercers to revoke all the orders they had given for foreign manufactures.†

Such was the state of public affairs which the King had to lay before the Duke of Cumberland. The Duke in his retired position and with his ruined health had nothing either to gain or to lose by any change of Government. But he had a high and strong sense of duty to the Crown, and when thus earnestly called on by his Royal nephew would not shrink from the task, however troublesome and thankless, of mediating to form a new administration. He sent an express to summon Lord Temple from Stowe, and himself repaired to visit the Great Commoner at Hayes. Meanwhile the King, without awaiting the result of his uncle's endeavours, intimated to Grenville with sufficient clearness, and with reference to the end of the Session, which was now close at hand, that he intended some change in the future conduct of his affairs.

These tidings rapidly spread, and public expectation was wound up to the highest pitch. We may gather what were the feelings at the time from the private letter of a man still young and little known, but destined to become the first philosophical statesman of his own, or perhaps of

* Memoirs, vol. ii. p. 158. We learn from Mr. Grenville that the Duke of Bedford had with great passion said the same thing to His Majesty. (Diary, May 19. 1765.)

† Annual Register, 1765, part i. p. 42.

any age. On the 18th of May Edmund Burke wrote as follows to Mr. Flood: "Nothing but an intractable spirit "in your friend Pitt can prevent a most admirable and "lasting system (of administration) from being put "together, and this crisis will show whether pride or "patriotism be predominant in his character. For you "may be assured, he has it now in his power to come into "the service of his country upon any plan of politics he "chooses to dictate, with great and honourable terms to "himself and every friend he has in the world, and with "such a strength of power as will be equal to anything "but absolute despotism over King and kingdom. A few "days will show whether he will take this part, or con- "tinue on his back at Hayes talking fustian." * This letter proves how large was the reliance which the nation at that time placed on Pitt, and how vast the consequent power that he wielded. It likewise denotes that the pompous and inflated style which may still be traced throughout his correspondence, and which no doubt also appeared in his less familiar conversation, did not even then escape the criticism of at least the discerning few.

It was found, however, that Pitt did not "talk fustian" when the chief Prince of the Blood Royal attended his leisure and entered his sick-room at Hayes. His tone might be lofty, but it was not intractable, and his statements as to measures were clear and plain. He made three principal demands: Condemnation of General Warrants for the future; Restoration of officers dismissed on political grounds; Alliance with Protestant Powers to balance the new Family Compact between France and Spain. The first article, said the Duke, would be accorded; the King himself had named the second; the third would be most subject to difficulty. As to appointments, Pitt was resolved that if he took office the statesman who was at this time the highest in his confidence—Chief Justice Pratt—should become Lord Chancellor; a scheme by no means welcome to the Court. On the other hand, the Court desired, as before, that the Earl of Northumberland might be placed at the head of the Treasury; and to that proposal Pitt, as before, demurred.

* Printed in Prior's Life of Burke, p. 81.

It seems probable that these difficulties might have been overcome, since sooner than fail the Duke was willing to offer Pitt almost CARTE BLANCHE. But it was observed that from the moment Lord Temple arrived, and had an opportunity of conversing with Pitt, the embarrassment and reserve of the latter visibly increased.

Pitt's intention had been to nominate Temple as First Lord of the Treasury; but not only did Temple reject the brilliant prize, he used every exertion to dissuade Pitt also from engaging. To explain this strange phenomenon in a man so ambitious as the Lord of Stowe, it must be mentioned that as it chanced he was then on the point of concluding a reconciliation with his brother George. It was now, it would seem, his wish that the family union might be perfected, and that "the three brothers," as Temple, Grenville, and the husband of their sister were commonly called, might form a ministry of their own, neither leaning upon Lord Bute and the Tories, nor yet upon the great Whig Dukes. It is probable that Pitt was not at all convinced by Temple's reasoning. He must have felt that in rejecting the overtures of the Duke of Cumberland he was foregoing a noble opportunity of good to the public and of glory to himself. But, on the other part, he could not be unmindful of the ancient obligations, personal and even pecuniary *, which he owed to Temple. Could he in honour begin his new administration by a breach with the only colleague who had adhered to him at the close of the former,—a breach, too, founded solely on the reconciliation of that colleague with their common brother, George Grenville? To feelings such as these we may presume Pitt yielded, but yielded with regret. When he took leave of Temple after the decision he mournfully repeated to him some lines from Virgil to imply: "Brother, "you have ruined us all!" †

It is remarkable that at nearly the same juncture Grenville in a long discourse announced to the King that poli-

* See vol. iv. of this History, p. 57., and its Appendix, p. xvi.

† "Extinxti me, teque, soror, populumque, patresque
"Sidonios, urbemque tuam!"

Æneid, lib. iv. ver. 682. Lord Orford's Memoirs of George III. (vol. ii. p. 174.) are fully confirmed by a passage in Wilkes's Letters to Humphrey Cotes (Corresp., vol. ii. p. 218.).

tics apart, and so far as private friendship was concerned, he had become reconciled with Lord Temple. The King answered drily, and with a well-timed allusion to Lord Bute: "I do not trouble myself about the friendships of "others, and wish nobody would about mine!"

The Duke of Cumberland, though disheartened at Pitt's refusal to treat, did not on that account immediately relinquish his commission. Other expedients were tried, or at least were talked of. It was suggested that Lord Lyttleton might be placed at the head of the Treasury, but Lyttleton himself with much good sense declined to engage in so unpromising a scheme.* The able were not willing, and the willing were not able, to serve, and thus in spite of Newcastle's tears and wailings no new Government could be formed. With bitter mortification the King found himself compelled to announce to his old Ministers that he intended to retain them in his service.

Grenville and Bedford, however, thinking that they had gained the vantage-ground, met the King's announcement by four fresh demands. The original minute of these is still preserved among the papers of the former.† First, would His Majesty promise to allow no further share or participation in his councils to Lord Bute? Secondly, would he dismiss Lord Bute's brother, Mr. James Stuart Mackenzie, from the office of Privy Seal of Scotland, and from the management of Scottish affairs? Thirdly, would he dismiss Lord Holland from the office of Paymaster? Fourthly, would he appoint Lord Granby Commander-in-Chief? This last demand might have for its pretext and justification the disturbed state of the country, but at the same time it had for its tendency, and no doubt also for its object, to disparage and insult the Duke of Cumberland. To Mr. Mackenzie the King had formerly pledged his word that he might retain his place for life. The King felt, however, that he ought not for the sake of one private

* Memoirs and Correspondence of Lord Lyttleton, vol. ii. p. 678. ed. 1845.

† Minute, at a Meeting at Mr. Grenville's in Downing Street, May 22. 1765. There were present only the Lord Chancellor, the Duke of Bedford, Lord Halifax, Lord Sandwich, and Mr. Grenville himself. They agreed also to a fifth demand, but this was rather prospective, pointing to the future selection of a Lord Lieutenant.

gentleman to run the risk of plunging the whole realm into confusion; and he knew that under such urgent circumstances Mr. Mackenzie himself would be willing to forego his pretensions.*

These terms—for terms they were, though Grenville called them only points or questions,—received from the King no immediate answer. On the same evening, however, he sent again for Grenville, and bade him carry to his brother Ministers the Royal reply. He declared himself ready to yield on all other points, but struggled hard against the dismissal of Mr. Mackenzie and the appointment of Lord Granby. Nevertheless, on another consultation, the Ministers resolved to stand firm on both; accordingly they carried through the former point, and they relinquished the latter only at Lord Granby's own desire and request. The King, as he surrendered, said at last, referring to Mr. Mackenzie's case: "I see that I "must yield; I do it for the good of my people."

Thus had the King bent his neck to the yoke; the iron had entered into his soul. His wounded feelings were shown by clouded looks to Grenville and Bedford; by smiles and gracious words to their opponents. He invited to Court the young Duke of Devonshire, a stripling of seventeen, who came attended by his uncles, and was welcomed as the son of a friend. Grenville and Bedford, both men of angry passions, both deeming that the King had now no resource beyond themselves, resented not less deeply this conduct of their Sovereign, and resolved to make him feel their power. The Duke said that he was determined, before he left town in the summer, to have an explanation with His Majesty. Accordingly, on the 12th of June, not three weeks from the previous discussions, Bedford entered the King's apartment, and after taking his orders on some current business, addressed to him an elaborate speech from notes which he had ready prepared, and appears to have held in his hand. His Grace complained of the kindness shown to the enemies of the pre-

* See a private letter from Mr. Mackenzie to Sir A. Mitchell, printed in the notes to the Chatham Papers, vol. ii. p. 312. Sir Denis Le Marchant observes that "he was a very amiable man, and no ob-"jection was ever raised to him beyond his relationship to Lord Bute."

sent administration,—inveighed against Lord Bute, "this "favourite," as he presumed to call him to his Master,—and, above all, ventured to question whether, as respected Lord Bute, the King had kept his own Royal word. The King, in deep displeasure, listened, nevertheless, with calmness and composure to this long harangue; he spoke a few words in the course of it, denying that he had, as was imputed to him, again consulted Lord Bute, but at the close he merely bowed as a sign that he desired to be left alone.*

Thus upbraided, thus set at defiance by one at least of his own official servants, and determined to bear them no longer, the King again applied to the Duke of Cumberland, and the Duke of Cumberland again applied to Pitt. On this occasion the Great Commoner, being at last nearly free from gout, came to town, and had an interview of about three hours' duration with His Majesty. Everything he asked was agreed to, especially a close alliance, if possible, with Prussia, an abolition of General Warrants for the future, a repeal of the Cyder impost, and a change in the American taxation.† On these terms Pitt declared himself ready to undertake the direction of affairs, if others

* On the details of this interview compare Walpole's Correspondence with Mann (June 26. 1765), his Memoirs (vol. ii. p. 182.), and a letter from the Duke of Bedford to his nephew of Marlborough, June 13. 1765. (Bedford Papers, vol. iii. p. 286.) These three accounts, although two are by the same hand, are far from agreeing with each other. The last is undoubtedly by far the most authentic, and is corroborated by several passages in the Grenville Papers. It is plain from this letter that the Duke had no intention, as Walpole alleges, to insult the King, and was unconscious of having done so. Yet such was certainly the public impression and belief at the time (see Burke's Works, vol. ii. p. 156. ed. 1815), and from the Duke's warm temper he was by no means unlikely to overstep the bounds proposed to himself in his notes. Even according to his own statement it appears that he presumed to ask the King whether "this (the Royal) "promise had been kept?"—a most offensive question surely, had it even been addressed to an equal or inferior.

† Private Diary of Mr. Grenville, June 26. 1765. These terms were repeated by the King to the Chancellor, and by the Chancellor to Grenville.—In the Memoirs of Rockingham by Lord Albemarle, vol. i. p. 185—203., may be seen a narrative of the negotiations through the Duke of Cumberland, written by His Royal Highness himself. It is very full and exact, but breaks off abruptly in the midst of the second interview with Pitt. (1853.)

would embark with him. He named Lord Temple for the Treasury, and the Duke of Grafton with himself as Secretaries of State. Accordingly an express was sent for the Lord of Stowe, to whom three days afterwards the King gave an audience in presence of Pitt. There Pitt once more expressed his willingness to accept office, but Temple peremptorily refused, saying, that he had "a "delicacy which must always remain a secret." Pitt would not take part without him, and thus the negotiation ended.—When afterwards referring to it, and speaking of Temple's desertion, Pitt in one of his striking phrases termed it "an amputation." And to one of his friends in a letter hitherto unpublished he wrote as follows: "All "is now over as to me, and by a fatality I did not expect; "I mean Lord Temple's refusing to take his share with "me in the undertaking. We set out to-morrow morn-"ing for Somersetshire, where I propose, if I find the "place tolerable, to pass not a little of the rest of my "days."* To Burton Pynsent he accordingly repaired, selling soon afterwards his house at Hayes to Mr. Thomas Walpole, a merchant in London, and a son of the elder Horace, Lord Walpole of Wolterton.

Pitt being thus for the present out of the question, the Duke of Cumberland had next recourse to the confederacy of the great Whig Houses. Several of the best heads in that party were against attempting to form a Government unless in combination with Pitt, but the old Duke of Newcastle was, as usual, whimpering for office, and his eagerness prevailed. At a meeting of their principal men it was agreed to put forward as their leader the Marquis of Rockingham, and to this arrangement, strangely as it sounded, neither the Duke of Cumberland nor the King made any objection. His Majesty was indeed no longer in a condition to cavil or dispute as to terms. Thus the Marquis of Rockingham was named First Lord of the Treasury. The new Secretaries of State were the Duke of Grafton and General Conway,—General Conway so lately dismissed with every feeling of anger, with every sign of ignominy, and now not only recalled but intended for the lead of the House of Commons! The Earl of

* To Countess Stanhope, July 20. 1765, Appendix.

Northington continued Chancellor. The Duke of Newcastle was soothed with the Privy Seal.* Another bygone statesman, the nearly octogenarian Earl of Winchelsea, became President of the Council. The Chancellorship of the Exchequer was bestowed on Mr. William Dowdeswell, hitherto a stranger to office, but a well informed and active country gentleman.

The new Government thus formed and installed on the 13th of July was beyond all question respectable in its character, fair and upright in its views. But consisting as it did in part of worn-out veterans, and in part of raw recruits, it held out little promise of stability whenever it should come to be tried in the ordeal of Parliamentary debate. "It is a jumble," writes Lord Chesterfield, "of "youth and caducity which cannot be efficient."† — "It "is a mere lute-string administration," — cried Charles Townshend, who, by the way, however, retained his place in it as Paymaster of the Forces; — "it is pretty "summer wear, but it will never stand the winter!"

Conscious of their weakness the new Ministers were from the first most eager to propitiate and gratify Pitt. His confidential friend, Chief-Justice Pratt, was immediately raised to the Peerage by the title of Camden. His confidential law-agent, Mr. Nuthall, was immediately appointed to the lucrative office of Solicitor to the Treasury. Pitt nevertheless continued cold and unbending. He called himself only "a Somersetshire by-stander;" but he desired it to be publicly known that this new administration had not been formed with his advice or concurrence. Above all, he expressed displeasure at the accession of the Duke of Newcastle. "Claremont," — thus he wrote in August, — "could not be to me an "object of confidence or expectation of a solid system for "the public good according to my notion of it."‡

The accession of the Duke of Newcastle need not have

* "The Duke of Newcastle gave up his claim to that post (the "Treasury) reluctantly, though most of his own friends felt that his "advanced age rendered him inadequate to fill it. . . . . . To keep "him in good humour the patronage of the Church was added to the "Privy Seal." Duke of Grafton's MS. Memoirs.

† To his son, August 17. 1765.

‡ Letter to the Duke of Grafton, August 24. 1765.

caused displeasure, nor have seemed important in any eyes, except his own, if the chief of the new administration had been a man of adequate ability and vigour. Charles, Marquis of Rockingham, was at this time thirty-five years of age. His paternal name was Watson, but in the female line he was a descendant of the great Lord Strafford, and inherited the honours of Wentworth. Horse-racing was his early passion and pursuit. He afterwards became a Lord of the Bedchamber, and was thought perfectly well fitted for that post. When in 1763 an idea was first entertained of appointing him to a high political office the King expressed his surprise, "for I "thought," said His Majesty, "I had not two men in my "Bedchamber of less parts than Lord Rockingham."* Indeed everything about him bore the stamp of the tamest mediocrity, except only his estate, which was extremely large and fine. On the merits of that estate his panegyrists were frequently compelled to rely. One of them, in relating his appointment as Prime Minister, bids us recollect "his Lordship's great interest in the "public welfare, in quality of one of the greatest land-"holders in England."† In the House of Lords, even as the leader of a party, he could seldom be persuaded or provoked to rise. One night, after Lord Sandwich had been plying him in vain with much raillery and eloquence, Lord Gower could not forbear to whisper, "Sandwich, "how could you worry the poor dumb creature so?" On the other hand, Lord Rockingham had clear good sense and judgment, improved by the transaction of business. His character was without a stain, marked by probity and honour, by fidelity to his engagements, and by attachment to his friends.

Such was the man whom the Whig party of 1765 selected from their ranks for their leader. Such was the man to whom they continued their allegiance in every variety of fortune during eighteen years. The selection might surprise us more were it not in some measure characteristic of that party. Since parties were formed

* Lord Orford's Memoirs of George III., vol. i. p. 291.

† Annual Register, 1765, part i. p. 44.; no doubt from the pen of Burke.

anew, though under the old names, early in the reign of George the Third, it has been the boast of the Tories that with them family and fortune have been no necessary qualities of leadership,—that many an esquire of no ancient lineage, or a younger son of no broad domains, and relying on no merits save his own, has been with joyful assent raised far above the heads of the wealthiest and proudest among them. The same boast, at least not to the same degree, could scarcely perhaps be made by their opponents. We find the Whigs most frequently prefer for chiefs the PORPHYRO-GENETS, as the Byzantines might have termed them,—men born and bred in purple,—the Marquis of Rockingham or the Duke of Portland, or, in our own times, Lord Althorp,—men no doubt of irreproachable character, public and private, and of excellent plain sense, but still without one single ray of eloquence or spark of genius. "Thoughts that breathe "and words that burn" have been far less sought in the selection than high-sounding titles and rich acres. Above all, it seemed to be imagined that a certain small cluster of great houses, as the original Whig Junta, should have the first choice of honours and employments. Whether such a system has always wrought injury I will not undertake to say. But sure I am that it must often have inflicted pain. How must, for example, the heart of Sir James Mackintosh have swelled within him when after long time and trials he saw his party at last attain to office,—when only a small nook at the India Board was assigned to that veteran friend and chief of many years,—when the Cabinet-door close shut against himself was opened wide from time to time to men who might have been his children, and who should have been his pupils,—the sons or the sons-in-law, the cousins or the nephews, of the Ruling Families!

Reverting to the early years of George the Third, let us rapidly glance at the state of parties as it then appeared. All party-cries had been hushed during the splendid administration of Pitt; at its close they were raised again. The previous names of Whig and Tory re-appeared, but no longer with the previous principles and views. Even the keenest of the Tories had ceased to dream of a foreign Pretender; their loyalty was fixed on the reigning Sovereign; their aim was not, as in bygone years, to subvert, but, on the contrary, to secure against any shock or change, the settled order of things. As a party, however, they were not as yet fully formed; they had then few statesmen in their ranks, and their influence was felt in the division rather than in the debate. — The Whigs of 1763, no longer the Whigs of King William or Queen Anne, may be justly termed the founders of that distinguished party which bears their name at the present day. But they were split into sections, and it was between these sections, rather than between Whigs and Tories, that the battle for office raged. The Rockinghams and the Bedfords, Mr. Pitt and Mr. Grenville, all equally called themselves good Whigs, all would equally have declared that they never had been, that they never could be, Tories. Yet these were the chiefs of warring parties and of rival administrations. Such a schism in the Whig party of those times has sorely grieved the Whig writers of our own. Several of these gentlemen appear to have begun their labours with the pleasant predetermination that any Cavendish, any Russell, any Wentworth, whom they met with, must have been of course a patriot and a sage. Deep is their sorrow, dire their perplexity, when they find, as in 1765, these patriots and sages arrayed on opposite sides, turning each other out of office, and bandying the fiercest invectives and the least complimentary epithets!

It was at this period and under such a condition of parties that rival Clubs for politics were formed, and rose into great vogue and importance. Under Lord Bute the Ministerial Club, as it was at first termed, used to meet at the Cocoa Tree Tavern, from which it soon derived its name. Gibbon has given a lively account of it in his Journal for November 1762: "It affords every evening "a sight truly English. Twenty or thirty perhaps of the "first men in the kingdom in point of fashion and fortune "supping at little tables covered with a napkin, in the "middle of a coffee-room, upon a bit of cold meat or a "sandwich, and drinking a glass of punch. At present "we are full of King's Councillors and Lords of the Bed- "chamber, who, having jumped into the Ministry, make "a very singular medley of their old principles and "language with their modern ones." * About a year from that time the Opposition, seeing the advantages of such a combination, established a Club of their own at another tavern, kept by Mr. Wildman in Albemarle Street. "Our Club goes on with new vigour," writes James Grenville to his sister, Lady Chatham. "I am "infinitely perplexed by the pressing of many quarters "to be of it." †

It is easy and plain to state by what name each of these parties called itself, or at what place it met, but hard is the task of defining by what principles or opinions they were kept asunder. At that period the line between the new divisions of Whig and Tory was very far less distinct than it afterwards became, and the line between the various sections of the Whigs was more shadowy still. Even when the differences were substantial it may be doubted how far they had arisen from clear and settled views on either side. Thus, for example, the Rockinghams warmly supported the American claim of equal rights, which the Bedfords as warmly opposed. Yet it might be rash to leap at once to the conclusion that on all other political questions a more liberal spirit prevailed at Wentworth than at Woburn. The accidents of office or opposition in the first instance, the progress of events, and the eagerness accruing from either course when once adopted, seem sufficient to account for the distinction.

Whenever there may rise in view any great public aim or object — as of aggression or defence, to reform or to maintain, — then the great public benefit of party will scarcely be denied by any one who has studied state-affairs in history. Still less will it be denied by any one who has seen them in action. But when no such aim exists, when no foreign danger threatens, when no internal change is contemplated, then the question suggests itself whether party may not grow an evil to the commonwealth, whether it be not, as it has been called, the madness of many for the gain of a few. Was it worth while for statesmen to combine in leagues and factions

* Gibbon's Miscellaneous Works, vol. i. p. 154. ed. 1814.

† Chatham Papers, vol. ii. p. 276.

only for the sake of some subaltern intriguers,—that Rigby might pin himself to the skirts of one of them,—that Wedderburn might sell his eloquence by turns to the best bidder?—So far as we can now discern, considerations such as these had much weight with many minds. Pitt was strongly impressed by them, although no doubt his sentiments to that effect were aided by the influence of his secluded habits and his haughty temper. He might, however, be forgiven for remembering how successfully and gloriously he had blended all parties together in his late administration, and how in all his attempts to form a new one he had been thwarted by the party-ties of others, entangled by his own. Thus also George the Third from the very commencement of his reign had found party-ties beset his path. By party-ties in various forms and times all his endeavours had been baffled, all his predilections overborne. He, too, may be pardoned for wishing that there might be no other checks to his power than those which the law and constitution had imposed. It should, therefore, be no ground for either surprise or blame if we find His Majesty in one of his letters during the year 1767 call upon his Ministers "to withstand with redoubled ardour that evil called "connection."*

The most valid plea, perhaps, for the existence of party at such times is, that it kept the machinery and framework ready and in use for other times when party combinations came to be in truth essential to the public good. It might be too late to forge the weapon when the warfare should begin. But it is natural that considerations like these should have little weight with men plunged in all the turmoil of active life, and feeling the present difficulty much more than the prospective advantage.

It was then at this period and under such circumstances that there arose another party, or, more exactly speaking, a number of persons, known by the name of

* Chatham Papers, vol. iii. p. 228. See also in the same collection the King's letter of November 28. 1766, in which he expresses his desire "to receive able and good men, let their private friendships be "where they will."

"the King's Friends." Several of these were men in office, many more were independent Members of Parliament. Of the former class Lord Barrington may be cited as an instance. From Treasurer of the Navy he was transferred to be Secretary-at-War under the Rockingham administration. He tells us that in his interview with the King shortly before his new appointment he renewed the most solemn assurances of his devotion solely and personally to His Majesty, and of his resolution to support the government, not because some of his oldest and best friends were of it, but because His Majesty had chosen it. He said that the Crown had an undoubted right to choose its Ministers, and that it was the duty of subjects to support them, unless there were some very strong and urgent reasons to the contrary. And he added, "Sir, I beg you will immediately dispose of my "place as shall be most convenient to you, and be as-"sured my conduct shall be exactly the same when I am "only your subject as if I continued your servant."*

Entering Parliament or accepting office with such feelings towards the Throne, it was natural that the King's Friends should on many occasions look rather to the supposed opinions of His Majesty than to the declared wishes of the Minister. The independent Members of Parliament would often shape their course accordingly. The holders of office would sometimes strain to the utmost that latitude on several public measures among the members of the same Government which has more recently obtained the name of "open questions." It was natural also that the Prime Minister, above all, if hard pushed in a division, should think that latitude exceeded, and should complain of them to his Royal Master. Nor can it be thought strange if the King had some tenderness to those who thus regarded him, if he pleaded their cause while he could to their angry colleagues, or if, when no longer able to defend them, he was desirous at least to soften or postpone their dismissal from his service.

Many and frequent were the shafts of calumny let fly

* Life of Lord Barrington, compiled by the Bishop of Durham, p. 96. (Unpublished.)

against the King's Friends. It was alleged that their secret chief and mover was no other than the Earl of Bute, whose ascendency over George the Third, it was thought, still continued. In vain did the Earl declare that he had renounced politics; in vain did he lead a studious and secluded life; in vain did he travel to Scotland; in vain did he travel to Italy. It was still imagined that by some occult means, invisible to vulgar eyes, he communicated with the King on all important occasions, and formed the mainspring of all the Royal movements. In fact, however, George the Third considered himself bound by his promise to Bedford and Grenville, even after the statesmen to whom he made it had quitted his service. Certain it is that from that day he never again either corresponded or conversed with Lord Bute. Once indeed the Princess Mother attempted, but without the least success, to renew the intercourse between them. As the King was one day walking with her in her garden at Kew Lord Bute suddenly appeared before him, having come out of a summer-house where he had been purposely concealed. The King many years afterwards told the story to his son the Duke of York, adding that he had effectually shown his displeasure at the intrusion of his former favourite.*

Strange as it seems, however, the belief in Lord Bute's continued ascendency over the Royal mind was by no means confined to the multitude, nor to those who had but scanty means of information. It was sincerely shared

* See Lord John Russell's Introduction to the third volume of the Bedford Papers, p. xxxiii. See also, in corroboration, the more guarded hints ascribed to Mr. Croker in the Quarterly Review, No. cxxxi. p. 236. But as to the main fact,—the cessation of all intercourse between the King and the Earl,—Lord Bute's own statement is quite sufficient and satisfactory. Thus writes his son, Lord Mount-Stuart, in a published letter, dated October 23. 1778: "He "(Lord Bute) does authorise me to say that he declares upon his "solemn word of honour that he has not had the honour of waiting "on His Majesty, but at his Levee or Drawing Room, nor has he "presumed to offer an advice or opinion concerning the disposition "of offices, or the conduct of measures, either directly or indirectly, "by himself or any other, from the time the late Duke of Cumberland "was consulted in the arrangement of a Ministry in 1765 to the present hour"

by many of the leading statesmen of the age. Several passages in Lord Chesterfield's letters which his first Editor suppressed show that prepossession in the strongest degree. Thus he writes to his son in 1767: "We must "soon see what order will be produced from this chaos; "it will be whatever Lord Bute pleases."* Thus also it is evident from the Wright and Addington transaction in 1778 that the same idea had to the last possession of Lord Chatham's mind.

Other charges equally groundless and far more grievous were brought against the King's Friends. They have been assailed by Burke with no common force and eloquence in his masterly Essay, "Thoughts on the Cause "of the Present Discontents," which appeared in 1770. But here it is needful to bear in mind how warm was Burke's attachment to the Rockingham party, and how much that very party had thought itself wronged by the King's Friends. Nor ought we to forget the distinction to be drawn in all Burke's writings. While the latest posterity may well recur to them for general maxims of philosophy and politics, no man should readily adopt their more narrow views of contemporary character. In these Burke ever displays the ardour of an advocate rather than the calmness of a judge. In these he ever mistakes the colouring of his own brilliant imagination for the hues of the objects around him.

But let us look more closely at the charges alleged by Burke against the King's Friends. In the first place he urges that they had no personal intimacy with their Sovereign, and therefore no just right to the name which they bore. "They are only known to the Sovereign," says he, "by kissing his hand for the offices, pensions, and grants into which they have deceived his benig-"nity."† It seems, however, equitable to remember that the name of the King's Friends was not assumed by themselves, but far rather applied by their opponents; that they did not claim or allege any peculiar intimacy

* Letter, July 9. 1767. The MSS. containing this and several other passages to the same effect had not been recovered at the time of the edition of 1845.

† Works, vol. ii. p. 285. ed. 1815.

with the Sovereign; and that they only professed special veneration for the Kingly office, and especial confidence for the personal character of George the Third.

Then again we find Burke ascribe to them a most refined and complicated scheme that no administration, however composed, should ever enjoy any real power, but that all affairs should be transacted by an interior and invisible Cabinet.— Surely the extreme refinement of this scheme is alone sufficient to prove its airy nature,— that it never could exist in real life, but only spring forth in an author's teeming brain. To resist some one measure or some one Ministry might be natural, but to resist all and every one of them upon system, and for the sake of another party in the clouds, is incredible. No one, I imagine, who now peruses Burke's eloquent pages on this subject, will adhere to them in their full extent. And I observe that later writers, as Mr. Macaulay and Lord John Russell, even while pursuing Burke's accusation against the King's Friends with undiminished fire and vehemence, have yet altogether shifted and altered its original ground.*

But further still it is urged by Burke against the King's Friends that their prevailing object was only to keep themselves in place. In such a charge Burke was no doubt justified by particular instances. In such a charge, however, he need not have confined himself to the King's Friends alone. The best party that ever existed in this or in any country has beyond all question comprised within it many selfish and sordid-minded men. Indeed parties are like coin which would never be fit for common use without some considerable alloy of the baser metals. But can it be proved, or even pretended, that the King's Friends under George the Third comprised a larger proportion of such men than the other contemporary factions? Was it to them that Lord Melcombe or Lord Sandwich, Mr. Rigby or Mr. Wedderburn, belonged?

Above all it is to be noted that the eloquent sally of Burke can apply only to such of the King's Friends as

* Edinburgh Review, No. clxii. p. 576. Introduction to the Bedford Papers, vol. iii. p. xxix.

contrived to hold paid offices of state, — amounting, perhaps at most, to eight or ten or twelve. The position of such gentlemen towards the head of the Government was no doubt a special one, — open to much cavil, — and only to be justified according to the latitude understood or agreed upon in regard to open questions. This was a point to be settled between them and the Prime Minister, between the Prime Minister and the King. But what charge is made, what charge can be made, against that far larger number of independent Peers and independent Members of Parliament to whom the name of King's Friends was commonly applied, — men without a wish or thought of office for themselves, but who loved and revered the Crown with all their heart, with all their mind, with all their soul, and with all their strength? Not freer from any selfish taint was the spirit, — such as Ormond felt, such as Clarendon describes, — the spirit with which the ancestors of many among them had stood by the Crown in its days of danger and distress, — in the days of the rout at Marston, or of the watch and ward at Carisbrook. Then the flame of loyalty beamed far brighter from the surrounding darkness, — now it was as pure though it paled before the day! Nor was it a blind unreasoning ardour of loyalty alone. Many of them throughout this reign fixed their faith on the personal integrity and upright intentions of the Sovereign, and felt more reliance on his character than on that of any of his Ministers, — the younger Pitt alone excepted. Such were the men to whom, as the last Lord Dudley states, his own parent belonged. "My father," — thus he writes to the Bishop of Llandaff, — "is a Tory of a very peculiar "breed; devoted to Courts and Ministers, and wholly in-"different to the favours they have to bestow." * Such were the men who formed in no slight degree the strength and support of the principal administrations in the reign of George the Third. It may be easy to misrepresent their views, — to call them abject, — to say that they were prompted, if not by sordid hopes, at least by a slavish mind. But there are some — themselves in truth anything but slavish to the prevailing temper of the day

* Letter of October 19. 1822.

— who will never join in that reproach. There are some who will remember that the most uncompromising assertors of the Crown have often proved no less the sturdiest champions of the people. There are some who know and feel how just a pride, how true a glory, may spring from the very meekness of legitimate obedience.

In Ireland the state of politics, though in some respects the same, was in others widely different. — The Parliamentary contest which commenced in 1753 * had now in a great measure died away. The two party-chiefs and rivals, Stone and Boyle, — the Lord Primate and the Earl of Shannon, — died in December 1764 within a few days of each other. At that time William Gerard Hamilton, as Irish Secretary, might still deliver some eloquent oration, first carefully learnt by heart, and Anthony Malone pour forth some able and unpremeditated sally. But in general the oratory of the Irish Parliament had sunk to a low ebb. A very competent authority assures us that at this period in Ireland "an unlettered style, almost "approaching to coarseness and vulgarity, was the only "one permitted by the House of Commons." † Nor in general were the subjects discussed of any Constitutional importance. One of the few exceptions was owing to the strong desire out of doors, which was manifested soon after the accession of George the Third, to limit for the future the duration of an Irish Parliament. For according to the law of Ireland at that time, as according to the law of England before the Revolution, a Parliament might, without any fresh appeal to the people, endure from the commencement to the very end of a reign. Dr. Lucas, once an apothecary, now become Member for Dublin, and a popular leader of the day, — "the Irish "Wilkes," as he was sometimes called, — brought in a Septennial or, as it afterwards became before the Privy Council, an Octennial Bill. At last in 1768 that Bill was carried through, but not without great difficulties, and contrary, as is alleged, to the secret wishes of many who had voted in its favour.‡

* See vol. iv. p. 128.
† Hardy's Life of Lord Charlemont, vol. i. p. 140.
‡ Lord Chesterfield's Letters, vol. iv. p. 468. ed. 1845.

In October 1761 there had gone as Lord Lieutenant the Earl of Halifax, a statesman of some reputation, but who impaired his constitution by drinking, and his fortune by neglect.* In September 1763 was installed the Earl of Northumberland, a grandee of princely wealth and magnificence; and in October 1765 the Earl of Hertford, a courteous and high-minded gentleman. But these appointments were too transitory to be beneficial; and indeed no choice of the Viceroy, however judiciously made, could reach the social evils of the kingdom. Disturbances, almost rising to the dignity of rebellion, broke forth at various times both among the Protestants of the north and the Roman Catholics of the south, — both in Armagh and Tipperary. In the former the moving grievance was the exorbitant exaction of tithe. The insurgents appeared in bodies of four or five hundred, headed, it was said, by farmers and yeomen of respectable property. All bore boughs of oak in their hats, from whence they were commonly called OAK-BOYS. Whenever any clergyman fell into their hands they compelled him to take an oath that he would not levy more than a certain proportion of tithe. One clergyman, by name Dr. Clarke, was especially obnoxious to them as having been the first to exceed what they thought the proper rate; so they seized him, held him fast on the top of his own coach, and drew him through several districts of the neighbourhood, amidst abundance of hisses and scurril jests. Thus their proceedings were not without some touch of the native Irish humour; and it is remarkable that though they insulted many persons, erected gallows, and threatened "ineffable perdition" to all their opponents, yet in fact they never took a single life nor maimed a single limb.

In the south, on the contrary, the rioters, all of the lowest class, showed ferocious cruelty, and committed dreadful crimes. They were known by the name of WHITE-BOYS, because as a mark among themselves in their attacks they frequently wore a shirt over their clothes. Their union was cemented by oaths of secrecy, and their vengeance wreaked upon any who betrayed,

* Walpole's Memoirs of George III., vol. iv. p. 326.

or who withstood, or even who refused to help them. The military force was sent against these banditti; many of them were killed or tried and sentenced, and one priest, Father Shehee, who had abetted them, was hanged. But disturbances of the same kind and in the same quarter, though often suppressed, as often broke forth anew until the close of that century,—the very period when the last highwaymen were disappearing from the lanes and commons of more happy England! Partly as the effect of these outrages may be noticed the low state of agriculture in the south of Ireland. But though in part their effect, it was also in part their cause. So early as 1727 Swift complains that "even ale and potatoes are imported from "England as well as corn." * Another grievance which was felt both in north and south was the pressure of the rates for the making of roads, which roads in too many cases were directed with a view to private mansions, rather than to public thoroughfares. In other matters also the conduct of the country gentlemen of the south of Ireland gave much handle for complaint. When in 1763 the Earl of Charlemont, a most unexceptionable witness, attempted to explain the causes of the White-Boy risings, we find as the first and chief which he assigns, "low "wages, exorbitant rents." † At nearly the same period another no less acute and practised observer, the Earl of Chesterfield, writes as follows to the Bishop of Waterford: "I see that you are in fears again from your White-Boys, "and have destroyed a good many of them, but I believe "that if the military force had killed half as many land-"lords it would have contributed more effectually to "restore quiet. The poor people in Ireland are used "worse than negroes by their lords and masters, and "their deputies, of deputies, of deputies." ‡

* Short View of the State of Ireland. Works, vol. vii. p. 329. ed. 1814.

† Hardy's Life of Lord Charlemont, vol. i. p. 172. In another place Lord Charlemont severely censures "the Protestant *Bashaws* "of the south and west."

‡ Blackheath, October 1. 1764. This passage and several others in his correspondence with the Bishop of Waterford were suppressed by the first Editors of 1777, and it was not till 1848 that the whole letters in MSS. came into my hands.

CHAPTER XLV.

From the train of events and the state of parties which have now been laid before the reader the weakness of the Rockingham administration is clearly manifest. It had hoped to lean on the resolute will and the lately returning favour of the Prince who had called it into being. But only a few weeks after its formation this its main prop was snatched away. — On the 30th of October the Duke of Cumberland was playing at piquet with his Groom of the Bedchamber, General Hodgson, when he grew confused and mistook the cards. Next morning he appeared at Court, and returned to dine at home, but after dinner was seized with a suffocation and ordered the window to be opened. One of his domestics accustomed to bleed him in such attacks was called, and attempted to tie up his arm, but the Duke calmly said: "Too late! "It is all over!" and expired.

The concern felt at the Duke's decease was, in England at least, deep and sincere. His former unpopularity was forgotten, or seemed only another claim in his behalf. It was observed that in London the middle and lower classes not only clad themselves in mourning, but wore it for a longer period than the Gazette prescribed.*

Of far graver import, however, both to the nation and to the Ministry, were the tidings which at this time came from North America. While the Assemblies were petitioning, the rabble were rioting, against the Stamp Act. Boston, above all, took the lead in such tumultuary proceedings. There, in the month of August, the house of Mr. Oliver, who had accepted the post of Stamp Distributor, was sacked and plundered, his effigy hung upon a tree†,

* Lord Orford's Memoirs of George III., vol. ii. p. 226.

† This tree was afterwards held in honour, and surnamed *Liberty Tree*; it stood "on the main street of Boston." (Holmes, American Annals, vol. ii. p. 271. ed. 1805.) In August 1775 some of the English soldiers or their friends "with malice diabolical" cut it down. (American Archives, vol. iii. p. 472.)

carried upon a bier, and finally burned in a bonfire, and himself compelled under terror of his life to promise to resign his office. The authorities had sent a written order to the Colonel of the Militia Regiment to beat an alarm; but the Colonel replied that it would avail nothing, for that as soon as the drum was heard the drummer would be knocked down and the drum broken; and to this he added a still more cogent reason that probably all the drummers of the regiment were in the mob. In short it became apparent that many of the principal persons in the town were inclined to approve and justify the act. Thus the populace unchecked and inspirited ere long betook themselves to fresh deeds of violence. "On the "26th of August," — writes one of the correspondents of the Government, — "towards evening some boys began "to light a bonfire before the Town-house, which is an "usual signal for a mob. Before it was quite dark a "great company of people gathered together crying, "'Liberty and Property!' which is their usual notice of "their intention to plunder and pull down a house!"* Accordingly they did proceed that night to plunder and in part demolish the houses of the Register-Deputy of the Admiralty, of the Comptroller of the Customs, and of the Lieutenant-Governor, destroying in the latter a large and valuable collection of papers. Next morning the streets were found strewed with money, pieces of plate, gold rings, and other effects which the depredators had dropped in carrying away. These last outrages had, however, the good effect of rousing the respectable inhabitants of the town and Colony to their own and the public defence. Moreover, the news of the change of Ministry in England might give them hopes of finding some more quiet method of redress. With such hopes the freeholders of Boston voted thanks to General Conway and Colonel Barré for their previous exertions against the Stamp Act, and directed that portraits of both should be placed in the Town Hall.

* Correspondence relating to America, laid before the House of Commons by the King's command January 1766, and printed in the Parl. Hist., vol. xvi. p. 112—133. See especially the letters from Boston of August 15, 16. 22. and 31. 1765.

A most thorough contrast to the popular tumults at Boston and some other cities was afforded by the staid and orderly proceedings of the General Congress at New York. There had come together the delegates from nine of the Colonial Assemblies. Some other Colonies had been withheld from sending any by legal technicalities thrown in the way by their Governors; others again, as Canada and New Brunswick, had calmly acquiesced in the obnoxious statute. When the delegates of Boston waited upon the Governor of New York he said that such a Congress was unconstitutional, unprecedented, and unlawful, and that he should give them no countenance; he made, however, no attempt to hinder or disturb their deliberations. The Congress having met early in October continued to sit for about three weeks. In compliment to Massachusetts, which had been the first to suggest the scheme, Mr. Timothy Ruggles from that Colony was appointed their Chairman.* All their proceedings were in form most cautious and respectful, but in substance decisive and firm. They passed fourteen Resolutions denying the right of the mother country to tax them without their own consent, and they agreed upon petitions to the King and to both Houses of Parliament. So temperate were they, so little of rashness or innovation seemed to pervade this Congress, that it has been but slightly noticed and well nigh passed over by several writers of the time. Yet a statesman's eye might have even then discerned the great importance of this the first example of combination among our Colonies in North America, of the correspondence thus established between the leading men of distant towns, of the seeds thus laid for future and further union.

Besides the popular tumults,—besides the General Congress,—besides the movements in the separate Assemblies,—other steps were also taken towards the same desired end. Associations were set on foot in nearly all the Colonies against the use or the importation of British manufactures after the 1st of January next. This obstruction it was announced by all and intended by most should endure no longer than until the Stamp Act was repealed. But it cannot be doubted that some few ardent

* Marshall's Life of Washington, vol. ii. p. 90. ed. 1804.

and ambitious spirits had already begun to carry their views much further. There is a remarkable letter of this time addressed to Franklin in England from one of his friends in Pennsylvania: "A certain sect of people," says the writer, "if I may judge from all their late conduct, "seem to look on this as a favourable opportunity of es-"tablishing their republican principles, and of throwing "off all connection with their mother country. I have "reasons to think that they are forming a private union "among themselves from one end of the Continent to the "other." *

Such was the state of public feeling in which drew near the 1st of November,—the day fixed for the first operation of the obnoxious Act. When shortly before ships arrived from England with the stamped papers on board, they found in many of the ports an exasperated multitude ready to oppose the use, nay even the unloading, of their freight. The persons, moreover, who had been named Distributors resigned their posts, in some cases, on the very day when it was intended that their duties should commence. At New York it was deemed necessary, after a tumult, that the stamped papers should be given up to the local magistrates, and deposited for custody in the City Hall; "a "step which," as Mr. Secretary Conway observes, "must "certainly be looked upon as greatly humiliating and de-"rogatory to His Majesty's Government." † Thus the due execution of the Act appeared in all the Colonies impolitic and in many impossible. The pursuits of commerce and the administration of justice, unless in criminal cases, were alike impeded. Some merchants, however, ventured to send forth their ships with certificates from the Governors that Stamps could not be obtained; and thus also the Courts of Justice, though suspended awhile in most of the Colonies, at length, from the necessity of the case, proceeded to transact business without the papers which the law required.‡

* Mr. Joseph Galloway to Benjamin Franklin, Philadelphia, January 13. 1766. Franklin's Works, vol. vii. p. 305.

† Despatch to Major-General Gage, Dec. 15. 1765. Parl. Hist., vol. xvi. p. 118.

‡ Holmes, American Annals, vol. ii. p. 139. ed. 1829.

This train of events and state of feeling as by successive packets it became known in England filled the Ministers with the utmost perplexity. To deal with it both promptly and wisely might indeed have tried a far stronger intellect than Rockingham's, a much less wavering temper than Conway's. They had themselves not approved the passing of the Stamp Act. But even had they approved it, how hard and painful the task to exact an impost from provinces beyond the Atlantic and at the point of the sword! On the other hand, how fatal the precedent to cancel any impost whenever it might be rebelliously resisted! Between these opposite difficulties the Ministers had yet come to no fixed resolution when it became needful to call Parliament together for another object, since either by deaths or by appointments to office in the change of Government there were now no less than forty-one new Writs to move. With that view Parliament was convened on the 17th of December, and the Ministers trusted to slip away from any present pledges or attacks by merely noticing American affairs in the King's Speech as "matters "of importance"—"deserving the most serious attention" —"after the usual recess." But they did not thus avoid the dreaded debate. Grenville, inflamed with anger at the ill reception which his own offspring, his favourite Stamp Act, had met with from the colonists, moved a fierce amendment expressing indignation at the dangerous tumults in North America, and calling on the Government to vindicate the law. He could obtain no reply from the Ministers, who were of course absent from the House as not yet re-elected. At last Charles Townshend and Sir Fletcher Norton, though mainly agreeing with his views, induced him to withdraw his motion.*

In the Christmas recess which ensued a meeting was held at the house of Lord Rockingham, comprising the Ministers and a few of their principal friends. There the various courses that might be followed in reference to America were brought forward and discussed. But it is

* See the letter of Mr. George Cooke to Mr. Pitt, dated Dec. 17. 1765, and published in the Chatham Papers, vol. ii. p. 350. A nearly similar scene in the Lords is described in another letter from Lord Shelburne (ibid., p. 353.), and Lord Lyttleton's own not very important speech may be seen in his Memoirs (vol. ii. p. 686. ed. 1845).

stated by a writer who had not only received oral information, but read the original minutes of the meeting, that the Ministers were not able to form any consistent plan of operations, and decided nothing beyond the terms in which the King's Speech should be expressed.*

When accordingly on the 14th of January the two Houses re-assembled, the second King's Speech which was delivered on that occasion did little more than commend the whole subject of America in general terms to the wisdom of Parliament. — The debate, however, which forthwith ensued in the House of Commons, is one of the most striking and memorable in our annals. Like nearly all debates at that period it might have passed unrecorded. The former practice of reporting as partially set on foot by Samuel Johnson and a few others under Sir Robert Walpole had long since died away. The present admirable skill and expertness in that department were as yet not even in their dawn. But as it chanced the public in Ireland felt deep interest in the question of the British claim to tax the Colonies, and thus the first debate upon it was taken down with some degree of minuteness by two gentlemen from that country, Sir Robert Dean assisted by the Earl of Charlemont. Their report was published in the course of the same year in the form of a pamphlet; and to evade the Resolutions of the House against the practice the title-page declared it to be printed at Paris.†

In these representations, as in the reality, the main figure was Pitt. It was above a year since he had been seen within the walls of Parliament. It was not known what sentiments he might express as to the Ministry. It was uncertain what course he might recommend as to the Stamp Act. Thus, as he stalked in, yet lame from

* Mr. Adolphus's History, vol. i. p. 198. ed. 1840.

† See this report as inserted in the Parl. Hist., vol. xvi. p. 95—110. I have had the opportunity of comparing it with two other reports now in my possession, and as yet unpublished, from Mr. Thomas Penn and Mr. Moffatt of Rhode Island, who were then in London. These I owe to the kindness of Mr. Bancroft while Minister at this Court; a gentleman whose worth and merit, high attainments and constant courtesy, gained him the respect of all parties, and will not soon be forgotten amongst us.

gout, but in part recruited by several weeks at Bath, the whole House closely scanned his aspect and eagerly awaited his words. Never, perhaps, has any man appeared more thoroughly the arbiter and lord of that great assembly. Even its rules and orders, as will presently be seen, were no obstacles in his path, and yielded to his lofty pleasure. He did not rise until not only the mover and seconder of the Address, but several other gentlemen, had spoken. The one who immediately preceded him was Edmund Burke, rising for the first time in Parliament, and Pitt began his speech by congratulating that "young Member,"—that "very able advo-"cate,"—on his success, and the friends of Burke on the value of the acquisition they had made. He then passed to more general topics. "I came to town," he said, "but this day. I was a stranger to the tenor of "His Majesty's Speech, and the proposed Address, till I "heard them read in this House. Unconnected and un-"consulted I have not the means of information; I am "fearful of offending through mistake, and therefore beg "to be indulged with a second reading of the proposed "Address."—Contrary to the common practice of the House, the Address was now read over a second time for the special convenience of one Member, and Pitt then resumed his observations in the same haughty strain: "I stand up in this place single and unconnected. As "to the late Ministry," (here he turned round to Mr. Grenville, who sat within one of him,) "every capital "measure they have taken has been entirely wrong. "As to the present gentlemen, to those at least whom I "have in my eye," (here he looked to the place where sat Mr. Secretary Conway,) "I have no objection; I "have never been made a sacrifice by any of them! "Their characters are fair;—but, notwithstanding, I "love to be explicit; I cannot give them my confidence; "pardon me, gentlemen," (here bowing to the Ministers,) "confidence is a plant of slow growth in an aged bosom; "youth alone is the season of credulity!"

Pitt in the next place touched on still more tender ground. "By comparing events with each other, by "reasoning from effects to causes, methinks I plainly "discover the traces of an overruling influence. . . . . . I "have no local attachments; it is indifferent to me "whether a man was rocked in his cradle on this side or "that side of the Tweed. I sought for merit wherever "it was to be found. It is my boast that I was the first "Minister who looked for it, and I found it, in the "mountains of the north. I called it forth and drew it "into your service; an hardy and intrepid race of men! "...... These men in the last war were brought to "combat on your side; they served with fidelity, as they "fought with valour, and conquered for you in every "part of the world. Detested be the national reflections "against them! they are unjust, groundless, illiberal, "unmanly. When I ceased to serve His Majesty as a "Minister it was not the country of the man by which I "was moved, but the man of that country wanted "wisdom, and held principles incompatible with freedom.

"It is a long time, Mr. Speaker, since I have attended "in Parliament. When the Resolution was taken in the "House to tax America I was ill in bed. If I could "have endured to have been carried in my bed,—so "great was the agitation of my mind for the conse- "quences—I would have solicited some kind hand to "have laid me down on this floor to have borne my "testimony against it. .... The justice, the equity, "the policy, the expediency of this Act I will leave to "another time. .... But since I cannot depend upon "health for any future day, such is the nature of my in- "firmities, I will say now thus much, that in my opinion "this kingdom has no right to lay a tax upon the Co- "lonies. On this point I could not be silent, nor repress "the ardour of my soul, smote as it is with indignation "at the very thought of taxing America internally with- "out a requisite voice of consent... Taxation is no part "of the governing or legislative power. At the same "time on every real point of legislation I believe the au- "thority of Parliament to be fixed as the Polar Star,— "fixed for the reciprocal benefit of the mother country "and her infant Colonies. They are the subjects of this "kingdom,—equally entitled with yourselves to all the "natural rights of mankind, and the peculiar privileges "of Englishmen,—and equally bound by its laws. The "Americans are the sons, not the bastards, of England.

"The distinction between legislation and taxation is "essential to liberty. The Crown, the Peers, are equally "legislative powers with the Commons. If taxation be "a part of simple legislation, the Crown, the Peers, have "rights in taxation as well as yourselves; rights which "they will claim whenever the principle can be sup- "ported by might.

"There is an idea in some that the Colonies are vir- "tually represented in this House. I would fain know, "by whom an American is represented here? Is he re- "presented by any knight of the shire in any county in "the kingdom? Would to God that respectable repre- "sentation were augmented to a greater number! Or "will you tell him that he is represented by any repre- "sentative of a borough,—a borough which, perhaps, "its own representative never saw! This is what is "called 'the rotten part of the Constitution.' It cannot "continue a century; if it does not drop it must be "amputated.—The idea of a virtual representation of "America in this House is the most contemptible idea "that ever entered into the head of man; it does not "deserve a serious refutation!"

On the close of this memorable speech a long pause ensued. At length rose the Ministerial leader, Secretary Conway. He declared that he entirely agreed with almost every word that had fallen from Mr. Pitt, and believed that such were the sentiments also of most, if not of all, the King's Servants. For himself he had been unworthily and accidentally called to the high employment he then bore; he had not thrust himself into it, and should think himself happy to resign it to the Right Honourable gentleman whenever he should please to take it. "But two things," he added, "fell from that "gentleman which give me pain, as whatever falls from "that gentleman falls from so great a height as to make "a deep impression. I must endeavour to remove it. "It was objected that the notice given to Parliament of "the troubles in America was not early. I can assure "the House that the first accounts were too vague and "imperfect to be worth the notice of Parliament. It is "only of late that they have been precise and full.—

"Secondly, an overruling influence has been hinted at. "I see nothing of it; I feel nothing of it. I disclaim it "for myself, and, so far as my discernment can reach, "for all the rest of His Majesty's Ministers."

In passing it may be observed as strange that considering the unimpeachable honour of General Conway, this statement as to the cessation of Lord Bute's secret influence should have made but slight impression, and commanded little credit. It does not appear to have in any degree arrested the popular rumours on that subject.

George Grenville was the next to rise. In a long and able speech he defended the justice and good policy of the Stamp Act. He denied that, according to Constitutional law, the right of taxation in the rulers depended on the right of representation in the people; resting his argument mainly on the cases of the County Palatine of Chester and of the Bishoprick of Durham, both made subject to taxation before they sent representatives to Parliament. For proof he appealed to the preambles of the very Acts which gave them representatives, the one in the reign of Henry the Eighth, the other in the reign of Charles the Second,—and these two preambles he desired might be read at length to the House. "The se-"ditious spirit of the Colonies," he added, "owes its birth "to the factions in this House. Gentlemen are careless "of the consequences of what they say, provided it "answers the purposes of Opposition."

Grenville had no sooner sat down than Pitt sprung up to answer him. At the outset he declared that he only wished to supply a portion of his former speech which he had expressly reserved to save the time of the House, but which was now forced from him. He was called to Order by Lord Strange; and indeed it is plain that his plea was no more than a shallow pretext, a flimsy evasion of the rules of the House against speaking twice in the same debate; nevertheless so great was then his personal ascendency that he was not only permitted but invited to proceed by loud cries of "Go on!" Thus authorized, he poured forth another oration by no means inferior to the first either in eloquence, in boldness, or in lofty disdain. "The gentleman,"—for thus, without the usual title of

Honourable or Right Honourable, does he appear to have designated Grenville, — " tells us America is obstinate; " America is almost in open rebellion. Sir, I rejoice that " America has resisted. Three millions of people so " dead to all the feelings of liberty as voluntarily to sub- " mit to be slaves would have been fit instruments to " make slaves of all the rest. I come not here armed at " all points with law-cases and Acts of Parliament, with " the statute-book doubled down in dogs'-ears, to defend " the cause of liberty. If I had I myself would have cited " the two cases of Chester and Durham. I would have " cited them to show that even under arbitrary reigns " Parliaments were ashamed of taxing a people without " their consent, and allowed them representatives. . . . . . " The gentleman asks when were the Colonies emanci- " pated? But I desire to know when they were made " slaves. . . . . I know the valour of your troops. I know " the skill of your officers. In a good cause on a sound " bottom the force of this country can crush America to " atoms. But in such a cause as this your success would " be hazardous. America, if she fell, would fall like the " strong man. She would embrace the pillars of the State, " and pull down the Constitution along with her! Is " this your boasted peace? Not to sheath the sword in " its scabbard, but to sheath it in the bowels of your " countrymen?"

After this noble burst of eloquence Pitt thus proceeded: " I consider the Stamp Act as a paltry mark of the nar- " row genius of the Minister who conceived and brought " it forward. The efforts of America against that impo- " sition were truly glorious, if they had not been clouded " over with tumult and confusion, and totally eclipsed by " the most odious steps of rage, violence, and rapine " against their brethren of a different opinion. The " Americans, I say, have not acted in all things with " prudence and temper. They have been wronged. They " have been driven to madness by injustice. Will you " punish them for the madness you have occasioned? " Rather let prudence and temper come first from this " side!"

Pitt then in a wholly different strain repeated and applied two lines from Prior on the behaviour of a husband to a wife *, and concluded his speech as follows: "Upon "the whole I will beg leave to tell the House what is "precisely my opinion. It is, that the Stamp Act be re- "pealed absolutely, totally, and immediately. That the "reason for the repeal be assigned, because it was founded "on an erroneous principle. At the same time let the "sovereign authority of this country over the Colonies "be asserted in as strong terms as can be devised, and "made to extend to every kind of legislation whatsoever. "That we may bind their trade, confine their manufac- "tures, and exercise every power whatsoever, except only "that of taking their money from their pockets without "their own consent."

This debate, most important as it was, and disclosing as it did a wide divergence of opinions, led to no present division, since all parties willingly concurred in the terms of the vague, inconclusive, inoffensive Address. But the declaration of Pitt on that night appears to have decided the American questions. It fixed at once the wavering minds among the Ministers, and induced them unanimously, after a brief interval, to bring in two Bills in respectful compliance with the councils of the Great Commoner, — the one Bill absolutely to repeal the Stamp Act, — the other declaratory of the supreme power of Parliament over the Colonies.

The first step, however, was to lay upon the table (this was on the very night of the Address) large extracts from the recent correspondence with America. Next were presented petitions from the traders of London, Bristol, Liverpool, Manchester †, and other considerable towns, stating that the colonists were indebted to the merchants of this country to the amount of several millions sterling,

* "Be to her faults a little blind,
"Be to her virtues very kind."

Mr. Croker observes: "This quotation in any other mouth would "have appeared trivial, but from his was accepted as the apo- "phthegm of a sage." (Quarterly Review, No. cxxxi. p. 245.)

† This is one of the earliest instances in our history in which Manchester appears as a place of much importance. General Conway stated in the February ensuing that in consequence of the American troubles nine in ten of the artisans in that town had been discharged from employment. (Lord Orford's Memoirs, vol. ii. p. 296.)

that up to this time they had always faithfully made good their engagements, but that now they declared their inability to do so on account of the interruption of their commerce through the oppression of the Stamp Act; and therefore relief from that grievance was prayed, not for the sake of the Colonies, but even for the advantage of the parent-state. Further still, evidence to the same effect was received at the Bar from several persons well acquainted with the subject; above all, from Dr. Franklin, the most eminent by far of the Americans then in England. His examination which is still preserved, and which included some sharp cross-questioning from Grenville, is a monument of his ready shrewdness and practical ability. Most strongly did he urge the distinction between internal and external taxation; the former, he said, the colonists would always resist; the latter they had never questioned. "Now," he was asked, "is there any kind of dif-" ference between a duty on the importation of goods and " an excise on their consumption?"—"Yes," answered Franklin, "a very material one. An excise, for the " reasons I have just mentioned, the Americans think you " can have no right to lay within their country. But the " sea is yours; you maintain by your fleets the safety " of navigation in it, and keep it clear of pirates; you " may therefore have a natural and equitable right to " some toll or duty on merchandize carried through that " part of your dominions towards defraying the expense " you are at in ships to maintain the safety of that " carriage."

Most skilfully again did Franklin parry what might seem an unanswerable argument against his countrymen's claim; the fact that some of their own Charters contradicted it. "I know —," he said, when closely pressed on the case of Pennsylvania, the very province which he represented: — "I know there is a clause in the Charter " by which the King grants that he will levy no taxes " on the inhabitants unless it be with the consent of " the Assembly or by an Act of Parliament." — "How " then could the Assembly of Pennsylvania assert that " laying a tax on them by the Stamp Act was an infringe-" ment of their rights?" — "They understand it thus: " by the same Charter and otherwise they are entitled to "all the privileges and liberties of Englishmen. They "find in the Great Charters and the Petition and Decla- "ration of Rights that one of the privileges of English "subjects is that they are not to be taxed but by their "common consent. They have therefore relied upon it "from the first settlement of the province that the Par- "liament never would or could, by colour of that clause "in the Charter, assume a right of taxing them till it had "qualified itself to exercise that right by admitting re- "presentatives from the people to be taxed, who ought to "make a part of that common consent."

Dr. Franklin likewise took occasion to describe with great force and effect the resolution of the colonists to refrain, unless the Stamp Act were repealed, from any further use of British manufactures. In that case they were fully determined, he said, to make hereafter the cloth for their own clothes. He was asked whether they could possibly find wool enough in North America? But here again he was ready with an answer:—"They have "taken steps to increase the wool. They entered into "general combination to eat no more lamb, and very few "lambs were killed last year. This course persisted in "will soon make a prodigious difference in the quantity "of wool. And the establishing of great manufactories "like those in the clothing towns here is not necessary, "as it is where the business is to be carried on for the "purposes of trade. The people will all spin and work "for themselves in their own houses."

The examination of Dr. Franklin concluded with two striking replies, no doubt concerted beforehand with the Member who put the questions: "What used to be the "pride of the Americans?"—"To indulge in the fashions "and manufactures of Great Britain?"—"What is now "their pride?"—"To wear their old clothes over again "till they can wear new ones." *

Amidst so numerous petitions and such weighty warn-

* The examination of Dr. Franklin has been often printed. As it stands in the last and best edition of his Works (Mr. Sparks's) there is appended a note by Franklin himself, giving an account of the Members who put the questions, and of his concert with some of them. (Vol. iv. p. 199. ed. 1840.)

ings there were laid before both Houses the Resolutions on which the Declaratory Act was to be founded. The Ministers, no doubt, had desired to frame them in most exact conformity with the expressed opinions of Pitt. But they found the Law Advisers of the Crown, backed by the high authority of Mansfield, denounce as fantastic and untenable the distinction laid down by the Great Commoner between taxation and legislation. Nor was that distinction welcome to any one party in the House of Commons. Accordingly the Ministers thought it expedient or found it necessary to state the authority of Parliament over the Colonies without any such reservation, and as extending to all cases whatsoever. In discussing the Resolutions Pitt adhered to his opinion, though owning the difficulty and intricacy of the subject, and though anxious, as he said, for an unanimous vote. Two Members only spoke in his support; and either in patriotism or in prudence he forbore from a division. In the Upper House, however, his friend Lord Camden took precisely the same ground of argument: "My position "is this," he cried, — "I repeat it, — I will maintain it "to my last hour, — taxation and representation are in- "separable. This position is founded on the laws of "nature, nay more, it is itself an eternal law of nature. "...... There is not a blade of grass growing in the "most obscure corner of this kingdom which is not, "which was not ever, represented since the Constitution "began; there is not a blade of grass which when taxed "was not taxed by the consent of the proprietor!" * At the close Lord Camden divided the House against the question, when only four Peers (Lords Shelburne, Paulet, Cornwallis, and Torrington) were found to vote with him.

Thus then the obstacles encountered by the Declaratory

* This speech of Lord Camden, as probably corrected by himself, was published at the time in the Political Register (vol. i. p. 282.) to the great ire of Mr. Grenville, who, on account of some of its expressions, wished to proceed against the printer. (See Parl. Hist., vol. xvi. p. 178.) "Lord Camden in the Lords divine — but one voice about "him," says Mr. Pitt in a letter to his wife. (Chatham Papers, vol. ii. p. 363., where, however, the editor has supplied the erroneous date of Jan. 15. 1766.)

Bill in its progress proved to be of no formidable kind. But with the repeal of the Stamp Act the case was directly otherwise. A large party combined against that healing measure. First, the chiefs of the late administration, Mr. Grenville in one House, the Duke of Bedford and Lord Sandwich in the other, opposed it with the utmost acrimony. Next, there declared against it many independent country gentlemen, who deemed it, and not without reason, a precedent of the most dangerous kind; indeed it could only be justified by such an emergency as had occurred. Lastly, Lord Bute with his kinsmen and countrymen, as likewise many persons both in and out of office, being those who were popularly termed the King's Friends, threw their weight into the scale against it. From this and other indications it was fancied that the King's private feelings were for maintaining and enforcing at all hazards the Act. In this, however, as in many other points at that period, the public voice did His Majesty injustice. His views in fact agreed with those which Lord Mansfield had formed, — to retain the Stamp Act in name, but to let go the greater part of the impost, repealing or amending every clause that could be deemed inconvenient or oppressive. On one occasion the King clearly explained himself to this effect, speaking to Lord Strange in the presence of Lord Rockingham: "My "Lord, the question asked me by my Ministers was "whether I was for enforcing the Act by the sword, or "for the repeal? Of the two extremes I was for the "repeal, but most certainly preferred modification to "either." *

It was therefore no light occasion, after all this stir of feelings, after all this clash of interests, when Conway in the name of the Government rose in the House of Commons and moved for leave to bring in a Bill to repeal the Stamp Act. It was understood that even this preliminary step would be opposed. The House was full of Members, while merchants from all the great ports thronged the gallery, the lobby, and the stairs. Conway performed his part with judgment and good feeling. He

* Lord Orford's Memoirs, vol. ii. p. 289. Lord Strange was then Chancellor of the Duchy of Lancaster.

lamented and condemned the popular outrages that had occurred in some parts of America. He declared that the Ministers would insist, according to a Resolution already passed in both Houses, on the Colonies making compensation to all persons whose property had suffered by those outrages. But at the same time he pointed out the danger of attempting to maintain a hateful impost on the other side of the Atlantic. In that case, he said, the Americans would neither take any more of our goods nor pay for those they had already. We had but five thousand men in three thousand miles of territory; the Americans were a hundred and fifty thousand fighting men. If we did not repeal the Act he predicted that both France and Spain would declare war and protect the malcontents. — Thus early was the final result foreseen!

Grenville, never wanting in ability or financial skill, and on this occasion inflamed by mortification and resentment, answered Conway well and warmly. On the other side the eloquence of Pitt shone supreme, as it had on almost every point in these transactions since the commencement of the Session. Some of his bursts of oratory we may still admire in the scattered fragments which alone remain to us. Others, as it seems, must have been indebted for the applause which they received to the charms of his voice or manner. Thus, for example, one night, alluding to his small number of adherents on the Declaratory Bill, he said that he appeared in the House of Commons, as Eve in the garden of God, single and naked, yet not ashamed! *

At an hour then unusually late, at half-past one in the morning, the House divided, and Conway's motion was carried by a triumphant majority; the votes against being 167, but for it 275. As the chiefs of the contending parties issued out each of them was greeted, though in very different terms, by the anxious multitude which had lately filled their galleries. Conway was welcomed by three loud cheers, by thanks and congratulations and pressing of hands. His own countenance was brightened

* Letter from Mr. Moffatt of Rhode Island, Feb. 1766, MS. His report is confirmed by Lord Orford's Memoirs (vol. ii. p. 283.).

by the joyful thought of a public duty performed and a civil war averted. But when Burke, who stood near him, declares in the words of Scripture, which he misapplies, that "we saw his face as it had been the face of "an angel,"* — his metaphor is so far overstrained that it borders on the ludicrous, and might fairly pair off with Pitt's mother of mankind. As the Great Commoner stepped forth that night the huzzas that had greeted Conway were renewed; every head was uncovered; and many persons, in token of their respect and gratitude, followed his chair home. On the other hand hisses and revilings assailed, but did not daunt, the haughty and resolute Grenville.†

So decisive had been the majority, and the public feeling on which it was founded, that Grenville's best friends besought him to forbear from further opposition. But, as Horace Walpole remarks, it was too much for him to give up his favourite measure, the Stamp Act, and his favourite occupation, talking, both at once. Thus on the third reading another fierce debate ensued. Pitt began by referring to a letter, which had been read, from Sir William Meredith to the Mayor of Bristol, and having for a postscript: "Mr. Pitt will soon be at the head of affairs." — "How could that prophet," cried Pitt, "imagine a thing "so improbable as that I should be at the head of affairs, "when I am so extremely at the tail of them? I with "five friends in the other House and four in this!" — Next he declared the heartfelt satisfaction with which he gave his vote for this repeal. "I have my doubts," he added, "if any Minister could have been found who would "have dared to dip the Royal Ermines in the blood of "the American people. That people like a fine horse, to "use a beautiful expression of Job, whose neck is clothed

* Acts, ch. vi. ver. 13., and Burke's Works, vol. ii. p. 408. ed. 1815.

† "The crowd pressed on Grenville with scorn and hisses. He, "swelling with rage and mortification, seized the nearest man to him "by the collar. Providentially, the fellow had more humour than "spleen: — 'Well, if I may not hiss,' said he, 'at least I may "'laugh,' — and laughed in Grenville's face. The jest caught; — "had the fellow been surly and resisted, a tragedy had probably "ensued." (Lord Orford's Memoirs, vol. ii. p. 299.)

"in thunder, if you soothe and stroke it you may do any-"thing,—but beware of an unskilful rider!"

Still undaunted, Grenville replied with a firmness and spirit which—the cause apart—is deserving of high admiration: "I am one who declare that if the tax were "still to be laid on I would lay it on. The enormous ex-"pense of the German war, an expense which I always "disapproved, made it necessary. The eloquence which "the author of that profusion now points against the Con-"stitutional powers of the Parliament makes it doubly "necessary. I do not envy him the huzzas. I rejoice in "the hiss. If it were to be done again I would do it."

In this debate, as in the first of the Session, Pitt, as though he were not bound by common rules, usurped the privilege of a reply. "I am charged," he said, "with the "expense of the German war. If the Right Honourable "Gentleman had such strong objections to that war, why "did he not resign his post as Treasurer of the Navy?"—To this troublesome question what answer could be made?

The last division in the House of Commons on the repeal of the Stamp Act proved even more decisive than the first. On reaching the Lords the measure had to encounter a most formidable party array. Lord Temple it appeared had forsaken the cause of Pitt, and allied himself with his brother. Lord Lyttleton, Lord Mansfield, and Lord Halifax spoke against the measure. The entire Bedford faction, the entire Bute faction, opposed it. But by far the greater number of independent Peers, though single and scattered, feeling the danger of the crisis, and the necessity for conciliation, came to the rescue; and the Bill was carried through their House by a majority of thirty-four.

It is to be observed that through all these transactions Lord Rockingham more than once complained to the King of the King's Friends in office, who had for the most part voted against the measure of repeal. Yet it is not easy to understand how Lord Rockingham could fairly blame any man's conduct, except his own. It was himself who had sanctioned the licence,—it was himself who, for example, had suffered Lord Barrington to become Secretary-at-War, with the express understanding that he might oppose the course recommended by the Government on such questions as the Stamp Act and General Warrants.* No wonder if under such circumstances the King, both in justice and feeling, shrunk from inflicting on the offenders, as Lord Rockingham now called them, the penalty of dismissal for doing only what Lord Rockingham had allowed their chiefs to do.

It is also to be noted that during the whole progress of the Stamp Act, and both before and after it, Lord Rockingham most earnestly applied to Pitt for his accession to the Government. Through Lord Shelburne, through Mr. Nuthall, through the Duke of Grafton, through every avenue, in short, that seemed to promise a favourable hearing, were these applications renewed. It was urged that on many of the chief questions, past or present,—on the terms of the Peace, on the use of General Warrants in the case of Wilkes, on the non-enforcement of the Stamp Act,—their opinions agreed. It was remembered that they sat in different Houses, and that Pitt had more than once declared that he would never under any circumstances be prevailed upon to become First Lord of the Treasury. Why then, Lord Rockingham thought, might not Mr. Pitt join the Ministry,—as before with the office of Secretary of State, and with the rank and honours of Prime Minister, but yet leaving Lord Rockingham and Lord Rockingham's principal friends securely fixed in their places?

To all these overtures Pitt made the same reply,—that if the King thought fit to summon him, and require his poor thoughts on the formation of a Government, he would be ready to submit them, but that, unless commanded by His Majesty, he would maintain silence. Such silence was by no means acceptable to Lord Rockingham, since it left as wholly doubtful whom in such a case Pitt might or might not recommend. In the words of Mr. Nuthall's report: "his Lordship feared if arrangements were not "previously settled it might end in breaking to pieces the "present administration." † Nothing more, however, could be wrung from Pitt, except indeed a haughty an-

* See Lord Barrington's Life, p. 119., and a judicious note by Sir Denis Le Marchant to Lord Orford's Memoirs, vol. ii. p. 331.

† Chatham Papers, vol. ii. p. 397.

nouncement, that he would not suffer the continuation either of office or of influence to the veteran Duke of Newcastle. So far had his Grace's double-dealings alienated that former and illustrious colleague, with whom he had so often sat side by side in Council, or lain bed by bed in secret consultations! *

Thus, then, notwithstanding Lord Rockingham's most persevering proposals,—his cries of Help at every fresh token of his weakness,—he could make no advance towards his much desired object,—the accession of Pitt as a head to the already formed administration.

In America the repeal of the Stamp Act was received with universal joy and acclamation. Fireworks and festivals celebrated the good news, while Addresses and Thanks to the King were voted by all the Assemblies. It was evident that though a small band of demagogues might already have set their minds on separation, the great body of the people were still firm in their allegiance,—proud of their parent country, and loyal to their prince. Not that the late events could pass away and leave no trace behind. It is beyond human skill or power that at the close of any quarrel the terms between the parties should again become precisely what they were at its commencement. The words of the Declaratory Act indeed gave the Americans slight concern. They fully believed that no practical grievance could arise from it. They looked upon it as merely a salvo to the wounded pride of England, as only that "bridge of gold" which, according to the old French saying, should always be allowed to a retreating assailant.† But they had been taught the secret

* M. Dutens relates how, in November 1759, the Duke of Newcastle went on important business to Mr. Pitt, whom he found ill in bed, and unable to bear a fire in his room.—"Le Duc ne pouvant "resister plus longtemps à la rigueur de la saison; permettez, dit-il, "que je me mette à l'abri du froid dans ce lit qui est à côté de vous; "et sans quitter son manteau il s'enfonce dans le lit de Lady Hester "Pitt, et continue la conversation sur le sujet qui l'avait amené! ". . . . . Le Chevalier Charles Frederick du departement de l'ar-"tillerie arrivant là-dessus, les trouva dans cette posture ridicule." (Memoires d'un Voyageur, vol. i. p. 143.)

† This was the saying of the Mareschal Anne de Montmorency during the invasion of Provence in 1536. (Robertson's Charles V., book vi.)

of their own growing strength, and were emboldened, even though on very slight occasions, to remonstrate or resist. In Massachusetts, Rhode Island, and New York the Assemblies slowly and unwillingly complied with the injunctions of the Secretary of State to award compensation to the sufferers by the recent riots. In many places murmurs were excited by a new clause lately added to the American Mutiny Act, according to which the Colonies were bound to supply the King's troops within their territory with vinegar, salt, and other small articles. Since, however, the enactment was but temporary, and the charge but very little, and since the joyful news of the repeal had so lately come over, the Colonies in general forebore from contest, and gave what was required. In New York only the Act was disobeyed and the Government defied. There the Assembly, after some sharp altercations with the Governor, at length went so far as to reject or new-model on their own authority the clause which had been passed by the Imperial Parliament.

So violent a step was the less expected or foreseen in England, since the repeal of the Stamp Act was not the only measure by which the Ministry in the Session of 1766 endeavoured to soothe and satisfy the Colonies. The duties of 1764 which touched the trade of America, and which had been complained of in that country as inconvenient or oppressive, were altered or removed. And another Act declared certain ports of Dominica and Jamaica to be free.

In the same yielding and accommodating spirit Lord Rockingham and Mr. Dowdeswell indulged the Spitalfields weavers by an Act restraining the import of foreign silks. The joy of the weavers was signalised, as their late dissatisfaction had been, by a numerous procession to Whitehall. Thus also, to gratify a powerful family connection, the name of Lord George Sackville was restored to the Privy Council. Pitt in his private conversations warmly denounced this measure as an insult to the late King and to the late King's Ministers, adding that he would never, never, consent to sit at the same Board with his Lordship.*

* Memoirs of the Duke of Grafton, MS.

Thus also the Cyder Counties were relieved, or rather, to speak more accurately, pleased and flattered, by a repeal of the Cyder Tax which Lord Bute had three years since imposed.

Thus again the complaints occasioned by the use of General Warrants in the case of Wilkes were not unheeded by the Ministers. They proposed to the House of Commons, and carried through, a Resolution preventing such a grievance for the future, by declaring General Warrants contrary to law. Another Resolution couched in like terms, and referring to the same transaction, condemned the seizure of papers in any case of libel.—All these measures were well and kindly meant. For the most part they were salutary and judicious. Yet still if we consider how decrepit was then the state of the Government, and how naturally every feeble Government leans towards the easier course of concession, and shrinks from the more rugged duty of resistance, we shall, I think, ascribe these measures in part to its weakness, and not solely, as Burke would persuade us*, to its wisdom.

The Session of 1766 indeed was not more remarkable for important measures than for the appearance in public life of that eminent man by whom the fame of those measures and of their framers has been mainly upheld. In that Session the House of Commons heard both the last speech of the elder Pitt and the first speech of Edmund Burke. REVIRESCIT might have been the motto of that year.

Edmund Burke was born at Dublin in 1728.† The original name of the family was Bourke, and thus Edmund himself appears to have spelled it until his

* See his masterly tract, "A short Account of a late short Administration." The mock answer, signed Whittington, and inserted in the Annual Register for 1766 (part ii. p. 213.), is believed, though not certainly known, to be also written by Burke. It is marked by great bitterness against Lord Chatham.

† The date assigned by Mr. Prior and other biographers of Burke is 1730; and Burke's own epitaph in Beaconsfield Church states him to have died in July 1797, "aged 68 years." But see a note (vol. i. p. 2.) to his Correspondence published in 1844. Earl Fitzwilliam, one of the joint Editors, has since favoured me with a letter, containing further evidence to the same effect.

manhood. His father was an attorney in good practice, and Edmund was the second son. His education was completed at Trinity College, Dublin. At that period his range of reading was already extensive, but his taste for the classics warm rather than pure. Thus he maintained that Plutarch is the first of all historians, that Euripides should be preferred to Sophocles, and Virgil be preferred to Homer. Virgil indeed much employed his pen at this period in a fragment of translation of such slight merit as might be expected from a boy of seventeen, but remarkable as his chief, and nearly sole, attempt in verse.

From Dublin in due time Burke passed to London, intending to keep the terms for the English Bar as a student of the Middle Temple. His first impressions of England were highly favourable. "Every village," he writes, "as neat and compact as a beehive; the inns like "palaces. What a contrast to our poor country where "you scarce find a cottage ornamented with a chimney!"* But his health was not strong, and he found the study of the law irksome and distasteful to him; ere long he wholly relinquished it, nor was he ever called to the Bar. In 1752 or 1753 he was a candidate for the Professorship of Logic in the University of Glasgow, but without success. All this time, however, his mind was rapidly accumulating large and varied stores of information. The law he had eschewed as too dry and abstract, but not because he wanted application, not because he ever yielded to "that master-vice, sloth," as his own words declare it. On the contrary, no form of knowledge came amiss to him if tinged in any degree with the golden hues of philosophy or poetry.

Three or four years later Mr. Burke married the daughter of Dr. Nugent, a physician, living at Bath, but like himself of Irish birth and parentage. Shortly afterwards he had intended to settle in America†, whether, as some say, in hope of a small Government appointment, or, as others suppose, in quest of a wider sphere for his abilities. Happily for England the design

* Letter to Mr. Matthew Smith, 1750.

† Letter to Mr. Shackleton, Aug. 10. 1757.

was soon abandoned. His resources at this time were but small; chiefly an allowance of 200*l.* a year from his father, and occasional supplies derived from the use of his pen. It is believed, though not certainly known, that he contributed largely to the periodical writings of the day. His first avowed work appeared in 1756, and was entitled " The Vindication of Natural Society." It is a most skilful and ingenious imitation of the style and reasoning of Lord Bolingbroke, provoked by the remark then often heard in society, that the style of the " all-" accomplished St. John" was not only perfect but inimitable. Even Lord Chesterfield and Bishop Warburton, familiar as they were with all Bolingbroke's writings, were, it is said, for a short time deceived.—A few months later in the same year 1756 Burke published another work: an Essay " on the Sublime and Beautiful." In this Essay, the fruit of keen discernment and diligent study, he strikes into a new and original path of criticism; wholly leaving that beaten track of Longinus, so dear, as Swift complains, to the shallow talkers of his time.* It was through this Essay that Burke during some years was chiefly known; it was through this Essay that he became familiar with Dr. Johnson, Sir Joshua Reynolds, and many more of literary taste or skill.

Among his associates of this class and of this time was Mrs. Anne Pitt, sister of the then Prime Minister. Of this lady Burke was wont to say, that she not only possessed great and agreeable talents, but was the most perfectly eloquent person whom he had ever heard speak. She had led an eccentric wandering life, and was no friend to her illustrious brother, of whom she declared that he knew nothing accurately but Spenser's Fairy Queen.†

* " A forward critic often dupes us,
" With sham quotations περι υψους;
" And if we have not read Longinus,
" Will magisterially outshine us."

On Poetry (1733). Works, vol. xiv. p. 317.

† Life of Burke by Prior, p. 65. Horace Walpole altering a French proverbial expression, used to say of the brother and sister that they resembled each other " comme deux gouttes de *feu*."

In 1758 Burke began a service to English history and literature which even now should be gratefully remembered. In conjunction with Mr. Dodsley, a bookseller of great note, he set on foot the well known "Annual "Register." For several years the political chapters were, it is believed, wholly written by himself, and for several years longer under his immediate direction. His remuneration for this task, as received from Mr. Dodsley, was 100*l*. a year.

An avenue to political life was first opened to Burke in 1761. When Lord Halifax proceeded to Ireland as Viceroy, and Mr. William Gerard Hamilton as Chief Secretary, Burke became Private Secretary to the latter. In those days the rules of the Pension List were far indeed from being clearly defined or vigilantly guarded. It is therefore no matter of blame either to the bestower or receiver that through the influence of Mr. Hamilton, and after little more than one year's official service, Burke obtained a pension of 300*l*. a year on the Irish Establishment. But this welcome boon was not long enjoyed. Mr. Hamilton broke asunder his ties of friendship with his Private Secretary under circumstances not clearly known, but so far as we can gather fraught on his side first with tyranny and afterwards with meanness. "To "get rid of him completely," says Burke, "and not to "carry a memorial of such a person about me, I offered "to transmit my pension to his attorney in trust for him. "This offer he thought proper to accept!" *

Mortifications such as these were not unexpected by Burke's philosophic mind. As he says in his own striking style: "I was not swaddled, rocked, and dandled into a "legislator. NITOR IN ADVERSUM is the motto for a man "like me."

But in July 1765 the fortunes of Burke were retrieved. The Marquis of Rockingham on becoming First Lord of the Treasury was induced, from the recommendation of several friends, to appoint Burke his Private Secretary. Still detraction and envy were not silenced, and they found a congenial mouthpiece in the veteran Duke of New-

* Letter to Mr. Flood, May 18. 1765.

castle. His Grace, so long the leader of the Whigs, exerted himself to the utmost to prevent the accession to that party of one of the brightest names that have adorned it. He rushed to Lord Rockingham eager and panting, and most earnestly besought his Lordship to be on his guard against this low adventurer, this wild Irishman, whom his Grace certainly knew to be a Papist, a Jesuit, a Jacobite in disguise. Lord Rockingham in some alarm communicated the warning to his secretary, but Burke justified himself with proofs so cogent, and a spirit so manly, as to banish every shade of distrust from Lord Rockingham's mind. Ever thenceforward he enjoyed that nobleman's full confidence and generous friendship. By the influence of the Marquis with Lord Verney, who then reigned in Wendover, Burke was immediately brought into Parliament; at a later period the Wentworth borough of Malton welcomed him; and when in 1768 he required a sum of money towards the purchase of a country house near Beaconsfield, that sum was spontaneously, and in the form of a loan, bestowed by his liberal patron.

Burke was now a Member of the House of Commons, and not long a silent one. On the Address in January 1766, as I have elsewhere mentioned, he spoke for the first time. The praises of Pitt on that occasion were echoed by many more; and the young orator became at once a statesman of high promise and renown. Some of his more distant acquaintances expressed wonder at his sudden rise. "Sir," said Dr. Johnson, "there is no "wonder at all. We who know Mr. Burke know that he "will be one of the first men in the country."

From this time forward the biography of Burke is blended with the public history of England. There is small risk of contradiction in asserting that his speeches as they may now be perused far outshine all earlier or contemporaneous ones that our Parliamentary Debate-book can afford. For this, besides their own high and undoubted merit, there is another cause to be assigned. These speeches were reported or revised by Burke himself; they appear with their original, perhaps even with added, ornaments, whilst of the oratory of his predecessors or his rivals, of Halifax, of Bolingbroke, of Walpole, of Mansfield, of Charles Townshend, none but most imperfect and disjointed fragments now remain. It is also to be borne in mind that our present just admiration for these speeches is no unerring test of their former or contemporary value. To the end of his days Burke never attained in any degree that mastery over the House of Commons which his great genius fully warranted. One of his kinsmen, writing to Barry the painter scarcely a month after Burke had for the first time risen in the House, observes: "Your friend Edmund has not only "spoke, but he has spoke almost every day."* This is declared in triumph, but through the whole of Burke's career his speeches were deemed both too frequent and too long. Three hours from him were no uncommon effort. His tone was likewise too didactic, and "at "length," says Horace Walpole, "the House grew weary "of so many essays."† His figure was not graceful, nor his action in speaking happy, it being usually marked by a peculiar undulating motion of the head. Some remains of the Irish brogue, which to the last he never overcame, formed another obstacle in the way of his success. Notwithstanding all these drawbacks, some of his harangues delivered in stirring times or on special occasions were hailed with much enthusiasm, and followed by much effect. But more commonly it happened that when he rose to speak the Members walked out to dine; and the great orator was nicknamed the "Dinner-bell."

In pamphlets, however, and political essays, — and even speeches when revised and sent forth singly may be comprehended in that class, — the personal disadvantages of Burke could no longer apply; and as regards that class of writings it may be doubted whether he has ever in any age or in any country been excelled. The philosophy and deep thought of his reflections, — the vigour and variety of his style, — his rich flow of either panegyric or invective, — his fine touches of irony, — the glowing abundance and beauty of his metaphors, — all these might separately claim applause; how much more then when all blended into one gorgeous whole! To give examples of these merits would be to transcribe half

* Letter of Mr. Richard Burke, Feb. 11. 1766.

† Memoirs of George III., vol. ii. p. 274.

his works. Yet still if one single and short instance from his maxims be allowed me, I will observe that the generous ardour and activity of mind called forth by competition has formed a theme of philosophic comment from a very early age. It is touched both by Cicero and Quintilian; it has not been neglected either by Bacon or Montaigne. Yet still as handled by Burke this trite topic beams forth, not only with the hues of eloquence, but even with the bloom of novelty. He invites us to "an "amicable conflict with difficulty.—Difficulty is a severe "instructor set over us by the supreme ordinance of a "parental Guardian and Legislator, who knows us better "than we know ourselves, as he loves us better too. "He that wrestles with us strengthens our nerves and "sharpens our skill. Our antagonist is our helper!"

If amidst so much of eloquence and feeling as Burke's writings display we are desired to seek for faults, we shall find them not in the want but only in the exuberance and overflow of beauties. The palate becomes cloyed by so much richness, the eye dazzled by so much glare. His metaphors, fraught with fancy though they be, are often bold; they seem both too numerous and strained too far, they sometimes cease to please, and occasionally border even on the ludicrous and low. Of this defect, as of his excellences, a single instance shall suffice me. In the "Letter to a Noble Lord" in 1796 Burke compares the Duke of Bedford to a lamb already marked for slaughter by the Marats and Robespierres of France, but still, unconscious of his doom, "pleased to the last," and who "licks the hand just raised to shed his blood!" Thus far the simile is conducted with admirable force and humour. But not satisfied with his success, Burke goes further; he insists on leading us into the shambles, and makes the Revolutionary butchers inquire as to their Ducal victim, "how he cuts up? how he tallows in the "caul or on the kidneys?"

Apart from the beauty of the style, the value, as I conceive, of Burke's writings is subject to one not unimportant deduction. For most lofty and far-sighted views in politics they will never be consulted in vain. On the other hand, let no man expect to find in them just or accurate, or even consistent, delineations of contemporary character. Where eternal principles are at stake Burke was inaccessible to favour or to fear. Where only persons are concerned he was often misled by resentments or by partialities, and allowed his fancy full play.

The rich stores of Burke's memory and the rare powers of his mind were not reserved solely for his speeches or his writings; they appeared to no less advantage in his familiar conversation. Even the most trivial topics could elicit, even the most ignorant hearers could discern, his genius. "Sir," said Dr. Johnson, "if Burke were to go "into a stable to see his horse dressed, the ostler would "say, 'We have had an extraordinary man here!'"—On other occasions also the author of Rasselas extols him as never unwilling to begin conversation; never at a loss to carry it on; never in haste to leave it off.*—His attempts at wit indeed were not always successful, and he might be accused of an inordinate affection for quibbles and puns. His favourite niece, and latterly his guest, was sometimes provoked into an: "Really, uncle, "that is very poor." † But upon the whole it may be asserted that in social converse Burke was equalled by none of his contemporaries and his countrymen, except only Dr. Johnson himself and perhaps Lord Thurlow.

Born to a slender patrimony, and endowed with liberal tastes, Burke was exposed in public life to very many trials and temptations. It is difficult, says a quaint old Spanish proverb, for an empty sack to stand upright. By him, however, these trials were ever courageously borne, these temptations ever nobly surmounted. The welfare of his country and his kind was at all times, I am persuaded, his great, his ruling, his all-absorbing thought. He was no doubt a keen partisan, for his friendships were warm, and his own disposition was eager and empassioned. Like most other partisans he was sometimes hurried into deeds or words of which his calmer judgment may have disapproved. But the higher we may rate his party-spirit, the higher is his praise when on one most momentous occasion he flung his

* Boswell's Life of Johnson, under the dates of May 15. 1784, and August 15. 1773. I have given the spirit rather than the words of the latter passage.

† Life by Prior, p. 492.

party-spirit aside, deliberately preferred his country to his friends, and rather chose to rend asunder the cherished ties of many years than to encourage, to connive at, or even forbear to raise his voice against, the doctrines and examples of Revolutionary France. How venerable does the "desolate old man" appear to us in his retreat of Beaconsfield! How, as we ponder on his living pages, do we seem to share his private sorrows when bereaved of his only son, and how admire that public spirit which could rise superior to such sorrows, and impel him to bequeath the noblest of all legacies— his last words of counsel and of warning — to his country!

The excellent intentions and for the most part excellent measures of Lord Rockingham's administration were not sufficient to avert the evils arising from Lord Rockingham's personal deficiencies. For want of a great controlling centre, the whole system was deranged; several of the satellites were drawn from their orbits and wandered in the realms of space. Towards the close of May the Duke of Grafton resigned his office as Secretary of State. He declared his reasons publicly in the House of Lords. He stated that he had no objection to the persons or to the measures of the present Ministers, but that he thought they wanted strength and efficiency to carry on proper measures with success, and that he knew but one man (meaning of course Mr. Pitt) who could give them that strength and efficiency. Under this person, he added, he should be willing to serve in any capacity, not only as a General Officer but as a pioneer, and would take up a spade and mattock and dig in the trenches.* — It was with great difficulty that the other Secretary of State, General Conway, could be withheld from following the example of his colleague.

Another proof of the weakness of the Ministry appears from their behaviour to Wilkes. That adventurer had by this time spent his money at Paris, and exhausted his credit in London. But the Resolution of the House of

* On the Duke of Grafton's speech compare the Chatham and the Chesterfield Letters (vol. ii. p. 422. of the former, and vol. iv. p. 423. of the latter).

Commons against the legality of General Warrants revived his hopes. He ventured, though still under sentence of outlawry, to come secretly to England, and threatened to attack and annoy the Government unless they agreed to his terms. As was said by himself very plainly: "If the Ministers do not find employment for "me, I am disposed to find employment for them!"* Lord Rockingham properly declined to see him, but sent Burke as his negotiator. No less than five interviews ensued. The terms of Wilkes were found to be: a free pardon, a sum of money, and a pension of 1,500*l.* a year on the Irish Establishment. The Ministers refused compliance, but so much in their feeble condition were their fears excited that they raised amongst themselves by private contributions a sum of several hundred pounds, which being displayed to the best advantage by the eloquence of Burke, and being tendered to the needy patriot, induced him to retrace his steps to Paris.†

The Seals which had been flung away by the Duke of Grafton were refused by several Peers in succession, and at last were bestowed upon the Duke of Richmond for no better reason apparently than because he asked for them. No man, however, even affected to believe this or any other nomination of Lord Rockingham likely to be lasting. In short, when the Session came to a close on the 6th of June, the Ministry, though not yet fully one year old, exhibited the most unequivocal symptoms of infirmity and decrepitude, and seemed at the very last gasp.

This languishing condition was speedily brought to a crisis by a disagreement in the Cabinet on a plan for regulating the civil government of Quebec. Lord Chancellor Northington told the King that he and his colleagues could not go on as they were, and the King then decided that he would send for Mr. Pitt. Accordingly on the 7th of July His Majesty entrusted the Chancellor with a letter of invitation to that statesman, which the Chancellor inclosed in a letter of his own. With perfect

* To Humphrey Cotes, Dec. 4. 1765. Correspondence, vol. ii. p. 218.

† Prior's Life of Burke, p. 99.

fairness and frankness the King on the same day informed the other Ministers of the step which he had taken. Their feelings at the news were very various. Conway answered boldly: " Sir, I am glad of it; I al-" ways thought it the best thing your Majesty could do. " I wish it may answer; Mr. Pitt is a great man, but as " nobody is without faults he is not unexceptionable."*

Few retiring Ministers, however, are thus candid and good humoured. Lord Rockingham appears to have been much and lastingly offended. The Duke of Newcastle, above all, who knew that he should be proscribed by Pitt, could not conceal his mortification. It is a picture which from the former scenes recorded of his Grace it is sure and easy to portray. We may well conceive to ourselves how the old placeman half ran, half tottered, from house to house and from room to room,—profuse of those hugs and kisses which sooner or later all his associates in office had the gratification to receive from him†,—with tears in his eyes at the loss of office, tears such as the bereavement of a wife or child would draw from other men,—and loudly lamenting that his friend, his dearest friend, Pitt had become so far estranged from him,—from him who would have been so proud to be his colleague,—from him who had always loved him in his heart even when he had outwardly reviled him! No doubt had Pitt but deigned to woo, Newcastle would have been ready as any young bride with a vow to love and to honour,—aye, and to obey, him!

Yet at this period, as on a former one, Newcastle, with all his love of place, may be justly praised for his contempt of lucre. In 1766, as in 1762, a large pension was tendered to him by the King, but was respectfully refused.

Pitt was at Burton Pynsent when the Royal mandate reached him. Only a few days before he had written as follows to a personal friend: " France is still the object

* Lord Orford's Memoirs of George III., vol. ii. p. 338.

† " I have heard much of the Duke of Newcastle's kisses, but " never had one from him till to-day." Mr. Rigby to the Duke of Bedford, April 22. 1761.

"of my mind whenever a thought calls me back to a public "world, infatuated, bewitched; in a word, a riddle too "hard for Œdipus to solve. . . . . Farming, grazing, "haymaking, and all the Lethe of Somersetshire cannot "obliterate the memory of days of activity." * — Those days of activity were now for a brief period to return.

On receiving the King's and the Chancellor's letters Pitt wrote suitable replies to both, wishing in pompous phrase that he could "change infirmity into wings of ex-"pedition," and promising to set off, as he did, without delay to London. The journey, in those days a long and weary one †, was rapidly travelled by Pitt, and severely tasked both his exciteable body and exciteable mind. When he arrived he was suffering from fever, and after his first interview with the King at Richmond found it necessary to retire for a while to the cooler air of Hampstead. There, however, he could still continue to communicate by letters with his Royal Master, and by interviews with his intended colleagues.

The reception of Pitt by the King was most gracious. His Majesty declared that he had no terms to propose, but left Mr. Pitt at full liberty to form his administration as he pleased. At the Great Commoner's suggestion the first step taken was to summon Lord Temple from Stowe, and to offer him the headship of the Treasury. Lord Temple came accordingly, had an interview with the King on one day, and with Pitt on the next. In both of these his tone was not conciliatory. To the King he suggested "almost a total exclusion of the present men." To Pitt he did not propose the reinstatement of his brother George, but declared that for himself he expected an equal share of patronage and power with the new Prime Minister. Pitt, on the other hand, was resolved, if in office at all, to be Prime Minister not in name only but in fact. "I felt "indignation," writes Lord Temple, "at the idea of being

* To the Countess Stanhope, June 20. 1766. See Appendix.

† In Toulmin's History of Taunton it is stated that even "the "*flying* machine," as it was termed, did not finish its journey in less than four days. The editor of the Chatham Papers who quotes this passage adds with exultation: "Now in (1838) the journey is ac-"complished in fifteen hours!" (vol. ii. p. 423.) Only eight years afterwards it was accomplished in less than four hours.

" stuck into a Ministry as a great cypher at the head of " the Treasury, surrounded with other cyphers all named " by Mr. Pitt." * Thus he disdainfully rejected the offers made to him. There was no second interview between the two statesmen; only next day Lord Temple had a parting audience of the King, and immediately afterwards wended back his way to Stowe.

The refusal of Lord Temple did not, however, as on a former occasion, impede and stop short the intended administration of Pitt. The Great Commoner felt his own honour concerned in its completion. As his friend Lord Camden writes: " It does behove him now to satisfy the " world that his greatness does not hang on so slight a " twig as Temple. . . . . Let him fling off the Grenvilles, " and save the nation without them!" †—Accordingly as soon as his returning health enabled him to return to town and resume his conferences with the King the new arrangements were perfected. His fundamental principle, as he stated it at the time, was to dissolve all combinations, and thenceforward to conciliate and unite. With this view he endeavoured to draw the ablest men from all parties, but did not always prevail in his well-meant object. He found one or two sections, especially the Bedfords, hold fast together, most willing to come in, but resolved to come in wholly or not at all. Finally, the chief posts were filled from two sources,—the friends and adherents of Pitt,—and the members of the late administration. The Duke of Grafton, instead of " a spade and mattock " in the trenches," received a General's baton, being induced, though most unwillingly, to accept the headship of the Treasury. Charles Townshend, after a large dis-

* To Lady Chatham, July 27. 1766. Both from his statement and from Pitt's (Chatham Papers, vol. ii. p. 448.) it is plain that notwithstanding the unfavourable issue, the tone throughout this conversation "was kind and affectionate;" yet no sooner had Temple arrived once more at Stowe than we find him write a most violent letter to his brother George, inveighing against " all the insolence" of " that " great luminary," Mr. Pitt, and concluding: " Thus ends this political farce of my journey to town, as it was always intended." (Letter, July 18. 1766, Grenville Papers.)

† Letters to Mr. Thomas Walpole, July 1766, as printed in Lord Campbell's Lives of the Chancellors, vol. v. p. 256—259.

play of his characteristic indecision, allowed himself to be appointed Chancellor of the Exchequer. General Conway was continued Secretary of State and leader of the House of Commons; his colleague in the Seals was the Earl of Shelburne. Lord Camden became Chancellor, and Lord Northington President of the Council.* In the lower ranks places were bestowed on Lord North, on Mr. James Grenville, brother of Lord Temple, and on Colonel Barré, who during the last few years had closely attached himself to Pitt. Mr. Stuart Mackenzie was restored to his former office, but with a clear understanding that he should be allowed no influence nor control over Scottish affairs.

As each of these appointments in succession became known or surmised, the public curiosity redoubled to learn what place Pitt had fixed on for himself. Many even of his colleagues were not yet apprised of his determination to reserve for himself a peerage and the Privy Seal. At last the curtain was undrawn at Court; and the scene which immediately followed is described with much spirit in the Duke of Grafton's Memoirs: " Being appointed to " the Queen's House, I found Lord Northington and Lord " Camden already there. Mr. Pitt was in with the King. " The two Lords appeared to be in most earnest con- " versation and much agitated. On perceiving it I natu- " rally was turning from them after my bow. But they " begged to impart to me the subject of their concern, " asking me whether I had any previous knowledge of " Mr. Pitt's intention of obtaining an Earldom, and thus " placing himself in the House of Lords, whereas our " conception of the strength of the administration had " been till that moment derived from the great advantage " he would have given to it by remaining with the Com- " mons. On this there was but one voice among us, nor

* It appears from the Duke of Grafton's Memoirs that the first Cabinet consisted only of the following persons: Lord Camden, Lord Northington. Lord Chatham, Duke of Grafton, Lord Shelburne, General Conway, Lord Granby (as Commander in Chief), and Sir Charles Saunders (as First Lord of the Admiralty). A few weeks later Charles Townshend was added. " He was not at rest," says the Duke, " till he had, through me, teased Mr. Pitt to admit him " there."

"indeed throughout the kingdom. When Mr. Pitt left "the Closet we had only to receive notice of the measure "as a matter fixed, and not for deliberation. The re-"ception we gave to the communication was so evident "that it could not escape a penetrating eye."

So far back as the February preceding it had been rumoured in some circles that there was a wish at Court to prevail upon Mr. Pitt to go into the House of Lords.* Nothing of the kind, however, is manifest in the transactions of the time. The peerage appears to have been Lord Chatham's own spontaneous unconsulting act, and the King took no further part in the business than to comply with his Minister's request. The following is the letter in which his final compliance was announced: "Mr. "Pitt, I have signed this day (July 29.) the warrant for "creating you an Earl, and shall with pleasure receive "you in that capacity to-morrow, as well as entrust you "with my Privy Seal,—as I know the EARL OF CHATHAM "will zealously give his aid towards destroying all party "distinctions, and restoring that subordination to Govern-"ment which can alone preserve that inestimable blessing "Liberty from degenerating into licentiousness."

They were not merely the colleagues of Pitt who murmured at his taking a Peerage. On all hands it was either lamented as an error or condemned as a kind of crime. It seemed to be assumed that on leaving the popular branch of the legislature he had also deserted the popular cause. By his enemies William Pitt was now compared to William Pulteney,—each, they said, a man of high eloquence and high ascendency,—each in his day surnamed the Great Commoner,—each lured from the paths of duty and honour by an Earldom,—each doomed hereafter to oblivion and contempt. In the City which had been the stronghold of Pitt's popularity its decline was most apparent. There it had been designed to celebrate his return to power by a general illumination. Lamps for the purpose were already placed around the Monument. But no sooner did the Londoners read in the Gazette that their patriot Minister was now

* Letter from Mr. Gerard Hamilton to Mr. Calcraft, Feb. 20. 1766. Note to Chatham Papers, vol. ii. p. 386.

the Earl of Chatham than the festivity was countermanded and the lamps were taken down. From Blackheath Lord Chesterfield observes: "There is one very "bad sign for Lord Chatham in his new dignity, which "is, that all his enemies, without exception, rejoice at it, "and all his friends are stupified and dumb-founded."* From Dublin Mr. Burke exclaims: "There is still a little "twilight of popularity remaining around the great "Peer, but it fades away every moment."†

The effect of this peerage in Lord Chatham's own family may also, considering the event, be deemed worthy of commemoration. "My Lord Pitt,"—thus writes the tutor, Mr. Wilson,—"is much better, Lady Hester quite "well, and Mr. William very near it. The last gentle-"man is not only contented in retaining his Papa's name, "but perfectly happy in it. Three months ago he told "me in a very serious conversation: 'he was glad he "'was not the eldest son, but that he could serve his "'country in the House of Commons like his Papa.'"‡

The Chatham peerage, though warmly censured by all contemporaries, has not in our own time wanted strenuous defenders. It has been urged that no peerage was ever better earned,—that Pitt was old in years and older still in constitution,—that it was impossible for him to go through the nightly labour of conducting the business of the Government in the House of Commons,—that his wish to be transferred to a less turbulent assembly was under such circumstances natural and reasonable.§ But no ability, as it seems to me, can palliate his utter and manifest impolicy in quitting that House which alone had brought him his power, and which alone could secure him in it. His regular attendance indeed could not be, and never had been, expected in his uncertain state of health; but even his occasional appearance would have sufficed, as heretofore, to awe his enemies to silence and his colleagues to submission.

* Letter to his son, Aug. 1. 1766.

† Correspondence, vol. i. p. 106. ed. 1844.

‡ Chatham Papers, vol. iii. p. 27. William Pitt was at this time only seven years of age.

§ See especially the able argument of Mr. Macaulay to this effect, Edinburgh Review, No. clxii. p. 583.

Nor can I regard as altogether destitute of foundation the popular outcry against the new-made Peer. If indeed Pitt, like Walpole, had been finally retiring from office, the Earldom of Chatham would have been as blameless as the Earldom of Orford. It is one great aim and purpose of the Peerage to receive and welcome such eminent Commoners at the close of their career. But since the design of Pitt was not the relinquishment, but the resumption, of power, the public, I conceive, might not unreasonably feel some disappointment and mortification at his title. They had set their pride on seeing one of themselves,—a younger son of new family and most scanty fortune,—raised by his genius and their favour high above the loftiest and richest of the Somersets and Seymours. He had now for the third time become the arbiter of the State by their determined will. For, as Dr. Johnson once observed, Walpole was a Minister given by the King to the people, but Pitt was a Minister given by the people to the King.* Could they then desire him at the very moment of his rise to lay aside the name which their enthusiasm cherished, and be decked by other honours than those they had themselves bestowed?

* Boswell's Life, under the date of May 9. 1772.

CHAPTER XLVI.

BOTH foreign and domestic affairs claimed the early attention of the new Prime Minister. He had ever regarded the Family Compact between France and Spain as threatening to the liberties of Europe. He had resigned office rather than forbear to strike a blow against it. But, besides the more open and manifest dangers attending the union of these two great Powers, Lord Chatham appears to have obtained intelligence of some secret and hostile designs which they had formed against us. There is reason to believe that at this very time, or shortly after it, French officers in disguise were perambulating our southern shores, and surveying the most favourable points for a future invasion. Among Lord Chatham's papers still exists, but without any indication how it came into his hands, a collection of most curious secret Memoirs, drawn up for the information of the French Cabinet; two especially are of great length, and bear the dates of 1767 and 1768. In the latter of these Memoirs the whole range of our coast, even far inland, is accurately described from recent observations, and all our means and powers of resistance are minutely discussed.* In Spain Grimaldi was not less our enemy than Choiseul had showed himself in France. The British Ambassador at Madrid discovered traces of a plot which he believed these two Ministers conjointly to hold in reserve; a plot to surprise and burn the dockyards both at Plymouth and at Portsmouth.†

To provide in time against any treacherous assault from the united House of Bourbon, Lord Chatham had

* MS. Memoirs among the Chatham Papers in the possession of W. S. Taylor, Esq. Some considerable extracts will be found in the Appendix to this volume.

† Secret Despatches of the Earl of Rochford, Sept. 1764 and Feb. 25. 1765, as printed in Coxe's Memoirs of the Bourbon Kings.

formed the design of a Great Northern, and for the most part Protestant, alliance. It was a noble scheme, which had he remained in office after 1761 would have worthily concluded and secured the triumphs of the war. It was now resumed at a far less auspicious time, and under difficulties which had since arisen. Mr. Hans Stanley, the negotiator of 1761, was at once appointed Ambassador to the Court of St. Petersburg, with instructions to visit Berlin upon his way, and to propose both to the King of Prussia and to the Czarina a defensive confederacy with us for the maintenance of peace, to which confederacy the Crowns of Denmark and Sweden and the States General should be afterwards invited to accede. The Duke of Grafton's Memoirs bear a striking attestation to the ability with which Lord Chatham's views upon this subject were expounded to his colleagues: — "On the "night preceding Lord Chatham's first journey to Bath "Mr. Charles Townshend was for the first time sum-"moned to the Cabinet. The business was on a general "view and statement of the actual situation and interests "of the various Powers in Europe. Lord Chatham took "the lead in this consideration in so masterly a manner "as to raise the admiration and desire of us all to co-"operate with him in forwarding these views. Mr. "Townshend was particularly astonished, and owned to "me as I was carrying him home in my carriage that "Lord Chatham had just shown to us what inferior "animals we were, and that much as he had seen of him "before, he did not conceive till that night his superiority "to be so very transcendent."

The departure of Mr. Stanley was, however, postponed until the ground at Berlin could be first felt by Sir Andrew Mitchell, the British Minister at that Court, and a personal friend of Lord Chatham. Sir Andrew's report was far from favourable. He found King Frederick mindful of the ill treatment he had received from Lord Bute at the time of the Peace of Paris, and descanting on the little reliance he could place on the strength of any government or the stability of any measures in England.* Nor was His Majesty moved even by the general

* Despatch to Mr. Secretary Conway, dated Sept. 1766, and printed

belief which prevailed that the House of Austria was engaged in a concert of measures with the House of Bourbon, and becoming, though not formally, yet virtually, a member of the Family Compact. In vain did Sir Andrew press the King in repeated audiences; in vain did Lord Chatham attempt by letter to alarm him for Silesia; the King resolutely kept aloof from the desired alliance. Thus during several months of preliminary negotiations Mr. Stanley's mission was still delayed, and these preliminary negotiations failing, it was at length wholly laid aside.

The return of Pitt to office was, however, in itself a tower of strength to England. "His dismissal,"—thus wrote an accomplished Frenchman in 1761,—"is a "greater gain to us than would have been the winning "of two battles."* In 1766 Horace Walpole, who had lately been at Paris, observes: "Their panic at Mr. Pitt's "name is not to be described. Whenever they were "impertinent I used to drop as by chance that he would "be Minister in a few days, and it never failed to occa- "sion a deep silence."† Thus in some parts of the Continent his name was pronounced with keen dislike, as in others with warm affection, but in all with respect and awe. His name, now transmuted to Chatham, lost some of its potent spell. Yet still it was felt at foreign Courts that so long as he really ruled England, England would endure no wrong; that all injurious acts must be forborne, all aggressive designs be postponed.

With respect to Ireland the views of Lord Chatham at this period are clearly set forth in a letter of the following year from his confidential friend Lord Camden. "The time must come (I wish it was come) when a dif- "ferent plan of Government must take place in Ireland.

in a note to the Chatham Papers. At this interview Frederick expressed himself satisfied with his own situation, and quoted the Italian proverb: *Chi sta bene non si muove!* To this Mitchell answered aptly: *Chi sta solo non sta bene!*

* "Il faut que vous sachiez que Monsieur Pitt est disgracié. Cela "vaut mieux pour nous que deux batailles gagnées." Diderot à Madlle Voland le 19 Octobre 1761. Corresp. Ined., vol. ii. p. 80. ed. 1830.

† To Sir H. Mann, July 23. 1766.

"Lord Chatham intended now to begin it; and to enable "himself to contend with the powerful connections there, "proposed to establish himself upon the basis of a just "popularity by granting the four favourite Bills."* Foremost among these was the measure which the Irish appeared to have much at heart for shortening the duration of Parliaments to the Septennial period. Deep cause is there for regret, deep cause even to the present day, that the power of Lord Chatham did not endure to give effect to his wise and healing policy.

In England almost the first public measure that engaged Lord Chatham's attention turned on the apprehended scarcity of corn. The weather had been most unfavourable for the harvest. On the 1st of August Lord Chesterfield writes: "There never was so wet a "summer as this has been in the memory of man; we "have not had one single day since March without some "rain, but most days a great deal."—It was found that the crops had to a large extent failed, and the prices risen not only in England but in Europe; and it was feared that our own supplies, scanty as they were, might soon be sent abroad. Great disturbances ensued in several counties, especially the western ones, where the mob rose and seized the corn by force, or burned down the barns of those who hoarded it. Under these circumstances Lord Chatham acted with characteristic energy. On the 10th of September came forth a Proclamation against "forestallers and regraters." On the 24th, the tumults having meanwhile increased, was issued,—wholly without precedent in time of peace,—the celebrated Order in Council laying an embargo upon corn, and thus keeping in port several ships laden with grain or flour, and preparing to sail. Nor did Lord Chatham deem it needful instantly to call Parliament together to sanction this last bold stretch of the prerogative; he decided that the Houses should not meet until the day for which they already stood prorogued, namely, the 11th of November.

Meanwhile, as for or against the new Prime Minister,

* Letter to the Duke of Grafton (Sept. 29. 1767) in the Grafton Memoirs. See also a note to Lord Orford's, vol. iii. p. 111.

an active paper war was waging. The partisans of Earl Temple, his "loving brother," were foremost in the field. On their side came forth a most acrimonious pamphlet, entitled "Inquiry into the conduct of a late Right Hon- "ourable Commoner." This was commonly ascribed to Humphrey Cotes, a brother of Alderman Cotes, and a thorough-going City-friend of Wilkes. It contains accounts of the private interview between Pitt and Temple, such as could only be derived from the private letters or the private conversation of the latter. Thus it says with truth that Lord Temple had complained of Mr. Pitt having chosen for himself "a side-place with little re- "sponsibility," while at the same time he "dictatorially "nominated" to all the other offices. Thus it says also with truth that Lord Temple had proposed first Lord Lyttleton and then Lord Gower for posts in the Cabinet. But, on the other hand, it alleges with absolute falsehood that Mr. Pitt had declared his readiness to grant several large pensions at the outset, while Lord Temple in a more patriotic spirit had exclaimed that he would not stain the bud of his administration with such burthens.*

To this pamphlet, in which truth and falsehood were thus ingeniously mingled, an answer soon appeared. It was called, "Short View of the Political Life of a late "Right Honourable Commoner." This was equally acrimonious and far more able. In some few passages there may even perhaps be traced Lord Chatham's master-hand. Thus it contains a wish that "private conversa- "tions had not thus been shamefully tortured into a thou- "sand time-serving forms." Thus also it disdainfully sums up the character of Earl Temple as follows: "Till "his resignation with Mr. Pitt he was looked upon "merely as an inoffensive good-natured nobleman, who "had a very fine seat, and was always ready to indulge "anybody with a walk in his garden or a look at his "furniture. How he has suddenly commenced such a "statesman as to be put in competition with Mr. Pitt is

* The falsehood of this story, though not suspected by the Quarterly Reviewer (No. cxxxi. p. 249.), is most frankly stated by Lord Temple himself in writing to Humphrey Cotes. (Letter, August 24, 1766, Grenville Papers.)

"what I am at a loss to determine. But this I will take "upon me to say that had he not fastened himself into "Mr. Pitt's train, and acquired thereby such an interest "in that great man, he might have crept out of life with "as little notice as he crept in, and gone off with no "other degree of credit than that of adding a single unit "to the bills of mortality." — A highly competent critic, Lord Chesterfield, observes of this last sentence, that it expresses such extreme contempt of Lord Temple, and in so pretty a manner, that he suspects it to be Mr. Pitt's own.* So rapid was the interchange of compliments that not only this attack and this answer, but a whole host of other pamphlets and half-sheets, had come forth before the middle of August.

Of all the party-writers at this time, since Junius had not yet appeared, none certainly was so dangerous as Wilkes. At first he had cherished hopes of some indulgence from the new administration. He came secretly to London, and on the first of November addressed to the Duke of Grafton as head of the Treasury a letter professing loyalty and imploring pardon. "That letter," says the Duke of Grafton, "I showed to His Majesty, "who, as well as I recollect, read it with attention, but "made no observation upon it. Lord Chatham on read- "ing it remarked on the awkwardness of the business "with which it was so difficult to meddle; and on my "pressing to know what was to be done, he answered, "'the better way, I believe, at present will be to take no "'notice of it.' And his advice I followed."† — Thus the baffled demagogue found it necessary to return to Paris, where soon afterwards he vented his spleen in a most angry pamphlet, entitled "Letter to the Duke of "Grafton," and inveighing in no measured terms not only against his Grace but against Lord Chatham, whom he terms "the first orator, or rather the first comedian, "of the age."‡

* To his son, August 14. 1766.

† Grafton's Memoirs, MS. Wilkes says in his pamphlet, that he received a message, or verbal answer, from the Duke, desiring him to apply to Lord Chatham, which he declined to do.

‡ Further still he calls Lord Chatham "the abject, crouching

No sooner had the Houses met than the Order in Council laying an embargo upon corn, and the delay in calling Parliament together, were eagerly assailed. Lord Mansfield to the public surprise, and perhaps to his own, appeared for the first time in his life as the assailant of Prerogative. It was on this occasion that Lord Chatham delivered his first speech in the House of Peers, which obtained the praise of eloquence, calmness, and dignity, and of resting his vindication on valid grounds. He defended the Order in Council from the national necessity, and the adherence to the day already appointed for the Meeting of Parliament from the desire of avoiding any needless alarm. Lord Camden who followed on the same side was far less judicious. Of the stretch of the prerogative he said that it was "at worst but a forty days' "tyranny;" and this unlucky phrase not only excited clamours at the time, but was used as a taunt against him for several years to come. The Opposition, urged especially by Earl Temple in one House and by Mr. Grenville in the other, called for an Act of Indemnity to the Ministers; this the Ministers at first disdained and refused, but finally accepted and passed. In one of the stages of the Bill Lord Chatham spoke for the second time, and took occasion in his most lofty tone to say that he would set his face against even the proudest connection in the land. These words of the great Dictator (as his enemies now began to call him) gave much offence, and drew him into a short but angry altercation with the Duke of Richmond. "I hope," cried Richmond, "the nobility will "not be browbeaten by an insolent Minister." — "I "challenge the Noble Duke," retorted Chatham, "to give "an instance in which I have treated any man with "insolence; if the instance be not produced the charge "of insolence will lie on his Grace." *

This scorn for aristocratical connections and family

"deputy of the proud Scot." But this seems to have been part of Wilkes's stock in trade, — used by him almost indiscriminately against every government. In his letter to Cotes of October 27. 1765, he says of Lord Rockingham and his colleagues: "I believe "the Scot is the breath of their nostrils." (Letters, &c., vol. ii. p. 214.)

* Lord Orford's Memoirs of George III., vol. ii. p. 409.

juntas was indeed prominent in Lord Chatham's mind at this time, as it had been during the formation of his Government. He did not fully consider the position in which that Government stood. When several small sections of different parties are combined in one administration they will always for some time forward remain at gaze, suspicious and jealous of each other. With such materials and at such a time even a slight spark can kindle a flame. The appointment of an insignificant man (Mr. Shelley) to a petty post (Treasurer of the Household), and the consequent removal of Lord Edgcombe who had refused, in exchange, a Lordship of the Bedchamber, incensed all those friends of the old administration who still continued in the new. General Conway as their chief was more especially perplexed and aggrieved. At length Lord Besborough, one of that little band, offered to accept the vacant office, provided, in return, Lord Edgcombe should be appointed to his own. The offer was eagerly forwarded by Conway to Chatham. But Chatham took offence, it would seem, at the kind of stipulation which the offer contained. He returned a haughty answer that he would not suffer connections to force the King. Upon which Conway was provoked into exclaiming that such language had never been held westward of Constantinople!

There seems indeed no reason to doubt that the demeanour of Lord Chatham to his colleagues on this and on most other occasions was overbearing and despotic. Conscious of his own upright motives and pre-eminent abilities he despised too much the common herd, or rather let them see too much that he despised them. In the present case Conway was with much difficulty appeased by his friend Horace Walpole, who during the last few years had been a most active meddler and go-between in party-politics. But the other placemen of that connection — Lords Besborough, Scarborough, and Monson, the Duke of Portland, and some others of less note — resigned their employments the next day. To supply the void thus created Lord Chatham reckoned on the Bedfords. That very evening he sent for Lord Gower, and offered places for himself and for others of his friends. Lord Gower hurried down to Woburn to consult the

Duke, and the Duke came up to confer with Lord Chatham in town; but his Grace, it was then found, insisted on a larger share of offices for his followers than the Prime Minister could or would afford. Thus that negotiation ended, and the vacant places were filled by the Duke of Ancaster, Lord Hillsborough, Mr. Nugent, now created Lord Clare, and other recruits from various sides.

In all these questions of office Lord Chatham's feeling as to party sections and connections has been already explained and may be well understood. But on other points also he showed himself untoward. Thus it was believed that Burke about this time was not unwilling to accept a place; and we find the Duke of Grafton recommend him to the Prime Minister strongly and justly as "the readiest man upon all points perhaps in the whole "House," and as "one on whom the thoroughest de-"pendence may be placed where once an obligation is "owned." But the reply of Lord Chatham, then still at Bath, was forbidding and cold.* There seems to me great reason to suspect that the terms, or at least the tenor, of that reply, may through some indiscretion have reached the ears of the young statesman, since otherwise it is not so easy to account for that constant and resentful feeling of dislike which even the studied compliments, but far more the private letters, of Burke reveal against Lord Chatham.

It is also in this affair remarkable how strongly Lord Chatham held the doctrine of a legislative preference to our own colonial industry. For on this he rests his main objection to the proposed recruit. "His (Mr. Burke's) "maxims and notions of trade can never be mine. Nothing "can be more unsound or repugnant to every first prin-"ciple of manufacture and commerce than the rendering "so noble a branch as the cottons dependent for all the "first materials upon the produce of French and Danish "islands instead of British."

Another affair on which at this time the mind of Chatham most eagerly turned was the state of the East India Company. Its territorial conquests had been gigantic,

* The Duke's letter of Oct. 17. 1766, is printed in the Chatham Collection. The reply, dated the 19th, will be found in my Appendix.

and were now ratified by treaty with the native Powers. Such conquests had not been in the slightest degree foreseen or expected either by the Parliaments which granted the Charter or by the merchants who held it. The proprietors of Stock thus suddenly transformed to Sovereigns had not hitherto shown any aptness for the new and extraordinary duties which devolved upon them. They had risen far above a trading Company in their fortunes, but not as yet in their conduct and opinions. Every mail from India brought dismal accounts of the rapine and insubordination of their servants, and of the sufferings of the Hindoos beneath their rule. At home their proceedings for the most part evinced a grovelling concern for their own selfish interests. Thus at a General Court held in September 1766 it was carried even against the wish of the Directors that the Dividends which had for some time past been at Six per cent. should be raised to Ten; and at the next General Court it was urged that no overtures from the Government should be accepted, unless with a further rise to Fifteen; that increase to be positively guaranteed for the ten ensuing years! *

Up to this time Parliament had given little attention to the state or the prospects of the East India question. Many politicians who called themselves statesmen deemed it a slight affair, and when they were in power they made or left it so. But far different were the views of Chatham. "I think it" (thus he writes to the Duke of Grafton) "the greatest of all objects, according to my sense "of great." So early as the 28th of August the Duke by his directions intimated to the Chairman and Deputy Chairman that they would do well to be prepared, for that the affairs of the Company would probably be brought before Parliament in the ensuing Session. At this time accordingly we may observe how the mind of Chatham brooded over a vast and daring scheme. Its precise details are nowhere to be found recorded, since

* Thornton's History of British India, vol. ii. p. 2. In February 1769 Lord Clive declared in the House of Commons: "The East "India Company have now twenty millions of subjects. They are "in the actual receipt of between five and six millions a year, out of "which revenue the Company, clear of all expenses, receive "£1,600,000 a year." (Cavendish Debates, vol. i. p. 261.)

to no one at its outset did Chatham fully entrust it, and since its further progress was arrested by that mysterious malady which closed his period of power. But we may trace its general import from some slight intimations at the time, and especially from Chatham's own words in his private letters to the Duke of Grafton. — Ought conquests which were never contemplated by the Charter to be deemed an essential part of that Charter? Could it be maintained that a document designed only to secure a few factories up the rivers and along the coasts had now, without check or control, bestowed the sovereignty of three vast provinces — Bengal, Orissa, and Bahar, — provinces larger in extent than the country from which the document came? Might not then these noble provinces be justly claimed as dominions of the British Crown, and governed as a part of such dominions? Were the merchants of the Company entitled as of right to more than a certain continuation of their commercial privileges, and a moderate return for their invested capital? On this basis, and without any real violation of plighted faith, might not a system be reared of lasting benefit to Hindostan, and of hitherto unparalleled prosperity to England, — a system which no longer enriching a band of greedy factors, but affording to the State a yearly stream of territorial wealth, would stand in the stead of all new taxes or imposts at home or in the Colonies, and gradually provide for the extinction of that National Debt laid on us by the pressure of recent wars?

Seven years afterwards when Lord Chatham, as retired from office, took a retrospect of the entire subject, we find him state his general view as follows to Lord Shelburne: "I always conceived that there is in substantial justice a "mixed right to the territorial revenues between the State "and the Company as joint captors; the State equitably "entitled to the larger share as largest contributor in the "acquisition by fleet and men. Nor can the Company's "share when ascertained be considered as private pro-"perty, but in trust for the public purposes of defence of "India and the extension of trade; never in any case to "be portioned out in dividends to the extinction of the "spirit of trade." *

* Letter, May 24. 1773. Correspondence, vol. iv. p. 264.

In the contest which Lord Chatham was thus preparing to commence between what he terms "the friends of the "Public" on the one side and "the advocates for the "Alley" on the other we should certainly not blame him if he failed to foresee (as who at that time could?) the great improvement which has since been wrought in the Company itself, and the large measure in which that Company has now become an instrument and agent in fulfilling some at least of the noble aspirations which the mind of Lord Chatham had conceived.

To carry out this bold and courageous scheme the first step needed was to institute an inquiry by the House of Commons. It seemed also most desirable that the inquiry should be proposed and conducted by some independent gentleman rather than by any member of the Government; the Government to step in afterwards as arbiter and umpire of the question. For this purpose Lord Chatham chose Alderman Beckford, his personal friend. Beckford was a man of neglected education, noted in the House of Commons for his loud tones and his faulty Latin*, but upright and fearless, and ever prompt and ready; of much commercial weight and especial popularity in the City of London which he represented in Parliament. On the 25th of November accordingly Beckford brought forward a motion for inquiry into the affairs of the East India Company on a future day and in a Committee of the whole House. It was the very time when Lord Chatham had become in a great measure estranged from Conway and Charles Townshend on account of the Edgecombe episode. This circumstance has afforded some colour for a strange misrepresentation which was afterwards made. It was alleged that Chatham having framed a measure touching the East India Company concealed it from his own administration, and entrusted a personal friend who held no office in that administration to take charge of it in the House of Commons.† But it is clear that Chatham did

* On one occasion, for example, (this was in 1770,) Beckford quoted: *Non omnium meum mecum porto!* (Cavendish Debates, vol. i. p. 489.) He must have been thinking of the *Omnium* in the City.

† See the statement of Lord Orford (Memoirs, vol. ii. p. 393.), in which he is followed too implicitly by the Edinburgh Reviewer (No. clxii. p. 586.).

precisely what the most judicious party-chiefs have often done; he selected an adherent out of place to call for papers and to search for facts, and he reserved himself and his colleagues to act upon the state of things which should be proved and ascertained.

The motion of Beckford on the 25th was warmly opposed by Charles Yorke and George Grenville, who defended the East India Company, and invoked the faith of Charters. Nevertheless on a division a large majority declared in favour of the proposed inquiry. Some days afterwards when the subject was resumed another fine speech against it was heard from Burke; in this he referred to Lord Chatham with no slight asperity, painting him as a great Invisible Power that had left no Minister in the House of Commons. "But perhaps," he cried, "this House is not the place where our reasons can be of "any avail. The great person who is to determine on "this question may be a being far above our view; one "so immeasurably high that the greatest abilities" (here he indicated Townshend) "or the most amiable dis-"positions" (here he pointed to Conway) "may not gain "access to him; a being before whom thrones, domina-"tions, princedoms, virtues, powers," (here he waved his hands over the whole Treasury Bench behind which he sat,) "all veil their faces with their wings!" *

Through the keen instinct usually found in Opposition on such subjects Burke had here divined the truth. Ever since the incident of Lord Edgcombe the Prime Minister had wholly withdrawn his confidence both from Conway and Charles Townshend. On their part they were in secret averse to his East India measures, and reluctant to render the inquiry as full and searching as was needed. It was only by vehement threats in letters to the Duke of Grafton that Lord Chatham had succeeded in spurring them forward.†

Thus, when after one active month of Session the Parliament adjourned for the Christmas holidays, the Govern-

* See a note to the Chatham Papers, vol. iii. p. 145. Lord Orford adds, that this was "one of his finest speeches." (Memoirs, vol. ii. p. 407.)

† See in the Appendix the letter of December 7. 1766.

ment had sustained keen attacks both on the Inquiry and on the Embargo, and had suffered loss by the resignations of several of its members. Nevertheless so great was still the ascendency remaining to the name of Chatham (let me rather say of Pitt) that his power was not as yet shaken or impaired. The Opposition was disunited and dispirited. The General Court of the East India Company far from daring another Parliamentary conflict with the administration came to an unanimous vote recommending the Directors to treat for terms. "We have had a busy "month," writes Horace Walpole, "and many grumbles "of a State-quake; but the Session has, however, ended "very triumphantly for the Great Earl." *

The "Great Earl," trusting in these holidays to recruit his health, proceeded once more to Bath. When Parliament met again in the middle of January his return was eagerly expected by his colleagues. But instead of himself the sad news came that he had been seized with gout and was shut up in his chamber. Week after week passed away and still the Prime Minister was absent. At length, only half recovered, he set out, but relapsed upon the road, and lay in bed for another fortnight in the Castle Inn at Marlborough.† Evils speedily grew forth from the absence of the master-mind. The Cabinet became divided, and the Parliament unruly. A jealousy, never after extinguished, was kindled between Grafton and Shelburne. Charles Townshend began to assume the airs of a great Minister in the House of Commons, and almost openly thwarted Beckford as to the East Indian Inquiry. Even the highest colleagues and most trusty friends of Chatham

* H. Walpole to G. Montagu, December 12. 1766.

† According to the Edinburgh Reviewer, "footmen and grooms "dressed in his family livery filled the whole inn, though one of the "largest in England. The truth was, that the invalid had insisted "that during his stay all the waiters and stable-boys of the Castle "should wear his livery." (No. clxii. p. 586.) I was assured by my excellent and lamented friend Mr. Thomas Grenville, almost a contemporary of that period, that this story had no foundation in fact. It used to be told by the late Lord Holland, and most clearly, as I think, arose from his imperfect recollection of a passage resembling it, but really quite different, (since referring only to Lord Chatham's own servants brought from Bath,) in Lord Orford's (then MS.) Memoirs. See, in these, vol. ii. p. 416. and 417.

complained that they were not thoroughly apprised of his views and intentions. The Duke of Grafton asked his leave to travel down to his bedside at Marlborough for one hour of conversation,—for one gleam of light. But he was answered in stately phrases that the same illness which hindered Lord Chatham from proceeding on his journey must likewise disable him from entering into any discussions of business.

The reins of power thus relaxing, all the parties out of office gathered courage and combined for a common blow. Charles Townshend as Chancellor of the Exchequer had to propose the annual vote for the Land Tax, amounting since the war to four shillings in the pound, but he pledged himself that if he continued in office another year he would reduce it to three. This pledge might have sufficed for economy, but could not for party-spirit. Dowdeswell, supported by Grenville, moved that the reduction to three shillings should take effect at once; and much to their own surprise they prevailed in the division, the numbers being 206 and 188. Thus no less a sum than half a million was struck off from the Ways and Means of the current year. It was the first defeat on any financial question of importance which had been sustained by any Government since the fall of Sir Robert Walpole. No wonder if the Opposition greatly plumed themselves upon it. Yet their triumph was perhaps more specious than real, for there was no settled majority against Lord Chatham, and "it is plain," writes Lord Chesterfield, "that "all the landed gentlemen bribed themselves with this "shilling in the pound." *

This untoward event occurred on the 27th of February. Three days afterwards Lord Chatham arrived from Marlborough still afflicted with gout, and scarce able to move hand or foot. His wrath was now fully kindled against Charles Townshend for the part which that gentleman had taken in respect to the East India Inquiry. In a few vehement lines to the Duke of Grafton we find him declare that "the writer hereof and the Chancellor of "the Exchequer aforesaid cannot remain in office to-

* To his son, March 3. 1767.

"gether."* He applied for and obtained the King's permission that the Exchequer Seals might be offered to Lord North, but Lord North, from an undue diffidence of his own merit, declined them.†

It is probable that a few days more would have seen the acceptance of some new overture and the naming of another Chancellor of the Exchequer. But at this very period Lord Chatham began to be afflicted by a strange and mysterious malady. His nerves failed him; he became wholly unequal to the transaction of any public affairs, and secluding himself in his own house he would admit no visitors and open no papers on business. In vain did the King address him in repeated messages and letters. In vain did his most trusted colleagues sue to him for one hour's conversation. As the spring advanced he retired to a house at Hampstead, and was able at intervals to take the air upon the heath, but was still at all times inaccessible to all his friends. His illness was of course no secret to his enemies, who conjectured that he must speedily quit either his post or the world; to them it little mattered which.

The utter secession of Lord Chatham from his own government broke the mainspring by which that government had moved. Even during his earlier periods of office his ascendency had been very far greater than most Prime Ministers possess. The old Duke of Newcastle was wont to describe with comic terrors "the dread the "whole Council used to be in lest Mr. Pitt should "frown!"‡ But at his last accession to power his ascendency was not only great but paramount; it was truly, as I just now termed it, the mainspring of the machine which alone could bring into harmonious action so many jarring parts. Even his retirement from the

* Letter, March 4. 1767. See Appendix.

† The Duke of Grafton adds in his MS. Memoirs, that "Mr. Town-"shend remained in his office quite uninformed of Lord Chatham's "intentions in regard to himself." But the Duke is here mistaken, as plainly appears from a passage in the Chatham Papers, vol. iii. p. 235.

‡ Mr. Rigby to the Duke of Bedford, Oct. 13. 1761. Bedford Correspondence, vol. iii. p. 56.

one House of Parliament to the other had been felt as a great blow to his colleagues, but how much greater still his retirement from all business and control! Then immediately the patchwork of administration loosened and rocked. Then indeed did that administration become what the caustic pen of Burke has afterwards so well described: "He (Lord Chatham) made an administration "so chequered and speckled; he put together a piece of "joinery so crossly indented and whimsically dovetailed; "a Cabinet so variously inlaid; such a piece of diversi-"fied mosaic; such a tesselated pavement without ce-"ment, here a bit of black stone and there a bit of white; "patriots and courtiers; King's Friends and Repub-"licans; Whigs and Tories; treacherous friends and "open enemies, that it was indeed a very curious show, "but utterly unsafe to touch and unsure to stand on."*

Foremost among the Ministers Charles Townshend now broke loose from all restraint. He delivered in the House of Commons several speeches justly admired for their eloquence, and no less justly censured for their levity and wildness. One especially was called his "Champagne speech," because he had returned to make it from a convivial dinner-table. Horace Walpole who was present vividly describes it as "a torrent of wit, "parts, humour, knowledge, absurdity, vanity, and fic-"tion, heightened by all the graces of comedy, the hap-"piness of allusion and quotation, and the buffoonery of "farce. To the purpose of the question (the East Indian "Inquiry) he said not a syllable. It was a descant on "the times, a picture of parties, of their leaders, of their "hopes and defects. It was an encomium and a satire "on himself; and he excited such murmurs of wonder, "admiration, applause, laughter, pity, and scorn, that "nothing was so true as the sentence with which he "concluded when speaking of government; he said it "was become what he himself had often been called A "WEATHER-COCK!—For some days men could talk or "inquire of nothing else. 'Did you hear Charles Towns-"'hend's Champagne speech?' was the universal ques-

* Speech on American Taxation, 1774.

"tion. For myself I protest it was the most singular "pleasure of the kind I ever enjoyed." *

It plainly appears that ever since Lord Chatham had left the House of Commons there was no man in that assembly who could either control or vie with Townshend. "He is the orator, the rest are speakers," remarks another of his hearers.†

As Chancellor of the Exchequer Townshend had been more than once taunted in the House of Commons with the necessity of providing in some manner for the loss occasioned by the reduction of the Land Tax. In one of his rash and heedless moods he threw out a pledge in reply, that he would find means free from offence to raise some revenue from America. That pledge he had given without the assent or knowledge of his colleagues, and in the teeth of their declared opinions. He now attempted to fulfil it, at least in name, by proposing certain small taxes on glass, paper, painters' colours, and tea, to be paid as import duties, and to bring in according to his own computation only from 35,000*l.* to 40,000*l.* a year. On this proposal Lord Chatham, as we have seen, could not even be consulted. Had he retained any degree of health it is clear that he would both have rejected the proposal and turned out the proposer. To the last Lord Camden protested against the scheme, though not pressing his resignation on that account. But the other Ministers and the Cabinet in general yielded a sullen and reluctant acquiescence, seeing no other alternative for them except the dismissal of Townshend, which in Lord Chatham's absence they durst not attempt.‡ The

* Lord Orford's Memoirs of George III., vol. iii. p. 24., and note at p. 26. Sir George Colebrooke states in his MS. Memoirs, that he and another gentleman were the only persons who dined with Townshend that day, "and we had but one bottle of Cham- "pagne after dinner;" so that the speech was not, as supposed, a drunken one. Nor was it extemporaneous; "it was a speech he had "meditated a great while upon, and only by accident did it find "utterance that day."

† Mr. H. Flood to Lord Charlemont, Nov. 1766.

‡ See in the Appendix to this volume an extract from the Duke of Grafton's MS. Memoirs (May 1767). See also the Cavendish Debates (vol. i. p. 213.), and the solemn declaration of Lord Camden

Acts for the purpose passed both Houses without opposition and almost without remark, since it was believed from Dr. Franklin's evidence of the preceding year that the Americans themselves acknowledged the laying on of Import Duties as an undoubted right of the British Parliament. Yet it might have been foreseen that, as really happened, the Americans would be emboldened by their recent victory to rise in their pretensions; that the new Import Duties would grow nearly as distasteful as the Stamp Act; and that the nice distinctions of Dr. Franklin as soon as they inconveniently pressed would be disavowed by his countrymen and renounced by himself.

Two other transactions of the same period, and also relating to America, are likewise deserving of attention. The Assembly of Massachusetts had reluctantly complied with the requisition of the Secretary of State, Lord Shelburne, to award compensation to the sufferers in the recent riots, but had inserted a clause in their Bill granting a free pardon to the rioters. This clause was deemed an encroachment on the Constitutional rights of the Crown, and their Bill was accordingly annulled by an Order of the King in Council. In New York, as I have already related, the Assembly had presumed of their own authority to set aside the American Mutiny Act as fixed by Parliament. There were not wanting Members of Parliament to propose rigorous measures of coercion in return, but at length there was carried through a law which Lord Chatham's Ministry had framed, and which prohibited the Legislature of New York from passing any other Act for any purpose whatsoever till the terms of the American Mutiny Act should be complied with. This law, for the moderation of which the Duke of Grafton many years afterwards takes credit in his Memoirs, was thoroughly successful; it induced the Assembly of New York to desist from their pretensions, and concede the points required.

Nor did the Session close without the passing of a measure relative to the East India Company. But that measure was no longer such as the genius of Chat-

nine years afterwards in the House of Lords. (March 5. 1776. Parl. Hist. vol. xviii. p. 1222.)

ham had shadowed forth,—such as that genius only could complete and mature. No sooner was it deprived of his vigorous aid than it became shorn of its fair proportions, and from a statesmanlike conception dwindled down to a petty compromise. The Directors were maintained for the next two years in their territorial possessions, they undertaking, in return, to pay 400,000*l.* each year towards the public service. By two other Acts it was sought to limit the exorbitant dividends of the Company, and to curtail the evil practice of creating fictitious votes at the India House.

All this time the Opposition were not idle. They showed in several debates how far the secession of Lord Chatham had both inspired them with courage and endowed them with strength. In one debate in the House of Lords upon the Massachusetts Bill they reduced the Government to a majority of only two—65 against 63. Under such circumstances the Duke of Grafton harassed and perplexed earnestly implored by letter a few minutes' conversation with Lord Chatham. He was again refused on the plea of continued illness; and then not knowing where else to turn, he conjointly with Lord Northington laid his difficulties fully and fairly before the King.

The King had from the first dealt with the Prime Minister most frankly and most kindly. The Royal letters to him as since published display throughout the greatest esteem and respect for his high qualities,—the greatest anxiety to aid him in all his views and arrangements,—the greatest consideration and forbearance to him in his infirmities. No master more gracious and confiding could ever be desired by a subject. On this occasion, unwilling as His Majesty felt to break in upon Lord Chatham's illness, he wrote to him at some length, pointing out the imminence of the crisis, since the First Lord of the Treasury, the Lord President, and the Lord Chancellor had declared themselves on the point of resignation. A few words of counsel or direction might yet retain them. "If," added His Majesty, "you cannot "come to me to-morrow, I am ready to call on you." Then, and not till then, did the sick man agree to what he deemed the lesser evil or fatigue—a visit from the Duke of Grafton. He promised to receive his Grace on the morrow — Sunday the 31st of May, — and on the morrow accordingly his Grace appeared.

An account of this interview so hardly obtained is given by the Duke of Grafton in his Memoirs. He states: "Though I expected to find Lord Chatham very "ill indeed, his situation was different from what I had "imagined. His nerves and spirits were affected to a "dreadful degree, and the sight of his great mind bowed "down and thus weakened by disorder would have filled "me with grief and concern even if I had not long borne "a sincere attachment to his person and character. ". . . . . The interview was truly painful." — In the conversation of full two hours which took place Grafton explicitly declared all the difficulties of the Government. In reply Chatham entreated him to remain in his present station, taking any method his Grace might think best to strengthen the Ministry by new accessions and allies; "and," the Duke adds, "he assured me that if Lords "Northington and Camden as well as myself did not "retain our high offices there would be an end to all his "hopes of being ever serviceable again as a public man."

As had been foreseen the Duke of Grafton was in some measure cheered and animated by the aspect of his chief. He refrained from his intended resignation, and found himself able to bring the Session to a close as Minister on the 2d of July. Still, however, his difficulties had thickened so fast around him that in the course of June he again appealed to the King, and the King again appealed to Lord Chatham. The Great Earl was most earnestly requested to make some effort to strengthen and support his own Ministry. "Such ends to be ob- "tained," writes the King, "would almost awaken the "great men of former ages, and therefore should oblige "you to cast aside any remains of your late indispo- "sition." — But to all such appeals His Majesty could only obtain such answers as the following in Lady Chatham's hand: "Under health so broken as renders at present "application of mind totally impossible, may I prostrate "myself at your Majesty's feet, and most humbly implore "your Majesty's indulgence and compassion not to re- "quire of a most devoted unfortunate servant what in "his state of weakness he has not the power to trace "with the least propriety for your Majesty's considera-"tion." *

Thus left to his own resources, but by no means relying on them, the Duke of Grafton had no sooner closed the Session than he commenced overtures to several of the parties opposed to him, especially the Bedfords and the Rockinghams. It was found, however, that none of these parties would agree on terms either with the Government or with one another, and thus, after various interviews and letters, the negotiations ended in failure. The administration continued as Lord Chatham had formed it, but henceforth was called and was in fact not Lord Chatham's but the Duke of Grafton's, since the Duke had ceased perforce to be a deputy, and became obliged to fulfil all the duties of Prime Minister. It is surely no slight proof what great things Lord Chatham might have achieved in office had health and strength been spared him, since even the remnant of his system when deprived of his aid and presence was yet able, though tottering, to stand and to proceed.

It is probable, however, that ere long the main power of the State would have centered in Charles Townshend. Of late he had found no rival in the House of Commons, and would bear no superior in the Cabinet. He had retired to his country house in Oxfordshire, and, as is believed, was busily employed in planning a new scheme of government, in which he was to be the Prime Minister and his friend Charles Yorke the Chancellor. But a fever which he at first neglected most unexpectedly put a period to his life on the 4th day of September and in the forty-third year of his age,—the very period when it might have been hoped that his brilliant genius would have cast aside the levity and fickleness by which it had hitherto been clouded.

In his stead the Duke of Grafton proposed the office of Chancellor of the Exchequer to Lord North, who, after sundry misgivings and one refusal, at last accepted it. In the winter which followed other changes ensued. Lord Northington was anxious to resign from age and growing infirmities; and General Conway had long been

* Chatham Papers, vol. iii. p. 277.

uneasy in political office, to which his temper and habits disinclined him. Brave though he was in the field, spirited and ready though he was in debate, he ever seemed in counsel irresolute and wavering; so eager to please all parties that he could satisfy none, and quickly swayed to and fro by any whisperer or go-between who called himself his friend. At the King's earnest request, however, he consented to remain, though out of office, for some time longer a Member of the Cabinet, and its spokesman in the House of Commons. Meanwhile his retirement and Northington's gave another opening to the Bedfords. The Duke himself would accept no office; he had lately lost his only son by a sudden and violent death; his own eyesight was impaired, and his own health failing; he expired indeed in only two years from this time. But he wished to see honourable provision made for his principal adherents. In the course of December the new party combination was complete. Earl Gower became Lord President; Lord Weymouth, the head of the Thynnes of Longleat, became Secretary of State; and the Earl of Sandwich obtained the promise of the Post Office; while another place rich and easy was secured for Rigby. Moreover at this time the rapid increase of business with our American settlements suggested, or at least justified, the nomination of a third Secretary of State "for the Colonies," a post which was bestowed upon the Earl of Hillsborough.

Some of these arrangements it was supposed would have been by no means pleasing to that illustrious statesman, if he could have been consulted, who still held the Privy Seal. "What will Lord Chatham say?" asked Horace Walpole of the Duke of Grafton. But it is impossible to deny the force of the Duke's answer: "If "Lord Chatham will do nothing, and leaves us to do "the best we can,—why then we must do the best we "can!"*

The great Earl indeed continued wholly incapable of business. His grievous plight is described as follows by the secretary of his brother-in-law, Mr. Grenville, who had no doubt excellent means of information: "Lord

* Lord Orford's Memoirs of George III., vol. iii. p. 128.

"Chatham's state of health is certainly the lowest dejec-"tion and debility that mind or body can be in. He "sits all the day leaning on his hands which he supports "on the table; does not permit any person to remain "in the room; knocks when he wants anything; and "having made his wants known gives a signal without "speaking to the person who answered his call to re-"tire."* Other accounts of a rather later period state that the very few who ever had access to him found him sedate and calm, and almost cheerful, until any mention was made of politics, when he started, trembled violently from head to foot, and abruptly broke off the conversation. During many months there is no trace in his correspondence of any letter from him, beyond a few lines at rare intervals and on pressing occasions which he dictated to his wife. Even his own small affairs grew a burthen too heavy for his enfeebled mind to bear. He desired Mr. Nuthall, as his legal adviser, to make ready for his signature a general power of attorney drawn up in the fullest terms, and enabling Lady Chatham to transact all business for him.† At the close of the summer he was removed from Hampstead to Burton Pynsent, and thence to Bath, some benefit to his health being looked for from the change. But all his own thoughts and wishes at this time were centered in the repurchase of Hayes. In that air he had enjoyed good health; in that air he might enjoy it again. There in former years he had made improvements which his memory fondly recalled,—plantations, for example, pursued with so much ardour and eagerness that they were not even interrupted at night-fall, but were continued by torch-light and with relays of labourers.‡

* Letter from Thomas Whately (private Secretary of Mr. Grenville) to Lord Lyttleton, dated July 30. 1767, and printed in Lord Lyttleton's Memoirs, vol. ii. p. 729. ed. 1845.

† Chatham Correspondence, vol. iii. p. 282. August 17. 1767.

‡ In an article of the Edinburgh Review (No. clxii. p. 581.) it is stated that these torch-light plantations were made at Burton Pynsent, and at the time of Lord Chatham's last administration and grievous sickness. But on referring to the authority for that statement (Lord Orford's Memoirs, vol. iii. p. 41.) it will be found that the place was Hayes, and the time long previous. In 1849 the very *belts* thus planted were pointed out to me at Hayes.

On inquiry, however, it was found that the new owner of Hayes, Mr. Thomas Walpole, was by no means willing to part with his purchase. His refusal was conveyed to the invalid by Lady Chatham and Mr. Nuthall with every possible preparation and in the gentlest terms. Lord Chatham on hearing the answer only said with a sigh: "That might have saved me!"* Lady Chatham now addressed to Mr. Walpole renewed and most earnest entreaties, as for a matter of life or death to her husband, and she at last prevailed. To Hayes, again become his property, Lord Chatham was removed in December 1767. But there during many months ensuing he continued to languish in utter seclusion, and with no improvement to his health.

It is not surprising that a malady thus mysterious and thus long-protracted should have given rise to a suspicion in some quarters that it was feigned or simulated, with a view to escape the vexations or avoid the responsibilities of office. This idea, however natural, was certainly quite unfounded. But, on the other hand, we may not less decisively discard the allegation of gout which his friends put forth to the public at the time. Gout, — this I have heard physicians of high eminence referring to the case declare, — could never have produced such and so unremitting effects. In truth it was not gout but the absence of gout which at this period weighed upon Lord Chatham. On the 2d of March, as we have seen, he had arrived in London from Marlborough, still lame, and no more than half recovered. Then his new physician, Dr. Addington, eager no doubt to restore him to his public duties with the least delay, had rashly administered some strong remedies which did indeed dispel the gout from his limbs, but only to scatter it about his body, and especially upon his nerves. This fact was discovered, and has been recorded by two separate and equally shrewd observers at the time.†

* Lord Orford's Memoirs of George III., vol. iii. p. 43.

† Lord Chesterfield in his letter to his son of December 19. 1767; Lord Orford in his Memoirs, vol. ii. p. 451. We find Lady Chatham also, when writing confidentially to Lord Shelburne in the autumn of 1767, observe: "I wish I could say there was any material change in

Hence arose the dismal and complete eclipse which for upwards of a year his mental powers suffered. There was no morbid illusion of the fancy, but there was utter prostration of the intellect.

The mental incapacity of Lord Chatham at this period could not remain altogether a secret to the public. In September 1767 there appeared one of the earlier letters from the pen of JUNIUS, but with the signature CORREGGIO; and in that letter we find Lord Chatham glanced at as "a lunatic brandishing a crutch." *

It may be asked, since Lord Chatham was now wholly unable to fulfil the duties of Prime Minister or even of Lord Privy Seal, why did he not resign his post? He did not resign his post for the very reason that he did not fulfil his duties. His mind was almost equally incapable of either effort. It was only, as we have seen, with the utmost agony and tremblings that he—so lately the most intrepid of statesmen—could speak or think of any public affairs whatever; nor was he ever impelled to that agony but on some most special and unavoidable occasion,—when close pressed by a letter from the King, or by a visit from a colleague.

Once, however, on such an occasion, in January 1768, Lord Chatham did express his desire to resign. A nobleman of the house of Berkeley, Lord Bottetort, was concerned in some copper-works in Gloucestershire; and a charter was required to pass the Privy Seal, but as there were some objections made, it was requisite in the first place to hear the parties. For this task Lord Chatham, then confined to his sick-room at Hayes, was of course unfit. Lady Chatham would not venture even to name the subject to her lord. Impatient of delay, Lord Bottetort threatened to lay his complaint before the House of Peers. An expedient was then suggested by the Duke of Grafton and Lord Camden, that the Privy Seal should be put into commission for the purpose of deciding this case, and immediately afterwards be restored to Lord Chatham. When at last Lady Chatham

"the state of my Lord's health, but we are forbid to expect that until "he can have a fit of the gout."

* See Woodfall's Junius, vol. ii. p. 474. ed. 1812.

was most reluctantly induced to consult the invalid, he bade her say, that he feared it could not be for the King's service that he should continue long to hold the Privy Seal. These few words gave great alarm not only to his colleagues but to his Sovereign. Grafton and Camden in their letters most anxiously besought him to forego his resignation. The King himself wrote to him as follows: "I am thoroughly convinced of the utility you are of to "my service; for though confined to your house, your "name has been sufficient to enable my administration "to proceed. I therefore in the most earnest manner "call on you to continue in your employment."* Yielding to these wishes Lord Chatham suffered the expedient proposed to take effect; and after the decision on Lord Bottetort's business, the Privy Seal was returned to him at Hayes by the hands of Lord Camden and a deputation from the Privy Council.

During this time there had been proceeding a short and not important winter Session, chiefly memorable for a measure which was termed the Nullum Tempus Bill. It took its rise from some recent transactions in Cumberland and Westmoreland. There the Portland family enjoyed the Honour of Penrith by a grant from King William the Third; and they had likewise for almost seventy years possessed the adjoining forest of Inglewood, though not strictly included in the terms of the original grant. In the local politics they had for their antagonist Sir James Lowther, a man of princely fortune and state in these counties, but hateful from his overbearing and tyrannical temper, and still more hateful to many persons as the son-in-law of the Earl of Bute. Sir James now determined to avail himself of the ancient legal maxim that the rights either of Crown or Church are not lost by any lapse of time: NULLUM TEMPUS OCCURRIT REGI VEL ECCLESIÆ. He solicited a lease of the King's interest in the forest of Inglewood, and this lease was too readily and too partially yielded by the Ministry, not displeased to mortify a political opponent as the Duke of Portland had now become. It may well be imagined how odious was the aspect, how loud the clamour, that a much-

* Chatham Correspondence, vol. iii. p. 318.

respected family, well-known for its zeal in the Protestant Succession, should be thus disturbed in property, perhaps in the first instance acquired without right, but certainly during many years enjoyed without molestation. In this state of public feeling Sir George Savile, one of the Members for Yorkshire, and already conspicuous in the ranks of Opposition, brought forward a measure commonly called the Nullum Tempus Bill, for securing the property of a subject at any time after sixty years' possession from any dormant pretension of the Crown. Lord North and the other Ministers did not venture to withstand this measure openly, but they pleaded the impropriety of the time — at the very close of a Parliament, — and they requested postponement till the next. Even on this special and chosen ground they only prevailed by a majority of twenty — 134 against 114. And when in the ensuing year the Bill was introduced again, it was allowed to pass quietly and almost as a matter of course.

The Parliament which had now approached its Septennial period was on the 11th of March dissolved. In the General Election which ensued the buying and selling of seats was probably more prevalent, and certainly more public and notorious, than in any former. Indeed it had begun even before the Dissolution took place. The Mayor and Aldermen of Oxford had written word to their Members that they should be re-elected if they would pay 7,500*l.* to discharge the debts of the Corporation. With proper spirit the Members laid the case before the House, and the House committed the peccant Mayor and Aldermen to Newgate for five days, when, having acknowledged their guilt, and asked pardon, they were discharged, being first, however, severely reprimanded by the Speaker at the Bar and on their knees. But their punishment had little effect as an example, even upon themselves. During their very imprisonment, as is said, they completed another bargain for their borough with the Duke of Marlborough and the Earl of Abingdon. Lord Chesterfield writes to his son in December 1767: "I have looked out for some venal borough "for you, and I spoke to a borough-jobber and offered "five and twenty hundred pounds for a secure seat in

"Parliament, but he laughed at my offer, and said that "there was no such thing as a borough to be had now, "for that the rich East and West Indians had secured "them all at the rate of 3,000*l.* at least, but many at "4,000*l.*; and two or three that he knew at 5,000*l.*" — Some weeks later we are told on the same authority, that "George Selwyn has sold his borough of Ludgershall to "two Members for 9,000*l.*" * — In the borough of Northampton, it is said, that a contested election and the petition which followed it cost Earl Spencer no less than 70,000*l.*† Some of the humbler boroughs which acted for themselves had commissioned attorneys (one of these was Hickey, that "most blunt, pleasant creature," as Goldsmith terms him,) to ride about the country and ply for bidders. But, although the assertion may be deemed a bold one, no place at these elections could vie in venality with Shoreham. There bribery had been reduced to a system, and the electors combined in a confederacy for the equal partition of whatever money was received. And as in the first age of the Apostles all things had been common among their followers, so this confederacy by a most profane and irreverent misapplication of the name called itself the "Christian Club." These scandalous practices, though long continued, were not brought to light until 1771, when one of the Members having died, and a new election ensuing, a Committee of the House investigated and disclosed the whole case. By an Act of Parliament in the same year the members of the Christian Club were deprived of their votes, and the franchise was extended from the small town of Shoreham to the adjacent Hundreds.‡

It was not merely by selling and buying that these elections were distinguished; tumults also and riots occurred in several places. The cause appears to have been the high price, which still continued, of provisions, and

* Letters to his son, December 19. 1767, and April 12. 1768.

† Note by Sir Denis Le Marchant to Lord Orford's Memoirs, vol. iii. p. 198.

‡ Parl. Hist. vol. xvi. p. 1346—1355. The doings at Shoreham have supplied Foote with his main points for the character of *Touchit* and the borough of *Bribe'em* in his play of *The Nabob.*

the consequent resentment of the people, though they scarcely knew against what or whom.

Among the new accessions to the House of Commons at this juncture by far the most eminent in ability was John Dunning. Of humble parentage and most mean appearance, this remarkable man was born in 1731 at Ashburton, from whence in after years he derived his Baron's title, to that town's honour and his own. When called to the Bar he speedily shot above all competitors in Westminster Hall. In January 1768 he was appointed Solicitor General; and in the March following, through the influence of Lord Shelburne, he was returned for Calne. Wilkes had been one of his earlier clients; — a circumstance which embarrassed and in a great measure silenced him during the first few years of his Parliamentary career. He was a man both of quick parts and strong passions; in his politics a zealous Whig. As an orator none ever laboured under greater disadvantages of voice and manner; but those disadvantages were most successfully retrieved by his wondrous powers of reasoning, his keen invective, and his ready wit. At the trial of the Duchess of Kingston for bigamy, when he appeared as counsel against her Grace, Hannah More who was present thus describes him: "His manner is "insufferably bad; coughing and spitting at every word; "but his sense and expression pointed to the last degree. "He made her Grace shed bitter tears." Still more striking is the impression which he made upon Chatham at their earliest interview in 1770. "He is another "being," — thus Chatham writes to Shelburne, — "from "any I have known of the profession. I will sum up "his character as it strikes me upon the honour of a first "conversation. Mr. Dunning is not a lawyer, at the "same time that he is the law itself!" *

But greatly as Dunning surpassed in ability every other accession to the House of Commons at this time, there was one as far beyond him in popular acceptance and applause. This was no other than John Wilkes. At the Dissolution of Parliament he had returned to England determined to push his fortune either with the Court or with the country. Finding his overtures to the first

* Letter, December 3. 1770. Correspondence, vol. iv. p. 41.

for pardon slighted, he boldly threw himself upon the latter. He declared himself a candidate for the City, but did not prevail; there were four favourite Aldermen in the field already; and indeed of seven candidates Wilkes was the lowest on the poll. With an undaunted spirit he immediately stood for Middlesex. Meanwhile his ancient popularity was day by day reviving. The discontent which had been ill-defined and was vaguely floating fixed upon him as its expression and its symbol. Crowds began to gather round him wherever he passed with loud cries of "Wilkes and Liberty for ever," and other crowds were no less busy in obstructing the voters of the opposite side. At five o'clock on the morning of the day of election Piccadilly and all the other roads or thoroughfares that lead to Brentford were beset by a multitude of weavers and other artisans who suffered no man to pass without blue cockades or papers inscribed "Wilkes and "Liberty," or "Number 45." At night, elated with the success of the day's polling, they renewed their outrages, compelling every person they met to huzza for Wilkes, scratching their mystic number 45 on the pannels of carriages, and insisting that all the houses in some streets should be illuminated. "Several Scotch refusing," adds Walpole, "had their windows broken."*—By such means, through the enthusiasm of his friends and the intimidation of his opponents, Wilkes was returned at the head of the poll.

Few events could have been more unwelcome to the Court. None could have been more embarrassing to the House of Commons. No sooner had the new Parliament met on the 10th of May, though but for a few days, than a doubt was started how far Mr. Wilkes as an outlaw

* To Sir H. Mann, March 31. 1768. In his Memoirs he adds: "When Wilkes first arrived in town I had seen him pass before my "windows in a hackney chair attended but by a dozen children and "women; now all Westminster was in a riot!" (Vol. iii. p. 187.) The excitement was by no means confined to the metropolis. Franklin writes to his son, April 16. 1768: "I went last week to Winchester, "and observed that for fifteen miles out of town there was scarce a "door or window-shutter next the road unmarked (with 'Wilkes and "'Liberty' and 'Number 45.'), and this continued here and there "quite to Winchester, which is sixty-four miles."

could be deemed rightfully elected or allowed to take his seat. It was agreed, however, to postpone the case until next Session, so as to await the result of the legal steps which were still proceeding. Wilkes on his arrival had pledged himself upon his honour to surrender to his outlawry on the first day of the ensuing Term. Accordingly he had appeared in the Court of King's Bench on the 20th of April, attended by his able Counsel, Mr. Serjeant Glynn. After some hesitation he was committed to custody, and on the 8th of June the Court by the mouth of Lord Mansfield gave judgment in his case. Then the outlawry was declared to be null and void from a technical flaw in the pleadings, but the original verdict was affirmed, and on a subsequent day Wilkes was sentenced to two years' imprisonment computed from the day of his arrest, and also to two fines of *500l.*, — the first for the "North Briton," the second for the "Essay on Woman."

It is not to be supposed that these legal proceedings passed without tumults, — tumults even worse than had disgraced and had carried the Middlesex Election. On the day of the arrest Wilkes was rescued by an admiring mob; they took off the horses from his carriage and drew him themselves to a tavern in Cornhill, insisting that he should remain at liberty and defy the law. Wilkes, however, was wiser than his friends; he slipped out by a back door and surrendered at the King's Bench Prison. Next morning another mob assembled before the prison gates, tore away the railings, and lighted a bonfire, but were at length dispersed by a detachment of the guards. Many other outrages took place on other occasions. But by far the most alarming scene was on the day of the meeting of Parliament, when there gathered in St. George's Fields great crowds of people, expecting that their favourite by virtue of his privilege would be released from his confinement, and allowed to take his seat in the House. Loud was the outcry as they demanded him at the prison gates; fierce the tumult when they found their request denied. Stones and brickbats were flung at Mr. Gillam and other magistrates who attempted to read the Riot Act, and also at the troops which had been sent for and had come in considerable numbers. Some soldiers thus ill-used pursued a young man who had seemed to be one of the most forward in assailing them, and shot him dead in an outhouse belonging to a publican, his father. His name was Allen, and it was afterwards alleged, as it never fails to be on such occasions, that he had taken no part in the affray, and had been only a spectator. The riot increasing, Mr. Gillam gave the officers authority to fire; the troops accordingly did fire, when five or six persons were killed and fifteen, including two women, wounded.

The riot was quelled, but the spirit of riot remained. It happened unfortunately that the regiment employed on this occasion consisted for the most part of Scots; a circumstance which added not a little to the frenzy of the multitude. A coroner's inquest on the death of Allen brought in a verdict of Wilful Murder against Donald Maclean, the soldier who shot him, implicating also Ensign Murray, the commanding officer. Mr. Gillam was indicted on a like charge, but when brought to trial both the soldier and the magistrate were honourably acquitted. The Government also deemed it necessary to stand forward and protect the troops which had protected their peaceful fellow-subjects. Some such encouragement was the more needed since, as Lord Barrington a year afterwards declared in the House of Commons, "repeated attempts had been made by handbills to seduce "the troops, and many individuals had come up to them "to tempt them to be on the side of the mob." All these attempts had, however, failed; and on the very next morning after the tumult Lord Barrington, as Secretary-at-War, conveyed both to officers and men in writing the Royal approbation of their conduct.*

Other riots ensued at other times and places. — In the City the main object of popular resentment was the Lord Mayor, Harley, a rich merchant and younger son of the third Earl of Oxford. As one of the Sheriffs in 1763 it had been his duty to direct the burning of the North

* Annual Register, 1768, part i. p. 111. On the same day (May 11.) there was issued a Royal Proclamation against "tumults "and unlawful assemblies," more especially, however, of "the large "bodies of seamen." For Lord Barrington's statement respecting the attempted seduction of the troops, see the Cavendish Debates, vol. i. p. 335.

Briton, Number 45; as a candidate for London in 1768 he had prevailed over Wilkes; as the chief magistrate he had striven fearlessly to maintain the public peace. For all these reasons, and especially the last, he was hateful to the mob; and it was found necessary to station a company of the footguards for his protection before the Mansion House. Many trades and callings also availed themselves of this favourable juncture to push their particular views. "There is a mob of tailors now collected "about the House!" cried a Member in some alarm on the 16th of May.* Large bodies of seamen left their work, and marched to and fro in procession with threats and cries for an increase of wages. In some cases they proceeded to acts of violence, seizing and detaining several outward-bound ships in the river that were ready to sail. On the other hand, the coal-whippers, hindered from unloading the colliers as usual, took the field as it were against the sailors. In one affray between them the seamen were worsted with the loss of several lives; after which the coal-whippers marched round in triumph, with drums beating and colours flying, and calling out that they would give five guineas for a sailor's head! Such deplorable scenes of violence extended to several of the seaport towns, especially to Newcastle. It was Midsummer ere general tranquillity was restored; and even then the painful thought remained how slight and precarious was its tenure when the mere return from exile of one worthless demagogue, — the "libeller of his King "and the blasphemer of his God," as Pitt emphatically called him, — had been sufficient to unsettle and disturb it.

With the Middlesex Electors, however, the popular flame already kindled was kept alive by an untoward event — the death of Mr. Cooke who had been returned as Wilkes's colleague. A new contest ensued. Serjeant Glynn, well known as the constant and strenuous advocate of Wilkes, was put forward as candidate; and through the same influence was elected the second Member.

From the American Colonies, and, above all, from Massachusetts, there came at nearly the same period

* Cavendish Debates, vol. i. p. 19.

tidings of still more painful, because more permanent, discontents. These and their consequences will be further in my narrative more fully stated.

On the Continent of Europe also the horizon so lately serene was clouded over. A war had broke forth between Russia and Turkey, so contrived that while all the real provocations had come from the Czarina, the first seeming act of hostility — the sudden arrest of an ambassador — proceeded from the Porte. The Turkish rulers indeed had for some time sunk to the lowest pitch of decrepitude and imbecility. Such was their ignorance that when one place close adjoining their own frontier was mentioned, it was found necessary to apply to the English ambassador and to ask him confidentially where that place might be! Such was their weakness that the Sultan had to dismiss and even to hang several of his favourites, for no better reason than because some anonymous handbills against them had been scattered up and down in the principal Mosques! *

At Madrid the Court and people were still agitated by the arrest and expulsion of the Jesuits in the preceding year; a measure planned with profound secrecy, and executed on the same day and same hour in every part of Spain. Important as the measure itself,—the adoption of that example elsewhere,—and the speedy ensuing abolition of the Order by its head the Pope †,—proved to the Roman Catholic states, and even to the Roman Catholic religion, it touches the History of England only thus far, that it engaged in another direction the designs of an unfriendly Power. — In France the restless spirit of Choiseul was ever impelling him to schemes of conquest. On a flimsy pretext he seized the Papal province of Avignon. By a still more iniquitous proceeding he sought to obtain the dominion of Corsica. The people of that

* On these two last cases see in the Appendix two secret despatches from my great grandfather, Mr. Henry Grenville, then ambassador at Constantinople (August 1. and Sept. 2. 1765). These, with the rest of his MS. correspondence, are preserved at Chevening.

† A modification of the Order had been at first proposed, but their *General* Ricci answered: (" avec une franchise et une roideur peu " Jesuitiques," adds Sismondi,) *Sint ut sunt aut non sint!* (Histoire des Français, vol. xxix. p. 368.)

island had for some centuries felt the republican sway of Genoa press grievously upon them. For some years they had made more than one endeavour to cast off the yoke. In 1736 they had chosen for their chief, with the attributes of Royalty, Theodore de Neuhof, an adventurer of Westphalian origin. The lofty title of King Theodore formed during many years a strange contrast to his abject fortunes. After a series of wanderings and expedients he came to London, where he was flung into prison for debt, and died in 1756 immediately after his release. The movement which he headed had been long since put down by the Genoese through the means of French auxiliary troops. But in the next insurrection the Corsicans found a chief of a far higher order, Pascal Paoli, a brave and skilful soldier, an upright and disinterested statesman. So long and so successfully did he make head against the Genoese that they grew weary of their unprofitable and vexatious dominion, and in May 1768 concluded a treaty with the Duke de Choiseul agreeing to cede their rights on Corsica for a sum of money to France. It is hard to determine whether this traffic was most discreditable to those who bought or to those who sold.

The importance of Corsica as a province is by no means considerable; experience proves that in some respects at least it has been a burthen rather than a benefit to France.* But at the time its acquisition by our neighbours was thought by the people of England to disturb the balance of power, and there was also among us a generous feeling of sympathy for the oppressed. The Ministers were accused of supineness and want of energy on this occasion, but certainly were not deserving of that reproach. The Earl of Rochford, as ambassador at Paris, was instructed to make, and did make, the strongest remonstrances,—stopping short only of a declaration of war. At one time he was confident of prevailing, but in his interview of the

* In 1831 the public expenditure of the island was 4,941,000 francs, while the receipts amounted only to 1,144,000. (Mac-Culloch's Dict. *sub voce.*) Observe also the dark tint of Corsica in the crime-charts of M. Guerry (1833). He says of La Creuse: " On a compté " chaque année d'après la moyenne un accusé pour attentats contre " les personnes sur 37,000 habitans. C'est environ quinze fois moins " que dans le Corse !"

next week with Choiseul he found the favourable tone of the French Minister altogether changed. "In a private "letter to me," adds the Duke of Grafton, "he attributed "this strange alteration in Choiseul to the imprudent de-"claration of a great law-Lord (Mansfield) then at Paris, "at one of the Ministers' tables, that the English Ministry "were too weak and the nation too wise to enter into a "war for the sake of Corsica." Thus disappointed, the Duke of Grafton determined on another course. He despatched on a secret mission to Paoli Captain Dunant, a gentleman born at Geneva, and trained in the Sardinian service. Captain Dunant posted through France without his object being known. At Marseilles he could not readily find a passage to the part of Corsica occupied by the insurgents, upon which he proceeded to Genoa, embarked in an English man of war for the island, and at Corte held a private conference with Paoli. The General pressed especially for a supply of arms and ammunition. No time was lost in England; and several thousand stands of arms were immediately sent to his aid from the stores in the Tower, sent, however, in secret, and in such a manner as to leave the Duke de Choiseul no pretext to complain. But meanwhile large reinforcements being forwarded from France, Paoli, notwithstanding a most resolute resistance, was overpowered. His friends were scattered and disarmed, and himself compelled to seek refuge in London, where he was received with all the respect due to his merits and misfortunes. A pension was bestowed upon him by the King, and he passed many years in "affluent and dignified retirement," * with the chief men in art and letters—as Reynolds, Goldsmith, Johnson,—for his friends.

Although many exaggerations were no doubt current at this time,—although Burke might go the length of exclaiming "Corsica a province of France is terrible to "me!"—it was even then discerned that the object at stake had not been such as to warrant us in renewing hostilities. That was the feeling of the House of Commons when the subject came to be discussed. Then only eighty-

* The words on his monument in Westminster Abbey. As is there stated, he was born in 1725, and survived till 1807.

four members voted against the Government on a general motion for papers; and only one, Admiral Sir Charles Saunders, was willing to say plainly that "it would be "better to go to war with France than consent to her "taking possession of Corsica." *

In the autumn of this year died the veteran Duke of Newcastle of a second stroke of palsy. Until the first, a few months before, he had continued active and forward in the cherished object of his life, the cabals of party.

Another more important event, nearly contemporaneous with the former, was Lord Chatham's resignation. During the whole spring and summer he had remained at Hayes in the same weak state both of body and mind, and the same utter seclusion from his friends. Rumours of all kinds were afloat respecting him. Some men whispered that his illness was incurable, and some that it was only feigned.† It is remarkable how frequent, minute, and circumstantial were the accounts of his health which the French Ministers desired to receive, and which the French ambassador accordingly despatched. The archives at Paris prove that to this end no source of information was neglected,—from the statement of a Cabinet colleague down to the eavesdropping of a household spy. And considering the great stress laid on these accounts of Lord Chatham's political eclipse, it is quite clear that had the accounts been of a contrary tenor,—had they represented the great statesman as restored to health and likely to wield power,—the iniquitous French conquest of Corsica would never have been made.

In the autumn Lord Chatham's health grew stronger. Judging from the event we may conclude that the morbid humours had begun to leave his nerves and to concentrate for a fit—so long intermitted and so much needed—of his hereditary gout. He was still entirely shut out from

* Cavendish Debates, vol. i. p. 56. At p. 40. is the strange exclamation of Burke, as given above.

† In the Grenville Papers is a story of an architect going at this time to Hayes, and finding the "Great Earl" quite well; but, on reporting him as such in London, giving much displeasure to Lady Chatham. But Mr. Whately, from whom we learn the story, did not himself believe it, since he says that it is "too extravagant to deserve "a particular repetition." (To Mr. Grenville, July 12. 1768.)

his friends, and still unable to transact any business, but he could bear to hear it mentioned, and could form some judgment of its tenor. In this situation his mind, not yet restored to its full vigour, brooded over suspicions and discontents for which the behaviour of his colleages afforded him no just foundation. The Duke of Grafton became apprised of these feelings *, and was eager to counteract and, if possible, dispel them. All access to the Earl was, he knew, denied, but he solicited and obtained an interview with Lady Chatham one Sunday morning at Hayes.

"I began my discourse," — says the Duke in his Memoirs, — "by assuring Lady Chatham that notwithstanding the King had now for so long a time by Lord Chatham's dreadful illness been deprived of all assistance from him in his Councils, His Majesty did not despair of seeing soon his return to the head of affairs, which I was expressly commanded to deliver as the King's particular hope and expectation. I ventured to add my own declaration, namely, of being ready and anxious to return to him that lead in administration to which his experience and ability had just claim, and which had been imposed on myself at his Lordship's earnest request, and was considered by myself as a painful and temporary possession. I added, that every man whom Lord Chatham had left in the Cabinet desired as earnestly as I did his return to power; and that I had taken care in bringing those into Ministry whom his Lordship had more especially pointed out as the most desirable accession to support it, to have it plainly understood by them that His Majesty and his Ministers were looking out with impatience for the day on which Lord Chatham could again take the lead in the King's Councils." It may be added in passing, that there seems no reason whatever to mistrust the sincerity of these assurances; they were fully borne out by the Duke's conduct both in previous and in subsequent years.

* See Lord Camden's letter to the Duke of Grafton, Sept. 29. 1768, printed in Lord Campbell's Chancellors, vol. v. p. 277. Lord Camden had not seen Lord Chatham, and it does not appear from whom his information was derived.

The Duke then proceeded to explain to Lady Chatham two incidents which, if left without explanation, might, he feared, give umbrage to Lord Chatham; first, the recent removal of Sir Jeffrey Amherst from the government of Virginia; secondly, the intended removal of Lord Shelburne from the office of Secretary of State. As to Amherst there was no slight or injury intended. In requital of his great merits during the late war the government of Virginia had, according to former practice, been granted him as a military sinecure to be held in London. But the troubled state of that province would no longer safely admit of a non-resident Governor; and its Assembly while voting the salary had made complaints that they received no service in return. With the unanimous assent of the Cabinet Amherst was informed that the King must call upon him to resign his post, but was willing to grant him an adequate pension until another appointment of the same value could be found for him. Sir Jeffrey, however, proved intractable, and refused all terms; and indeed might be justly offended at a point of form, since his successor was appointed before his answer had been obtained. It must also be acknowledged that the choice of that successor, namely, Lord Bottetort, was such as greatly to weaken the argument on which the Ministers relied, and to lay them open to a biting taunt as though it was not Virginia that wanted a Governor but a Court favourite that wanted a salary.*

The Earl of Shelburne had for some time past been at variance with the Duke of Grafton. They could only have been kept from jarring by the strong hand of a superior, and that strong hand, Lord Chatham's, being now withdrawn, the alienation between them grew wider and wider, and became for the time irreconcileable. Lord Camden was a common friend to both; but the other members of the Cabinet sided with the Duke; and moreover, as his Grace assures us in his Memoirs, "instigations to remove Lord Shelburne fell daily from the King." †

* See the letter of August 23. 1768, and signed VALERIUS, in Woodfall's Junius, vol. iii. p. 103. ed. 1812.

† It has been said, or rather hinted, by Burke (Thoughts on the

On both these points Lady Chatham listened with attention to the Duke of Grafton's statements, and promised to report them faithfully to her lord. But the result was not such as the Duke of Grafton hoped. On the 12th of October, the third day after the interview, he received a letter from Lord Chatham requesting his Grace to lay before the King his resignation of the Privy Seal. The reason assigned was his weak and broken state of health which continued to render him entirely useless to His Majesty's service; but he likewise added that he could not enough lament the removals of Sir Jeffrey Amherst and of Lord Shelburne.

The resignation of Lord Chatham produced an impression upon his colleagues which cannot but appear to us strangely disproportionate to the part which he had lately taken in their councils. Such Ministers as were absent in the country were summoned by express to town. The Duke of Grafton replied to Lord Chatham, entreating him to forego his resolution. The King himself wrote in the same terms. "I think," says His Majesty, "that "I have a right to insist on your remaining in my ser-"vice; for I with pleasure look forward to the time of "your recovery, when I may have your assistance."* But Lord Chatham being resolute, it was necessary to accept his resignation. As a propitiatory compliment to him the Privy Seal was bestowed upon his personal friend and follower the Earl of Bristol; while in the room of Shelburne the Earl of Rochford, lately ambassador at Paris, became Secretary of State.

Thus in October 1768 did Lord Chatham retire from the office which he had assumed in July 1766. Until towards the middle of March 1767 he had been truly and in effect Prime Minister, since that time he had been — nothing. What was done thenceforward he was so far from directing that he scarcely knew. He had fallen

Discontents; Works, vol. ii. p. 274. ed. 1815) that Lord Shelburne's removal was a penalty for the warmth of his remonstrances to the French Court on the subject of Corsica. But this supposition is disproved by the Duke of Grafton's MSS., and by other contemporary documents. See a note of Sir Denis Le Marchant to Lord Orford's Memoirs, vol. iii. p. 245.

* Chatham Correspondence, vol. iii. p. 343.

not as other statesmen sink from office to opposition, or from a larger to a lesser share of influence and power, but he had fallen as a dead body falls *, blind, unheeding, unstirred. It is strange how large a space in the History of England at this period must be devoted to the details of his personal health and of his family feuds. The fate of the nation seemed to hang suspended on the gout and on the Grenvilles. Whether one sick man did or did not feel a twinge in his foot at Hayes, — whether that sick man would or would not shake hands with his brother from Stowe or his brother from Wotton, — such are the topics which we have here to treat as the most important State affairs!

* "Io venni men così com'io morisse,
"E caddi come corpo morto cade."
Dante, Infern., canto v.

CHAPTER XLVII.

" I HAVE suffered myself," — thus writes the Lord Chancellor to Lady Chatham, — " I have suffered myself to " be overcome by the King's pressing entreaties,—I might " almost say commands, — not to desert his service at this " juncture; the Duke of Grafton declaring at the same " time that he could not safely or honourably continue " without me. Thus have I unwillingly and with the " utmost reluctance consented to halt on a while longer " with this crippled administration; for so it now is, " being deprived of the main prop that gave it support." * — At that time indeed the Duke of Grafton and Lord Camden, — although Lord North was daily rising in importance, —were still the two leading Ministers. Let me here attempt a slight sketch of both.

Augustus Henry, Duke of Grafton, was born in 1735, and succeeded to his title and estate at the age of twenty-two. Great expectations were formed of him at his outset. He had in a high degree that practical good sense which is called common, but which is far indeed from being so.† He was upright and disinterested in his public conduct, sincere and zealous in his friendships, and by no means wanting in powers either of business or debate. Unhappily, however, as his career proceeded, experience showed that these excellent qualities were dashed and alloyed with others of an opposite tenor. He was wanting in application, and when pressed by difficulties in his office, instead of seeking to overcome them, would rather speak of resigning it. Field-sports, and, above all, his favourite pack of hounds at Wakefield Lodge, too much employed his thoughts, or at least his time; New-

* To the Countess of Chatham, Oct. 22. 1768.

† " Le Roy nostre maistre (Louis XI.) avoit le sens naturel par- " faitement bon, lequel precede toutes autres sciences, qu'on scauroit " apprendre en ce monde." Comines, Mem. lib. ii. ch. vi.

market also had great charms for him; nor could he resist a still more dangerous fascination. His frequent appearance in public with Nancy Parsons, a well-known courtesan, gave offence even to the laxer age in which he lived. His contemporaries beheld with surprise that woman seated at the head of the Ducal table, or handed from the Opera House by the First Lord of the Treasury in the presence of the Queen. Such frailties were not likely at any period to escape the host of Opposition libellers. Still less could they pass unnoticed and unimproved in the age of a Junius. Other circumstances, some owing to no fault whatever of his own, tended to lower the reputation and to limit the term of his official power. Still, however, in spite of every disadvantage and defect, he continued through a long life (he survived till 1811) much respected by all who knew him for the uprightness and integrity of his public motives; and for a considerable period he exercised no mean influence upon parties. Mr. Fox in a letter hitherto unpublished intimates that there was no man under whom he would rather act as a leader*; and when in 1783 Mr. Pitt undertook to form a new administration, one of the first persons whom he asked to join it was the Duke of Grafton.

Lord Chancellor Camden was the younger son of Chief Justice Pratt,—a case of rare succession in the annals of the law, and not easily matched, unless by their own contemporaries, Lord Hardwicke and Charles Yorke. Charles Pratt, the future Chancellor, was born in the last year of Queen Anne. As a boy at Eton he formed a friendship, which through a long life never varied, with William Pitt. Lyttleton also and Horace Walpole were among his playmates. His classical studies were completed at Cambridge, and his legal studies pursued at the Inner Temple. During several years he remained without a client. "He sat patiently in chambers," says Lord Campbell, "but no knock came to the door, except that of a dun, or of a companion as briefless and more volatile."† The first case in which he

* To the Duke of Grafton, December 4. 1775. See Appendix to the next volume.

† Lives of the Chancellors, vol. v. p. 232. The same high au-

attracted the public notice was in 1752, on a prosecution for libel which grew from the commitment of Alexander Murray. The question then arose whether the Jury should decide on the intent and meaning, or merely on the fact, of the publication. On this point Pratt as junior Counsel spoke with all the eloquence of earnestness. On this point he now made his first great forensic pleading; on this same point, forty years afterwards, when contending with Lord Thurlow, he delivered his last Parliamentary speech. "Are you impannelled, Gentlemen of the Jury," said he, "only to determine "whether the defendant has sold a piece of paper, value "twopence?" The verdict in accordance with his views was ascribed in no slight degree to his ability; and he much eclipsed his leader in the cause, whose fame is now entirely forgotten. From that time forward the junior Counsel found no lack of clients. In 1757 the friendship of Pitt, then becoming Prime Minister, raised him to be Attorney General over the head of his rival, Charles Yorke. In 1762, as we have seen, he became Chief Justice of the Common Pleas; in 1765 a Peer, and in 1766 Chancellor.

The decisions of Lord Camden while filling the highest legal office have received the rightful meed of public approbation; only one of his decrees was reversed, and even that one reversal was probably wrong.* His style in the Court of Chancery was extremely simple and colloquial. It could not vie with Lord Mansfield's lofty dignity,—his luminous order and skilful array of facts. Dunning indeed was wont to say that a statement by Lord Mansfield was equal to any other man's argument. But how greatly does Lord Camden shine superior in Constitutional doctrine and zeal for public liberty! When contending with Lord Mansfield for the rights of Juries, —when against that great magistrate again and again advising justice to the Middlesex electors, and conciliation to the North American Colonies,—their contemporaries

thority states, as one cause of his "*impecuniosity*," his "not inviting "attorneys to dine with him, and never dancing with their daughters!"

* Such at least seems to have been the opinion of Lord Eldon. See 13 Ves. Jun. 492., as quoted by Lord Campbell.

might be divided in opinion, but does at this day any one man doubt to whom the palm should be awarded?

One especial characteristic of Lord Camden was his gentleness of temper. With many political opponents, he had not one personal enemy; and a circle of attached friends was always the gainer when he could allow himself, as he did most willingly, intervals of leisure and of ease. He did not love labour for its own sake, but only when prompted by some strong emotion or some worthy object. It may also be owned of him without disparagement that his mind wanted something of energy and firmness, preferring, and perhaps requiring, to lean on another's more resolute will, — first on the elder and subsequently on the younger Pitt. With this turn of mind he was sometimes a little too apt to despond of the public weal. "From politics, my dear Lord," — thus he writes in 1777, — "I am almost entirely weaned. I can-"not prevail upon myself to go with the tide; and I "have no power to struggle against it."* But if destitute of that earnest and eager ambition which glowed in the breasts of Loughborough or Thurlow, he was no less wholly free from those dark blots by which the fame both of Loughborough and Thurlow is stained. He never bartered his principles for place. He never plotted against his colleagues. He never betrayed nor yet ever fawned upon his Sovereign. Such things far from tainting his conduct did not even sully his thoughts. On the contrary, while among his own contemporaries some displayed more vigour in the fierce contentions of his party, none perhaps evinced more honourable steadiness in those friendships and those principles for the sake of which alone party is desirable, for the sake of which alone party can be justified. His descendants may well be proud not merely of his talents but also of his virtues. And his country "will not willingly let die" the honoured remembrance of an orator so accomplished, a judge so firm a friend to liberty, a statesman so far-sighted and pure-minded.

The Duke of Grafton and Lord Camden, as chiefs of the Government at the beginning of 1769, had lost the

* Letter to the Duke of Grafton, January 7. 1777.

valuable co-operation of their late colleague Lord Shelburne and of his adherent Colonel Barré, both of whom henceforth joined the ranks of Opposition. — William, second Earl of Shelburne, and afterwards first Marquis of Lansdowne, was sprung on his father's side from the Fitz-Maurices Earls of Kerry, one of the oldest and most illustrious houses of Ireland, whose barony dates even from the days of Henry the Second. By female descent he inherited the name, and what was far better the fortune, of that most shrewd and selfish of calculators, Sir William Petty. The future Minister was born in 1737, and at his father's death in 1761 succeeded both to the Irish Earldom of Shelburne and to an English peerage derived from the borough of Wycombe. Over that borough I may observe in passing that he held considerable influence (he sat for it indeed during a few weeks of 1761) as possessing near it a house (an ancient Abbey) and estate which afterwards passed by purchase to the first Lord Carrington. The Abbey has since been wholly rebuilt, though still in the abbatial style, but the beauty of its hills and glades as in Lord Shelburne's day, — the double beechwood above it, — the stately plane-trees by its side, — and below the shaded mossgrown dell with its cascade and crystal stream, — might justify a partial fondness even from the owner of Bowood. — Lord Shelburne's first destination was the army, which he entered very young. He was present in the battle of Minden, and on the accession of George the Third was appointed an aide-de-camp to His Majesty with the rank of Colonel. But on entering the House of Lords he applied to its business with undivided care, and ere long attached himself especially to the person and the principles of Chatham. It is remarkable at how early a period of life he attained high office. We find him at twenty-six chief of the Board of Trade, at twenty-nine Secretary of State.

Lord Shelburne had indeed some of the highest qualities that fit men for public affairs. As a debater in the House of Lords, a great authority, — no other than Lord Camden, — considered him second to no one, Lord Chatham alone excepted.* In business he was quick, assiduous, and ready, and amidst his political cares did not neglect the prudent administration of a large estate. He was wont to say that a man of high rank who looks into his own affairs may have all that he ought to have, all that can tend either to use or ornament, for five thousand pounds a year.†

On many questions, and, above all, it may be said on points of foreign policy, his knowledge was both extensive and profound. He might not be destitute of vanity nor insensible to praise‡, yet he always felt the subordination due to the superior genius of Chatham, and throughout the life of that great man continued one of his most zealous followers and most devoted friends.

There was, however, one defect, as the public deemed it, — or, as Lord Shelburne himself would have said, one misfortune, — that greatly detracted from the weight of his abilities. He could never attain a reputation for sincerity. Hollow and plausible, — such were the epithets bestowed on him by common report; and he was speedily nick-named Malagrida, from a plotting Jesuit of the name in Portugal. Thus also his friends were sometimes designated as "Malagrida's gang."§ Even at a much later period, after his character had been so long before the public, — after he had been for years the leader of a party, — after he had been for months the chief of an administration, — we still find the same reproach urged against him in the satirical writings of the time.‖ — One cause (perhaps it may be deemed the only one) of this

* Sketch of Life by Mr. George Hardinge. See Lord Campbell's Chancellors, vol. v. p. 362.

† As repeated by Dr. Johnson; Boswell's Life, under the date of April 10. 1778.

‡ In an unpublished passage of one of the letters to Mr. Philip Stanhope, then Envoy at Dresden, Lord Chesterfield observes: "He "(Lord Shelburne) has abilities, but is proud above them, so pray "lay him on pretty thick in your answer to his Circular." (August 1. 1766. From the original MS.

§ As in Wilkes's private letter to Junius of Sept. 12. 1771.

‖ Hence the speech which the *Rolliad* puts into his Lordship's mouth:

"A noble Duke affirms I like his plan;
"I never did, my Lords! — I never can!

general imputation on his sincerity was the overstrained politeness of his address. As I have heard from some who knew him, he could scarcely meet with or part from any acquaintance without a profusion of high-flown compliments and earnest inquiries. Such an address has never proved successful in this country. It has never been practised by the great masters of politeness among us. Lord Chesterfield, versed as he was in all courtly graces, did not intersperse his conversation with touches of panegyric, but far rather with strokes of satire. The Duke of Marlborough, whose charm of manner has been celebrated as one element of his invariable success,—of whom it was said that he gained hearts not less readily than towns,—the Duke of Marlborough says of himself in one of his most familiar letters: "You know I am not "good at compliments." *

But even in the more congenial sphere of France we may observe that Lord Shelburne's compliments were, sometimes at least, deemed fulsome and excessive. Thus an old blind lady of eighty-two writes as follows from Paris: "Lord Shelburne has flattered me extremely; he "assures me that he shall come again next year singly "and solely for the pleasure of seeing me!" †

At the beginning of 1769, as I have already observed, it was certainly no slight disadvantage to the Ministers to find the Earl of Shelburne, so late their colleague, turned to their opponent. But at the very same period, —in January 1769,—an enemy still far more formidable suddenly rose up against them. A new knight entered the lists with his vizor down, and with unreal devices on his shield, but whose arm was nerved with inborn vigour, and whose lance was poised with most malignant skill. Even now the dark shadow of JUNIUS looms across that period of our annals with a grandeur no doubt much enhanced and heightened by the mystery. To solve that mystery has since employed the most patient industry, and aroused the most varied conjectures; and a full

"Plain words, thank Heaven, are always understood;
"I *could* support, I said, but not I *would!*"

* To the Duchess, June 15. 1704.

† Lettres de Madame Du Deffand, vol. ii. p. 597. ed. 1810.

statement at least, if not a full solution of it, may justly be required from the historian of that time.

One of the newspapers in London at this period was the "Public Advertiser," printed and directed by Mr. Henry Sampson Woodfall. His politics were those of the Opposition of the day; and he readily received any contributions of a like tendency from unknown correspondents. Among others was a writer whose letters beginning at the latest in April 1767 continued frequent through that and the ensuing year. It was the pleasure of this writer to assume a great variety of signatures in his communications as MNEMON, ATTICUS, and BRUTUS. It does not appear, however, that these letters (excepting only some with the signature of LUCIUS which were published in the autumn of 1768) attracted the public attention to any unusual extent, though by no means wanting in ability, or still less in acrimony. Of late indeed a highly acute and ingenious writer has expressed his doubts whether all at least of these letters came from the same pen as JUNIUS.* The original printer, Mr. Sampson Woodfall, had died before the date of the first collective edition in 1812, and may not have left to the editors, — his son, namely, Mr. George Woodfall, and Dr. Mason Good, — a clue for every letter. It is possible that in some cases these gentlemen may have decided on conjecture rather than authority. But, on the other hand, Mr. Sampson Woodfall was not likely to be silent to his son on such a subject, and his means of judging at the time as derived from the identity of the handwritings, of the seals, and of the signals, must, I conceive, be admitted as unquestionable. Moreover the assertion of the editors of 1812 will be found borne out in a most remarkable degree by the letters, as yet unpublished, from the archives at Stowe, in which the writer, who certainly was Junius, avows in explicit terms not only the authorship of the papers signed Atticus and Lucius, but also, as he says, of many more.

Such was the state of these publications, not much

* See the series of papers which have appeared in the *Athenæum* on this subject; those especially of July 22. and 29. 1848, February 2. and 9. 1850.

rising in interest above the common level of many such at other times, when on the 21st of January 1769 there came forth another letter from the same hand with the novel signature of Junius. It did not greatly differ from its predecessors either in superior merit or superior moderation; it contained, on the contrary, a fierce and indiscriminate attack on most men in high places, including the Commander-in-Chief, Lord Granby. But, unlike its predecessors, it roused to controversy a well-known and respectable opponent. Sir William Draper, General in the army and Knight of the Bath, undertook to meet and parry the blows which it had aimed at his Noble friend. In an evil hour for himself he sent to the Public Advertiser a letter subscribed with his own name, and defending the character and conduct of Lord Granby. An answer from Junius soon appeared, urging anew his original charge, and adding some thrusts at Sir William himself on the sale of a regiment, and on the nonpayment of the Manilla ransom. Wincing at the blow, Sir William more than once replied; more than once did the keen pen of Junius lay him prostrate in the dust. The discomfiture of poor Sir William was indeed complete. Even his most partial friends could not deny that so far as wit and eloquence were concerned the man in the mask had far, very far, the better in the controversy. It was scarcely an exaggeration when Junius addressed Sir William as follows in the tone of lofty scorn: "I "should justly be suspected of acting upon motives of "more than common enmity to Lord Granby if I con-"tinued to give you fresh materials or occasion for writing "in his defence!" *

These victories over a man of rank and station such as Draper's gave importance to the name of Junius. Henceforth letters with that signature were eagerly expected by the public, and carefully prepared by the

* Letter v., Feb. 21. 1769. In the notes which Junius himself afterwards supplied to his letters it is added: "Sir William Draper "certainly drew Junius forward to say more of Lord Granby's charac-"ter than he originally intended. . . . . In private life he was un-"questionably that good man who, for the interest of his country, "ought to have been a great one."

author. He did not indeed altogether cease to write under other names; sometimes especially adopting the part of a by-stander, and the signature of PHILO-JUNIUS; but it was as Junius that his main and most elaborate attacks were made. Nor was it long before he swooped at far higher game than Sir William. First came a series of most bitter pasquinades against the Duke of Grafton. Dr. Blackstone was then assailed for the unpopular vote which he gave in the case of Wilkes. In September was published a false and malignant attack upon the Duke of Bedford,—an attack, however, of which the sting is felt by his descendants to this day.* In December the acme of audacity was reached by the celebrated letter to the King.

All this while conjecture was busy as to the secret author. Names of well-known statesmen or well-known writers—Burke or Dunning, Boyd or Dyer, George Sackville or Gerard Hamilton—flew from mouth to mouth. Such guesses were for the most part made at mere hap-hazard, and destitute of any plausible ground. Nevertheless the stir and talk which they created added not a little to the natural effects of the writer's wit and eloquence. "The most important secret of our times!" cries Wilkes.† Junius himself took care to enhance his own importance by arrogant, nay even impious, boasts of it. In one letter of August 1771 he goes so far as to declare that "the Bible and Junius will be read when "the commentaries of the Jesuits are forgotten!"

Mystery, as I have said, was one ingredient to the popularity of Junius. Another not less efficacious was supplied by persecution. In the course of 1770 Mr. Woodfall was indicted for publishing, and Mr. Almon with several others for reprinting, the letter from Junius to the King. The verdict in Woodfall's case was: Guilty of printing and publishing only. It led to repeated discussions and to ulterior proceedings. But in the temper of the public at that period such measures could end

* See the remarks of Lord John Russell, Bedford Correspondence, vol. iii. Introduction, p. lxv—lxx.

† Letter to Junius, Sept. 12. 1771, vol. i. p. 297. ed. 1812.

only in virtual defeat to the Government, in augmented reputation to the libeller.

During the years 1770 and 1771 the letters of Junius were continued with little abatement of spirit. He renewed invectives against the Duke of Grafton; he began them against Lord Mansfield, who had presided at the trials of the printers; he plunged into the full tide of City politics; and he engaged in a keen controversy with the Rev. John Horne, afterwards Horne Tooke. The whole series of letters from January 1769, when it commences, until January 1772, when it terminates, amounts to sixty-nine, including those with the signature of Philo-Junius, those of Sir William Draper, and those of Mr. Horne.

Several other communications from Junius, but no longer with that signature, nor known to proceed from him, appeared in the Public Advertiser during the spring of 1772. They referred mainly to some matters at the War Office, and were for the most part subscribed VETERAN or NEMESIS.

If then we discard the name, and look only to the author, of Junius, we shall find that the series of letters coming from his pen, and published in the Public Advertiser, extends from April 1767 until May 1772.

But besides the letters which Junius designed for the press, there were many others which he wrote and sent to various persons, intending them for those persons only. Two addressed to Lord Chatham appear in Lord Chatham's correspondence. Three addressed to Mr. George Grenville have until now remained in manuscript among the papers at Wotton, or Stowe; all three were written in the same year, 1768, and the two first signed with the same initial C. Several others addressed to Wilkes were first made known through the son of Mr. Woodfall. But the most important of all, perhaps, are the private notes addressed to Mr. Woodfall himself. Of these there are upwards of sixty, signed in general with the letter C.; some only a few lines in length; but many of great value towards deciding the question of the authorship. It seems that the packets containing the letters of Junius for Mr. Woodfall or the Public Advertiser were sometimes brought to the office-door, and thrown in, by an unknown gentleman, probably Junius himself; more commonly they were conveyed by a porter or other messenger hired in the streets. When some communication from Mr. Woodfall in reply was deemed desirable, Junius directed it to be addressed to him under some feigned name, and to be left till called for at the bar of some coffee-house; both the name and the coffee-house being frequently changed. It may be doubted whether Junius had any confidant or trusted friend. One among his private notes to Mr. Woodfall mentions a "gentleman who transacts "the conveyancing part of our correspondence."* But on a more solemn occasion, when dedicating his collected letters to the English people, he declares: "I am "the sole depository of my own secret, and it shall perish "with me."

After the letters of Veteran and Nemesis which ceased in May 1772 no communications from Junius, either public or private, were received by Mr. Woodfall during many months. In his "Notices to Correspondents" the printer inserted from time to time, but without effect, certain signals and catch-words as previously agreed upon between them to invite the re-appearance of his unknown friend. At length on the 19th of January 1773 Junius in a private note addressed him once more, and finally, as follows: "I have seen the signals thrown "out for your old friend and correspondent. Be assured "that I have had good reason for not complying with "them. In the present state of things if I were to "write again I must be as silly as any of the horned "cattle that run mad through the City, or as any of your "wise Aldermen. I meant the cause and the public. "Both are given up. I feel for the honour of this "country when I see that there are not ten men in it "who will unite and stand together upon any one ques-"tion. But it is all alike,—vile and contemptible.— "You have never flinched that I know of, and I shall "always rejoice to hear of your prosperity."† Such were the last words of Junius.

* Private Note of January 18. 1772. See also the Note, No. viii., Sept. 10. 1769.

† Woodfall's Junius, vol. i. p. *255. As a postscript Junius adds:

Like other pamphlet-writers, Junius may be viewed in two separate aspects,—as an author in regard to his style, as a politician in regard to his principles. In the former class it is certainly no slight proof of his merit that his popularity should so long have survived the fleeting topics of the day to which alone he applied himself. That popularity endures even now when those topics have altogether ceased to be appreciated or even clearly understood. Indeed his terseness and perspicuity of statement,—his terrible energy of invective,—the force and fire with which he pleads any political opinion,—the poised and graceful structure of his sentences,—and, above all, the elaborate polish of his sarcasms,—can never be denied. So ably does he make his illustrations subservient to his arguments, his fancy to his reasoning, (in this how unlike to Burke!) that we might almost say of Junius as Junius says of kingly splendour: "the "feather that adorns the Royal bird supports his flight."* But while freely owning the great merits of Junius as a writer, I yet believe that these merits have been often and extravagantly over-rated; I cannot look upon them as wholly surpassing and unrivalled. Mr. Fox, as we learn on high authority, never thought them so.† Another eminent statesman, one whose personal friendship I had the honour of enjoying,—the same to whose most able suggestions on the character of Walpole I have elsewhere acknowledged myself as much beholden‡,—and why, now that he has gone from us, need I forbear to name Sir Robert Peel?—observed to me in 1832 that in his judgment several of the leading articles of THE TIMES newspaper during the last year were not at all inferior in ability to Junius.

The opinions of Junius were by no means uniformly on the popular side. He maintained the right, although

"If you have anything to communicate (of moment to yourself) you "may use the last address, and give a hint." Mr. Woodfall did write accordingly and transmit some books (copies of Junius) on March 7.; after which all communication between them absolutely ceased.

* Letter xlii., January 30. 1771.

† See Lord John Russell's Introduction to the Bedford Correspondence, vol. iii. p. lxx.

‡ See vol. i. p. 264.

he questioned the policy, of taxing the Americans by an Act of the British Parliament. He defended the practice of press-warrants for seamen. He warmly supported a return to Triennial Elections, but no less warmly opposed any disfranchisement of the smaller, or as they were termed the rotten, boroughs. "I would not," he adds, "give representatives to those great trading towns which "have none at present. If the merchant and the manu-"facturer must be really represented, let them become "freeholders by their industry, and let the representation "of the counties be increased."* Such doctrines do honour as some may think to his judgment; as few will deny to his courage. But at all events they contrast a little strangely with the spirit of republican liberty, or rather licence, that breaks forth in other parts of his writings, — with all his hints of armed resistance, — his sneers against the Bishops, — and his insults to the King.

Of all the statesmen then living the one for whom this writer appears to have felt the most of esteem and reverence was George Grenville. It was to Grenville's party, if to any, that Junius in truth belonged. In 1767 some of the earlier letters inveigh with great bitterness against Lord Chatham, who was then at variance with the houses of Wotton and of Stowe.† But after their reconciliation the asperity of Junius was much softened; he owns in 1771 that the character of Lord Chatham has "grown "upon his esteem," and he refers to him at last in terms of high, though not unqualified, admiration. To lawyers or to Scotchmen he can seldom allude without a sneer. Thus in one place he observes of the former: "The in-"discriminate defence of right and wrong contracts the "understanding, whilst it corrupts the heart. Subtlety "is soon mistaken for wisdom, and impunity for virtue. "If there be any instances on record, as some there are "undoubtedly, of genius and morality united in a lawyer, "they are distinguished by their singularity and operate

* Private letter to Wilkes, Sept. 7. 1771.

† From this great bitterness the authenticity of the earlier letters has been called in question, but, I think, without sufficient ground. See Mr. Wright's note to the Chatham Papers, vol. iii. p. 305.

"as exceptions."* But no doubt his fiercest rancour was reserved for the Duke of Grafton and the King. Thus on one occasion he writes to the Duke: "Though "I am not so partial to the Royal judgment as to affirm "that the favour of a King can remove mountains of "infamy, it serves to lessen at least, for undoubtedly it "divides, the burthen. While I remember how much "is due to his sacred character, I cannot with any decent "appearance of propriety call you the meanest and the "basest fellow in the kingdom. I protest, my Lord, I "do not think you so."† Far from blushing at this ribald strain of calumny, Junius viewed it with especial pride. He says of it in a private note to Mr. Woodfall: "I am strangely partial to the inclosed. It is finished "with the utmost care. If I find myself mistaken in "my judgment of this paper I positively will never write "again." Nor are his invectives by any means confined to political affairs. He delights to stir and exacerbate any private wound. George the Third is taunted with the suspected frailty of his mother! The Duke of Grafton is reminded of the recent elopement of his wife! The Duke of Bedford is accused of displaying indifference at the death, and of pocketing money from the wardrobe, of his only son!

With all this, however, and contradictory though it seems, the feelings of Junius, so far as we can trace them, were certainly on some points good and generous. He loved to assail the mighty, not to trample on the fallen; and malignant as he was in his language, he was never sordid in his views. There are many indications that a real regard for what he deemed the welfare and honour of his country was often present in his thoughts. But he was plainly under the dominion of a temper arrogant and proud beyond all ordinary limits of pride,—liable to gusts and sallies of anger, or I should rather say of fury,—and when once offended both implacable in his resentments, and unscrupulous as to the method of indulging them.

But who was Junius? Who lurked beneath that

* To Lord Mansfield, January 21. 1772.

† Letter xlix., June 22. 1771.

name, or rather, according to the motto he assumed, that "shadow of a name?"* This question, which has already employed so many pens and filled so many volumes, cannot be fully dealt with in these pages. But I will not affect to speak with doubt when no doubt exists in my mind. From the proofs adduced by others, and on a clear conviction of my own, which I am bound thus frankly to express, I affirm that the author of Junius was no other than SIR PHILIP FRANCIS.

Philip Francis was born at Dublin in the year 1740. His father, the Rev. Dr. Francis, still remembered from his translation of Horace, was domestic tutor in the family of the first Lord Holland, then Mr. Henry Fox. By Mr. Fox's favour young Francis obtained in 1756 a small place in the Secretary of State's office. When shortly afterwards Mr. Pitt became the head of that office he extended his protection to the client of his recent rival. In 1758 Philip Francis was named Secretary of General Bligh in the expedition against Cherbourg, and in 1760 Secretary of the Earl of Kinnoul on a special embassy to Lisbon. After the retirement of Mr. Pitt he found other friends in Mr. Grenville's party, and in 1763 obtained a clerkship of considerable value in the War Office. This post he held until March 1772 when he resigned or was removed, full of ire against Lord Barrington, who had promoted Mr. Chamier over his head to be Deputy Secretary at War. Francis then went abroad, visiting both France and Italy. He returned to England about the beginning of 1773, and shortly afterwards discovered that he had been much in error in supposing Lord Barrington to be his ill-wisher and his enemy. On the contrary, Lord Barrington "most honourably and most generously," as was afterwards acknowledged on the part of Francis, recommended

* *Stat Nominis Umbra;* the motto affixed to Woodfall's first collective edition of 1772.—I observe, on referring to the files of the Public Advertiser at the British Museum, that according to the custom of the time the letters of Junius, as originally published, abound in blanks and dashes,—but such as it was easy for readers to fill up. Thus the famous letter to the Duke of Bedford (Sept. 19. 1769) is addressed "To the Duke of——;" and W——n and G——n stand for Woburn and Grafton.

him to Lord North, and Lord North inserted his name in an Act of Parliament which passed in June 1773, and which appointed him with General Clavering and Colonel Monson members of the new Council to be constituted for the government of Bengal.

Important as was this office, and large as were its emoluments*, the choice of Francis may, perhaps, be sufficiently explained by the good opinion which Lord Barrington must have formed of his abilities, and the regret which he may have felt at his estrangement. Some persons, however, are rather disposed to rely on a vague traditionary story that the King in one of his rides about this time let fall to a trusted attendant: "We "know who Junius is; and he will write no more."† These persons then suppose that the authorship of Junius having by some means become known to His Majesty and to the Ministers they had conferred this place on Francis as a bribe for his future silence.

Early in 1774 Philip Francis sailed for Calcutta.— In this History, should it further be continued, I shall have occasion to relate the fierce struggle which he forthwith commenced against Warren Hastings,—the long altercations and the final duel between them. It may be said with truth that the character to be deduced of Junius from his writings,—most arrogant and angry, and yet on many points high-minded,—exactly tallies with the character to be deduced of Francis from his life. To the end of his days indeed Francis was noted among his friends both for his testy temper and his pithy sayings.‡

In 1781 Francis returned to England; and in 1784 obtaining a seat in Parliament took a forward and eager part in the prosecution of Hastings. On other questions also he spoke sometimes with great force and spirit, but even by his own account with no easy flow of words. Upon the accession of the Whig party to power in 1806

* No less than 10,000*l.* a year as fixed by the Act, 13 Geo. 3. c. 63. sect. 21.

† See "Junius Identified," p. 399. ed. 1818. Sir Philip's widow, in her letter to Lord Campbell, admits this story as certainly true, but for my own part I consider it apocryphal.

‡ See as an instance the anecdote in Moore's Life of Sheridan, vol. ii. p. 300. ed. 1825.

he was invested with the red riband of the Bath, and became Sir Philip. Hitherto he had never been suspected as the secret libeller of 1769.* But the publication of Woodfall's edition in 1812, comprising all the secret notes and unacknowledged letters of Junius, gave a new turn to the inquiry, and was followed at no long interval by "Junius Identified," an able and ingenious work by Mr. John Taylor, fixing on Sir Philip by many cogent proofs the authorship of Junius. Sir Philip, however, on no occasion, at least not on any public one, acknowledged the impeachment, but, on the contrary, always denied, or more commonly evaded it. — He died in 1818.

In considering this question of identity the first point is to compare the two handwritings. The hand of Junius was plainly a disguised one; it is upright, while that of Francis is slanting. But on examining especially the fragments of sentences from each, which have been engraved and placed in collocation, it is impossible to doubt that the two hands closely agree in the form of several letters and the junction of several words; as also in some peculiarities both of spelling and punctuation.

Next as to the style. To compare with the letters of Junius we may take the speeches of Francis as prepared by himself for the press. Thus in one of them does Sir Philip advert to lawyers: "It belongs to the learning of "these gentlemen to involve, and to their prudence not "to decide. . . . . . . In the name of God and common "sense what have we gained by consulting these learned "persons? It is really a strange thing, but it is certainly "true, that the learned gentlemen on that side of the "House, be the subject what it may, always begin their "speeches with a panegyric on their own integrity. You "expect learning and they give you morals; you expect "law and they give you ethics; you ask them for bread "and they give you a stone! . . . . Equality is their "right. I allow it. But that they have any just pre-"tensions to a superior morality, to a pure and elevated "probity, to a frank, plain, simple, candid, unrefined in-

* "Until the work before us, Sir Philip Francis had never, as far "as we know, been suspected." (Edinburgh Review, No. lvii. p. 96. Nov. 1817.)

"tegrity, beyond other men, is what I am not convinced "of, and never will admit." *

In another speech Sir Philip refers to Chatham as follows: "I hope it will not appear improper in me to say "that in the early part of my life I had the good fortune "to hold a place, very inconsiderable in itself, but imme- "diately under the late Earl of Chatham. He descended "from his station to take notice of mine; and he honoured "me with repeated marks of his favour and protection. "How warmly in return I was attached to his person, "and how I have been grateful to his memory, those "who know me know. I admired him as a great, illus- "trious, faulty, human being, whose character, like all "the noblest works of human composition, should be de- "termined by its excellencies, not by its defects." Sir Philip adds elsewhere: "But he is dead, and has left "nothing in this world that resembles him!" † — these last words being designed for a cruel stab against the policy and character of Mr. Pitt. It seems to me that even the most cursory reader cannot peruse these extracts, — and many more besides that might be given, — without feeling in the strongest manner their complete family likeness, both in sentiment and in style, with parallel passages of Junius.

Thirdly, there are several points in the position of Junius that are best elucidated by referring to the position of Francis at that time. Thus it is clear from several passages that Junius was anxious to forbear from any attack upon Lord Holland; and Lord Holland it will be remembered was Francis's first patron. Thus again it appears that Junius attended the House of Lords in 1770 and took some notes of Lord Chatham's speeches; and we find that many years afterwards several of Lord Chatham's speeches in that very Session were printed by Mr. Almon from the notes that Sir Philip had supplied.— But above all, how else can we sufficiently explain the passionate resentment which the man in the mask betrays at the promotion of Mr. Chamier? How else account for those most rancorous and numerous letters

* Speech in the House of Commons, March 12. 1788.

† Speech of July 26. 1784, and February 12. 1787.

which he poured forth on so trifling a question during the whole spring of 1772, desiring the printer at the same time not to allow it to be known that these letters came from the same hand as Junius?—Let it also be observed how well the dates of the last letters agree with the dates in the career of Francis,—their interruption with his Continental tour,—their cessation with his Indian appointment.

The strongest perhaps and most convincing of all the arguments in support of Francis still remains to be given. It has often been urged as an argument upon the other side that Junius in February 1769 put with much solemnity a question to Sir William Draper, whether he did not take a certain oath on receiving his half-pay, which question Sir William was able to answer with a triumphant negative. How, it was asked, could such a blunder have proceeded from one of the War-Office Clerks? But when Mr. Macaulay was himself Secretary at War he made some inquiries on the subject in his department, eliciting in the clearest manner that this mistake was likely to be made by some person closely connected with the English War-Office, and by no person besides.*

It may be asked, however, why, Sir Philip being the author of Junius and surviving till 1818, he did not in his later years avow his secret, and claim his meed of literary fame. But perhaps he may have felt that in adding to his literary fame he should lose at least as much in moral estimation. Of his style in Junius, a style which had so powerfully and so permanently stirred the nation, he might be justly proud; of his venom and injustice, and of the high office accepted from the very hands that he most loathed, he must sometimes at least have been ashamed. Forward as he was moreover in the Whig politics of the day, he was throughout his later years living on familiar terms with many of the nearest kinsmen of those whom he had anonymously slandered. The Duke of Grafton himself did not die till 1811. The

* The letter of Mr. Macaulay on this subject dated January 3. 1852, and hitherto unpublished, will, through his kind permission, be found in the Appendix to the present edition of this volume. (1853.)

grandsons of the Duke of Bedford, and the sons of George the Third, one of these a zealous Whig, were still alive in 1818. Such reasons sufficiently explain Sir Philip's desire to retain the mask. But we learn from his widow in her interesting letter to Lord Campbell, that though Sir Philip did not wholly drop the mask even to herself, it was then of the lightest texture and meant to be seen through.*

Strong as this, the "Franciscan," theory appears when separately viewed, it becomes, I think, far stronger still when compared with the other claims that have been urged. In no other can many strained inferences and many gratuitous assumptions fail to be observed. In no other do the feelings and the circumstances which must be ascribed to Junius, or the dates applying to the cessation of his letters, admit on all points, or even on most points, of simple explanations from the theory adduced. Even the claim on behalf of Lord George Sackville, which at first sight has dazzled many acute observers, will not, as I conceive, endure the light of a close and critical examination.†

The Session of 1769 (for here I resume my course of narrative) having begun in the previous November continued until May. Two questions mainly engrossed its time; the case of Wilkes and the news from North America. In the former as in the latter the Government had displayed a grievous want of foresight and discretion. Just before the meeting of Parliament one of the Ministers asked another how the House of Commons ought to deal with the convict Knight of the Shire; and the answer was only: "I do not know!"‡ The Duke of

* The letter of Lady Francis is printed in the Lives of the Chancellors, vol. vi. p. 344. On this point, as on many others, the public is greatly indebted to Lord Campbell's judicious spirit of inquiry.

† "In our conviction the weight of suspicion still preponderates "towards Lord George Sackville." (See the article ascribed to Mr. Croker in the Quarterly Review, No. cxxxi. p. 256. June 1840.) On the other hand, there will be found in the Appendix to my present volume a long and able letter from Sir James Mackintosh which I have had the good fortune to obtain, giving most decisive reasons, as they seem to me, against Lord George's claim.

‡ Earl of Chesterfield to General Irwine, Nov. 21. 1768.

Grafton indeed makes no scruple of owning in his Memoirs that at the first Cabinet held upon this subject not one of its Members, not even the Lord Chancellor, contemplated or anticipated the difficulties which so soon afterwards arose. Wilkes himself now made the first move in the game by presenting to the House through the hands of his friend Sir Joseph Mawbey, Member for Southwark, a petition complaining of his past grievances and present imprisonment. Several gentlemen cried out against this imprisonment as a breach of privilege. Other gentlemen cried out no less against his election, and asked for his expulsion.

But before this last, as the main point, was brought forward for debate, several new incidents occurred further to perplex the case.—In the previous April Lord Weymouth as Secretary of State had addressed a letter to the Surrey magistrates at Lambeth advising them to be on their guard against riots and tumults, and to make early application if needful for a military force. Wilkes having now obtained a copy of this letter published it with a comment of his own, but without his name; in this he called it a "hellish project" tending to a "horrid "massacre." Lord Weymouth complained to the House of Lords of a breach of privilege. By means of a Conference the main question was transferred to the House of Commons, and several witnesses were summoned for examination. Baldwin, the printer, acknowledged that he had received the letter from Wilkes. Wilkes was brought to the Bar in custody, and was asked what defence he could make to the charge; when he boldly said that he did not deny the publication, but rather gloried in having brought to light that "bloody scroll."

By a large majority the House of Commons determined that Wilkes's comment on Lord Weymouth was an "in-"solent libel." He had also made a complaint against Lord Mansfield touching some points in a Writ of Error which he had moved, and this complaint the House of Commons no less readily voted to be a "groundless asper-"sion."—Thus unworthily had the House of Commons come to bandy invectives with a single man! Thus lavish had they grown of their own and the public's leisure! Well might Captain Phipps exclaim on one occasion:

"Ever since the opening of the Session we have been putting off affairs of the greatest consequence; and the time of Parliament has been taken up — in what? — in examining horse-waterers and newspaper-jackals!" *

During these contests with the House of Commons, and in fact by means of them, the popularity of Wilkes in the City rose higher and higher. In January he was chosen Alderman of the Ward of Farringdon Without, polling thirteen hundred out of fifteen hundred votes. And thus did Wilkes become by right of office a magistrate of the metropolis while still denounced by the law as a criminal, and confined by the Government as a prisoner.

These were by no means the only incidents that arose collaterally in the case of Wilkes, but to recount them all in minute detail would be, as I conceive, both tedious and unprofitable. On the 3d of February Lord Barrington brought forward the decisive motion, first recapitulating the offences of Wilkes and the judgments against him, and then proposing that he "be expelled this House." It was natural that Honourable Members deserving of the epithet should view the election of Wilkes as an insult, and his sitting amongst them as a contamination. It was natural also that such feelings should be shared, as shared they were by a man so upright and high minded as the King.† But indignation, however just, is no safe counsellor in State affairs. Some cool observers, among whom was Horace Walpole, thought that considering Wilkes's utter want of Parliamentary ability, the House of Commons was the very place where he could do the least mischief.‡ A similar point was

* Cavendish Debates, vol. i. p. 111.

† So early as April 25. 1768, I find the King write as follows to Lord North: "Though entirely relying on your attachment to my person as well as on your hatred of any lawless proceeding, yet I think it highly expedient to apprise you that the expulsion of Mr. Wilkes appears to be highly expedient, and must be effected. The case of Mr. Ward in the reign of my great grandfather seems to point out the proper mode of proceeding." (MS. Extracts.) John Ward of Hackney being convicted of forgery had been expelled the House in May 1727.

‡ H. Walpole to Sir H. Mann, March 31. 1768.

urged with great force by George Grenville. If, he cried, we expel Mr. Wilkes, and if afterwards any untoward accident or sudden distress should befal us, what then will the common people say?—"Aye, if Master "Wilkes had been in the House he would have prevented "it; they knew that, and therefore would not suffer him "to come amongst them!"

But this was not the argument on which Grenville mainly relied. In his most able speech on this occasion, the best perhaps that he ever made, he pointed out the Constitutional objections to an expulsion on such grounds, and warned the House against the perilous contest in which it was engaging. Many of the friends of Government were shaken in their purpose; Dunning, though Solicitor General, remained absent; and General Conway left the House without voting. Nevertheless such numbers still remained that the proposed expulsion was carried by a majority of 82, and a new Writ for Middlesex was consequently issued. And thus ends, said Burke, the last act of this tragi-comedy; a tragi-comedy acted "by His Majesty's Servants," at the express desire of several persons of quality, for the benefit of Mr. Wilkes, and at the expense of the Constitution!

It soon appeared, however, that this act was by no means the last. The freeholders of Middlesex took fire at the indignity attempted to be set upon their representative. At a meeting held in the assembly room of Mile End it was formally resolved to put him again in nomination. Such was the enthusiasm that at Brentford no other candidate durst appear upon the hustings, and Wilkes was unanimously re-elected, all the proceedings being carried on with the most strict and studied order so as to afford no ground or plea for a petition.

The prevailing party in the House of Commons had now no other choice,—so at least it seemed to themselves,—than to pursue the path which they had entered. A motion was made to the effect that John Wilkes, Esquire, having been once expelled, was incapable of being returned to the same parliament. For such a course the precedent mainly cited and relied on was that of Robert Walpole in 1712. "But at this rate," said Mr. Dowdeswell, "no man's seat will be secure. There "is one worst man in the House—turn him out! Is "there not now a worst man left?—turn him out too! "In short when will you stop?"—Against the motion there were likewise speeches from all the other chief men in the Opposition ranks: Burke and Barré, Sir George Savile and Alderman Beckford, Serjeant Glynn and Grenville. Nevertheless a majority even much larger than on the last occasion,—a majority increased from 82 to 146,—affirmed the incapacity of Wilkes, and declared the last election for Middlesex to be null and void.

At the news of this decision the popular flame only blazed the higher. Another meeting was held at Mile End, and proved to the full as zealous as the first. At the London Tavern many gentlemen of note assembled, and set on foot a subscription not only to defray the election expenses of Wilkes, but also to free him from his private debts and liabilities. A sum amounting to upwards of 3,000*l.* was subscribed in the room, and many more donations speedily accrued. At the next meeting of these gentlemen they assumed the name of "Supporters of the "Bill of Rights;" and the Society thus formed grew for a time to some importance, taking part in political discussions not less than in pecuniary affairs.*

At the King's Arms Tavern a meeting of some gentlemen was attempted on the opposite side. This was promoted chiefly by Mr. Dingley, a mercantile speculator, who desired to become the Ministerial candidate for Middlesex. A loyal Address to the King was prepared and agreed to, and other measures were designed; but a party of the Wilkites breaking in, a scuffle ensued, and the gentlemen dispersed. On their way some time afterwards to present their Address at St. James's they were again assailed with insult and violence. A hearse had been made ready to precede them adorned with paintings of the death of Allen; and their coaches were pelted with mud and stones, several among them being compelled to turn back. It was attempted to continue such outrages

* An account of the origin and first proceedings of this Society is given in Almon's Memoirs and Correspondence of Wilkes, vol. iv. p. 7—14.

even within the palace gates, but the Lord Steward, Earl Talbot, a bold resolute man, stepped forward, and though deserted by his own servants, secured two of the most forward of the rioters with his own hands.

A new incident at this period added not a little to the popular flame. At the election of Serjeant Glynn for Middlesex in the previous December Mr. Clarke, one of his supporters, had been struck by two chairmen of the opposite party, and soon afterwards died. Against these chairmen, whose names were Balfe and Macquirk, a verdict of Wilful Murder was returned by an exasperated Jury. A doubt, however, had arisen as to the true cause of the death of Mr. Clarke. His Majesty through the Secretary of State referred this point to the examination of the College of Surgeons, who gave it as their unanimous opinion that Mr. Clarke had not died from the consequences of the blow he had received. Upon this as a matter of course a free pardon was granted to Macquirk and to Balfe.—Clear and plain as this transaction seems, it provoked at the time much popular resentment, and afforded materials to Junius for one of his most venomous attacks.*

Another step, far from welcome at this critical period, was taken—not in right season surely—by Lord North. He proposed to the House of Commons to grant half a million for the discharge of the debts upon the Civil List of 800,000*l.* a year. The money was voted, but invidious comments, both in the House and out of it, were not forborne.—In all personal tastes and habits George the Third, as I have elsewhere shown, was beyond most men plain, unpretending, and domestic. But the expenses in the various departments of State in the Royal Household, and the profits and perquisites expected from them, were enormous, growing as yet without the check of any due system of control. Thus, for instance, the state-coach built in 1762 had been charged to His Majesty at no less a sum than 7,562*l.*† Such were the magnitude and extent of these abuses as to need for their correction

* Letter to the Duke of Grafton, March 18. 1769.

† See the items in the Annual Register, 1768, part ii. p. 138.

some years later all the ability of Burke and all the authority of Parliament.

Amidst such a combination of untoward circumstances came on the new election at Brentford. Mr. Dingley — "the miserable Dingley," as Junius calls him, — had announced himself as a candidate, but being roughly handled by the populace did not venture to urge his claim, nor to appear upon the hustings. Again therefore was Wilkes unanimously returned as the Member of Middlesex. Again did the House of Commons declare his incapacity, vote his election to be null and void, and issue a new Writ for the county. On this occasion, however, the Ministers took care to provide a candidate of their own. Colonel Henry Lawes Luttrell, son of Lord Irnham, and member for Bossiney, was persuaded by his friends in office to relinquish his safe seat and to stand for Middlesex. As the appointed time for this election (the 13th of April) drew near great fears were entertained of tumults and riots on that day; but none at all occurred, so careful were the people to cast no slur or discredit on their cause, or so placable from the sure confidence of victory. The nomination took place in perfect order; Stephen Fox, eldest son of Lord Holland, proposing Mr. Luttrell. The polling followed in due course, when it appeared that in a few hours Wilkes obtained upwards of eleven hundred votes, and Luttrell less than three hundred. — A large party of the freeholders on horseback, with colours flying and music playing, and blue ribands streaming from their hats, rode to the King's Bench prison to congratulate Wilkes upon his triumph; and at night illuminations ensued through all the city.

Thus was Wilkes for the fourth time proclaimed Knight of this great Shire. The result had been foreseen by the Ministers as inevitable, but as they hoped would be provided against through their care. Mr. Onslow, son of the late Speaker, and member for Surrey, brought forward a motion, supported by the whole strength of Government, that not Wilkes but Luttrell should have been returned at this election; thus, in fact, bestowing the seat upon the latter. Long and fierce was the discussion which arose, and the motion was carried by a majority reduced to 54. Shortly afterwards, on the last day but one of the Session, the subject was renewed on a petition of the freeholders of Middlesex against this vote, when after another keen debate the original decision was affirmed.

A step so violent and so unpopular was defended by Lord North and his friends with some force on the ground of expediency. Must not the House of Commons maintain its own determination, so recently and so solemnly taken, of closing its doors on Mr. Wilkes; and if so, would not utter confusion and disgrace attend a longer struggle,—an interminable series of expulsions by the House and of elections by the county? It may in fairness be acknowledged that the Ministerial majority had scarcely left themselves any other course to follow. But on the ground of Constitutional right their arguments were weak indeed! There were ample precedents, no doubt, for excluding any Member subject by law to disability, and for seating in his place a candidate who had obtained a much smaller number of votes. But here lies the distinction, and it is a vital one,—that Wilkes was not subject to disability by any law, but only by a Resolution of the House of Commons. Therefore to exclude him as not eligible, and to seat another candidate in his place, was to make a Resolution by one branch of the Legislature equal to the Law by all three; and that, moreover, on the tenderest of all points, as touching the freedom of election. It might seem to be a question, if such a course were followed, whether henceforth the country was to choose Members for the House of Commons, or the House of Commons to choose Members for the country. With these views full upon the public mind, the following words which fell in debate from Mr. Henry Cavendish were warmly applauded and adopted; they were called "Mr. Cavendish's Creed," and were drunk as a toast at political dinners. "I do from my "soul detest and abjure as unconstitutional and illegal "that damnable doctrine and position that a Resolution "of the House of Commons can make, alter, suspend, "abrogate, or annihilate the Law of the Land."* At

* Compare a note in the Chatham Correspondence, vol. iii. p. 360. with the Cavendish Debates, vol. i. p. 428. Mr. Henry Cavendish was

the present day few or none could be found to controvert that Creed, though many in the House of Commons are still eager on occasion to set Privilege above Statute; they are still heretics in action, though at last orthodox in faith.

In 1769 the course of the Duke of Grafton and Lord North in Wilkes's case was much disapproved by Lord Chancellor Camden, who nevertheless consented to remain their colleague. A support far more strenuous was afforded them by another great lawyer, Mr. Blackstone, sometimes called Dr. Blackstone, as practising in Doctors Commons. He was at this time Solicitor General to the Queen and Member for Westbury, but became promoted to a judgeship in the ensuing year. Only the first volume of those Commentaries which have since given lustre to his name had as yet appeared. In his speech on this occasion he warmly maintained the legal incapacity of Wilkes, but was answered by Mr. Grenville from a passage in his own book where all the rightful grounds of disqualification were enumerated, and where no such case as Wilkes's was assigned. Hence there grew to be another favourite toast at the Opposition banquets: "The First edition of Dr. Blackstone's "Commentaries on the Laws of England." Still more bitter is the taunt of Junius: "For the defence of truth, "of law and reason, the Doctor's book may be safely "consulted; but whoever wishes to cheat a neighbour "of his estate, or to rob a country of its rights, need "make no scruple of consulting the Doctor himself!"*

Thus at the close of the Session of 1769 the Court party had prevailed in their favourite object—the exclusion of Wilkes from the House of Commons. But

in descent an illegitimate scion of the great house of Devonshire. In 1776 he became a Baronet on the death of his father, and in 1792 his wife was raised to the Irish peerage as Baroness Waterpark. The MS. notes which he took of the debates in the House of Commons from 1768 to 1774 were partly published in 1841, and were ably edited by Mr. Wright, although their own historical value has been perhaps a little overrated. Some of the most important debates of the period (as those in January 1770) are wholly omitted by Sir Henry.

* Letter xiv., June 22. 1769.

how heavy was the cost of that insignificant victory! Wilkes had in consequence grown to be the idol of the people, the champion as they deemed of the Constitution; and from within his prison walls he wielded a more powerful and extensive influence than as a member of the Legislature he could ever have attained. Meetings were held in various places—as in Westminster among the cities, and in Yorkshire among the counties,—to declare that the people had lost all confidence in their present representatives, and praying His Majesty to exert his prerogative for a Dissolution. In the autumn there came on for trial the long pending action of Wilkes against Lord Halifax as Secretary of State for the seizure of his papers, when the jury gave a verdict in Wilkes's favour, and awarded him for damages no less than 4,000*l.* Large as these damages may seem, they by no means fulfilled the eager expectations of the populace; and the jurymen were obliged to withdraw privately for fear of insults by the way. But perhaps the strongest testimony to the extent of the popular agitation at this period is afforded by a most shrewd observer, Benjamin Franklin, then resident in London. Many years afterwards at Paris in conversation with Lord Fitzmaurice he was, as he tells us himself, descanting on the value of fair repute with the world. He adds: "To express my "sense of the importance of a good private character in "public affairs more strongly, I said that I even believed "if George the Third had had a bad private character, "and John Wilkes a good one, the latter might have "turned the former out of the kingdom!"*

From Franklin the transition is easy to Franklin's native country. There the import duties laid on in 1767 had unhappily revived all the dissensions of the Stamp Act. The ferment increased when the new Commissioners, appointed to enforce and direct these duties, were seen to land and to fix themselves at Boston. For this reason, among others, Boston took the lead in opposing them. So early as October 1767 the principal gentlemen of the town had met and formed a non-importation agreement; that is, they had subscribed a bond pledging

* Private Diary, July 27. 1784.

themselves to encourage the consumption of their own manufactures, and to buy nothing from Great Britain beyond a few articles of indispensable necessity. Great efforts were also made through the American press. In Massachusetts Mr. James Otis was forward in circulating the Resolutions of the Assembly, which he had been no less forward in urging *; and in another quarter Mr. John Dickinson wrote the well-known "Letters "from a Farmer in Pennsylvania." Some members of the Government in England it appears suspected Franklin as the author of that most popular work. In fact, however, he had merely republished it in London with a preface of his own †; and he also upon the strength of it retracted his former opinion, so confidently given, as to the just difference to be made between internal taxation and external. But in private he could not always forbear a little civil scorn at the want of logic in these and the like effusions. "I know not what the Boston people "mean; what is the subordination they acknowledge in "their Assembly to Parliament, while they deny its "power to make laws for them?" ‡

The Governor of Massachusetts at this time was Francis Bernard, afterwards Sir Francis, a man of ability and firmness, but harsh and quarrelsome. He had become much disliked by the Assembly of the province from their conviction, — certainly well-founded, — that he constantly wrote home the most unfavourable statements of their motives and designs. Between him and them there now arose a long train of painful altercations. They complained especially of his conduct in refusing to confirm the nomination of several members of the Council, and of a letter from Lord Shelburne which had approved that conduct. In February 1768, notwithstanding his most earnest endeavours, they addressed a Circular Letter to all the other Colonies, inviting them

* Of Mr. Otis's own pamphlets on Colonial rights the first had appeared in the summer of 1764. Yet in 1765, on reading the Virginian Resolutions, he declared them "a treasonable composition." See Grahame's History, vol. iv. p. 185. and 271.

† Works, vol. iv. p. 256. The date of the Preface is May 8. 1768; it is signed only N. N.

‡ To his son, March 13. 1768. Works, vol. vii. p. 391.

to take measures to defeat the obnoxious taxes latterly imposed. The terms of that letter must be acknowledged as moderate, but its purport might be suspected as dangerous. At all events it gave the utmost displeasure to Lord Hillsborough, the new Secretary of State for America. He directed Governor Bernard to require of the Assembly that they should rescind the Resolution on which their Circular Letter was founded. This they refused to do. "If the votes of this House," they said, "are to be controlled by a Minister, we have left us but "a vain semblance of liberty." In that spirit several of their Members who had voted against the Resolution for the Circular Letter, now gave their votes against rescinding it; and thus on the division there appeared ninety-two Nays with only seventeen Ayes.—Upon this, according to Lord Hillsborough's positive instructions, they were immediately dissolved.

This irritating Dissolution took place on the 1st of July 1768. Only twenty days before, another incident had happened not less untoward, and adding full as much to the popular ferment which prevailed. A sloop named the "Liberty," and belonging to Mr. John Hancock, a merchant of Boston, had anchored in the harbour laden with wine from Madeira. According to one of the American authorities, "it had been a common practice, "upon the arrival of a vessel, for the tide-waiter to "repair to the cabin, and there to remain drinking "punch with the master, while the sailors and others "upon deck were employed in landing the goods;"* the goods in this manner being landed duty-free. But the new Commissioners, as was their duty, had determined to enforce the law. On this occasion, therefore, the tide-waiter when he came on board refused not only the usual punch, but several other, perhaps more tempting, "proposals;" upon which the skipper laid violent hands upon him, locked him up in the cabin, and carried the wine to shore without further ceremony. Next morning he entered a few pipes of his Madeira at the custom-house, declaring that they had formed the whole cargo; but the Commissioners knowing the contrary ordered

* Dr. Gordon's History of the Revolution, vol. i. p. 230.

the sloop to be seized in the King's name, and for security to be towed under the guns of the Romney man-of-war. As the sloop was being moved from the wharf there gathered on the shore a great mob, consisting chiefly of boys and negroes, but urged on by Malcolm, a captain in the smuggling trade; and they assaulted the custom-house officers with the utmost violence. On the ensuing day the tumult was renewed. The houses of the Commissioners and other officers of the customs were attacked and their windows broken, and their collector's boat was dragged through the town to the Common, where it served for a bonfire. Meanwhile the Commissioners in terror for their lives fled for refuge to Castle William, a fortress at the mouth of the harbour.

Neither the Assembly, which was still sitting at the time, nor yet the leading merchants of the town, appear to have shown any great zeal to check the riot or chastise the rioters. They were far more ready to complain of the insult which they said they had sustained by the removal of the sloop from the wharf, since this removal implied the apprehension or allowed the possibility that such good worthy men as they were could ever be guilty of a rescue. They offered a reward, however, for the discovery of the ringleaders in the affray, and some of the lower orders were pointed out as such, but Malcolm himself, the chief abettor of these riots, and other men like Malcolm sat upon the Grand Jury and prevented true bills being found.

It was in the midst of the twofold agitation arising from the seizure of the sloop and the dissolution of the Assembly that a fresh source of difference unhappily sprung forth. Governor Bernard and the Board of Commissioners at Boston had for some time past represented to the Ministry their apprehension of disturbance, and their desire of an armed force for their support. Lord Hillsborough had taken measures accordingly; he informed Governor Bernard that orders had been sent to General Gage as Commander-in-chief for North America to despatch from Halifax to Boston two regiments and four ships of war. It so chanced that Lord Hillsborough had sat down to write that letter at St. James's on nearly the same day that Hancock's sloop—the cause of so grievous riots—had anchored at Boston. But the subsequent experience of these riots did not serve as any justification of that letter in the eyes of the New Englanders. The utmost irritation prevailed at Boston at the news, early in September, that troops were coming. A meeting of the inhabitants was immediately summoned. There a Committee of management was appointed, and a Resolution was passed: "That as there is an apprehen-"sion in the minds of many of an approaching war with "France, those inhabitants who are not provided be re-"quested to furnish themselves forthwith with arms." It is scarcely needful to add that no such idea of a war with France was really entertained, and that arms were desired with a wholly different view. Even amidst the irritation of that time there were not wanting many loyal men in Boston to reprobate loudly both the factiousness of the proposal and the falsehood of the plea.*

In a more peaceful spirit the Boston meeting desired the Ministers of the town to set apart an early day for fasting and prayer throughout the province. They also addressed a petition to the Governor, referring to his dissolution of the late Assembly, and requesting him to call another forthwith. Mr. Bernard in reply declined to do so unless he should receive His Majesty's commands to that effect. The petitioners were well aware that according to the terms of their Charter a new Assembly could not be postponed beyond the month of May ensuing. Such delay, however, in their then excited state seemed to them intolerable. They resolved to hold an Assembly through their own act and by another name. A "Convention" was summoned to meet at Boston before the close of the month, to consist of deputies, or, as they were termed, "Committee-men," from the several districts and towns in Massachusetts. Elections accordingly ensued, and on the 22d of September the Members sent to this Convention met in Faneuil Hall, so called from Peter Faneuil, a wealthy citizen, who had built and bequeathed it to the town.† On their meeting the Governor addressed to them a letter in a firm yet temperate tone;

* Note to Mr. Grahame's History, vol. iv. p. 274.

† Holmes's Annals, vol. ii. p. 20. ed. 1829.

he told them that as a friend to the province he must warn them of the perilous and illegal path they were about to tread. Either his firmness or their own returning sense of moderation (to say nothing of the daily expected arrival of the troops) caused them, it would seem, to falter and recede from their first design. After only five or six days of sitting, several communications with the Governor, and one petition to the King, they quietly dissolved themselves.

On the very day of this Dissolution the ships of war from Halifax cast anchor in the port; and the soldiers—seven hundred in number, commanded by Colonel Dalrymple,—prepared to come on shore. Great difficulty was made by the Council in providing them quarters*, and great dissatisfaction was expressed by the inhabitants at the unhallowed sound of many a fife and trumpet, which even on the Sunday did not wholly cease its clangour. Thus did Boston from a mart of commerce bear for a while the aspect of a garrison-town; and other detachments speedily arriving, no less than four regiments were mustered within its walls. Quiet was maintained, but content was not restored.

It is not to be supposed that the ferment in any other Colonies of North America,—and in some there was, it may be said, no ferment at all,—bore any proportion to that in Massachusetts. In no other had the King's Representative given so much provocation. In no other was there the same Cromwellian leaven at work. Yet still the Circular from Boston of February 1768 found an echo, though a fainter one, in many places. Non-importation agreements were formed far and wide by the "Sons "of Liberty," for thus did the Opposition parties in

* Bernard's despatches on this subject were communicated from England to the Members of the Council, and by them were published, with a very able counter-statement of their own, dated April 15. 1769. In this they observe: "It hath been the happiness of His "Majesty's Council from the grant of the Charter till lately to be on "the best terms with the King's Representative. There have indeed "been frequent disputes between the Governor and the House of "Representatives, but never that we know of between the Governor "and the Council till now. That it is so at this day is our unhap-"piness, not our crime."

America continue since 1765 to call themselves. Even ladies, assuming the name of "Daughters of Liberty," combined among themselves to refrain from the use of tea. Such merchants as hung back and refused to take part in these associations were in many cases goaded forwards and compelled to sign by threats or even deeds of violence. In several Colonies, moreover, dissensions arose and grew between the Governor and the Assembly, — not always prudently conducted by the former. Indeed the ill-choice of such officers in England deserves to be noted as among the secondary causes of the Revolution which ensued. On this point no testimony given on either side since the commencement of the troubles can be deemed wholly free from suspicion. But here are some words from a private letter, written by a meritorious officer, General Huske, so far back as 1758: "As to the civil "officers appointed for America, most of places in the "gift of the Crown have been filled with broken Mem-"bers of Parliament of bad, if any, principles, valets-de-"chambre, electioneering scoundrels, and even livery "servants. In one word, America has been for many "years made the hospital of England."* I may add, that even at the present time abuses of this kind have not altogether ceased.

At the meeting of Parliament in November 1768 the news from America, and above all from Massachusetts, could not fail to engage the earnest attention of both Houses. On Lord Hillsborough's motion they passed votes of censure on several measures of the late Assembly and of the Meetings of Boston. That censure on their part might be just, but whether it was also politic may be fairly questioned. Such as it was, it proved by no means sufficient to satisfy the more eager opponents of the American pretensions. Foremost among these was the Duke of Bedford. It seemed to his Grace, as to many others besides, that the partiality of the Boston jury to the rioters had been so flagrant and so heinous that no juries in that whole Colony could hereafter be relied on. Accordingly he proposed and carried through

* This remarkable letter is published in Mr. Phillimore's Memoirs of Lord Lyttleton, vol. ii. p. 604.

both Houses a joint Address to the King, entreating His Majesty to obtain the fullest information respecting the actors in the late outrages, so that His Majesty might then, if he saw sufficient grounds for such a course, set in force against them a statute passed in the thirty-fifth year of King Henry the Eighth, and under that statute direct them to be brought over to England and tried before a Special Commission. Thus was it designed to draw forth the mouldering edict of a tyrant from the dust where it had long lain, and where it ever deserved to lie, and to fling it—instead of bread, a stone,—not merely at the guilty, but also at the innocent, whom it equally despoiled of their rightful native Juries! Such a proposal, made at such a time, to me at least appears utterly unjustifiable. Well and truly and almost prophetically might Burke exclaim in these debates: "If "your remedy is such as is not likely to appease the "Americans, but rather to exasperate them, you fire a "cannon upon your enemy which will recoil upon your-"selves. And why take such a course? Because, as "you say, you cannot trust a Jury of that country. Sir, "that word must convey horror to every feeling mind. "If you have not a party among two millions of people, "you must either change your plan of government or "renounce your Colonies for ever." *

In pursuance of the same views of policy it was thought proper to reward Governor Bernard, and the King at this very period was advised to bestow the dignity of Baronet upon him,—a most ill-timed favour surely when he had so grievously failed in gaining the affections or the confidence of any order or rank of men within his province; when even the Council, that steady friend of all former Governors, had become his enemy; when even Members of that Council had sent home a petition for his recall.—Success is indeed no unerring test of merit, but for promotions it is probably the surest guide.

A more important question still remained,—whether the new import-duties laid upon America should or should not be persevered in. The latter alternative was urged

* Speech, January 26. 1769. Cavendish Debates, vol. i. p. 199.

in Parliament by Governor Pownall* and some others, but the Ministers gave equivocal replies, and had come as yet to no decision among themselves. At last a Cabinet-meeting was held upon it on the 1st of May. The Duke of Grafton as Prime Minister proposed to his colleagues that at the commencement of next Session they should bring in a Bill for the complete repeal of these obnoxious duties. Lord North, on the other hand, thought that a concession so entire might argue timidity and weakness in those who made it. He desired rather that, so far at least as any present promise or announcement was concerned, the article of Teas might be excepted from the repeal. On a division the proposal of Grafton was rejected by the casting vote of one, — that one Lord Rochford, whom the Duke himself had so lately nominated as his colleague! The Duke in his Memoirs enumerates this result among the evil consequences which he ascribes to Lord Chatham's resignation. "But for that unhappy "event," says he, "I must think that the separation from "America might have been avoided. For in the following "spring Lord Chatham was sufficiently recovered to have "given his effectual support in the Cabinet to Lords "Camden and Granby and General Conway, who with "myself were overruled in our best endeavours to include "the article of Teas with the other duties intended to be "repealed." — The Duke adds, that from this time forward he felt himself ill at ease in his high post. Lord Camden on his part was so much offended at finding his opinion set aside both in that affair and in Wilkes's, that although he continued to hold the Seal of Chancellor, he ceased to attend the meetings of the Cabinet.

The Session was closed on the 9th of May, and four days afterwards Lord Hillsborough communicated the resolution of his colleagues in a Circular Letter addressed to the Governors of the several Colonies in North America.

* Mr. Pownall had been Governor of Massachusetts, and still retained the title. He was a worthy well-meaning man, and often spoke on Colonial affairs, but in a very tedious strain, so that as Franklin laments, "he is very ill heard at present." (To Dr. Cooper, Feb. 24. 1770.) It is probable therefore that very little of his speeches would have reached posterity had they not been carefully reported by himself.

That letter was drawn up in harsh and ungracious terms, and omitted all those softening expressions which the minority in the Cabinet had, as they thought, prevailed in introducing. No wonder that concessions so curtailed in their amount, and so far from courteous in their announcement, gave little satisfaction, and called forth little gratitude.

CHAPTER XLVIII.

A FEW weeks only after Lord Chatham's resignation his gout so long intermitted, but for some time past giving symptoms of approach, returned.* Bowed down as he was by a far more grievous malady, it proved to him a healing visitation. It raised his drooping spirits, and it strung his feeble nerves. The clouds which had obscured that great intellect wholly passed away. Never indeed, as we shall see hereafter, did either his splendid eloquence or his wise and resolute counsels shine forth more brightly than during the next following years.

Another event which followed close upon Lord Chatham's retirement from office was his reconciliation with the Grenvilles. At his desire Lord Temple came down to visit him at Hayes, and departed on most friendly terms both private and political. An event so favourable to Lord Temple's views of ambition was not likely to remain a secret in his hands. He took care to have it announced in the publications of the day with no small pomp, and—since this alliance had already proved unstable—with a prophecy of its eternal duration; just as the frailest ladies are ever the most prodigal in their vows of constancy.†

Some considerable time, however, still elapsed ere Lord Chatham resumed his part in public affairs. His first appearance beyond his own domestic circle was at the Levee in July 1769 to present his duty to the King. Men

* "Lord Chatham has got a regular fit of the gout after so long "an intermission. Many think this indicates his re-appearance." (H. Walpole to Sir H. Mann, Nov. 18. 1768.) Another fit of gout occurred in the March following. (Chatham Correspondence, vol. iii. p. 351.)

† "In consequence of repeated solicitations on the part of the Earl "of Chatham a most cordial, firm, and perpetual union this day took "place with his noble brother-in-law, Earl Temple. Mr. Grenville "has heartily acceded." Political Register, Nov. 25. 1768.

gazed at him with eager curiosity as on one risen from the grave; above two years and a half had elapsed since he last had shown himself in public. The King was very gracious, and whispered him to come into the Closet after the Levee, which Lord Chatham did accordingly, and remained in conversation with His Majesty for twenty minutes.* He stated his objection to the course pursued both in Wilkes's case and in East India affairs, but added that with his broken health he could have no desire of office, and that therefore if in Parliament he should dissent from any of the Ministerial measures he hoped His Majesty would do him the justice to believe that it would not arise from any interested views. To the Duke of Grafton at this Levee he behaved with only cold politeness, — much to the chagrin of his Grace, whose feelings of respect and admiration for Lord Chatham had not at all abated.

The fact of Lord Chatham's conversation with his Majesty (the last that ever took place between them) was speedily noised abroad, but its details remained unknown, and thus a large scope was left to rumours and conjectures. Perhaps he was sent for, says Burke, or perhaps he came of his own accord, "to talk some significant, "pompous, creeping, explanatory, ambiguous matter in "the true Chathamic style!"† These words, it must be owned, describe with considerable aptness, though not without exaggeration,—as even now we may trace them, — Lord Chatham's epistolary faults. "The best orator "and the worst letter-writer of our age!" cries Wilkes.‡

Of these two unfriendly critics, the former, writing from Beaconsfield, portrays with no less graphic force the unusual pomp and needless train of servants that

* The Court was surprised with an unexpected phenomenon. ". . . . . . He (Lord Chatham) was perfectly well, and had grown "fat." (Lord Orford's Memoirs, vol. iii. p. 373.) See in my Appendix a minute of Lord Chatham's conversation with the King as taken down by the Duke of Grafton the same evening, no doubt on His Majesty's report.

† To Lord Rockingham, Beaconsfield, July 9. 1769. Correspondence, vol. i. p. 173.

‡ To Humphrey Cotes, December 4. 1765. Memoirs, &c. vol. ii. p. 217.

Chatham maintained. The "Great Earl" was then on his way to Lord Temple's,—his first visit since their reconciliation. "I ought to tell you," says Burke, "that "Lord Chatham passed by my door on Friday morning "in a JIMWHISKEE drawn by two horses, one before the "other; he drove himself. His train was two coaches "and six, with twenty servants, male and female. He "was proceeding with his whole family, Lady Chatham, "two sons, and two daughters, to Stowe." *

Thus, according to Burke's description, did Lord Chatham proceed on his visit to Stowe, Lord Temple's mansion, where he was warmly received, and where the freeholders drank to the union of the three brothers. The rest of the summer and autumn he passed at Chevening, which his kinsman and friend Lord Stanhope had placed at his disposal during his own absence abroad.

Lord Chatham now was eager for the opportunity of declaring his views in Parliament. Accordingly he did not fail to appear in his place at the opening of the next Session on the 9th of January following. The King's Speech on that occasion began by lamenting a distemper which had lately broke out among the Horned Cattle of the kingdom, and towards the checking of which some measures had been taken by the Privy Council without the assent of Parliament. Much ridicule at the time was showered upon this reference in the Royal Speech; the whole Session was in consequence surnamed the "Horned-"Cattle Session;" and Junius, for example, charged the Duke of Grafton with having put into His Majesty's mouth not the true sentiments of a King, but rather "the misery of a ruined grazier." † Trifling indeed might this calamity appear to those in whose eyes the squabbles of party and the prizes of office were alone important! Yet since we find that the murrain had been so destructive and deadly that public prayers for its cessation were offered up in the churches, we may presume to think it not altogether beneath the dignity of the Royal notice.

After this mention of the Horned Cattle the King's

* To Lord Rockingham, July 30. 1769.

† Letter xxxvi., February 14. 1770.

Speech touched generally on foreign affairs; recommended to attention the North American Colonies, to some proceedings in which the epithet of "highly un-"warrantable" was applied; and concluded with an earnest exhortation to both Houses to avoid all heats and animosities among themselves. The Address in reply was moved by the Duke of Ancaster, and seconded by the Earl of Dunmore. No sooner had Dunmore sat down than Chatham rose. He began with some expressions of his loyalty and duty to the King, and proceeded to bewail the unsatisfactory state of our foreign affairs, which he ascribed to the manner in which the treaty of Paris was concluded. Having then, he said, deserted our allies we were left without alliances, and during a peace of seven years had been every moment on the verge of a war; while, on the contrary, France had carefully cherished her alliances, especially with Spain. But important as foreign affairs might be at this juncture, he felt that they sunk to nothing when compared to the distractions and divisions within our own empire. Here he lamented the unhappy measures which had estranged the Colonies from the mother country, and which he feared had drawn them into excesses that he could not justify. He owned his natural partiality to America, and was inclined to make allowance even for those excesses. They ought to be treated with tenderness, for in his judgment they were ebullitions of liberty which broke out upon the skin, and were a sign, if not of perfect health, at least of vigorous constitution, and must not be driven in too suddenly lest they should strike to the heart. With such feelings he objected to the word "unwarrantable" in the proposed Address. The Americans, he cried, had purchased their liberty at a dear rate; they had left their native country and gone in search of freedom to a desert! — Passing from these topics, Lord Chatham inveighed in the strongest terms against the votes of the House of Commons seating Luttrell in the place of Wilkes, which he pronounced to be a flagrant outrage against the common right of the subject, and the real root of the public discontents; and he concluded by moving an Amendment that the House would with all convenient speed take into their most serious consideration "the late proceedings in the House "of Commons touching the incapacity of John Wilkes, "Esquire."

It is truly astonishing, even on the fullest admission of Chatham's weight and abilities, how great was the effect of this his return to public life, and declaration of his sentiments. It immediately produced a Ministerial crisis as keen and strange as any in our party annals. It stirred at that very hour Lord Chancellor Camden to cast aside his recent reserve, or acquiescence in measures that he disapproved, and to take henceforward a firmer and a nobler course. Rising with much emotion from the Woolsack he spoke nearly as follows: "I accepted the "Great Seal without conditions: I meant not therefore "to be trammelled by His Majesty, — I beg pardon, by "His Majesty's Ministers, but I have suffered myself to "be so too long. For some time I have beheld with "silent indignation the arbitrary measures of the Min-"ister; I have often drooped and hung down my head "in Council, and disapproved by my looks those steps "which I knew my avowed opposition could not prevent. "I will do so no longer, but openly and boldly speak my "sentiments. I now proclaim to the world that I entirely "coincide in the opinion expressed by my Noble Friend, "whose presence again reanimates us, touching this un-"constitutional and illegal vote of the House of Commons. "If in giving my opinion as a Judge I were to pay any "respect to that vote I should look upon myself as a "traitor to my trust and an enemy to my country. By "their violent and tyrannical conduct Ministers have "alienated the minds of the people from His Majesty's "government, — I had almost said from His Majesty's "person!"

The Earl of Marchmont, Lord Lyttleton, and perhaps other Peers also, took part in this debate. Lord Mansfield especially referring to Lord Chatham's amendment condemned it as an encroachment on the privileges of the other House, and adverting to the measures of the Government in the case of Wilkes offered for them an apology, — for so qualified was his language that it could scarcely be called a defence. The Government, however, had no reason to rejoice in his advocacy, able as it was, since it immediately called forth from Lord Chatham a reply, or rather a second speech. In that second speech occurs his celebrated burst of eloquence on the old Magna Charta Barons. "They did not," cried Chatham, "con-" fine to themselves alone that great acknowledgment of "national rights which they had wrested from their "Sovereign, but delivered it as a common blessing to the "whole people. They did not say, these are the rights "of the great Barons, or these are the rights of the great "Prelates. No, my Lords, they said in the simple Latin "of the times: NULLUS LIBER HOMO, — uncouth words, "and sounding but poorly in the ears of scholars, but "they have a meaning which interests us all; these three "words are worth all the classics. Those Iron Barons, "for so I may call them when compared with the Silken "Barons of modern days, were the guardians of the "people; yet their virtues, my Lords, were never en-" gaged in a question of such importance as the present. "A breach has been made in the Constitution, — the "battlements are dismantled, — the citadel is open to the "first invader, — the walls totter, — the Constitution is "not tenable. What remains then but for us to stand "foremost in the breach to repair it or perish in it?"

The amendment of Lord Chatham was negatived by a large majority of the Peers, but Lord Rockingham desired that their Lordships might be summoned for the morrow, as he intended to bring forward a motion of great importance on the state of the nation. The Ministers pleaded, as they reasonably might, for further delay, and this was granted, though not without demur. Lord Temple said: "It is clear to the House for what purpose "an adjournment is sought, — to dismiss the virtuous "and independent Lord who sits on the woolsack, and to "supply his place with some obsequious lawyer who "would do as he was commanded!" And Lord Shelburne added: "The Seals it seems are to go a-begging; "but I hope there will not be found in the kingdom a "wretch so base and mean-spirited as to accept of them "on the conditions on which they must be offered!"

In the other House that day the scene was far less interesting and important. There also, however, an amendment was brought forward, being moved by Mr. Dowdeswell, and supported by a large minority. For that amendment the Marquis of Granby both spoke and voted, though still Commander in Chief and a Member of the Cabinet. His Lordship took this occasion to express his sorrow for the vote which he had rashly given last Session declaring the incapacity of Wilkes.

Notwithstanding the course thus publicly taken by Lord Granby, both the King and the Duke of Grafton were earnest with him to continue in office. But he resisted all their entreaties, and after a few days resigned all his employments. Lord Camden, on the other hand, determined by the advice of his personal friends to forbear from resignation, and to leave the invidious task of removing him to his recent colleagues and present adversaries. Under these circumstances the Duke of Grafton applied to Charles Yorke. The Great Seal, the darling object of his life, was now at last within the reach of that accomplished and amiable man. Yet though within his reach, his hand was not free to grasp it. The offer found him closely bound and pledged to Lord Rockingham's party. He took a day for deliberation, during which he consulted both his brother, Lord Hardwicke, and his chief, Lord Rockingham, and yielding to their influence he reluctantly declined the glittering prize.

Three days afterwards there was a Levee at St. James's, which Mr. Yorke thought it his duty to attend. To his surprise the Lord in Waiting came up and whispered that His Majesty desired to see him in his Closet as soon as the Levee was over. There and then the offer of the Great Seal was renewed. The King declared it a point most essential to his service, and earnestly besought Mr. Yorke to rescue his Sovereign from the factious combination by which the throne was now besieged. The pleader was too powerful and the temptation too strong. In an evil hour for himself Mr. Yorke consented; he sank down on his knee; and the King giving him his hand to kiss hailed him as Lord Chancellor.

Next day accordingly Lord Camden was summoned to the palace to surrender the Great Seal into the King's own hands; and a Privy Council being then convened, Mr. Yorke was sworn into office, and carried away with him the Great Seal in his carriage. A patent also was ordered, raising him to the peerage by the title of Lord

Morden. But how different his reception when he left his Sovereign and his colleagues in the Council Chamber, and drove to see his Opposition friends assembled at Lord Rockingham's! He was stung to the very heart by their angry reproaches or their indignant silence. Returning home, the first frenzy of his anguish wrought so far on his sensitive mind that he turned a rash hand against himself, and three days afterwards expired. His family endeavoured to assign some natural causes for his death; and such were the respect and sympathy felt for him that even those who might know the truth were unwilling to divulge it.*

Another death at this crisis, but marked by no uncommon circumstance, was that of the Speaker, Sir John Cust. It became necessary to proceed without delay to fill the vacant Chair. Sir Fletcher Norton was proposed and carried by Lord North; an excellent choice so far as ability and knowledge were concerned, but by no means as unexceptionable on the score of temper and discretion.

The decease of Mr. Yorke took place on the 20th of January; the election of Sir Fletcher on the 22d. On the latter day also Lord Rockingham, according to his notice, moved the Peers to consider the causes of the public discontents. "He was driven on," says a contemporary, "by his friends who were ashamed of their "attachment to a mute, but he delivered his proposal with "all the ungracious agitation of terrified spirits, and "hobbling through the grievances of the nation." † He was ably answered by the Duke of Grafton, and far more ably supported by Lord Chatham. Notes of these speeches, not published till long afterwards, were taken at the time by Philip Francis. To one memorable expression of the Great Earl in this debate Francis thus alluded many years

* The various testimonies on this subject are drawn out in array by Lord Campbell, but he shrinks from expressing any opinion of his own upon them. (Lives of the Chancellors, vol. v. p. 415.) It seems to me that the statements of Lord Orford and of the Duke of Grafton in their respective Memoirs can leave no reasonable doubt as to the truth.

† Lord Orford's Memoirs of George III., vol. iv. p. 57. The *Claude Lorraine* glass, as applied to Lord Rockingham's speeches, is held up in Lord Albemarle's Memoirs, vol. i. p. 141. &c. (1853.)

later in a pamphlet under his own name: "Let the war "take its course, or, as I heard Lord Chatham declare in "the House of Lords with a monarch's voice: 'Let dis"'cord prevail for ever!'"—As if these words had not been strong enough, Lord Chatham went on to say: "I "know to what point this doctrine and this language will "appear directed. But rather than the nation should "surrender their birthright to a despotic Minister, I hope, "my Lords, old as I am, I shall see the question brought "to issue and fairly tried between the people and the "government." In this speech also Lord Chatham took occasion to explain his plan for reform in our representative system. He desired that each county should return one member more, which he called, "to infuse a portion "of new health into the Constitution." But against any idea of disfranchisement he strongly protested. "In my "judgment, my Lords, these small boroughs, corrupt as "they are, must be considered as the natural infirmity of "the Constitution. The limb is mortified, but the am"putation might be death."

The Duke of Grafton as Prime Minister was now beset with difficulties. He found himself unable to provide a Chancellor, having since Mr. Yorke's decease applied, but in vain, both to the Attorney General, Mr. De Grey, and to Sir Eardley Wilmot, the Chief Justice. The Government moreover had sustained other losses besides Lord Camden's and Lord Granby's. James Grenville had flung up his sinecure and rejoined his brothers. Dunning had declared that he would only continue in office until a new Solicitor General was found. Several great noblemen in the Royal Household had withdrawn their support and relinquished their places. Under such dispiriting circumstances the vehement attacks of Lord Chatham appear to have fixed the Duke in his determination to resign; and on the very day of Lord Rockingham's motion he announced that determination to the King.

Thus no sooner had Lord Chatham emerged from his retirement and raised his voice against the Ministry than the Ministry crumbled to pieces. It was now imagined that George the Third must needs send for the chiefs of Opposition and submit to whatever terms they might require. Only one expedient remained by which this degrading submission—for so His Majesty deemed it—could be averted. By his commands Lord Weymouth and Lord Gower waited upon Lord North with an earnest entreaty that, in addition to his post as Chancellor of the Exchequer, he would assume that of First Lord of the Treasury. Lord North would have greatly preferred to continue in a second place, but yielded at last and reluctantly to the Royal desire; a proof of his devotion to his Sovereign which the King never afterwards forgot.* General Conway, who had lately held a seat in the Cabinet without office, now withdrew; Mr. Thurlow was named Solicitor General; and the Great Seal was put into Commission, but few other changes that could be avoided were made.

Such then was the outset of Lord North as Prime Minister,—the seventh within the ten first years of this reign. Of all his six predecessors none had entered office under less favourable circumstances, with less freedom of choice, or with less prospect of permanence. Yet so strange are the chances and changes of public life that, as will be seen, this administration endured longer than all its six predecessors combined.

In some part or degree, however, this permanence of power may be fairly ascribed to the amiable and conciliatory qualities of him who held it. Frederick Lord North, eldest son of the Earl of Guilford, was born in 1733. He went through the usual course of an English education at Eton and at Oxford, and afterwards proceeded to the Continent, where he remained three years. He had become, and what is far more rare he continued through life, an excellent classic scholar; and of French, German, and Italian, the first especially, he made himself master in his travels. On coming of age he was returned to Parliament for the family borough of Banbury; and in 1759 he was named a Lord of the Treasury through the influence of his kinsman the Duke of Newcastle. He retired from office at the formation of the Rockingham Ministry, but in 1766, as we have seen, he was named by Lord Chatham joint

* See in the Appendix the King's letters to Lord North;. the entreaty (Jan. 23. 1770), and the permanent sense of obligation (Sept. 1777)

Paymaster of the Forces, and in the year following succeeded Charles Townshend as Chancellor of the Exchequer. Through all these promotions it may be said with truth that he did not seek honours; it was rather that honours sought him. He was by no means of an eager and aspiring temper, nor ever feeling tempted to deviate from principle in quest of popularity. "I do not "dislike popularity," he said in 1769, "but it so happens "that for the last seven years I have never given my vote "for any one of the popular measures. In 1763 I sup- "ported the cyder tax; and I afterwards opposed the re- "peal of that tax; a vote of which I never repented. In "1765 I was for the American Stamp Act; and when "in the following year a Bill was brought in for the re- "peal of that Act I directly opposed it, for I saw the "danger of the repeal. And when again in 1767 it was "thought necessary to relieve the people by reducing the "land tax to the amount of half a million I was against "that measure also. Then appeared on the public stage "that strange phenomenon of popularity, Mr. Wilkes. I "was the first to move his expulsion in 1764. Every "subsequent proceeding against that man I have sup- "ported; and I will again vote for his expulsion if he "again attempts to take his seat in this House. In all "my memory therefore I do not recollect a single popular "measure I ever voted for; no, not even the Nullum "Tempus Bill, nor the declaration of law in the case of "General Warrants. I state this to prove that I am "not an ambitious man. Men may be popular without "being ambitious, but there is rarely an ambitious man "who does not try to be popular." *

Of outward advantages Lord North was altogether destitute. His figure was overgrown and ungraceful, and his countenance gave little promise of ability. He was extremely near-sighted; a great obstacle in the way of Parliamentary eminence, which has never perhaps been wholly overcome, except by himself and in our own time by Lord Derby. A few days only before he became Prime Minister one of his keenest opponents, Mr. Burke,

* Speech in the House of Commons, March 2. 1769. Cavendish Debates, vol. i. p. 299.

thus described him in the House of Commons:—"The "Noble Lord who spoke last, after extending his right "leg a full yard before his left, rolling his flaming eyes, "and moving his ponderous frame, has at length opened "his mouth!"* But Mr. Burke might have added, though he did not, that no sooner was that mouth opened than it made ample amends for every defect of form or gesture. Out there came, fresh at each emergency, a flow of good sense and sterling information, enlivened by never failing pleasantry and wit. During his long and for the most part disastrous administration it was frequently his fate to maintain almost alone a contest with some of the ablest orators whom the world had ever seen. Yet by his natural and acquired gifts of mind, conjoined with high character and with steady courage, he was enabled to stand firm during so many years against all the efforts of Fox and Burke, of Dunning, Savile, and Barré, and at last the younger Pitt. Unequal as he might be to some at least of these in powers of eloquence, he far surpassed them, and indeed all men of his time, in his admirable mildness and placidity of temper. So cheerful was ever his mien, and so unruffled his composure, that it seemed scarcely an effort to him to wage the warfare of debate even against such adversaries. Indeed his great difficulty during the violent volleys of attacks that were often poured upon him as he sat upon the Treasury Bench was to keep himself awake! Many a keen opponent charging him to his face with the heaviest crimes and misdemeanors must have felt not a little disconcerted at seeing opposite the object of all his vehemence dropping by degrees into a gentle doze, and only roused by his neighbours' elbows into starts of watchfulness.

Whenever Lord North rose to reply the same good-humoured unconcern was still more apparent. Thus, for instance, on one occasion interposing in a quarrel he observed that there was often far too much readiness to take offence. "That is not my own case," he added. "This "very evening one Member who spoke of me called me "'that thing called a Minister.' Well to be sure,"—

* Speech of January 9. 1770. Parl. Hist., vol. xvi. p. 720. This is one of the debates omitted by Cavendish.

continued Lord North, here patting his ample sides,—"I am an unwieldy thing; the Honourable Member there-"fore when he called me 'a thing' said what was true, "and I could not be angry with him. But when he "added, 'that thing called a Minister,' he called me that "thing which of all things he himself wished most to be, "and therefore I took it as a compliment!" *

This sweetness of temper in Lord North was by no means confined to public life; it was no less manifest and no less delightful in his domestic circle. His youngest and long surviving daughter—herself a person of no mean attainments—has recorded that she never knew him really out of humour. She tells us that he had one drunken stupid groom who used to provoke him, and who from this uncommon circumstance was called by the children "the "man that puts Papa in a passion." Yet it seems this drunken stupid groom was never discarded, but died in the service of the same indulgent master.†

As an upright public servant the character of Lord North stands above all suspicion or reproach; indeed but for the Wardenship of the Cinque Ports, which the King's spontaneous act bestowed upon him as afterwards upon Mr. Pitt, he would have left office a poorer man than he had entered it. On all occasions his feelings as his manners were those of an honourable and high-bred gentleman. He had great sagacity in unravelling, and great quickness in mastering, the most intricate details of public business. But in conducting that business it cannot be denied that he lacked something of energy, of firmness, of fixed and resolute will. These qualities—needful to a statesman at all times, but doubly needful at a period so fraught with

* Reminiscences of Mr. Charles Butler, vol. i. p. 159.—On another occasion (Jan. 27. 1778) when Fox had accused him of indolence and love of flattery, Lord North observed in answer that "he passed "a great deal of his time in that House, where he could not be idle, "and where it was plain that he was not flattered!" See Lord John Russell's Memorials of Fox, vol. i. p. 165. (1853.)

† Letter, on the character of Lord North, from Lady Charlotte Lindsay to Lord Brougham, February 18. 1839. This interesting and excellent letter, creditable alike to its object and to its writer, has been published by Lord Brougham in the Appendix to his Historical Sketches.

difficulties as the American contest,—never certainly shone forth in this too amiable, too complying, Prime Minister. It is his main reproach as he stands before the tribunal of History, nor can History absolve him from the charge, that he frequently yielded his own deliberate judgment to the persuasion of his Sovereign or of his friends. His daughter owns it as his weakness, which, she adds, followed him through life,—"the want of power to resist the in-"fluence of those he loved."—Thus it is that on several occasions, though not from any base or sordid or unworthy motive, he stooped to be an instrument of measures which he did not in his heart approve; thus it is that on many questions of policy at least, though not perhaps on any question of principle, we find his public speeches defend the very course which his private letters arraign.

The success of the Opposition in driving the Duke of Grafton from the helm could not fail to animate them to many a fresh onset against Lord North. During the whole remainder of the Session he was assailed in both Houses with every topic of reproach or ridicule. Above all there was urged against him the old and stale, but by no means worn out, accusation of his being the mere puppet and secret tool of Lord Bute, even although Lord Bute was then in Italy. In allusion to the title of his ancestor, a Lord Keeper, the new Prime Minister was nick-named Lord Deputy North.* It is with sorrow I observe that no one was more factious on this topic, more unsparing in his hints against the King, more forward with this party charge of continued Scottish influence, than Lord Chatham. Only a month after the new appointments he took occasion in the House of Lords to thunder against the "invisible, irresponsible, and most pernicious counsels "of a Favourite. . . . . That Favourite is at the present "moment abroad, yet his influence by his confidential "agents is as powerful as if he were at home. Who does "not know the Mazarinade of France,—that Mazarin "absent was Mazarin still,—and what is there I would "ask to distinguish the two cases? . . . . When I was "earnestly called upon for the public service I came from "Somersetshire with wings of zeal. I consented to pro-

* See the Chatham Papers, vol. iii. p. 443.

"serve a peace which I abominated; a peace I would not "make, but would preserve when made. . . . . I own I "was credulous; I was duped; I was deceived; for the "same secret invisible influence still prevailed, and I found "that there was no original administration to be suffered "in this country!"

On hearing this attack, which while aimed against Lord Bute glanced also at Royalty itself, the Duke of Grafton felt it his duty, though no longer a Minister, to rise in vindication of his Sovereign, and to declare, as General Conway had done on a like occasion, that while in office he had never seen or felt such an influence as was described. He added with great force and point that the charge was so utterly groundless that it could only be "the effect of a distempered mind brooding over its own "discontents."—Upon this, Lord Chatham rose again, and with a monarch's voice (as Sir Philip Francis termed it) spoke as follows: "I rise, my Lords, neither to deny, "to retract, nor to explain away the words I have spoken. "As for His Majesty, I always found everything gracious "and amiable in the Closet; so condescending as to promise in repeated audiences not only to forgive but to "supply the defects of health by his cheerful support. "Instead of this, all the obstacles and difficulties which "attended my public measures were suggested, nourished, "and supported by that secret influence to which I have "alluded. . . . . A long train of these practices has at "length unwillingly convinced me that there is something "behind the Throne greater than the Throne itself!"

This visionary charge—which coming from Lord Chatham can only in my opinion be explained as the Duke of Grafton did explain it—was by no means the last of Lord Chatham's attacks in this year. The Duke of Grafton observes in his Memoirs that he had never under any Ministry seen his Lordship in more active opposition. He was sometimes disabled by the gout, but when his health allowed him to be present he brought forward several uncompromising motions against the measures of the Government. One of these motions was for a Bill reversing the adjudications of the House of Commons in the case of Wilkes; another was for an Address to the King praying him to dissolve the Parliament. In all these he was defeated by large majorities or without a division. In all these, however, it may be said that his eager party spirit coincided with just views for the public good. The adherents of the Ministry endeavoured to comfort and re-assure themselves by whispers of his recent insanity. "A mad motion of the "mad Earl of Chatham!"—says that disinterested patriot, Mr. Rigby. * But the main difficulty with which at this period Lord Chatham had to strive lay in the qualms and fears of Lord Rockingham and Lord Rockingham's followers. Thus on one occasion does the Earl write from Hayes to his confidential friend Mr. Calcraft: "I was in "town on Wednesday last, saw Lord Rockingham, and "learnt nothing more than what I knew before; namely, "that the Marquis is an honest and honourable man, but "that 'Moderation! Moderation!' is the burden of the "song among the body. For myself I am resolved to be "in earnest for the public, and shall be a scare-crow of "violence to the gentle warblers of the grove, the mo-"derate Whigs, and temperate statesmen." †

At this period indeed the Opposition were far from being a compact or united body. The followers of George Grenville looked with great dislike to the followers of Lord Rockingham, — a feeling not less heartily returned. In the year but one preceding Mr. Knox, lately the Secretary of Mr. Grenville, and writing under his eye, had published a pamphlet, entitled "The present "State of the Nation." That pamphlet (as usual with secretaries out of place) contained many fond recollections of his chief while Minister, and many lugubrious statements of the evils which had followed his retirement. Some strokes in it at the Rockingham party had provoked Burke to draw his pen; the more so since many persons in the public believed Grenville himself to be the author.‡ The celebrated answer of Burke: "Observations on a "late State of the Nation," which was published in 1769,

* Bedford Correspondence, vol. iii. p. 412.

† Letter dated July 28. 1770.

‡ Mr. Knox to Mr. Grenville, Nov. 1. 1768. Grenville Papers. Mr. Knox adds, that he "did not discountenance the supposition." This was on the appearance of the third edition.

proved a masterpiece of skill and eloquence. But the brighter the weapon the deeper the wound which it gave. Thus in one passage Burke refers to Mr. Grenville as foremost among "the ravens who have always croaked "out this kind of song. They have a malignant delight "in presaging mischief when they are not employed in "doing it!" Nor is this all. Burke goes on to compare the eminent retired statesman to the Spirit of Envy, as Ovid has portrayed her, gazing down upon Athens in all its wealth and glory, and scarcely able to restrain her grief because she could see nothing to grieve at! *

It is plain also at this very period, from Burke's private correspondence, that however respectful the tone adopted in public towards Lord Chatham, he did not in reality regard his Lordship with a much more favourable eye. Pursuing his ornithological similes, we find him liken the great orator not indeed to a raven, but to a hawk: "The style of Lord Chatham's politics is to keep hovering "in air over all parties, and to souse down where the "prey may prove best!" †

Thus when Lord Chatham came forth again to public life he had found himself on the Opposition side between two jarring parties, and not without some resentful feelings turned against himself. On many points, as on the Middlesex Election, he combined them to harmonious action, but on others he could not so prevail. Nor indeed did his own opinions entirely agree with either party. On several questions of domestic policy he differed from Lord Rockingham. On several questions of Colonial policy he differed from Mr. Grenville. But there speedily gathered round himself a band of personal adherents, a band far from numerous, but strong in their leader's

* "Vixque tenet lachrymas quia nil lachrymabile cernit!" See Metam., lib. ii. p. 796. and Burke's Works, vol. ii. p. 75. ed. 1815.

† To Lord Rockingham, Oct. 29. 1769. Correspondence, vol. i. p. 206. — Lord Chatham's own opinion of Burke's pamphlet was that "however well intended it has done much hurt to the cause." This he says in a private letter of next year to Lord Rockingham; which private letter the Marquis, perhaps not quite fairly, allowed the author to read; as we may find from a much later note by Burke himself, published by Lord Albemarle in his Memoirs of Lord Rockingham, vol. ii. p. 195. (1853.)

talents and their own. To this small band belonged Lord Camden, Lord Shelburne, and Lord Stanhope, Colonel Barré and Alderman Beckford, Mr. Calcraft and Mr. Dunning.

Such was the state of parties when an attempt was made to remedy one of the most flagrant evils that party spirit had produced, and from which no party had stood clear. A Bill to regulate the trial of Controverted Elections was drawn up and brought in by Mr. Grenville. That able statesman, though not yet fifty-eight years of age, was already declining to his grave. It was observed of him during the debates of 1769 that on sitting down after an eager speech he spat blood.* Next winter he sustained a most grievous bereavement by the death of his wife, the daughter of Sir William Wyndham. Some time afterwards Mr. Knox, his former secretary, paid him a visit at Wotton, and, as Mr. Knox has recorded, was assured by him that he had given up all thoughts of office. "And indeed," he continued with a deep sigh, and putting his hand upon his side, "I am no "longer capable of serving the public. My health "and spirits are gone. The only thing I have any in-"tention of doing is to endeavour to give some check to "the abominable prostitution of the House of Commons "in elections by voting for whoever has the support of "the Minister, which must end in the ruin of public "liberty if it be not checked."† In pursuance of this public-spirited design Mr. Grenville prepared a measure which, as is well known, transferred the trial of controverted elections from the House at large to a Select Committee, gave to that Committee the power of administering an oath, and bound the Members of that Committee by an oath of their own. The Bill encountered a zealous resistance from Mr. Rigby and Mr. Dyson, while other Members more faintly expressed their doubts and objections to it ‡, but a majority declared in its favour; and

* Cavendish Debates, vol. i. p. 371.

† Extra-official State Papers by William Knox, Esq., 1789, vol. ii. p. 41.

‡ Compare the fuller and better report in the Parl. Hist., vol. xvi. p. 907—924. with that in the Cavendish Debates, vol. i. p. 513. and

in the other House Lord Mansfield, much to his honour, discarded all party ties to give it his support; by that support ensuring its success. No man in our own day will deny how great was the improvement wrought by this Bill. Yet even this Bill proved so inadequate to the demands of justice as to have been repeatedly altered and new modelled, so that now scarce a trace of the original remains. Thus manifold has been the endeavour to reconcile privilege with justice; so hard and well nigh hopeless the task to turn on each occasion warring partisans into impartial judges!

In this state of parties also Lord North found it necessary, according to his pledge last Session, to deal with the difficult question of taxes in America. From that quarter the news had continued to be far from favourable. That rash and yet feeble course proposed by the Duke of Bedford and adopted by both Houses, — the appeal to an obsolete and arbitrary Act of Henry the Eighth, and the neglect of any measures to enforce it, — had produced the usual effect of empty threats, — to irritate rather than alarm. In May 1769 the House of Burgesses in Virginia voted some strong Resolutions against the policy lately pursued towards the Colonies, and also an Address to the King praying him on no account to revive the statute of Henry the Eighth against them. Upon this they were dissolved in displeasure by their newly appointed Governor, Lord Bottetort. But the principal members immediately repaired to "the Apollo" (a tavern room), and formed, what they had hitherto forborne to do, an association engaging upon their honour to import no British merchandize so long as the duties laid on in 1767 should continue unrepealed. Among the names put down to this agreement were some still obscure, but destined to become illustrious on the side of American independence. It bears the signatures of Patrick Henry and Peyton Randolph, of George Washington and Thomas Jefferson.

514. Mr. Dunning, still Solicitor General, declared that as the law of Election Petitions had lately been administered, "decisions in "Turkey would in my apprehension be far preferable!" The first fruit of Mr. Grenville's Bill in the ensuing year was the exposure of those corrupt practices at Shoreham to which I have elsewhere referred.

In several more of the Colonies similar irritation was displayed at the announcement of the Parliamentary proceedings. In Massachusetts, according to the terms of the Charter, the new Assembly was convened in the same month of May. They met in no complying humour. Nearly their first business was to complain of the King's ships and the King's troops which had come among them, and to apply to Governor Bernard that he would give orders for the removal of both. The Governor answered drily: "Gentlemen, I have no authority over His Majesty's ships in this port, or over his troops within this town." Hereupon the House of Representatives refused to transact any further business, surrounded as they were, and threatened as they alleged themselves to be, by an armed force. Sir Francis hoped to remove this objection by adjourning them to Cambridge, a town divided from Boston by an arm of the sea, and in which there were no troops. But their resentful spirit still continued; they refused to make any, even the smallest, provision for the soldiers; and at last there appearing no prospect of any reconcilement they were prorogued by the Governor, not to meet again until January 1770.

At this period, and after so many provocations given and received, Sir Francis Bernard was most judiciously summoned back to England. He was not indeed formally recalled, but sent for partly to answer the charges brought against him, and partly on the honourable plea of consulting him in person; and he continued nominally Governor of Massachusetts two years more. Still, however, he was never permitted to return to his province; and the government was administered in his place by Lieutenant Governor Hutchinson. Great hopes were entertained that on his departure greater concord and cordiality might prevail in his province. Such hopes were not fulfilled. The leaders of the non-importation movement were more vehement than ever. They were far from trusting solely to persuasion or argument upon their fellow-citizens; they set on foot a system of terror against the disinclined. It was not even permitted to the merchants to keep the goods they had imported in store, as if bonded, until the duties should be repealed in England. One merchant bolder than the rest who had so far presumed was waited upon by a chosen Committee with an axeman and a carpenter in their front-rank, — as though ready to cut off his head or to make his coffin! They told him that there were a thousand men close by awaiting his answer, and that if he did not comply they could not answer for the consequences. Such cogent logic was decisive; the unlucky merchant sent back his goods to those who had shipped them, and much against his will was enrolled as an eminent member of the patriot band. But while the patriot chiefs were thus inflexible to strangers, they are accused of showing undue favour to their own especial friends, allowing some of these to sell the prohibited articles in secret, and in fact to set their own prices upon them since the articles could not be obtained elsewhere. All informers, and indeed all such as gave any aid or support to the Government, were seized upon by the populace to be tarred and feathered. This process was to strip the patient naked, bedaub his body with tar, and roll him round in feathers, and then turn him out into the streets. Such a process may be treated as a jest, and indeed was sometimes talked of as such in England*; but attended as it was too commonly with blows and violence, it put its victims to considerable suffering as well as to shame.

Tarring and feathering although the most effectual were not the only methods by which the good men of Massachusetts manifested their displeasure. Another favourite device with any obnoxious person was to smear over his whole house with pitch or filth, so as to render it for a time almost uninhabitable.

It was natural and just that respectable Americans should disavow any share in such outrages, and impute them solely to the rabble in the streets. No doubt in a

* The tarring and feathering at Boston is humorously referred to by Foote in his play of the *Cozeners*. There the *Cozener*, Mr. Flaw, promises to the Irishman, O'Flanagan, "a tide-waiter's place in the "inland parts of America."—And he adds, "a word in your ear! "if you discharge well your duty you will be found in tar and "feathers for nothing. . . . When properly mixed they make a "genteel kind of dress, which is sometimes worn in that climate; it "is very light, keeps out the rain, and sticks extremely close to the "skin!"

large majority of cases these disavowals were perfectly well-founded; still however the suspicion remains that the rabble on these occasions was set in movement and directed by some persons of higher rank and larger views of mischief than themselves. Even if we avert our eyes altogether from such acts of violence, and look only to the votes of formal meetings and legislative assemblies at that period, even then in more than one of the Colonies, and above all in Massachusetts, we shall still find scope for censure and complaint. We shall find that even the statesmen in England most zealous for the rights of that Colony, and most mindful of the provocations it had received,—we shall find that even Lord Chatham, staunch friend as he was to America,—felt it a duty to express public and strong disapprobation of the language there used, and of the tendency there displayed.*

It must be confessed, however, that some encouragement from England was not wanting even for the most anti-English of these men. Colonel Mackay, who had just returned from his regiment at Boston, declared in the House of Commons: "I have read letters from Eng-"land advising them to persevere, and they would be "sure to obtain their ends. And can you suppose that "men at that distance, having such advice given to them "by men pretending to be their friends, will not pay a "regard to such advice, and more particularly in a "matter of taxation?"†

Under such circumstances, and on the 5th of March 1770, Lord North brought forward his motion on the subject of American Revenue. His speech was temperate and able. He declared himself ready to abide by the terms of Lord Hillsborough's letter, and to propose the repeal of all the duties laid on in 1767, except only the duties on Teas. "Would to God," he added, "I "could see any reason from the subsequent behaviour of "the Americans to grant them further indulgence, and "extend the proposal to the removal of the other duties

* See in the Appendix to this volume an extract of Lord Chatham's speech, March 2. 1770, as reported at the time by Mr. Johnson, agent for Connecticut.

† Cavendish Debates, vol. i. p. 493.

"which it was my intention at that time to do!" But from what had lately passed at Boston and elsewhere it was scarcely prudent, he argued, nay scarcely even possible, for the Government to make any further concession. In truth they were not called on to redress a grievance, but only to relinquish a right. For the whole probable amount of these duties on Tea was no more, according to Lord North's estimate, than eleven or twelve thousand pounds a year. Nor was even this small amount in reality any additional charge on the Americans. The Colonial tax of three pence a pound had been laid upon this article of Tea at the very time when Parliament had taken off the English duty of twenty-five per cent. upon Teas exported to America. Under the whole transaction therefore, — such a duty taken off in England, and such a tax laid on in America, — it was clear that Tea might be sold to the colonists even cheaper than before.*

The remission of the English duty to which Lord North referred, — that is, a drawback to the full amount on all the Teas belonging to the East India Company, and exported to the American Colonies, — had been granted in 1767, as part of the agreement between the administration of that day and the East India Company. But it might be described as resembling an experiment rather than a full concession. The period of the Act was limited to five years, and by one of its clauses the Company undertook to make good the consequent deficiency in the revenue, should any such be found to have arisen on an average of the annual returns within that period.†

Against Lord North's proposal, as stated to the House of Commons, there appeared two opposite classes of objections. Mr. Welbore Ellis and Lord Barrington, though holding office under him, declared that they could not support his scheme, nor, after the recent behaviour of the Americans, allow them any, even the smallest, indulgence. On the other hand, Burke, Barré, Dowdes-

* See further on this point Mr. Strahan's Queries to Dr. Franklin, November 21. 1769. Franklin fairly admits in his reply: "It is not "the sum paid in that duty on Tea that is complained of as a bur-"then, but the principle of the Act expressed in the preamble." (Works, vol. iv. p. 262.)

† Act 7 Geo. III. c. 56.

well, Governor Pownall, and General Conway, and the whole force of Opposition (excepting only Mr. Grenville who spoke irresolutely and did not vote at all), declared in favour of including the article of Teas, and repealing the entire Act of 1767. For how mere a trifle, it was urged, was the Government then struggling! Such had been the effect of the non-importation agreements, or such the prevalence of smuggling, that the whole receipt from the Tea duties in America during the last financial year, was less than three hundred pounds.* Thus the right was but a shadow, and the profit but a peppercorn. How much wiser, if conciliation were attempted at all, to conciliate clearly, finally, and fully! Arguments such as these wrought so far with the House that the usual majority of Ministers was greatly lessened in this vote; they carried the partial as against the entire repeal by only 204 against 142.

The same day on which the question of American taxes had been discussed and decided in the House of Commons was marked by a painful and long remembered affray at Boston. To that town the stationing of the regiments, now again reduced to two, had been hitherto, to say the least, no unmitigated evil. Upwards of 60,000*l.* had been spent by them, and many a farmer was heard to exult that he could now get ready money for his goods; while, on the other hand, they had cost the province nothing or next to nothing. No other provision had been made for them by the Assembly beyond straw, wood, and candles, and a barrack, which, as one of their officers afterwards said in Parliament, was a building "in which no gentleman of this House would keep his "hounds!"† Unhappily on political grounds the troops were most obnoxious to many of the upper class, and to all the lower, in the town. A man in a red coat could scarcely go through some of the streets without being

* Alderman Beckford said, April 19. 1769: "This duty upon tea "has produced in the southern part of America only 295*l.* 14*s.*; in "the northern part, nothing; and all this with a great army to col- "lect it!" (Cavendish Debates, vol. i. p. 400.) Yet Franklin writes in 1773: "It is supposed that at least a million of Americans drink "tea twice a day." (Works, vol. iv. p. 385.)

† Cavendish Debates, vol. i. p. 493.

insulted; nor could discipline always prevent retaliation. On Saturday the 3d of March a quarrel took place at a rope-walk between some soldiers and towns-people. The latter were the aggressors, but were beaten and pursued, and though much incensed allowed the Sunday to intervene between them and their revenge. But at nightfall on Monday the 5th a large crowd, armed with sticks and staves, assailed the main guard; pelting the soldiers with snowballs, lumps of ice, and logs of wood, and not sparing abuse and execrations at the "lobster scoundrels." The commanding officer, Captain Preston, showed an humane and soldier-like forbearance; and the men for a long time remained steady to their arms; but at length were provoked to fire without orders, when three persons were killed, and several others (one mortally) wounded.

To prevent any further bloodshed, and at the earnest desire of a deputation, Governor Hutchinson and Colonel Dalrymple removed all the troops from the town to Castle William. Meanwhile every effort was made by the popular leaders to magnify and distort the late transaction, which they insisted on calling "the Massacre;" and represented as a deliberate and concerted scheme of slaughter by the troops. "The Murderers" was now the common term applied by them and their correspondents to all the King's troops at Boston*; and no pains were spared to agitate and inflame the minds of the people from whom the Jury in the trial of Captain Preston must be chosen. When, however, that trial did take place, in due course of law a few months afterwards, it was conducted with perfect fairness. At first indeed Captain Preston had great difficulty in obtaining Counsel. Many, either from popular principles, or in personal terror, refused their aid. Finally, one of his friends, Mr. Forrest, waited upon Mr. John Adams, a young lawyer of great ability then first rising into fame. With tears streaming from his eyes Mr. Forrest said: "I am come "with a very solemn message from a very unfortunate "man, Captain Preston, in prison. He wishes for "Counsel, and can get none. I have waited on Mr. "Quincy, who says he will engage if you will give him

* See Franklin's Works and Correspondence, vol. vii. p. 478, &c.

"your assistance; without it he positively declines. "Even Mr. Auchmuty declines, unless you will engage." Mr. Adams was warm and zealous on the popular side, and on that side all his ambitious hopes depended. Yet with a noble spirit, and without any hesitation, he answered Mr. Forrest that Counsel ought to be the very last thing that an accused person should want in a free country, and that the Bar ought, in his opinion, to be independent and impartial at all times and in every circumstance. Upon this Mr. Forrest offered him as a retaining fee, a single guinea, which Mr. Adams cheerfully accepted.* As he had foreseen, there immediately arose a violent clamour against him among his political friends. But it did not long endure. Ere long his upright conduct was acknowledged and respected; and in later years, after many other public services, John Adams became the second President of the United States.

At this trial the skill of the young advocate, supported by a host of witnesses, established beyond dispute the true facts of the case; and a verdict of Not Guilty was returned. All the four Judges present expressed their concurrence with that verdict, and by one of them the entire case was summed up as follows: "Happy I am to "find that after such strict examination the conduct of "the prisoner appears in so fair a light; yet I feel my-"self deeply affected that this affair turns out so much "to the disgrace of every person concerned against him, "and so much to the shame of the town in general."

The soldiers of Captain Preston being in like manner brought to trial were also acquitted, excepting the two who had first fired without orders, and who were found Guilty of Manslaughter only. But neither the evidence adduced, nor the verdicts returned, wrought any change in the feelings or the language of the popular leaders on this question. During several successive years they observed with much solemnity the anniversary of "the "massacre," as they continued to call it, employing their ablest spokesmen to deliver annual harangues, by which

* See the Autobiography of John Adams, as recently printed from the MS. in his Works (vol. ii. p. 230. ed. 1850).

the public resentment might be stirred, and the irritating remembrance kept alive.

From these trials there may justly, as I conceive, be deduced two general and not immaterial considerations. In the first place, the perfect fairness with which they were conducted, and the satisfactory verdicts with which they closed, afford the best reply to that most unjust and most impolitic proposal of the Duke of Bedford in the preceding year that American prisoners should be brought before Juries in England. Secondly, however good may have been upon the whole the conduct of Captain Preston and his soldiers, a heavy responsibility seems to rest upon the Government at home for having sent them without absolute necessity into the very streets and lanes of these exasperated townsmen. The probability of some such collision should certainly have been foreseen, and might perhaps have been averted.

Notwithstanding both the untoward events on March the 5th, 1770,—the retention of the Tea Duties by the House of Commons, and the bloodshed in the streets of Boston,—there ensued at this time a calm or lull in American affairs. The repeal of the other Duties by Lord North had, after all, narrowed to a slender point the grounds of difference. By a large majority of the people in a large majority of the provinces it was felt as unwise and undesirable to continue altercations with their mother country on such narrow grounds as these. Their non-importation agreement had proved far more inconvenient to themselves than had been expected or foreseen when they engaged in it. One Colony, New York, had already broken loose from the tie; and in spite of remonstrances from Boston it was gradually relinquished by the rest. Satisfaction or confidence indeed were far from being restored. But trade with England was resumed on nearly the same footing as before the Stamp Act; except only as to the article of Teas, which were either abstained from or more commonly purchased elsewhere. Thus it may be said that the next three years passed quietly over. Some districts, however, and above all Massachusetts, did not share in the general tranquillity, but continued to bear a troubled aspect. There the Government was still administered by Hutchinson, who, although an American by birth, and highly prepossessing in manners, found himself full as much assailed and upbraided and beset with controversies as was ever Sir Francis Bernard. There the course of opposition was no longer guided by Otis, who about this time became insane. His friends had with deep concern beheld him borne away in a postchaise as a maniac bound hand and foot.* But among the principal and most zealous leaders at this period may be mentioned John Hancock, James Bowdoin, Royal Tyler (most unaptly named!), and the two Adams, Samuel and John; these were distant kinsmen and close friends, and both men of much ability, but far different in character; the first a demagogue; the second a statesman.

In April this year the term of Wilkes's sentence having expired, he was set free from the King's Bench. Some riots had been apprehended on that occasion as tokens of the popular joy, but any such he prudently prevented by going for several days out of town. On his return he was sworn in to fill his new office of Alderman, and eagerly embarked in the full stream of City politics. The Common Council indeed and the Court of Aldermen comprised many of his most strenuous partisans and brother agitators, — at their head William Beckford now again Lord Mayor. It was their pride or their policy at this juncture to strain to the utmost their ancient right of presenting Addresses to the King, to be received by His Majesty in person and in state, — a privilege enjoyed by no other City Corporation in England, and shared only with both Houses of Parliament and both the Universities. First came a Petition, to pray that Parliament might be dissolved, and to protest against every vote of the House of Commons as invalid since the exclusion of Wilkes. Next in the month of March fol-

* Dr. Gordon's History, vol. i. p. 308. I observe that Mr. John Adams in his private Diary from time to time mentions Otis with no high respect. Thus, Dec. 23. 1765: "Otis is fiery and feverous; "he is liable to great inequalities of temper, sometimes in de-"spondency and sometimes in a rage." Thus again, Sept. 3. 1769: "Otis talks all; he grows the most talkative man alive; no other "gentleman in company can find space to put in a word."

lowed a Remonstrance to the same effect, but of wider scope and less respectful language,—especially inveighing against a "secret and malign influence" at Court. The King, as was proper, and as his Ministers advised him, answered them in terms of high displeasure. But vain was the Royal rebuke. Vain was a Resolution passed by a large majority of the House of Commons, and levelled at them and their language. Not at all disconcerted by either censure they speedily came forward with a second Remonstrance still more vehement than the former,—again complaining of secret influence,—again calling for a Dissolution of Parliament.* This second Remonstrance was presented at St. James's on the 23d of May by Lord Mayor Beckford, attended by the Aldermen and Common Councillors. In all these cases it was customary to transmit to Court by a private hand a copy of the intended Address, so that the King might consult and be prepared. Thus, as usual, His Majesty was ready with an answer to read; it was on this occasion brief and firm, referring to the sentiments he had lately expressed, and declaring that they continued unchanged.

No sooner had the King concluded than to the general astonishment the Lord Mayor stepped forward and asked leave to say a few words. The King, like every other person present, was taken by surprise, and neither granted nor yet refused the permission thus suddenly sought. Beckford then proceeded boldly to declare that His Majesty had no subjects more loyal or more affectionate than the citizens of London. Should any man dare to insinuate the contrary, or attempt to alienate His Majesty's affections from them, "that man," continued Beckford, "is an enemy to your Majesty's person and "family, a violator of the public peace, and a betrayer of "our happy Constitution as it was established at the glo-"rious Revolution!" Such at least was Beckford's own account of his expressions, but there is great reason to think that in the hurry of his spirits at the time he did

* It is supposed that this Remonstrance was drawn up by Lord Chatham. (Lord Orford's Memoirs, vol. iv. p. 153.) It is certain at least that he entirely approved it. (Chatham Papers, vol. iii. p. 459.)

not really utter all that he intended or supposed.* The King, with proper dignity, forbore from making any answer; but, according to the usual form, allowed the citizens in withdrawing to kiss his hand.

This extemporaneous address on the part of the Lord Mayor was most unprecedented, and surely also most unconstitutional. For if it be in truth a paramount maxim of our Constitution that the King can do no wrong, and that his words are to be taken as only the words of his Ministers, what course can be more plainly repugnant to that maxim than the endeavour to draw His Majesty into a personal altercation, and obtain from him an answer on which he could not have consulted his official servants? Or supposing that answer an improper one, in what manner or on what plea could the Government have been arraigned for it? Yet so prevalent was party spirit at this juncture that two days afterwards the Common Council by a large majority of votes approved and applauded the behaviour of Beckford. Beckford himself died in less than a month from this time from a violent fever into which, it is said, his blood had been thrown by the agitation of his spirits. In honour to his memory the citizens voted that his statue should be placed in their Guildhall, and they also decided that the words which he had ventured to speak to the King on the 23d of May should be engraved upon the pedestal. And there they remain to this day.

The death of Beckford was a grievous blow to his party in the City,—strong as he had been in wealth, in boldness, in recent reputation, in the confidence and friendship of Chatham. As heir to his enormous fortune he left an only son, Lord Chatham's god-child, then a boy ten years of age †, afterwards well known in a sphere wholly different from his father's—the author

* It is remarkable that Horace Walpole writing only the day afterwards, mentions "my Lord Mayor's volunteer speech" as being "wondrous loyal and respectful." To Sir H. Mann, May 24. 1770.)

† Three years latter Lord Chatham thus describes him to his own son William: "Little Beckford is just as much compounded of the "elements of air and fire as he was. A due proportion of terrestrial "solidity will, I trust, come and make him perfect." (Burton Pynsent, Oct. 9. 1773.)

of Vathek, — the fastidious man of taste, — the fantastic decorator of Ramalhao and Fonthill. To supply the loss of Beckford during the remainder of his year of Mayoralty his party selected their next best man, Barlow Trecothick, a rich merchant engaged in the American trade; one of Beckford's brother-members for the City, and like Beckford also an occasional speaker in the House of Commons.

Amidst the difficulties and embarrassments which at this period from so many quarters and so many causes beset the Ministry, it would be strange indeed if Ireland had not contributed her share. Lord Townshend, a man of more ability than sound judgment, was now Viceroy. He had obtained a vote for the augmentation of the army by a public and solemn promise on the part of the Crown that not less than twelve thousand effective men should at all times be kept in Ireland, unless in cases of invasion or rebellion in Great Britain. Such a pledge afforded scope for many Opposition attacks in England. "An absurd dishonourable condition!" cried Lord Chatham. "The army is the thunder of the Crown. But "the Ministers have tied up the hand which should "direct the bolt!"* Not long afterwards, however, there ensued a misunderstanding with the House of Commons on the ground of privilege. They rejected a Money Bill because it had not taken its rise with themselves, but had been sent over by the English Privy Council. This pretension on their part was deemed a direct infraction of the Act of Henry the Seventh for the government of Ireland, known by the name of Poyning's Law. The Lord Lieutenant, after applying to England for instructions, suddenly, and with a public reproof, prorogued the Parliament for some months, — to the great detriment, they said, of its business, and certainly to the great displeasure of its Members. This measure also gave rise to angry attacks in the British Parliament. Why not dissolve instead of proroguing? cried the Opposition. Yet had a different course been taken no doubt the same

* Speech of January 22. 1770. See also in Cavendish Mr. Grenville's and Colonel Barré's speeches of May 3. in the same year. There were only five thousand men in Ireland before.

gentlemen would have asked with equal earnestness: Why not prorogue instead of dissolving?*

In the course of this autumn the administration found itself suddenly freed from two of its most formidable adversaries by the deaths of Lord Granby and Mr. Grenville. They expired within a month of each other, each scarcely past the prime of manhood, each already in the meridian of fame. Had life and health been spared to them, and had they continued to take part against the Government, it may be questioned,—such was now their weight in the House of Commons, derived in the one case from personal character, and in the other from financial skill,—whether Lord North and his colleagues could much longer have maintained themselves in place. For the loss of Grenville and Granby was not merely so much ability or so much reputation withdrawn from the ranks of Opposition; it removed a strong curb on the discordant claims and views of other men; it left, in Grenville's case at least, a section without a chief; it greatly widened the interval that already divided the followers of Chatham from the followers of Rockingham.

It may also be a matter for curious speculation had Grenville returned to office either as the colleague or successor of Lord North, what influence his counsels would have exerted on the coming contest with America. Strange though it may seem in the author of the Stamp Act, I believe that he would thenceforth have been ranged on the side of concession. His last recorded expressions on American taxation are the following, delivered in the month of March previous to his death: "Nothing could ever induce me to tax America again, "but the united consent of King, Lords, and Commons, "supported by the united voice of the people of Eng- "land. . . . . I will never lend my hand towards forging "chains for America, lest in so doing I should forge "them for myself." †

* Cavendish Debates, vol. i. p. 552—560. Some Members it seems mourned over the good old times of Henry the Seventh. "The Hon- "ourable Gentleman," said Lord North, referring to Mr. Boyle Walsingham, "has contrasted the present times with those of Henry "the Seventh, when Ireland was so well governed."

† Cavendish Debates, vol. i. p. 496.

CHAPTER XLIX.

In the autumn of this year, as the time for reassembling Parliament drew near, the Ministry and the nation had before them a momentous alternative, — the alternative of peace or war. That chance had arisen from a quarter wholly unexpected, from a region almost unknown. A desert archipelago in the southern hemisphere, first discovered at the close of the sixteenth century (by whom is not quite clear), had been called by the English Falkland Islands, and by the French Iles Malouines, a name derived from St. Malo. These "miserable islands," as in our own day a voyager terms them *, were long unsettled, and to any settler little worth; their soil a mass of peat, their climate a succession of storms. In Anson's voyages, however, their fertility had been presumed, and their situation vaunted as most favourable for any purpose either of trade or war in the Pacific Ocean. Accordingly in 1748 an expedition to explore them had been fitted out in England, but was laid aside, though without any acknowledgment of the Spanish right, on some remonstrances from the Spanish ambassador, General Wall.

After the peace of 1763 it so chanced that the Duke de Choiseul also cast his eyes to this quarter, and sent forth an expedition under M. de Bougainville to form a settlement. The Court of Spain which claimed these isles as part of her South American dominion again remonstrated; and Choiseul readily yielded to the complaints of his ally. The new settlement was transferred from French to Spanish hands, and its appellation altered in like manner from Port Louis to Port Soledad. Meanwhile, at nearly the same time as Bougainville's, an ex-

* See the instructive and agreeable Journal of Mr. Charles Darwin (vol. i. p. 188.). Mr. Darwin visited these islands in March 1833 and again in March 1834.

ploring expedition had been sent from England under Commodore Byron. A British settlement was formed on another of the islands; a small blockhouse was reared, and a small garrison stationed, the place receiving the name of Port Egmont in honour of the Earl of Egmont, First Lord of the Admiralty.

Thus for some years the English garrison continued; deriving annually at a great and unprofitable charge its supplies from England. The Spanish rulers in South America had attempted no disturbance and uttered no complaints. "We supposed," says Dr. Johnson in his able treatise on this question, "that we should be per-" mitted to remain the undisputed lords of tempest-beaten "barrenness." * But towards the close of 1769 Captain Hunt of the Tamar, being then stationed at Port Egmont, received various protests and remonstrances against the occupation from the Governor of Port Soledad. Captain Hunt replied by counter-statements that the islands belonged to His Britannic Majesty by the double claim of discovery and settlement. Some threats also passed on each side.

The first account received in England of any discontent expressed by the Spaniards was conveyed by Captain Hunt himself on his landing at Plymouth in June 1770. By that time, however, their discontent had assumed a more practical form. In the same month of June there appeared off Port Egmont a Spanish armament, which had been despatched by Don Francisco Buccarelli, the Governor of Buenos Ayres; it consisted of five frigates and no less than 1,600 men. Against such a force the handful of English at Port Egmont could not pretend to make resistance. A few shots were fired for form's sake; and then a capitulation was accepted. All the honours of war were granted to the English. But by the terms of the capitulation, and with a view to enable the Court of Madrid to have the first word in Europe, their departure was delayed for twenty days; and the better to secure their stay the rudder was removed from a King's ship, the Favourite. Such were the tidings which in the October following Captain

* Works, vol. viii. p. 107. ed. 1820.

Maltby of the Favourite brought with him to England. The event had already been announced in softening terms by the Prince de Masserano, the Spanish ambassador in London.

At the news of this insolent aggression in the midst of peace the English Government appears to have displayed a proper combination of spirit and of prudence. We must insist on most ample reparation for the insult to the British flag. But we must not assume or take for granted that no such reparation could be peacefully obtained. Orders were sent to the British Envoy at Madrid to demand in peremptory terms the restitution of the Falkland Islands, and the disavowal of Buccarelli's attack. And in case these demands should not be complied with, immediate and active preparations were made for war. Ships were refitted, commanders named to them, and stores put on board; press-gangs for sailors were sent round in all directions; and thus ere long a formidable fleet was ready at Spithead. Lord Mansfield advised the King to postpone the opening of Parliament until the final answer from Spain could be received. But His Majesty declined to take that course, deeming that both the Courts of Versailles and Madrid might probably misunderstand it, and hold it to indicate his resolution to settle the dispute at all events.* The Parliament met therefore on the day previously fixed, the 13th of November. The King in his Speech from the Throne declared his deep sense of the wrong which his people had sustained, and his full determination to obtain redress; he detailed to his Peers and Commons the steps he had already taken, and as to the future desired their advice and assistance.

Of their advice indeed the Opposition in both Houses were far from chary; but certainly with no view whatever of assistance. They raised a loud cry against what they termed the tameness, the supineness, the pusillanimity of Ministers. It was not their fault if the pride of Spain was not aroused. It was not their fault if we did not become involved in immediate war for the sake of a doubtful right and of a worthless object. Among all the vehement speeches at this period and for this purpose there

* The King to Lord North, Nov. 9. 1770. MS.

were none more vehement than Chatham's. Yet even in his fiercest bursts of party spirit he could show a noble disregard of popularity when he thought his country's good concerned. The press-warrants had been opposed in the City. Wilkes sitting as Alderman, and athirst for some new grievance, had refused to back them. Several of his colleagues followed his example. Trecothick, the Lord Mayor, attempted, much to his honour, to stem the torrent on this question, but his term of office expired a few days before the meeting of Parliament, and his successor, Alderman Brass Crosby, leaned to the popular side. Lord Chatham was consulted, but Lord Chatham disdained such demagogue arts. Thus he wrote: "The "City, respectable as it is, deems of itself as I do not if "they imagine themselves exempt from question." * And in one of his speeches at this time he did not scruple to advise that the refractory Aldermen should be brought to answer for their conduct at the Bar of the House of Lords.

Unlike the common race of popular leaders, Lord Chatham, it appeared, had power not only to impel but to restrain. His voice was, although reluctantly, obeyed by the City, and no further serious obstacle was cast in the way of the press-warrants.

At this period, and during the Ambassador's absence, our Chargé des Affaires at Madrid was Mr. Harris, son of the author of Hermes. He was only twenty-four years of age, but already gave indication of that eminent skill and ability which have since shed lustre on his well-earned title of Malmesbury. His letters to Lord Weymouth as the Secretary of State are now before me.† He reports

* Chatham Letters, vol. iv. p. 24. See also the Parl. Hist., vol. xvi. p. 1101. On the general question of the Falkland Islands Dr. Johnson inveighs severely against Lord Chatham's violence. (Works, vol. viii. p. 118.) He seems disposed to award him "that equipoise of praise "and blame which Corneille allows to Richelieu, a man who, I think, "had much of his merit and many of his faults:

"'Chacun parle à son gré de ce grand Cardinal,
"'Mais pour moi je n'en dirai rien;
"'Il m'a fait trop de bien pour en dire du mal,
"'Il m'a fait trop de mal pour en dire du bien!'"

† The despatches of Mr. Harris from Madrid are published in his Diaries and Correspondence (vol. i. p. 33—78.). See also Coxe's Bourbon Kings of Spain, vol. iv. p. 385. et seq.

that the Catholic King and several of his Ministers felt themselves unprepared for war, and were sincerely desirous of peace. Still, however, they could not be brought to yield the full measure of retribution that England claimed. Others among the Spanish statesmen partook in the designs of Choiseul, and like him no doubt looked forward to a vigorous attack on England, Under such circumstances it is probable that hostilities would have been renewed had the power of Choiseul himself stood firm. But the nearer did these aggressive schemes approach the time for execution, the more did the repugnance to them of Louis the Fifteenth grow manifest. Towards the close of 1770 he wrote with his own hand to his "good brother" of Spain. "My Minister wishes for war, "but I do not."

Moreover at the same period a different train of events was leading to the downfal of this lately all-powerful Minister. Madame de Pompadour had died several years before. In the selection of herself and of the other favourites of the King of France some regard to station, to rank, nay even to character, had been observed. But the woman to whom henceforth Louis the Fifteenth without disguise or reserve attached himself,—a new Nell Gwyn,—had none of the "decencies of a mistress," according to the phrase employed by Bishop Burnet.* By a singular contrast she was born at Vaucouleurs, the same village in Lorraine from which the heroic Joan of Arc had sprung. Her lovers in her early youth were both numerous and various. Some of them, in admiration of her beauty, used to call her "the angel;" and thus she became known by the name of Mademoiselle L'Ange. But no sooner had she attracted the Royal notice than a ruined spendthrift of quality—a Comte Du Barry—was induced to secure her rank and his own fortune by giving her, for form's sake, his hand in marriage. In state affairs she showed much greater aptitude than might have been imagined, and her influence over the amorous monarch grew to be unbounded. Sometimes indeed he seemed conscious of

* History of his Own Times, vol. i. p. 263. folio ed. The reader may recollect Swift's caustic note upon the margin of that passage. (Works, vol. x. p. 266.)

his degradation; nor were there wanting many significant hints even from the most servile of his courtiers.* But love, or what he called so, never failed to resume its sway.

Madame Du Barry had no desire or design to enter the lists against Choiseul had not Choiseul himself haughtily set her at defiance. His temper, always overbearing, was now elated by long possession of power. He deemed also that he had fully secured that power by the support of Austria, having only a few months since negotiated and solemnized a marriage between the King's eldest grandson, the heir apparent to the Crown, and a daughter of the Empress Queen, the Archduchess Marie Antoinette. By his arrogance he added Madame Du Barry to the number of his enemies, while his ambition and his perfidy supplied them with formidable weapons. He was denounced to the King for his perpetual thirst of war, for his restless machinations against England, for his unauthorized promises to Spain; and the whole dispute of the Falkland Islands was said to be raised and fomented by his arts. Early in December Choiseul received secret information that his downfal was resolved upon; and on the 24th of that month there was put into his hands a LETTRE DE CACHET dismissing him from office and banishing him from Court, the place of his banishment, however, being fixed at his own country seat of Chanteloup in Touraine. Then, subject to the smiles of Madame Du Barry, did an unworthy Triumvirate rule the King and kingdom; D'Aiguillon at the head of foreign affairs; Terray at the head of the finances; and Maupeou at the head of the law. Then did the Crown of France lose all influence, all dignity, in the eyes of other nations; then for a while did it wholly cease to weigh in the balance of European powers.

The effect of Choiseul's retirement on the Spanish councils was immediate and decisive. In the course of December the Prince de Masserano had transmitted to

* "Un jour qu'il contait son abjection, Louis dit au Duc de "Noailles: 'Je sais bien que je succède à Sainte Foy.'—'Oui, Sire,' "dit le Duc en s'inclinant, 'comme Votre Majesté succède à Pharamond!'" (Sismondi, Hist. des Français, vol. xxix. p. 401.)

Lord North the answers from his Court. They had refused the terms demanded, and only offered that the King of Spain would disavow the expedition of Buccarelli if the King of England on his part would disavow the threats of Captain Hunt. Upon this Lord Rochford declared the negotiation at an end, and sent orders to Mr. Harris to quit the Spanish capital. Mr. Harris therefore in the January ensuing set out on his journey homewards. But he had not proceeded beyond a small hamlet twenty leagues from Madrid when he was stopped by a second courier from Lord Rochford informing him of a subsequent and satisfactory communication from the Prince de Masserano. Spain at last conceded everything that England had asked. The attack of Buccarelli was expressly disavowed. The settlement of Port Egmont was respectfully restored. It was stipulated that this restitution was not to affect any claim of right which His Catholic Majesty might have to the territory, but it is wholly false as alleged by the Opposition of that day that there was a secret article pledging England at some future time to surrender it to Spain.

The Court of St. James's, however, had learnt by experience how great and how unprofitable was the charge of this distant settlement. Nor had we then as now other settlements and Colonies in the Southern Seas, giving to the possession of the Falklands a value beyond its own. Thus after recovering Port Egmont, and retaining it for nearly two years more, the English of their own accord abandoned it. Even then they did not surrender it to Spain. They left their flag flying from the rocks, and affixed large sheets of lead with engraved inscriptions declaring to all other states that the Falklands were the sole right and property of the King of Great Britain. The Spaniards at that time showed not the least desire to seize or people the sterile island which their rivals had forsaken, and it continued during many years the same bleak desert we first found it.* And thus while the dignity of the

* The island was re-colonized in 1826 by the Republic of Buenos Ayres, and was held by that Republic, chiefly as a place of banishment, until 1831. (Note to Cavendish Debates, vol. ii. p. 306.) In 1833 the British flag was for the second time unfurled at Port Eg-

British name had not been stained or lowered, the dangers of an European conflict were happily averted.

The Opposition did not fail during the remainder of this Session to exclaim most vehemently against the provisions of the Treaty; but in both Houses a large majority approved it. Far less happy was the chance which at the same period involved the House of Commons in unseemly and unprofitable altercation, first with the House of Peers, and next with the City of London. In the first the immediate cause was one of the debates on the Falkland Islands, before the negotiation was concluded and while war was deemed imminent. The Duke of Manchester was descanting on the neglected and insecure condition of Gibraltar, when a motion was made to clear the House of strangers that the weakness of the nation, if weakness there were, might not be publicly disclosed. This motion was warmly resisted by Lord Chatham and the Duke of Richmond, but such was the agitation that the former could not even obtain a hearing, and they finally retired with their friends to the number of eighteen, and all in the utmost anger. Then the order for clearing the House was enforced, and extended also to such Members of the Commons as were present, some of whom had come not from curiosity but on business with a Bill. Colonel Barré who was among them gave to his own House an inflamed and passionate description of what had passed. "I could not suppose," said he, "that a single "Peer remained in the House. It seemed as if the mob "had broke in, and they certainly acted in a very ex"traordinary manner. One of the heads of this mob— "for there were two—was a Scotchman. I heard him "call out several times: CLEAR THE HOOSE! CLEAR "THE HOOSE! The face of the other was hardly human; "for he had contrived to put on a nose of enormous size "that disfigured him completely!"* In this coarse caricature the two Peers aimed at were the Earl of March-

mont, a British officer being again sent out in command, and "We "found him," says Mr. Darwin, "in charge of a population of which "rather more than half were runaway rebels and murderers!" (Journal, vol. i. p. 188.)

* Cavendish Debates, vol. ii. p. 162. See also the Chatham Papers, vol. iv. p. 58.

mont and the Earl of Denbigh. The Commons were provoked into some retaliation, and had not the Ministers displayed more judgment and temper than their adversaries this small spark might have been blown into a violent flame.

It is worthy of note in these debates as an indication of the state of parties that Burke seized the opportunity of paying high compliments to Chatham. "Conscious of my "own natural imbecility I endeavour to get knowledge "wherever I can. I desire to hear the discussions of the "other House. I desire to learn the opinions of that "great man who, though not a member of the Cabinet, "seems to hold the key of it, and to possess the capacity "of informing and instructing us in all things." Chatham himself was to the full as indignant at the diminution of his audience. Thus he writes to the Countess Stanhope: "The House being kept clear of hearers, we are reduced "to a snug party of unhearing and unfeeling Lords and "the tapestry-hangings; which last, mute as Ministers, "yet tell us more than all the Cabinet on the subject of "Spain, and the manner of treating with an insidious and "haughty Power."—These tapestry-hangings, it will be recollected, portrayed the defeat of the Spanish Armada.

Of all the Members of the Commons there was none more eager and zealous in resenting the alleged insult they had received than Lord George Sackville, who about this period to inherit an estate had taken the name of Germaine. In reply to him Governor Johnstone said sarcastically, that a man ought to clear his own honour before he set himself up as the champion of the honour of the House. As might be expected after such a taunt a duel ensued between them. They met in Hyde Park, and exchanged pistol-shots without hurt on either side, but Lord George displayed so much intrepidity and coolness on this occasion that, in the estimation of his friends at least, it might efface the memory of the evil day at Minden.

The contest shortly afterwards with the City of London was not unconnected with the former. The more immediate cause, however, was the growing practice of reporting the debates in Parliament. It would be far from candid to judge of the measures adopted then by the feelings prevalent now. In the earlier days of our Constitutional history, from the Revolution downwards, it was deemed, even by the ablest and the wisest men, that they had everything to dread from the publication, if permitted, of any false or garbled statement of their conduct or opinions. Even Marlborough, so sagacious in estimating perils, and so serene in confronting them, warmly urges his colleague Godolphin to discover, if possible, and to pursue the author of a libel; "for," he adds, "if such liberties may be taken of telling scandalous "lies without being punished, no government can stand "long." * In 1728 and again in 1738 under the administration of Sir Robert Walpole the House of Commons, by the concurrence of all parties, and without a single dissentient voice, agreed to stringent Resolutions against any person who should presume to give any account of their Debates. By the same Resolution they pledged themselves to proceed against such offenders "with the "utmost severity." † Nevertheless the practice was never put down. It was found that at periods especially of party-struggle and excitement the news-writers were not restrained from gratifying at any risk the public curiosity. Various disguises and evasions were assumed for safety. The London Museum published the "Debates "in the Political Club," and the Gentleman's Magazine published the "Debates in the Senate of Lilliput." The names given of the speakers were fictitious, often those derived from Roman History, and afterwards explained in advertisements separate from the volumes. If the real names were used at all they were designated at most by the first and concluding letter with a dash or asterisk between. In some few cases, as at present, the reports were supplied or corrected by the speakers themselves. ‡ But in general they were most brief and

* To Lord Godolphin, August 24. 1705. Coxe's Life of Marlborough.

† Resolutions of the House of Commons, February 26. 1728, and April 13. 1738.

‡ "As to the speeches printed by Members themselves, we never "have prevented their publication," said Burke in February 1771. Cavendish Debates, vol. ii. p. 259. There are, however, some remote cases to the contrary; Lord Digby's in 1641, Sir Edward Dering's in 1642.

imperfect, and drawn up with such glaring partiality and passion on one, chiefly the Opposition, side as to afford at the time a specious argument against the practice itself. No one as yet foresaw how much, when itself became improved, it would improve and instruct the people. The practice was then considered only on most narrow grounds; by timid men who dreaded a libel on themselves; or by formal men who deprecated a breach of the Privileges of the House.

It was not until 1770 that the practice of reporting nearly in its present form may be said to have commenced. In that year the Parliamentary debates began to be given, not only at wide intervals or on special occasions, but both more frequently and more fully, and with less of disguise or concealment. Such an innovation could not fail to be displeasing to many Members. It was noticed more especially when in consequence of the quarrel with the House of Lords the exclusion of strangers came to be in question. Colonel George Onslow, Member for Guildford, and nephew of the late Speaker, moved that certain printers whom he named should be summoned to the Bar to answer for their disobedience. It did not appear easy for the House when thus called upon to refuse to give effect to its own Orders. Some of the printers being therefore summoned did accordingly appear at the Bar, and were reprimanded by the Speaker upon their knees; after which they were discharged. Others evaded compliance with the requisition; and one of them, Miller by name, took his stand upon his rights as a liveryman of London. In quest of him one of the messengers was despatched to his shop by the Serjeant-at-Arms. A scuffle ensued, and at last this messenger, instead of taking Miller, was himself taken by a City constable, and carried before Brass Crosby, the Lord Mayor. The Lord Mayor, when after some hours' delay he admitted the parties, was attended by Alderman Oliver and Alderman Wilkes. With their full concurrence he declared that to lay hands upon a citizen within the precincts of the City, and without the knowledge or authority of the City Magistrates, was a flagrant violation of the City's Charters. On this ground the three Magistrates not only refused to give up Miller, but took the bold course of holding the Messenger to bail for an assault,—that is, for the arrest he had attempted.

At the news of this occurrence the House of Commons were fired with indignation. They began to feel, as the King more wisely foresaw at the outset*, that they had entered upon a rash and unsafe course, but they felt also that they could not recede from it with honour. It was ordered by a large majority that the Lord Mayor and Alderman Oliver, who were Members, should attend in their places, and that Alderman Wilkes should appear at the Bar. Wilkes wrote a letter in reply to this order, declaring that he was the lawful representative of Middlesex by the free choice of the electors, and refusing to appear unless as a Member in his place. Three times was the order repeated, three times distinctly declined. Yet so great was the unwillingness on all sides to meddle any further with this formidable patriot, that notwithstanding his open defiance of the House, the order for his attendance was allowed to drop,—to the great disappointment no doubt of Wilkes himself, who had reaped a most abundant and profitable harvest from each of his former prosecutions.

Of the two remaining magistrates, the Lord Mayor being ill of gout, and compelled to quit the House abruptly, the case of Oliver was first decided. That Alderman appeared in his place, but refused to make the smallest submission. "Do what you please," he said; "I defy you." † After a violent debate, but by a large majority, Alderman Oliver was sent a prisoner to the Tower. Two days afterwards, on the 27th of March, the turn of Brass Crosby came. In consideration of his sickness it was moved that he should not be sent to the Tower, but committed to the gentler custody of the Serjeant-at-Arms. But the Lord Mayor with a noble spirit disdained the proffered lenity. He said that his health was much amended; that he had no favour to ask of the House; that in justice to his honourable friend he ought to share the like confinement; that in maintaining the City Charters he had done no more than his duty, and that in the same circumstances he

* Letter to Lord North, March 17. 1771.

† Cavendish Debates, vol. ii. p. 461.

should certainly do the same again. An amendment was then moved by Mr. Welbore Ellis that he should be sent to the Tower; an immense majority approved, and to the Tower the Lord Mayor was sent accordingly.*

It is not to be supposed that measures so violent were adopted by the House without as violent resistance from some of its own Members. A minority, small indeed in numbers, but resolute in their spirit, and historically important in their names, (they were joined by Burke; they were approved by Chatham †;) offered every opposition in their power. One evening they divided the House no less than twenty-three times. At other times they tried the moral effect of a secession; Colonel Barré, Sir George Savile, and several more withdrawing from the House in much wrath, and exclaiming it was clear that justice would not be done. Still less did these violent measures pass without riots and tumults in the streets. Large multitudes gathered as during the Middlesex Elections, greeting the City Magistrates with cheers, their opponents with hisses and stones. On the day, above all, when the Lord Mayor was ordered to attend, and was finally sent to prison, it was with great difficulty that the Ministerial members could make their way into the House. Lord North's chariot was broken, and himself wounded in the hand, and he might not improbably have been torn to pieces but for the rescue of an honourable enemy, Sir William Meredith. Mr. Charles Fox, then a Lord of the Treasury, and among the foremost on the anti-popular side, was almost as roughly handled as his chief. There had been at that time a prevalent rumour that Lord North intended to resign. But when he addressed the House that same evening, moved even to tears, though speaking with manly firmness, the Prime Minister adverted to that point as follows: " I certainly did not come into office at

* According to Lord Orford: " When he (the Lord Mayor) " entered the Tower he was half-drunk, swore, and behaved with a " jollity ill becoming the gravity of his office or cause." (Memoirs, vol. iv. p. 304.)

† " If the Ministry proceed to punish the Lord Mayor, the stand " against such injustice and oppression cannot be made with too " much vigour and firmness." (Chatham Correspondence, vol. iv. p. 136.)

"my own desire. Had I my own wish I would have "quitted it a hundred times. My love of ease and re-"tirement urged me to it, but as to my resigning now, "look at the situation of the country, look at the trans-"actions of this day, and then say whether it would be "possible for any man with a grain of spirit, with a grain "of sense, with the least love for his country, to think of "withdrawing at such a moment from the service of his "King and his country. . . . . . There are but two ways "in which I can go out now: — by the will of my Sove-"reign which I shall be ready to obey, or by the pleasure "of the gentlemen now at our doors when they shall be "able to do a little more than they have done this day." *

The City supported its magistrates zealously and warmly. Three other Aldermen in the House of Commons, Trecothick, Sawbridge, and Townsend, declared that they made common cause with their chief. At a Court of Common Council, convened in Guildhall and presided over by Trecothick, thanks were voted to the Lord Mayor and to Aldermen Wilkes and Oliver for their public spirit and courage, and a Committee was appointed to assist in their defence. It was also resolved that the expense of the Lord Mayor's table and of Alderman Oliver's during their confinement should be defrayed from the City funds. Further still, by the desire and at the charge of the City, Writs of Habeas Corpus were sued. Crosby and Oliver were brought before Lord Mansfield and Lord Chief Justice De Grey. Serjeant Glynn and Mr. Lee appeared as their counsel. But after a full hearing the Judges declared themselves bound to acknowledge under such circumstances the power of commitment by the House of Commons, and thus the prisoners were sent back to the Tower.

Whatever man, not himself belonging to the House of Commons, shall calmly review its proceedings from the Revolution to the present day, will scarce be able to deny that whenever its own privileges were in question it has shown itself prone to petty acts of tyranny. Nor is this any matter of especial blame, for what other council or

* Cavendish Debates, vol. ii. p. 480. At this very page, that useful publication was, for want of funds, abruptly ended. The MS. extends to 1774.

assembly or body of men could be safely entrusted with an absolute power of deciding how far under the name of Privilege their own dignity and power should extend? But considering that perhaps unavoidable and certainly often recurring proneness, it is a most happy, a most beneficent, provision in our law which limits the duration of such petty acts of tyranny to the House's own period of sitting. Thus when on the 8th of May 1771 this busy and anxious Session was closed by a Prorogation, then without controversy or doubt or delay, and as a matter of course, the prison doors were thrown open to the Lord Mayor and Alderman Oliver. A gorgeous procession of the City officers in their robes attended them from the Tower to the Mansion House; and a large concourse of spectators testified their approbation and good-will; while in the evening bonfires and illuminations gave further tokens of the general joy. Warned by such signs of the popular feeling the House of Commons in the ensuing Session more wisely forbore any renewal of the conflict; neither Miller nor any other printer of their debates was again molested on the general plea of Privilege; and the freedom of the press, grown only the stronger and the firmer from the blow which had been aimed against it, has continued until our own times to thrive and grow, until at last, as it has been said, the Reporters' Gallery has become almost a fourth Estate of the Realm.

In the course of these proceedings some readers may feel surprise at finding the name of Charles Fox thus amongst the foremost opponents of the popular cause. Such, however, was at that time his position,—in the very vanguard of Prerogative and of Privilege—"Privi-"lege, that eldest son of Prerogative," says Burke, "and "inheriting the vices of its parent." * It was the position at that time not of Charles Fox alone but of his house. The latest official connexion of Lord Holland had been with Lord Bute and Lord Bute's friends. With them he continued linked during great part of his retirement. This connexion did not indeed prevent him from soliciting from others also that Earldom which had

* Speech in the House of Commons, March 20. 1771.

become the darling object of his life. Thus in 1767 he had not deemed it beneath the station he had filled in the eyes of men to implore that favour from his ancient rival and enemy, Lord Chatham; applying in most submissive terms, and declaring that he would sooner owe that aim of his ambition to Lord Chatham than to any man alive! * But until his death in 1774 he might be, and was, upon the whole regarded as one of that band of statesmen who held the highest notions of Royal and aristocratical power, and were most disposed to stand firm against the claims and pretensions of the people. Such were the auspices under which his two sons, Stephen and Charles James, entered public life, the first as Member for Salisbury, the second as Member for Midhurst. Both took a forward part in the Middlesex Elections, espousing with their father what is now universally admitted to be the unconstitutional side. Stephen Fox proposed Colonel Luttrell on the hustings; Charles Fox argued in the House that in spite of Luttrell's minority of votes he should be declared the sitting Member. Both zealously withstood on other questions that new Whig phalanx to which in after years Charles himself and the son of Stephen, Henry third Lord Holland, were destined to become the brightest ornaments.

Charles Fox when first elected for Midhurst was not yet twenty years of age. Little more than a twelvemonth afterwards when Lord North became Prime Minister he was named a Lord of the Admiralty. It is not my intention in this place to attempt any sketch, however slight, of the character and career of that most eminent statesman; here I desire to state only the circumstances under which he rose. I may add that at his rising he did not as yet shine with his full lustre. It was only by slow degrees, as Burke long afterwards said, that he grew to be the most brilliant and accomplished debater that the world ever saw. But although at his outset he did not attain nor indeed attempt any high pitch of oratory, his speaking from the first was ready, ardent, clear, and to the point. I find a remarkable testimony to his Parliamentary powers before he was twenty-three years of age,

* See the Chatham Papers, vol. iii. p. 270.

from one of his keenest opponents at that time. In March 1771 Colonel Barré, in the very midst of a personal altercation with him, mentions him as "a very young Member "with great abilities, who already takes a sort of lead in "the House." *

The retirement of Lord Weymouth during the negotiations on the Falklands proved no heavy loss to the administration. Lord Weymouth had indeed good natural abilities and an easy flow of eloquence, which combined with a graceful person pleased the House of Lords, but he wanted steady application, and had injured both his fortune and his health by his taste for gaming and drinking.† He was then scarcely yet passed the mid-way of Dante, — only thirty-six years of age, — but he never rose to any higher fame in public life, although he once again, as Secretary of State, became a colleague of Lord North, and at a later period by the regard of Mr. Pitt was promoted to the Marquisate of Bath. His retirement; the death of Lord Halifax shortly afterwards; the promotion to the Bench of the Attorney General De Grey; and other changes of that period, afforded Lord North the means of greatly strengthening and improving his political position. The Duke of Grafton was induced to accept the Privy Seal, but with a kind of proud humility refused a seat in the Cabinet. The Great Seal was taken out of Commission and entrusted to one of the Commissioners, the eldest son of Lord Bathurst, now created Lord Apsley; a careful, painstaking lawyer, a mild, inoffensive man. To the first seat at the Board of Admiralty was promoted the Earl of Sandwich. Faulty as he was in his private, nay even in his public, conduct, his appointment was most unwelcome to his Sovereign. "Many others," says the Duke of Grafton in his Memoirs, "were not aware as I was of the King's strong "dislike to place Lord Sandwich, whose character he "disapproved, in any elevated post." Yet as regarded the duties of his office Lord Sandwich brought to them

* Cavendish Debates, vol. ii. p. 426.

† Observe the irreverent allusion in Junius; "If you deny Lord "Weymouth the Cup—" (June 22. 1771), and his subsequent attempt under the signature of Philo-Junius to explain that allusion away (August 26. 1771).

no common activity and zeal. A most unexceptionable witness, Mr. Charles Butler, speaks of him as follows: "Lord Sandwich rose early; he often appointed me to "attend him at six o'clock in the morning; and his time "from that hour till a late dinner was wholly devoted to "business." * The Earl of Suffolk became Secretary of State. Though himself pompous and shallow, his accession was much prized, because since the death of Mr. Grenville he had, for want of a better, been looked upon as chief by many of Mr. Grenville's followers, as distinguished from Lord Chatham's or Lord Rockingham's. Thus did Lord North's Government become reinforced by and embodied with two detachments from the old Whig army; the squadron of George Grenville and the squadron of the Duke of Bedford.

But no appointments probably were of so much importance to Lord North as the legal ones connected with the House of Commons, when Mr. Thurlow became Attorney and Mr. Wedderburn Solicitor General. It was between them that Lord North during the succeeding years of his administration used in general to sit; it was on them that he mainly, nay almost entirely, relied for assistance in debate. Gibbon, himself in Parliament and afterwards in office, thus states the case, not without a sly allusion to the somnolent habits of his chief. "The "Minister might indulge in a short slumber whilst he "was upholden on either hand by the majestic sense of "Thurlow and the skilful eloquence of Wedderburn." †

Neither Thurlow nor yet Wedderburn were men whose characters can be dismissed in a few slight words. — A country clergyman was the father, and a Norfolk vicarage the birthplace, of Edward Thurlow. He was educated at Caius College, Cambridge, but ere long was desired to

* Reminiscences, vol. i. p. 71. Lord Sandwich was noted for his attachment to Miss Reay, an actress at Covent Garden Theatre. After having lived with him for many years and borne him nine children, she was one evening shot dead with a pistol by one Mr. Hackman, a clergyman who had become passionately and hopelessly enamoured of her. Mr. Hackman was in consequence hanged at Tyburn. See the details of this tragical story in the Annual Register, 1779, p. 206.

† Memoirs (Dean Milman's edition), p. 239.

remove his name from the books on account of his having dared to hint in public,—what every one freely acknowledged in private,—that Mr. Dean was ignorant of Greek. On leaving Cambridge thus abruptly he entered a Solicitor's office, where William Cowper was among his brother pupils. "There," says the future poet, "was I "and the future Lord Chancellor constantly employed "from morning to night in giggling and making others "giggle, instead of studying the law." But Thurlow had one of those rare and powerful intellects which can make better use of minutes than common minds of hours. By short but vigorous snatches of study he effectually explored the most hidden nooks and bypaths of the rugged land of Jurisprudence. He had been entered at the Inner Temple, and in 1754, being then twenty-two years of age, he was called to the Bar. For several years did he languish without business. He first attracted notice by the spirit and success with which he maintained the rights of the Junior Bar against the arrogance of an overbearing leader, Sir Fletcher Norton. At the General Election of 1768 he was returned for the borough of Tamworth, but his first speech was not delivered until the great political crisis of January 1770. Almost immediately afterwards, Lord North becoming Prime Minister and Dunning having resigned, Thurlow was appointed one of the Law Officers of the Crown.

The principles of Thurlow, at least until his final fall from office, were those of the brave old Cavaliers,—for Church and King. It must be owned, however, that his private life by no means eminently qualified him to stand forth as the champion of any Church or creed. He was licentious in his morals, and though never married he used in his later years to take about with him to the houses of his friends three young ladies, his daughters. His conversation even beyond his convivial hours abounded with profane oaths. And as immorality thus dimmed and tarnished his Church principles, so did inconsistency his politics. There is no doubt, as I believe, that he was sincerely and truly attached to those high Monarchical tenets which he professed. Yet on one memorable occasion in 1788 it was clear that he did not love them or conscience and honour so well as office; while four years later he showed that even office itself was not so dear to him as spleen and the indulgence of his froward and resentful humour.

With all his faults and shortcomings, however, there was that in Thurlow which overawed and daunted his contemporaries, and of which the impression is not wholly lost even on posterity. It was a saying of Mr. Fox that no man ever yet was so wise as Thurlow looked. His countenance was fraught with sense; his aspect stately and commanding, his brow broad, massy, and armed with terrors like that of the Olympian Jove, to which indeed it was often compared. His voice loud, sonorous, and as rolling thunder in the distance, augmented the effect of his fierce and terrible invective. Few indeed were they who did not quail before his frown; fewer still who would abide his onset in debate. Perhaps no modern English statesman, in the House of Lords at least, was ever so much dreaded. In Parliament, as at the Bar, his speeches were homethrusts, conveying the strongest arguments or keenest reproofs in the plainest and clearest words. His enemies might accuse his style of being coarse and sometimes even ungrammatical, but they could never deny its energy or its effect.

In private life Thurlow was remarkable for his thorough knowledge of the Greek and Latin writers; and no less for his skill in argument and brilliant powers of conversation. While yet at the Bar Dr. Johnson said of him to Boswell: "I honour Thurlow, Sir; Thurlow is a fine "fellow; he fairly puts his mind to yours." And after he became Chancellor the same high authority added: "I "would prepare myself for no man in England but Lord "Thurlow. When I am to meet him I should wish to "know a day before." Unless with ladies his manner was always uncouth, and his voice a constant growl. But beneath that rugged rind there appears to have lurked much warmth of affection and kindliness of heart. Many acts of generous aid and unsolicited bounty are recorded of him. Men of merit and learning seldom needed any other recommendation to his favour. Thus on reading Horsley's Letters to Dr. Priestley he at once obtained for the author a Stall at Gloucester, saying (what I earnestly wish all other Chancellors had borne in mind) that "those who "supported the Church should be supported by it." Nevertheless his temper, even when in some measure sobered down by age, was always liable to violent and unreasonable starts of passion. It is related by a gentleman who dined with him at Brighton only a few months before his death (for I must ever hold that great characters are best portrayed by little circumstances), that a plateful of peaches being brought in, the ex-Chancellor incensed at their ill-appearance ordered the window to be opened, and not only the peaches but the whole desert to be thrown out! * Apart from any such sallies or passing gusts of anger, strong shrewd sense was the especial characteristic of Lord Thurlow. As a judge he was acute, vigilant, and fearless; above all taint or suspicion of corruption. And on the whole of his career it may be said that rising as he did from an humble station to the highest, he owed his rise solely to his own talents and exertions, and in no degree, however slight, to any suppleness or subserviency or mean compliances, either as a flatterer of the great or as a demagogue among the people.

Alexander Wedderburn, afterwards Lord Loughborough, and later still Earl of Rosslyn, was born in 1733. His father was an advocate at Edinburgh, and a small landowner in East Lothian. Young Alexander having completed his legal studies commenced his practice at the Scottish Bar. But fired with ambition for a loftier sphere, and engaging in a quarrel with the Dean of Faculty, he stripped off and flung aside his gown in open Court, bid his country farewell for ever, and sought his fortune in London. His main difficulty in his new career lay in overcoming a stubborn Northern accent, but by great resolution and perseverance he succeeded in that object. Not a trace of its origin could hereafter be detected in his language or his tones during the long and vigorous prime of his manhood, but it is alleged that in the last few years of his life as his energies declined his Scottish speech returned. As a barrister, with chambers at the Temple, he had at first but moderate success. In politics his rise was more rapid. At the beginning of the new reign he attached

* MS. Diary of Mr. Creevey, 1805, as cited by Lord Campbell in his Lives of the Chancellors, vol. v. p. 628.

himself to his countryman Lord Bute, whose star was then in the ascendant. By Lord Bute's influence was he brought into Parliament, and with Lord Bute's body-guard was he numbered. As such he was lashed by Churchill in one of his satires.* He adhered to Lord Bute most faithfully while the Earl was still in office, or while there seemed a reasonable prospect that the Earl would return to office. But these hopes gradually fading away, Wedderburn deemed it best to plunge headlong into hot Opposition. He took part against the Government with eagerness on all the leading questions of the day. One speech and one vote of his in the case of Wilkes gave offence to Sir Lawrence Dundas, the patron of the borough of Richmond, which Wedderburn at that time represented. Wedderburn thereupon resigned his seat, and was forthwith hailed as a martyr by his new allies. His health was drunk at the Thatched House Tavern as "the Steward "of the Chiltern Hundreds" amidst thunders of applause; yet his martyrdom proved light and easy; a new seat being without delay provided for him by Lord Clive at Bishop's Castle. Lord Clive, — with a liberal spirit frequently found under the old close borough system, — assured him in writing that he left him altogether free and uncontrolled as to his future course in politics.

Wedderburn, even amidst all the sound and rage of opposition, had ever kept office in his view. As the Ministers by degrees grew stronger and firmer he felt his objections to them ooze away; and when at last Lord North proposed to him to become Solicitor General the pleasing offer was readily accepted.† For this desertion Wedderburn was soon afterwards taunted by Colonel Barré in the House of Commons. He defended himself by saying that his ties had been with Mr. Grenville, and were dissolved by Mr. Grenville's death. This, however,

* "A pert prim prater of the Northern race,
"Guilt in his heart, and famine in his face!
"Mute at the Bar, and in the Senate loud," &c.

† "This must be confessed," says Lord Campbell, "to be one of the "most flagrant cases of *ratting* recorded in our party annals." (Lives of the Chancellors, vol. vi. p. 87.) This biography of Wedderburn has been of especial service to me, abounding as it does with new and valuable information derived from the Rosslyn MSS.

was in great measure an after-thought; his pretext rather than his motive. During the whole preceding Session of 1770 it will be found on examination that his course in politics considerably differed from Grenville's.

In the ranks of Lord North the new Solicitor General inspired at first but little confidence. At that period Junius sums up as follows the character of the rising champions, as he deems them, of Prerogative: "Charles "Fox is yet in blossom; and as for Mr. Wedderburn, there "is something about him which even treachery cannot "trust!" *—But he speedily made himself most useful, and as useful prized. Without ever attempting the higher flights of oratory, he was on all occasions a most able and dexterous debater, seldom at loss for an illustration, and never for an argument. Unlike most lawyers he shone alike at the Bar and in the Senate; and when raised to the judicial Bench as Chief Justice and Lord Chancellor, the dignity and grace of his manner were no less justly admired. He had the rare gift of speaking speciously on any side of any question; his stock of learning, if not vast, was at least sufficient and ever at command; and he would have been upon the whole a great man were it possible to be so without some share of public virtue. But public virtue was in him altogether wanting. In political affairs, such at least is my own firm belief, he looked not to the merits of the question, but solely and singly to his prospect of deriving from it some personal advantage.

Nor can it with truth be pleaded that Wedderburn sought high office merely as affording a wider scope of public usefulness. On the contrary, he might be charged with a love of ostentatious splendour. He told the Earl of Haddington that on the very day he became Solicitor General he had ordered a service of plate which cost him 8,000*l.* He appears to have changed his political associates to and fro with little concern. Indeed a character so cold and selfish could scarce be expected to glow with any ardour of private friendship, and though he loved society he never shone in it. "What can he mean," cried Foote, "by coming among us? He is not only dull him-

* To the Duke of Grafton, June 22. 1771.

"self but the cause of dullness in others."—"I never "heard anything from him that was at all striking," said Dr. Johnson to Boswell.* But he deserves this high praise, that to men of genius he was uniformly kind. He always acknowledged fully their claim to public respect, and on several important occasions, even when most clearly on the other side in politics, he showed himself the enlightened and generous protector of literary merit.

While the Government of Lord North was thus fortified by new accessions and by a better distribution of its members, the Opposition was even more than proportionably weakened and divided.—Wilkes when he ceased to be a martyr was shunned as an ally. It was found that his name during his imprisonment had been far more potent than his presence and exertions after his release. In the former period the Society of the Bill of Rights, while taking a forward part in public agitation, had raised a sum of no less than 17,000*l.* for the discharge of his debts. Wilkes, however, was by no means satisfied, thinking that they ought not only to free him from embarrassment, but make some provision for his future ease and comfort.† The Society now lost its weight and influence, and finally came to be dissolved through the quarrels of its members. None of them had been more strenuous in supporting Wilkes both at Brentford and Mile End than the Rev. John Horne, afterwards Horne Tooke. His abilities were ill fitted for the profession of a clergyman, which indeed he at last renounced, but they highly qualified him for his favourite occupation as a demagogue. Between him and Wilkes there now arose a violent animosity and a keen altercation carried on in newspapers. Descending to the lowest and most selfish details they were not ashamed thus publicly to wrangle respecting a Welsh pony and a hamper of claret!

Even before the close of 1770 might be discerned the growing discord and weakness of Wilkes and his City friends. At a meeting which they convened to consider their course of action, some proposed a new Remonstrance

* Boswell's Life of Johnson, vol. viii. p. 168. ed. 1835.

† Almon's Memoirs and Correspondence of Wilkes, vol. iv. p. 10. and 14.

to the King, while others urged an impeachment of Lord North in the House of Commons. "What is the use of a "new Remonstrance?" cried Wilkes. "It would only "serve to make another paper kite for His Royal High-"ness the Prince of Wales!"—"What is the use of an "impeachment?" cried Sawbridge. "Lord North is quite "sure of the Bishops and the Scotch Peers in the Upper "House, and could not fail to be acquitted!" But although these ardent patriots might differ a little as to the means, they were bent on one and the same end; and the Remonstrance which was at last agreed upon appears to have been framed by their united wisdom. As thus drawn up it teemed with silly vagaries fit only to please the lowest order of intellects. Thus it prayed that His Majesty would for ever remove from his presence and councils all his Ministers and Secretaries of State, especially Lord Mansfield (who by the way was not one of them), and that His Majesty would not again admit any Scotchman into the administration! *

Extravagancies like these could not fail among Wilkes's own supporters to disgust the upright and reflecting. Such was Alderman Oliver. During his imprisonment with the Lord Mayor in the Tower Wilkes became ambitious to fill the office of Sheriff for the ensuing year, and pitched upon Oliver as a most eligible second candidate. But the Alderman when applied to answered coldly, that he differed from Mr. Wilkes in many views of public affairs, and declined to be his colleague in the London Shrievalty. Finally Wilkes succeeded in his own object, being chosen Sheriff in conjunction with Alderman Bull; but he must have keenly felt the alienation of so many among his best and worthiest allies.

It was not only beyond Temple Bar that the cause of Opposition languished. In Parliament it was still divided between the followers of Rockingham and the followers of Chatham; and worse still than division, its stock of grievances ran low. The Falkland Islands no longer held out a plea for war. The complaints of the American Colonies were hushed, and it was hoped appeased. The

* See the Annual Register, 1770, p. 160., and Wilkes's own account in the Gentleman's Magazine for the same year, p. 519.

blow to Constitutional freedom in the case of the Middlesex Election, however unjustifiable, had lost its novelty and therefore much of its popular effect. The tyranny of Privilege had ceased when the prisoners in the Tower were set free. Under these circumstances the whole country, so long troubled by the warring of parties, manifested its desire for repose. Then it was that Burke wrote to one of his friends as follows: "After the violent ferment "in the nation as remarkable a deadness and vapidity has "succeeded." * Then it was that Junius in despair flung down his pen.

This lull of parties in England may be said to have continued for nearly three years. Parliament was not again convened until the January following; and when it did meet, turned its first attention to subjects of religious policy. A Petition was presented to the House of Commons by Sir William Meredith from about two hundred of the clergy, and some thirty or forty physicians and civil lawyers, praying that at the Universities and elsewhere their professions might be relieved from the necessity of subscription to the Thirty-nine Articles. The prayer of this Petition appears to have been supported by the principal men then in Opposition, with the remarkable exception of Burke. He did not plead for the perfection of the Articles as they stood, but he showed the difficulty of dispensing with them, and of framing better in their place. "These gentlemen," said Burke, "desire, instead "of Articles, to make a profession of their belief in the "Holy Scriptures. But what are we to understand by "the Holy Scriptures? The Romish Canon admits the "books of the Apocrypha; the Canon of Luther excludes "some parts of the Pentateuch and the whole epistle to "the Hebrews; and some ancient Fathers have rejected "the book of Revelations. Mankind are as little likely "to be of one mind on this as on any other subject."

The reception of this Petition, or the very idea of entertaining it, was opposed with much zeal by Lord North, Mr. Charles Fox, and other Ministerial Members. Nevertheless this being considered as an open question, the now

* To Mr. Shackleton, July 31, 1771. Correspondence, vol. i. p. 256. See also p. 504.

Solicitor General ventured to take part in its support. "The Universities," said he, "which prepare for all the "learned professions, and to rear fit Members of Par-"liament, ought not to be confined to those of a particular "creed; and we must reform them if they will not reform "themselves."—A division being called for, the Petition was rejected by 217 votes against 71.

A similar fate attended shortly afterwards a motion of Mr. Henry Seymour. The object of his intended measure was to secure the possessions of the subject against dormant claims of the Church; this was called the Church Nullum Tempus Bill.

In the midst of these debates on questions of religious policy an incident occurred which gave fresh force and edge to them. According to annual custom Dr. Nowell, chaplain to the House of Commons, preached before them on the 30th of January. As usual also the discourse was but thinly attended; only the Speaker and four other Members being present, and these perhaps not very attentive. Motions of thanks and for printing the Sermon were afterwards carried without notice or remark. But when the Sermon came to be transmitted to the Members in its printed form it was found to convey most highflown doctrines from the school of Filmer and Sacheverell, inculcating passive obedience, and repugnant to the principles of the Revolution of 1688. Mr. Thomas Townshend, at that time a speaker of some note, and afterwards a Minister with the title of Lord Sydney, was the first to sound the alarm. He moved that Dr. Nowell's sermon should be burned by the hands of the common hangman; and his motion might perhaps have been carried had not the House remembered just in time their own former vote of thanks. That former vote combined with their more recent indignation made the situation of the House a little embarrassing, not to say ridiculous.—Several acrimonious discussions ensued. At length it was agreed that in the Journals the vote of thanks should be expunged.

These debates, as may be supposed, did not pass without many and some severe allusions to the words of the Service which the Church has appointed for King Charles's Day. In consequence Mr. Frederick Montagu moved to repeal the Act for its observance. He declared that to his mind the Service for that day was no less than blasphemous, as conveying a parallel between our blessed Saviour and King Charles. On the other hand Sir Roger Newdigate, Member for the University of Oxford, zealously stood forth in defence of the Liturgy, and on a division he was supported by 125 votes against 97.

This conjuncture seemed to the Protestant Dissenters opportune for urging their pretensions. Several expressions in their favour had been heard to fall in the course of these debates from the midst of the Ministerial ranks. A meeting of the principal pastors resident in London, and belonging to the various Nonconformist congregations, was thereupon convened; and it was resolved to unite their efforts towards one common end. Their first step was to seek to dispense with the obligation imposed by the Toleration Act of William, though not enforced, of subscribing certain of the Articles: their final object was no doubt the repeal of the Test Act. With their sanction and support a Bill for the first step was proposed by Sir Henry Hoghton as a leading gentleman in the county of Lancaster, and seconded by Sir George Savile as a leading gentleman in the county of York. The arguments on both sides were nearly the same which have been repeated and continued even down to the present day. On the one hand some zealous churchmen urged that since the laws in question were never on any occasion put in force the Dissenters could have no valid reason to complain; on the other hand it was contended that even when no injury was inflicted, a reproach might still be conveyed. Among the Ministers and Ministerial supporters the prevailing wish was to comply with the request of the Dissenters, and to unite with them so far as possible in a Protestant league against the Roman Catholics. With this feeling the Bill passed the House of Commons speedily, and with only a slight and insignificant minority against it. In the Lords it was supported by the high authority of Camden, of Shelburne, of Chatham, and even of Mansfield. But some of the principal prelates, — Drummond, Archbishop of York, Terrick of London, Lowth of Oxford, Hinchcliffe of Peterborough, and Barrington of Llandaff, — opposed it with much warmth, as did also Lord Bruce and Lord

Gower; and on a division the Bill was rejected by a large preponderance, if not of arguments, yet certainly of numbers.

It was apparently during one of these debates that Lord Chatham ventured to describe the Church of England as being Popish in her Liturgy, Calvinistic in her Articles, and Arminian in her Clergy, — "a shallow "witticism," observes Mr. Gladstone, "little worthy of "so illustrious a man." * Such light expressions are indeed of little weight, but they may serve for a sample of the vehemence and exaggeration which on both sides of this question prevailed. How strange to find such vast advantages promised and expected from either the repeal or the retention of a law which, while it remained, all parties by common consent agreed was not, and never would be, put in execution!

* See Mr. Gladstone's "Church Principles," p. 452. ed. 1840. This saying of Lord Chatham is not to be found in the meagre Parliamentary reports of that day, but was mentioned by Burke many years afterwards in the House of Commons (Debate, March 2. 1790). Another passage of the same speech, "the College of Fishermen," to which Burke also alludes, I have had occasion to cite elsewhere. (See vol. iii. p. 17., and the Parl. Hist., vol. xvii. p. 441.) That passage (unless indeed Lord Chatham twice repeated the same taunt) fixes the date of the whole speech in 1772, although Burke's expression, "on the Dissenters' *second* application," would rather point to 1773.

CHAPTER L.

While public affairs, so long perturbed, began to flow in a smoother and more tranquil current, the King, although in some measure relieved of care for them, was sorely tried by afflictions in his own family. Among his brothers and sisters he had to mourn over the untimely death of some, and the erring conduct of others. The next in birth to himself, Edward Duke of York, a young man as yet careless and unthrifty but of many generous feelings, had set forth upon his travels in 1767, and had died of a fever at Monaco. The youngest, Prince Frederick, at the age of only fifteen expired of consumption. Henry Duke of Cumberland had grown to manhood, but was noted only for his libertine amours. He attached himself to a young and beautiful woman, Henrietta Vernon Lady Grosvenor, whose husband, it must be owned, afforded her no slight grounds of alienation. This lady he secretly followed into Cheshire, meeting her in disguise, yet not unobserved, at various times and places. On the discovery which ensued Lord Grosvenor, though from his own conduct hopeless of divorce, brought an action for Criminal Conversation, at which for the first time a Prince of the Blood appeared in the situation of Defendant. Besides other evidence his own letters were produced, showing him to be no less faulty in his grammar than in his morals. The verdict was of course against him, and damages were awarded to the amount of 10,000*l.* Immediately afterwards the Duke deserting his victim openly engaged in a new intrigue with the wife of a wealthy timber merchant. Here at least there was no dread of a second trial, since, as Horace Walpole tells us, it seemed uncertain which was most proud of the distinction, the husband or the wife.* But His Royal Highness once more proving inconstant next became

* Memoirs, vol. iv. p. 356.

enamoured of Mrs. Horton, the daughter of an Irish Peer, Simon Luttrell Lord Irnham, and the widow of a private gentleman in Derbyshire. This lady required marriage, to which the weak Prince agreed, and in October 1771 carrying off his prize to Calais he there espoused her according to the rites of the Church of England. The King in high displeasure forbade them both his Court. Nevertheless another of his brothers, William Henry Duke of Gloucester, seized this opportunity to avow and declare a marriage contracted by him several years before with Maria, an illegitimate daughter of Sir Edward, and grand-daughter of Sir Robert, Walpole, and Countess Dowager of Waldegrave.

Of these two marriages thus made public at nearly the same time it might be hard to determine which was the more offensive to the just pride of the Royal Family. On the one hand the stain of illegitimacy, even in her inferior birth, attached to Lady Waldegrave. But on the other side there was an especial sting in finding that the scheming widow thus foisted into the rank of the princesses was no other than the sister of that Colonel Luttrell, by Court favour the candidate, and by a violation of the law the Member, for Middlesex. Such a circumstance was heightened to the best advantage in all the party libels of the day. Thus had written Junius: "The forced unnatural union of Luttrell and Middlesex "was an omen of another unnatural union. If one of "those acts was virtuous and honourable, the 'best of "'princes,' I thank God, is happily rewarded for it by "the other!" *

Degrading as these alliances may have been in Royal estimation they were wholly cast into the shade by the disastrous news which came from Copenhagen. A sister of George the Third, the Princess Caroline Matilda, had some years before espoused Christian the Seventh King of Denmark. Queen Matilda was young and beautiful, pure and gentle-minded. † She had borne her husband

* Letter lxvi. To the Duke of Grafton, November 28. 1771. In another passage he commemorates "the King's brother-in-law Colonel Luttrell, and old Simon his father-in-law."

† Queen Matilda is described as follows by an accomplished Dane, the Comte de Falckenskiold: — "la plus belle femme de la Cour,

two children; a son about four years of age, and a daughter whom at this period she was nursing. Unhappily in her marriage she was linked to an abject wretch, destitute alike of sense and of virtue. Already while travelling in England he had been noticed for his ridiculous figure and eccentric manners. But since that period his mind, never strong and unnerved by his early excesses, had given way, and he was verging by degrees to a state of utter imbecility. During his travels he had attached to himself one Struensee, then a physician at Altona; a young man of handsome person and aspiring talents. On his return to Copenhagen Struensee became at first in fact, and ere long also in name and title, his Prime Minister. To be Prime Minister under such a sovereign was in reality to be absolute master of the King and kingdom. It was by him, and next to him by his coadjutor Brandt, that all measures were decided and all appointments bestowed. In such a state of things it was natural, nay necessary, that Queen Matilda should have frequent communication with Struensee on public affairs. But her enemies alleged that during these communications she had forgotten, or rather perhaps remembered too well, her half-witted husband, and had betrayed her conjugal duty. And although, as I believe, this accusation was unfounded, it certainly derived no little colour from her own imprudence.

Imprudence of a different kind, but at least in an equal degree, may be justly imputed to Struensee himself. He entered upon a course of violent and arbitrary measures, some of them tending to useful reform, but many more partaking of rash innovation. The numerous persons whom he had offended, the numerous classes which he had alarmed, united in one common league against him, taking for their chief the step-mother of Christian, the Dowager Queen Juliana Maria. Under such auspices a secret and daring conspiracy was formed. The time fixed for its execution was at the close of a masqued ball to be given by the Court on the 16th of January 1772. Then

" d'un caractère doux et reservé, et qui aurait été vraisemblablement " fort heureuse, si son sort eut été lié à celui d'un bon et honnête " seigneur." (Memoires, p. 111. ed. 1826.)

some of the conspirators bursting into the King's chamber at midnight with well simulated zeal assured him that his life and throne were in peril, and that his consort was plotting to depose him. The stupified monarch nearly unconscious of what passed around him, and animated only by a dastardly terror for himself, signed at once the orders of arrest that were laid before him. Under such an order Struensee and Brandt were seized by a party of guards, loaded with irons, and cast into a dungeon. Under such an order Queen Matilda also was roused from her slumbers and informed of her arrest. Little respect was paid either to her station or her sex; and on her attempting to reach the chamber of her husband she found the bayonets of the soldiers crossed before her. Only half-attired (since no longer time was granted), and with her infant in her arms, she was led into a close carriage, an officer with a drawn sword being stationed by her side, and thus was she hurried away a prisoner to the castle of Cronenburg.*

So hateful had the Favourite become, that this revolution in the palace, however violent and sudden, was far from unwelcome to the people. The whole power of the State now devolved upon the Dowager and her confederates. Struensee and Brandt, who deserved dismissal, but not death, were brought to trial with only a slight semblance of the forms of justice; of course they were found guilty, and they ended their lives upon the scaffold. In like manner proceedings of divorce were commenced against the Queen, and various depositions, some from her own ladies, were produced. But these measures, so derogatory to the honour of both Crowns, were cut short by the resolute interposition of the King of England. After a

* Colonel (soon afterwards Sir Robert Murray) Keith was at that time the British Minister at Copenhagen. His despatches on this delicate transaction are missing from the series which I have seen at the State Paper Office, and his private letters, as published in 1849, seem to me of little value. I cannot forbear from here expressing my admiration of the skill with which the incidents of this conspiracy have been wrought by M. Scribe into his drama of *Bertrand et Raton*. The sketches (as was said) of Prince Talleyrand as *Bertrand* and of M. Laffitte as *Raton*, whether just or unjust, are drawn by the hand of a master.

captivity of four months the release of Queen Matilda was obtained. She received the first news of her deliverance with eager joy, speedily succeeded by a burst of bitter anguish when she was told of her intended separation from her infant child and nursling. With heavy heart and streaming eyes she was that very day led on board a British man of war, but remained on deck gazing on the castle of Cronenburg — so lately her own prison, yet still her dear daughter's abode — until its topmost battlements had faded from her view. She was conveyed to the dominion of her fathers, the Electorate of Hanover, where a residence and suitable household at the charge of her Royal brother was assigned her in the castle of Zell. There was not wanting a party in Denmark desiring her return, and planning a counter revolution in her favour.* But after three years of exile and only twenty-four of life Queen Matilda died at Zell of a malignant fever, or rather perhaps of a broken heart.

This unhappy princess, — the daughter, the sister, the wife, and the mother of Kings, and yet to whom the fate of the meanest peasant might seem enviable, — left behind her a dying declaration, recorded on high authority, but up to this time little, if at all, known in England. M. Roques, pastor of the French Protestant church at Zell, spoke of it as follows: "Almost every day Queen "Matilda used to send for me to read or converse with "her, or still oftener to consult me respecting the poor of "my district whom she desired to relieve. During the "last days of her life I became still more assiduous in "my visits, and I was with her till just before she drew "her last breath. Though very feeble in body she had "preserved all her presence of mind. After I had recited "to her the prayer for the dying, 'M. Roques,' said she, "in a voice that seemed to recover strength in the effort, "'I am going to appear before God. I now protest that "'I am innocent of the guilt imputed to me, and that I "'never was unfaithful to my husband.' — In all my con-

* This appears from one of George the Third's confidential letters Lord North, dated February 9. 1781. That extract, though brief, sufficiently corroborates the detailed narrative of Sir N. Wraxall in his Posthumous Memoirs (vol. i. p. 374—418.), a book which, without some such corroboration, is of no authority

" versations with the Queen she had never until that " moment alluded even in the most distant manner to the " charges brought against her." *

Ten days only after the first sorrowful tidings of the arrest and imprisonment of Queen Matilda her mother and the King's, the Princess Dowager, expired at Carlton House. She had not yet completed the fifty-third year of her age, but sunk beneath a grievous and incurable malady, a cancer at the breast. To the last she bore with unshrinking fortitude and firmness both the pangs of disease and the aspersions of party rancour. Thus, only a few months before her death, Alderman Townsend had inveighed against her by name in the House of Commons. " The people," he cried, " consider the Princess " Dowager of Wales to be the cause of the calamities that " have befallen us, and are anxious that an inquiry should " be made into the influence Her Royal Highness has " upon the councils of the kingdom." † Nay more, some of her ill wishers did not scruple to dwell with unmanly exultation on the anguish of her growing malady.‡ During the last few weeks of her life the King and Queen with affectionate duty came to pass every evening at her bedside. On the concluding night of all she took leave of her son as she was wont to do; nor did he perceive any discomposure or change in her demeanor, except that she embraced him with greater warmth and tenderness than usual. She then sank back to her pillow, and before the morning died.§

Such domestic misfortunes and mortifications as had thus in rapid succession befallen the Sovereign of England could admit on one point only of legislative preven-

* Memoires de Falckenskiold, p. 235, note by the editor of those Memoirs, M. Secretan, " premier juge du canton de Vaud." M. Secretan adds : " Ce que M. Roques me dit je l'écrivis le jour même (à " Hanovre le 7 Mars 1780) comme venant d'un homme distingué par " l'integrité de son caractère."

† Cavendish Debates, vol. ii. p. 447. Lord North replied with much good taste and propriety wholly denying the imputed influence. (Ibid. p. 459.) But as he forbore from any counter-panegyric on the Princess, the author of Junius attempted to found a taunt upon his silence. (Letter signed A WHIG, April 9. 1771.)

‡ Woodfall's Junius, vol. i. p. 241*. ed. 1812.

§ Gentleman's Magazine, 1772, p. 89.

tion for the future. To that point the King, with a just feeling of wounded dignity, applied his care. A Royal Message sent to both Houses recommended to them to consider the state of the law of marriage as applying to members of the Royal Family. Next day the new Bill prepared by the Government under the King's direction was laid upon the Table of the House of Lords. By that Bill every Prince or Princess, the descendant of George the Second, except only the issue of Princesses married abroad, was prohibited from marrying until the age of twenty-five without the King's consent. After the age of twenty-five, should the King's consent be refused, they might apply to the Privy Council, and if within a year of such announcement both Houses of Parliament should not express their disapprobation of the intended marriage it might then be lawfully solemnized. This measure, the "Royal Marriage Bill," was opposed in both Houses very vehemently and on various grounds; it passed nevertheless by large majorities and without any alteration; and happily for us it has continued in force until the present day.

The proposal of this measure led, however, to the resignation of Charles Fox. Lord Holland had ever regarded with the keenest animosity the Marriage Bill of Lord Hardwicke. That feeling appeared to have descended to his children; and the new statute might be said not only to extend, but also to confirm and ratify, the provisions of the former. Charles Fox therefore threw up his office, thus being at liberty both to oppose the Royal Marriage Bill, and to propose (as he did without success) the repeal of Lord Hardwicke's Act. At this period Gibbon writes as follows to a private friend: "Yesterday Charles Fox resigned the Admiralty. He "is commenced patriot, and is already attempting to "pronounce the words COUNTRY, LIBERTY, CORRUPTION, "and so forth; with what success time will discover."* But the patriotism, as it is here termed, of Mr. Fox extended no further at this juncture than to the question of Marriage. That question being disposed of, there

* To Mr. Holroyd, February 21. 1772. Miscellaneous Works, vol. ii. p. 77

was no motive to prevent his renewed connexion with Lord North. Thus in the January following we find him restored to Downing Street as one of the Lords of the Treasury; if not the same post, yet precisely the same rank, as he had held before.

In Sweden there took place a revolution nearly contemporaneous with the one in Denmark, but differing from it altogether in every circumstance except its time. —The Senate on the death of Charles the Twelfth had usurped, and ever since had held fast, by far the larger portion of the Royal prerogatives. These prerogatives Gustavus the Third, a young and ambitious monarch, who had recently succeeded to the throne, was eager to resume. Considering how much the Swedish oligarchy had abused its power the object might be free from blame, but in pursuing it the King did not shrink from false professions and violated oaths. After some cautious delays he succeeded, by fomenting an insurrection in Scania and a military movement at Stockholm. He had also been assisted by a subsidy from the Court of Versailles which hoped to resume its ancient influence in Sweden, while George the Third in a more rightful spirit had refused to contribute, as was required, large sums of money on the other side.*

The war between the Ottoman Porte and the Czarina still continued. Several bloody battles had been fought in the provinces adjoining the Danube; victory always inclining to the Russian side. But it was in truth, what King Frederick of Prussia with caustic wit has termed it, victory of the one-eyed over the blind. In the Turkish ranks the old religious enthusiasm had waned, not as yet succeeded by any portion of military discipline. Among the Russians, on the other hand, the soldiers were newly levied and ill-cared for; the Generals for the most part favourites of Catherine, promoted only from her partiality, and altogether destitute of skill or experience. Thus even when a battle had been bravely won it could seldom be judiciously improved. For naval operations the Empress had planned an enterprise, up to that time without a parallel, and by which she expected

* Letter to Lord North, February 28. 1771.

both to awe her rivals and to overwhelm her adversaries. A formidable fleet being equipped in the Baltic was ordered to sail round the continent of Europe into the Mediterranean and attack the Turkish dominions on that side. The nominal command was bestowed upon Count Alexis Orlof, a man wholly unversed in maritime affairs, and wanting even in personal courage, but brother of the ruling favourite. At the same time, however, the true efficient Admirals and Captains—as Elphinstone and Greig—were of British race. Appearing off the coast of the Morea in the spring of 1770 the Russians found little difficulty in raising an insurrection among the Greek inhabitants, but that insurrection being ill supported was soon suppressed. The Russians throve better with their schemes in the July following when they encountered the Turkish fleet; it was first defeated off the coast of Scio, and then destroyed by conflagration in the Bay of Tchesmé.

The victory of the Russians was great and might have been decisive. They proceeded to blockade the Dardanelles, and as a first step to further conquests laid siege to the castle of Lemnos. Thus assailed both by land and sea the Ottoman empire seemed in imminent peril and verging to its fall. But at this crisis it was saved by the genius and valour of one man, Gazi Hassan. Born on the frontier of Persia; sold in his boyhood as a slave to a Turk of Rodosto; employed during his youth as a boatman; he had in after-life gone through a range of romantic adventures, by turns a chief at Algiers, a fugitive in Italy, and a prisoner at Constantinople.* Far from the loose tenets so common in political adventurers, Hassan through all his wanderings most straitly held the faith, and most scrupulously practised the rites, of a Mussulman. At the naval battle off Scio he had commanded the Admiral-ship of the Turks which was attacked by that of the Russians. The Admirals on both

* For the character and early career of Hassan, see Rulhière Histoire de Pologne, vol. iii. p. 475—495. and vol. iv. p. 85—89. ed. 1807. This account closely agrees with the spirited sketch in *Anastasius* (vol. i. p. 29, &c.), which, as Mr. Thomas Hope assured me, was drawn in strict conformity to the information obtained by him in his Eastern travels.

sides, Cassim and Orlof, with equal prudence kept aloof. But Hassan towing close alongside his enemy, and locked fast to him by grappling-irons, continued to fight with the utmost fury, until from the Russian hand-grenades both vessels stood in flames. Both at length blew up with a terrific explosion, while Hassan, one of the last on deck, and one of the few survivors as it proved out of many hundreds, though severely wounded, swam safe to shore. Scarce yet recovered from his wounds he laid before the Grand Visier a scheme to raise the siege of Lemnos. He proposed to enlist four thousand volunteers from among the lower orders at Constantinople, — to arm each man with a sabre and pistol only, — and to transport them over to the island in rafts or small boats without artillery, trusting wholly to the force of courage and to the chances of surprise. This project seemed a mere chimera to all the best judges of the art of war; to none more than to Baron de Tott, a French engineer of great distinction in the Turkish service. De Tott felt it his duty to remonstrate on the subject with the Grand Visier. The Grand Visier heard him with attention, and then calmly replied: "I agree with you that "Hassan's scheme is absurd and hopeless; but at all "events it will rid us of four thousand rabble; and that "riddance is almost as good as any victory!"* Under such auspices, such prognostications, did Hassan proceed upon his enterprise. It was crowned with triumphant success. Landing in Lemnos unperceived, he fell sword in hand upon the enemy, who fled with precipitation and not without slaughter to the shore, where they re-embarked; the Russian fleet in a panic heaved anchor; and the Turkish fortress was saved.

After an exploit so brilliant and so wholly unexpected the Sultan named Hassan Capitan Pacha or Lord High Admiral. From that time forward, partly through his vigilance, and partly through their own dissensions, the Russians could achieve no further conquest, and make no further progress by sea; and they finally sailed back

* Memoires du Baron de Tott, vol. ii. p. 81. ed. 1785. The difficulty of access to this island was long since remarked by Homer (Iliad, lib. xxiv. v. 573.)

Ες Σαμον ες τ' Ιμβρον και Λημνον αμιχθαλοεσσαν.

with much disappointment to the Baltic. The King of England offered his mediation towards a peace, and conferences for that object were pursued with much activity through the summer of 1772. No such result, however, was at that time attained, and hostilities continued, though more languidly, till the summer of 1774, when they were terminated by the treaty of Cainardgi, the principal stipulation being that the Porte should relinquish its sovereignty over the Crimea.

Not unconnected with the warfare in Turkey were the troubles in Poland. That ill-fated country, owing to its own elective Royalty and defective constitution, had for many years past lain open to the rapacity or dictation of its neighbours. There, as Russia had often tried, everything might be had for asking or rather for taking. There, as the Empress Catherine had once declared, one need only stoop down and gather up.* Since the election above all of Stanislas Poniatowsky for King in 1764 the Russian influence which had mainly wrought his elevation assumed to rule the kingdom in his place. The chief cause or pretext of internal strife was the condition of the DISSIDENTS, under which term in Poland were comprised all other forms of Christian faith beyond the Roman Catholic pale. Russia as adhering to the Greek Church warmly espoused the cause of the Dissidents, obtaining for them by main force a repeal of penal statutes and a participation in political rights. As warmly did the party opposed to Russia resist and resent such concessions. And thus unhappily in the annals of Poland at this period the cause of religious intolerance is closely blended with the cause of national freedom. A confederation in favour of the Dissidents was formed at Radom; another confederation against them was formed at Barr. The former was openly upheld by the Court of Petersburg, while the latter received in secret some succour from the Court of Versailles. It was also mainly with a view to assist the Confederates of Barr that France in 1768 had impelled the Porte to its rash and ill-considered declaration of war. In the desultory hos-

* "Il semble, dit-elle en riant, qu'en Pologne il n'y a qu'à se "baisser et en prendre!" (Ferrand, Hist. des trois Demembremens, vol. i. p. 142. ed. 1820.)

tilities which ensued throughout Poland many districts were laid waste; and wherever the Russian troops were quartered they levied recruits or contributions as they might in a conquered province.

This treatment of Poland so repugnant to every principle of generosity or justice was not long in attracting the serious consideration of the King of Prussia. Generosity or justice had indeed little or no weight with Frederick in his conduct of foreign affairs; they served him only as flourishes for the adornment of his writings. But although he was perfectly willing that Poland should still be plundered, he was not willing that Russia should monopolise the spoil. Why might not Prussia claim a share? Why might not each of the three neighbouring Powers seize and incorporate in its own dominions the provinces most contiguous and most desirable to itself, leaving only the poor remainder to King Stanislas and his successors? Negotiations on this basis were actively pursued both at Petersburg and at Vienna. The Empress Catherine, though with some difficulty, was brought to acknowledge that Poland ought not to be a prey for herself alone. Far different were the feelings of that virtuous and noble-minded woman the Empress Maria Theresa. She expressed to her Minister, Prince Kaunitz, the utmost aversion and horror of the scheme as a flagrant violation of the public right.* But her age was now advanced, and her strength declining, while her son the Emperor Joseph the Second had become her colleague, or in truth more than her colleague, in the administration of the government. Thus at last she yielded, though not without a bitter pang. On the 5th of August 1772 were signed the definitive treaties of partition between the Three Powers; according to which the Prussians were to have Pomerelia, the Austrians Galicia, and the Rus-

* In the Appendix to this volume will be found her confidential note to Prince Kaunitz, as translated from the German. The original is in Preuss (Lebens Geschichte, &c., vol. iv. p. 38.). In January 1772 Frederick the Second wrote to D'Alembert as follows: " J'entreprendrais plutot de mettre toute l'histoire des Juifs en ma-" drigaux, que d'inspirer les mêmes sentimens à trois Souverains, — " entre lesquels il faut compter deux femmes!" (Œuvres Posthumes, vol. xi. p. 242. ed. 1789.)

sians great part of Lithuania. Poland, distracted and enfeebled, and standing alone against the Three, could offer no resistance, and obtain no succour to her cry; nay more, she was soon compelled to ratify the rapine which she could not hinder.

The iniquity of this transaction stands little in need of comment. An usurpation more shameless, more destitute of any plausible plea, is scarce to be found in any page of history. When Louis the Fifteenth was first apprised of it he is said to have exclaimed, "This would "not have happened had Choiseul still been here!" The successors of Choiseul indeed were not men either to foresee the crisis or to deal with it when come. They might express displeasure and resentment; they might threaten to send one fleet of observation to the Archipelago, and another to the Baltic; they might even commence preparations with that view in the harbours of France and Spain; but all men felt that theirs were but illusory schemes or idle boasts; that they would shrink from the moment of action; that they were neither to be feared as enemies nor trusted as allies. Under such circumstances the sole remaining Great Power, namely, the Court of St. James's, can scarcely, as it seems to me, be blamed in abstaining from hostile measures, and coldly acquiescing in the partition of Poland. To do otherwise England must have reversed her whole previous policy, and sought alliance with the Sovereigns of the Family Compact, Louis the Fifteenth and Charles the Third. She must have relied upon, and acted with, the abject Ministry of Madame Du Barry. She must have renounced the hope, on which at that time her ablest statesmen set the utmost value, of a close alliance with the Court of Russia. And if we could not take part in the conflict frankly and directly, still less could we do so indirectly; still less was it consistent with our dignity and honour, while ourselves remaining inactive, to fan the flames of war between Turkey and Russia, as our ambassador at Constantinople attempted at one moment contrary to his instructions.* Yet while acknowledging

* See in the Appendix the prompt rebuke addressed to him by the Secretary of State, July 24. 1772. It may be observed in that de-

the justice of these views in vindication of the British Ministers, we may still regret that their language at that time was scarcely adequate to the magnitude of the occasion. The Secretaries of State, the Rochfords and Suffolks, of the day, so far as we can judge from their own despatches, do not seem to have comprehended the full bearings of the question before them; they say nothing of the danger of disturbing the balance of power; they do not dwell on the ill example from such a violation of the public law; they are silent as to motives of compassion for the injured Poles; they descant only on the possible interruption and disturbance of the British trade! It was right under all the circumstances to abstain from hostile measures, but it might have been neither impolitic nor unbecoming to have placed on record a protest to the Three Powers, declaring in strong terms the disapprobation which their conduct had excited and deserved.

The year 1773 is memorable for the measure which in its result, though certainly not in its intention, finally estranged the North American Colonies from England. It so chanced that the affairs of the East India Company had fallen into confusion and arrear through their own mismanagement, and that they found it necessary to apply to the Government for a loan of 1,500,000*l.* The loan was granted, but it was accompanied by a stringent Bill carried through Parliament for the better administration of their affairs in future. Amidst the reform of abuses, a reform by no means palatable to them, there was one point designed for a welcome boon, as providing for the more ready sale of their Teas. Of that commodity there was then a vast accumulation in their warehouses, amounting to no less than seventeen millions of pounds. The decline in their sales was ascribed in no slight degree to the growth of illicit traffic in America. And the Five Years Act passed in 1767 having expired in 1772, a new Act had then been carried, also for the period of five years, granting a drawback of three fifths

spatch how much weight the Ministry placed on the hope of future alliance with Russia. Such was also the view of their antagonist Lord Chatham. He writes to Lord Shelburne, October 20. 1773: "Your Lordship knows I am quite a Russ."

of the English duties of customs on all the Teas sent over to the trans-Atlantic Colonies.* Lord North now proposed that whenever any Teas belonging to the East India Company should be exported to any of the British plantations in America, a drawback should be allowed of the whole duty payable in England.† It was also part of Lord North's scheme that the remission thus made should not, as before, extend only to a specified term of years, but be granted absolutely without any limitation of time. By the new Bill, moreover, the East India Company were empowered to export Teas direct from their own warehouses and on their own account. Arriving in America the Teas would still be subject, under the Act of Parliament passed in 1767, to a Colonial tax of threepence on the pound, but, considering the remission of the English customs duties, might be sold to the Colonies at a lower rate than before the Colonial tax had been imposed. It was hoped that under such circumstances the change, though likely to prevent the illicit traffic, would not be unacceptable to the Americans themselves. Thus Lord North's Bill appears to have passed without opposition, nay, almost without remark. Subsequently, indeed, it has been asserted, that some of the leading men of the East India Company were by no means convinced of the utility of the scheme, — that on consulting some of the principal tea merchants they were assured that it was wild and visionary, and would afford them no relief, — and that in consequence they remonstrated against it.‡ But as the same writer proceeds to state, although far too broadly, the East India Company had been by the late regulations brought entirely under the direction of the Government. Certain it is that the Company as a whole eagerly embraced the new privilege accorded them. In the course of the summer, they

* Act 12 Geo. III. c. 60.

† Mr. Stedman states, and so stating has misled Mr. Grahame and many more, that by this Act of Parliament the Company had "leave "to export their Teas duty free, wherever they could find a market "for them." (Hist. of War, vol. i. p. 85.) But the words of the Act itself (13 Geo. III. c. 44.) limit the privilege expressly to "the "British Colonies or plantations in America."

‡ Annual Register, 1774, p. 47.

freighted several vessels with Teas for the different Colonies, appointing also in each Colony consignees or agents for the disposal of the cargo.

At this period the American Secretary of State was no longer Lord Hillsborough; he had resigned in the previous year on some difference with his colleagues, and had been succeeded by a man superior both in talent and in temper, William Legge, Earl of Dartmouth. No member of the Ministry (this was acknowledged on all sides) had more upright or candid views, or a more earnest desire to conciliate the Colonies. But his character is best painted by a single anecdote. Once, when Richardson was asked if he knew any original answering to his portrait of Sir Charles Grandison, he observed that it would apply to Lord Dartmouth if Lord Dartmouth were not a Methodist.*

At this period the Colonies, with only two exceptions, were in the enjoyment of tranquillity. In Rhode Island indeed there had taken place a most daring outrage during the past year, when a King's ship, the Gaspee schooner, which had been employed against the illicit traders, was boarded, set on fire, and destroyed. Other scenes or symptoms of irritation, though much slighter, might be discerned elsewhere. But in general the aspect was peaceful and serene; overcast and troubled chiefly in the Colonies of Virginia and Massachusetts. In Virginia the Assembly and the people were divided between two parties; the party of conservation, to which the principal land-holders, as Colonel Washington, belonged; and the ardent democratic band, headed by Patrick Henry, and by another young lawyer of eminent abilities, Thomas Jefferson. In Massachusetts the spirit of opposition was far-spread, bitter, and unceasing. The populace still continued its pastime of tarring and feathering the objects of its ill-will, and above all the revenue officers; while the House of Assembly, so far from affording them protection, refused to acknowledge their exist-

* See a note to Lord Orford's Memoirs of George III., vol. i. p. 253. Lord Orford says that he spoke in the House of Lords "with decency and propriety." He is commemorated by Cowper as one "who wears a coronet and prays."

ence. Thus they say, in one of their Addresses: "We "know of no commissioners of His Majesty's customs, "nor of any revenue His Majesty has a right to establish "in North America; we know and we feel a tribute "levied and extorted from those who, if they have pro- "perty, have a right to the absolute disposal of it."*

Revenue, or the collection of revenue, was by no means the only ground of difference. On other questions also the Assembly continued to wage war with the utmost keenness against the servants of the Crown. Hutchinson, their new Governor, was a native of New England, and therefore a countryman, nay almost a townsman, of their own; he was moreover acknowledged to be of courteous and pleasing manners, and of apparent moderation in his counsels; yet in dealing with the local authorities, or those that claimed to be so, he fared no better than his predecessor Bernard. In his rapidly increasing unpopularity were involved his two brothers-in-law, Andrew and Peter Oliver, who had been appointed, the first, Lieutenant Governor, and the second, Chief Justice, of the province. It is needless to follow in full detail discussions which so speedily merged in others more momentous. But it may be mentioned that especial indignation was excited by the desire of the Crown to take into its own hands the payment of the salaries to the Governor and Judges. On the one side, it was argued that there was strong objection to leave the payment of those dignitaries dependent on the yearly votes of the very men whose angry passions it might be part of their duty to control. On the other side, the cry was loud that such a project was an insult to the Assembly, a breach of the Charter, a step to the establishment of arbitrary power. So far did this conflict proceed that at last the Assembly moved to impeach the Chief Justice for having, unlike his brethren, agreed to accept the salary tendered by the King.

Another measure arising from these altercations was much less violent in its appearance, yet much more important in its consequences. In the winter of 1772 the

* Address to the Governor, July 5. 1771.

people of Boston proceeded to elect twenty-one of their fellow townsmen as a "Corresponding Committee." In that measure the prime mover was Mr. Samuel Adams, and the chief instrument was the system of CAUCUS. The derivation of that word has appeared doubtful and mysterious, even to inquirers on the spot*; much more then may it elude those of another country and another age. But whatever was the origin of the phrase it continued for many years a favourite at Boston, denoting a private meeting or council of leaders, to carry out their schemes. It was mainly the Caucus that gave birth to the Corresponding Committee.

This last body, convoked on its own authority, and controlled by no power either of Prorogation or Dissolution, speedily became a formidable engine of the popular will. Early in 1773, the example was followed and even exceeded by what the Boston leaders termed "our noble "patriotic sister" — namely Virginia. The object in the first mentioned Colony had been correspondence within its own limits; but the second, grown bolder, aimed at correspondence and a concert of measures with the rest.

Dr. Franklin was at this time the agent in London for the Assembly of Massachusetts. He had resided in England ever since the period of the Stamp Act, but had continued to retain his lucrative office as Deputy Postmaster General in America. In the autumn of 1773, he signalized both his talents and his zeal by two satirical pieces of considerable merit, which first appeared, like Junius, in the pages of the Public Advertiser. The one was a pretended "Edict of the King of Prussia." In this piece His Majesty puts forward a claim that the people of England shall in future, on account of their Teutonic origin, contribute to his Prussian revenue. It was of course intended to imply that the claim of England to American taxation was almost equally frivolous and futile. The other piece was entitled "Rules for reducing "a Great Empire to a Small One." Of these rules, likewise composed in the manner of Swift, the following may

* Dr. Gordon's History of the American Revolution, vol. i. p. 365. The verb "to caucus" was also, he tells us, in vogue at Boston.

serve as a sample of the rest: "In the first place, Gen-"tlemen, you are to consider that a great empire, like a "great cake, is most easily diminished at the edges. Turn "your attention therefore first to your remotest provinces, "that, as you get rid of them, the rest may follow in "order!"*

In these Essays, published cautiously and without his name, Dr. Franklin had by no means exceeded the fair limits of political or literary warfare. But we cannot affirm the same of another transaction in which at nearly the same period this shrewd philosopher became engaged. Mr. Thomas Whately, at one time private secretary to Mr. Grenville, and, after several years' interval, Under Secretary of State to Lord Suffolk, had died in the summer of 1772. During some time he had carried on an active correspondence as a personal friend of old standing with several officers of the Crown in Massachusetts, especially with Thomas Hutchinson the Governor, and Andrew Oliver the Lieutenant Governor, of the province. Their letters he may have shown in confidence to one or more of the Ministers at the public offices. Either from those offices or from his own house these letters were purloined at or after the period of his death. Later in the same year they were brought to Dr. Franklin. Who it was that so brought, or who had at first obtained them, was never discovered.† Dr. Franklin received them under an injunction of secrecy and a solemn pledge, which he kept, not to reveal the name of the person or persons concerned. It was quite plain, however, that they could not have been obtained by any other than dishonourable means. Nevertheless, Dr. Franklin thought himself at liberty to forward

* Franklin's Works, vol. iv. p. 387—404. ed. 1844.

† The honour of the theft was in 1820 claimed by Dr. Hosack of New York for Dr. Hugh Williamson. But the last editor of Franklin's Works has conclusively shown from a comparison of dates that Dr. Williamson was then in the West Indies. (Note, vol. iv. p. 442. ed. 1844.) Mr. John Adams, in a letter to Dr. Hosack, dated January 28. 1820, states: "Mr. Temple, afterwards Sir John Temple, "told me in Holland that he had communicated these letters to Dr. "Franklin." But on the other hand, as Mr. John Adams goes on to remark, "Dr. Franklin declared publicly that he received them from "a Member of Parliament," which Mr. Temple was not.

these letters, with a private note of his own, to Mr. Cushing, the Speaker of the House of Assembly in Massachusetts.

In the letters thus forwarded, the direction of each to Mr. Whately had been either omitted, as being on a cover, or else erased. It did not therefore appear to whom they were addressed, but by the signatures as well as the handwriting it was evident from whom they had proceeded. On perusal they were found to contain many strong and unguarded expressions against the opposition party at Boston. There were also some hints as to the popular licentiousness which had grown from several provisions in the Charter. Thus Hutchinson wrote: "I doubt "whether it is possible to project a system of govern-"ment in which a Colony three thousand miles from the "parent state shall enjoy all the liberty of the parent "state. . . . . . I wish the good of the Colony when I "wish to see some further restraint of liberty rather than "that the connexion with the parent state should be "broken."* Containing such expressions and such sentiments, the letters were no doubt well adapted, when made known to the popular leaders in Massachusetts, to feed the flame which already blazed high in that Colony against the officers of the Crown. But it is to be observed that all these expressions, and all these sentiments had been put forth in the strictest confidence. "If I have wrote "with freedom," says Oliver, "I consider I am writing "to a friend, and that I am perfectly safe in opening "myself to you."† It is also to be noted that during the years 1767, 1768, and 1769, to which years the letters thus abstracted were confined, Mr. Whately did not fill any official station, and was merely a private Member of Parliament.

To make use of private letters so obtained for such an object would be, in our own time at least and in our own country, and by all parties alike, equally and warmly condemned. Several Americans of high character have indeed attempted to palliate or to justify the conduct of Franklin

* Letter, January 20. 1769.

† Letter of Andrew Oliver, August 12. 1769. See also to the same effect Mr. Hutchinson's letter of October 26. in the same year.

in that transaction. But I have so much respect for these gentlemen, my brethren in blood, in language, and in feeling, as to believe that every one of them would utterly shrink from doing what from mistaken zeal they still labour to defend.

In transmitting these letters to Mr. Cushing, Dr. Franklin had stated that in pursuance of the terms upon which he had received them, he must insist that they should not be printed nor made public, but only circulated among a chosen few. As might have been foreseen, this restraint was quickly overleaped. The temptation was too strong for eager politicians to hold such a weapon in their hands and yet forbear from wielding it. Accordingly in the summer of 1773, after many previous rumours of these letters, they were laid before the Assembly. The name of Franklin as connected with them was still carefully concealed; it was only said in general terms that they had come from one of their friends in England. It was added that he their unknown friend had forbid these letters being published. Under this prohibition, the Assembly for some time paused. But at length it was alleged, though without a shadow of truth, that other copies of these letters had arrived from England by the last ships.* That assurance was deemed sufficient to absolve the House from any engagement of secrecy. It was voted by a majority of 101 against only 5 that the letters thus revealed were designed to subvert the Constitution and establish arbitrary power. A petition was likewise passed, and transmitted to Franklin for presentation, beseeching His Majesty to remove both Hutchinson and Oliver from their posts within the province.

The letters having been published in Boston, printed copies of them came to England in the course of the ensuing autumn, and produced of course no slight degree both of resentment and surprise. Public curiosity was upon the stretch by what possible means they could have been obtained. The person most aggrieved was Mr.

* Dr. Samuel Cooper to Franklin, June 14. 1773. Franklin says in answer, on the 25th of July, "As to the report of other copies "being come from England, I know that could not be. It was an "expedient to disengage the House." (Works, vol. viii. p. 50. and 79.)

William Whately, the surviving brother of Thomas, and the rightful heir to his papers. His suspicions fell, and apparently not without good grounds, on Mr. John Temple, lately one of the Commissioners of Customs at Boston, but a partisan of the popular side*, and a close friend of Franklin. A duel ensued between them, in which Mr. William Whately was wounded. Under these circumstances Dr. Franklin felt it necessary to avow, and so far as he could to vindicate, his part in the transaction. The whole tide of obloquy was now turned against himself. He was assailed by Mr. William Whately, although not quite with the same weapons as Mr. Temple; he received no challenge, but he found a suit in Chancery commenced against him.

Meanwhile the petition from Massachusetts, praying for the dismissal of Hutchinson and Oliver, had been through the hands of Lord Dartmouth laid before the King; and was by His Majesty referred to a Committee of His Privy Council. Accordingly, the Lords of the Council, after one adjournment and full notice to the parties concerned, met for that purpose in solemn conclave on the 29th of January 1774. No less than thirty-five Privy Councillors took their seats on this memorable day; at their head, the Lord President, Earl Gower. There also was seated the Prime Minister, and on the other side stood Benjamin Franklin. The public expectation was eager, and the Council Chamber thronged. Among others struggling, the most part vainly, for admittance was Dr. Priestley, who has left us a lively description of the scene. "We shall never get through!" cried he to Mr. Burke. "Mr. Burke said, 'Give me your arm,' and locking it "fast in his, he soon made his way to the door of the "Privy Council. I then said, 'Mr. Burke, you are an "excellent leader.' He replied, 'I wish other persons "thought so too!'"†

* This apparent contradiction is explained by Dr. Gordon. "Mr "Temple was not obnoxious to the populace, being averse to the "establishment of the Board of Commissioners, which lessened both "his salary and power. He wished the dissolution of it, and to be "restored to his former place of Surveyor General of the Customs." (History of the American Revolution, vol. i. p. 237.)

† Letter of Dr. Priestley in the Monthly Magazine, November 10. 1802.

The business of the day was opened by the Counsel on the part of the petition, Mr. Dunning and Mr. John Lee. They spoke but feebly; Dunning being hoarse and ill; and both it was thought labouring under an uneasy consciousness of the means by which the letters must have been obtained. Wedderburn, the Solicitor General, then rose on behalf of the Crown. Besides his public duty he was, it seems, on some personal grounds, stirred by a feeling of ill-will to Franklin; and he had carefully prepared himself for the part he was to play. In an able and brilliant but most bitter speech he turned the full force of his ready rhetoric against the agent of Massachusetts. Private correspondence, he observed, had hitherto been held sacred, even in times of the greatest party-rage. Into what companies, he asked, could Dr. Franklin hereafter go with an unembarrassed face? Men would hide their papers from him and lock up their escritoires. Hitherto he had aspired to fame by his writings, but henceforth he must esteem it a libel to be termed a man of letters! Wedderburn even went so far as to apply to his opponent the Roman by-word, as "a Man of three Letters," namely FUR, a thief! He next drew an elaborate parallel between him and the character of Zanga, in Young's fine play of THE REVENGE. And that parallel he wound up as follows: "I "ask, my Lords, whether the vengeful temper attributed "by poetic fiction only to the bloody-minded African, is "not surpassed by the coolness and apathy of the wily "New Englander?"

Such language on such an occasion was certainly most ill-judged and impolitic. A strong case can scarce ever be stated too gently. Had Wedderburn dwelt on the transmission of the letters in terms of greater moderation, his hearers would have felt with him how far from justifiable had been the conduct of Franklin. But his keen philippic caused, on the contrary, a rebound in Franklin's favour. The audience and the public inclined amidst all these taunts to remember how eminent was the character of Franklin as a man of science; how from an humble station he had risen, solely by his own merits and exertions, to enjoy the confidence of America and the esteem of Europe.—What added to the ill-effect of the invective was its too favourable reception by those to whom it was addressed. At each sally of Wedderburn's sarcastic wit, the Lords of the Council, with the single exception of Lord North, forgetting their judicial character on this occasion, frequently laughed outright. Dr. Franklin, on the other side, showed perfect self-command, calmly listening to the words of his accuser, and never swerving a hair's breadth either in the attitude of his body or the expression of his face. There is no doubt, however, that the iron had entered into his soul; and that the resentment he conceived not only against the English Government but against the English people was both deep and lasting.*

The decision of the assembled Privy Councillors was

* It has often been related how, in token of his deep resentment, Franklin carefully laid by the dress of "figured Manchester velvet" in which he had stood before the Privy Council, and as carefully resumed it some years afterwards on the day of signing that treaty by which England first acknowledged the independence of America. Mr. Jared Sparks, in his Life of Franklin (note, p. 488.), has given some strong reasons against the truth of this story, above all, that on the day when the treaty was signed there was a Court mourning at Versailles, and that therefore Dr. Franklin came attired, not in "figured Manchester velvet," but in a suit of black. But Mr. Sparks is scarcely justified in proceeding to say that the statement is therefore "entirely erroneous"—"eagerly seized upon to gratify the ma-" levolence of a disappointed party." For it appears from a narrative published by Mr. Sparks himself in Franklin's Writings (vol. iv. p. 453.)—the narrative namely of Dr. Bancroft, an American, and an intimate friend of Franklin—that the incident in question did really occur—not indeed at the Peace of Versailles in 1783, but at the Treaty of Alliance with France in 1778. Here are Dr. Bancroft's words: "When Dr. Franklin had dressed himself for the day (Feb. 5.) " I observed that he wore the suit in question, which I thought the " more extraordinary as it had been laid aside for many months. " This I noticed to Mr. Deane, and soon after, when a messenger " came from Versailles (to postpone the signatures till the next " evening), I said to Mr. Deane, 'Let us see whether the Doctor will " 'wear the same suit of clothes to-morrow: if he does I shall suspect " 'that he is influenced by a recollection of the treatment which he " 'received at the Cockpit.' The morrow came, and the same clothes " were again worn, and the treaties signed. After which these clothes " were laid aside, and, so far as my knowledge extends, never worn " afterwards. I once intimated to Dr. Franklin the suspicion which " his wearing these clothes on that occasion had excited in my mind, " when he smiled, without telling me whether it was well or ill " founded." (1853.)

not doubtful, nor yet long delayed. They reported that the petition from Massachusetts had been framed upon "false and erroneous allegations," and was "groundless, "vexatious, and scandalous." Two days afterwards Dr. Franklin was apprised that the King had no further occasion for his services as Deputy Postmaster General. Several writers, both American and English, have censured this last step of the Government as a fatal error of policy. Yet, considering the transaction relative to the private letters which had now been brought home to Franklin, and considering his position during that transaction as an officer of the Crown, and above all in the department of the Post Office, it appears to me that his subsequent dismissal, however unhappy in its effect upon the Colonies, was scarcely a matter even of choice or option for the Ministers, but rather of clear and unavoidable duty.

Shortly before this period, there had commenced the Session of Parliament. Its first votes were of slighter interest, — as to render perpetual the Grenville Act, till then passed only for a term of years, and to convict Mr. Horne the clergyman and Mr. Woodfall the printer of a libel against the Speaker. At the time, however, these were deemed the measures of importance, while the coming resentment of the Colonists was not foreseen, and while one cause of their resentment, the recent scene before the Privy Council, was little dreamed of, or remembered only to exult in. A statesman, even then of some and since of pre-eminent fame, thirty years later took occasion to refer in striking terms to that false and delusive feeling of joy. In May 1803, on the impending renewal of the war with France, Mr. Fox was answering some splendid philippics of Mr. Pitt against the ambition of Bonaparte, —philippics which Mr. Fox admired even while he condemned, — philippics which, he said, "Demosthenes himself, were he among us, would hear with "pleasure, and possibly with envy. But such philip-"pics," he added, "are not new to us." He bade the House recollect, as he did, the eloquent invective of Wedderburn before the Privy Council; how the future Chancellor of England had called the future plenipotentiary of the United States "a hoary headed traitor;"

and how, as they walked away, men were ready to toss up their hats and clap their hands for joy, as if they had obtained a triumph. " Alas, Sir, we paid a pretty dear " price for that triumph afterwards ! " *

This very period, — the month of February 1774, — proved to be a turning point in Mr. Fox's own career as well as in Dr. Franklin's. His father, Lord Holland, had recently relieved him from embarrassment by paying his debts, contracted mainly through his passion of high play, and amounting (and yet he was not twenty-five) to the enormous sum of 140,000*l*.† Freed from this burthen Fox became less patient of any other trammels. At the opening of Parliament a few weeks afterwards, though still holding a subordinate office, he showed little regard for the advice or opinion of his chief. On several occasions he appears to have pursued his own independent course. Once, in his zeal against the licentiousness of the press, — in his eagerness, as he declared, " to bring " libels of all denominations on the carpet," — he urged a complaint against the printer of the Public Advertiser for having inserted a letter reflecting on the principles of the Revolution. Lord North found it necessary to join him in this vote, though against his wishes, and with a hint to that effect to several of his friends. The King in his secret notes at this juncture expresses much resentment at the presumption of this ill-disciplined Lord of the Treasury.‡ So high did the Royal or Ministerial indignation rise, that on the 24th of February there was put into Fox's hands a letter from Lord North, couched in the following laconic terms : " Sir, His Majesty has " thought proper to order a new commission of the " Treasury to be made out, in which I do not perceive " your name." Certainly it was no common provocation which could call forth such a letter from the most courteous and good-natured of Prime Ministers.

* Parl. Hist., vol. xxxvi. p. 1484. Lord Brougham's Characters, vol. i. p. 74.

† Gibbon to Holroyd, December 16. 1773. In a previous letter (February 8. 1772) it is stated that on one occasion Fox was engaged at hazard for twenty-two hours without intermission; in that sitting he lost 11,000*l*. See Gibbon's Miscellaneous Works.

‡ To Lord North, Feb. 16. and 17. 1774.

Thus dismissed from office Fox eagerly threw himself into all the counsels of Opposition. There, so far as the House of Commons was concerned, he found few rivals to compete with him. Burke had greatly impaired his influence, at least on American questions, by accepting two years before the post of agent to the State of New York, with a salary little short of 1,000*l.* a year.* Since that time his suggestions on the affairs of the Colonies, however wise and however eloquent, were regarded as in some degree the words of a hired advocate. Dowdeswell, for a different reason, received perhaps even less favour from the House. He was acknowledged to be well-informed and upright, but there was some foundation for the epithet — "dull Dowdeswell" — which Lord Chatham had once applied to him.† Moreover his health was rapidly declining; in the course of this spring he found it necessary to retire from politics, and a few months afterwards he died.

The gap thus left on the front Opposition benches was much more than supplied by Mr. Fox. Through frequent and assiduous practice he acquired most consummate powers of debate, displaying a degree of ability which had never been suspected either by his opponents or his friends. His new career might leave him open on several questions to a taunt of inconsistency. But fortunately for him the affairs of America had scarce ever come forward during his tenure of office; and thus, amidst all the troubles which followed quick on his dismissal, he was enabled with full energies, and without fear of any taunt, to espouse the popular side. With Burke and with others of his new connection he speedily formed a close and cordial friendship. And indeed the qualities which raised him so high as a party leader were not merely his eloquence, his wit, his genius, but also his engaging warmth of heart and kindliness of temper. To these a strong testimony may be found in the memoirs of a great historian, by no means blind to his faults, and by no means attached to his principles. On summing up his character many years afterwards, Gibbon writes

* Life by Prior, p. 154.

† Chatham Papers, vol. iv. p. 105.

of Fox as follows: "Perhaps no human being was ever "more perfectly exempt from the taint of malevolence, "vanity, or falsehood."* It will serve in no slight degree to the enhancement of this praise if we consider how much at that period the temper of Fox had been tried by grievous provocations given and received, — how office had more than once already been wrested from his grasp, and was then receding from his view, — how the tide of popular favour, for which he was so ably striving, had wholly ebbed away from him, and bore high upon its waves the vessel of a younger and triumphant rival.

* Memoirs, p. 287. Dean Milman's edition.

APPENDIX.

APPENDIX.

ACCOUNT OF THE RESIGNATION OF THE DUKE OF DEVONSHIRE, October 28. 1762. BY LORD JOHN CAVENDISH.

[Grafton MSS.]

"As soon as my brother came to town he went to "Court, and sent in one of the pages to desire an au- "dience. The page returned, and told him that the King "*would* not see him. He desired him to go again and "inquire in whose hands he should leave his Staff. The "King sent back word that he would send him his orders. "Upon this he went immediately to Lord Egremont's, "and desired him to take the Staff and Key to the King "as he wanted to go out of town, and so left them in his "Lordship's hands. Lord Besborough and George were "to resign the next day."

It also appears from the Grafton Memoirs that the King was offended with the Duke of Devonshire for having failed, notwithstanding a special summons, to attend a Council held on the Preliminaries of the Peace. With these accounts Lord Orford's very nearly agrees.—(Memoirs, vol. i. p. 201.)

MR. PITT TO THE COUNTESS STANHOPE.

Hayes, July 20. 1765.

Madam,

I am not the first who, under the impressions of a strong impulse, has attempted the impossible thing. I am now set down to try to write without a hand, for such my lameness continues to be, that I may almost as well be without one. The lively sense of Lady Stanhope's goodness to me makes it no strange thing that I should attempt a letter with my own pen, rather than employ any of the small secretaries who would be too proud and happy to undertake the work. The honour of your Ladyship's most obliging letter found me confined still to my room, and mostly to my bed; gout without end, and, to close all, an ague and fever, have disabled me from expressing some part of what I feel from the flattering marks of a friendship which makes me so justly proud. The letters marked as accompanying a pacquet came safe, but, alas, the various pamphlets which your Ladyship's goodness had destined for your invalid servant's comfort and recreation lost their way, nor have I been able ever to recover them; but the circumstance the most valuable could not be lost to me, the knowledge of your Ladyship's obliging intentions. I find my hand begins to admonish me how ridiculous *a Secretary* I should have proved upon the large scale, where I was so near engaging. All is now over as to me, and by a fatality I did not expect, I mean Lord Temple's refusing to take his share with me in the undertaking. We set out for Somersetshire to-morrow morning, where I propose to pass not a little of the rest of my days, if I find the place tolerable. Lady Chatham joins in every warm wish for the health and happiness of our respectable and kind friends at Geneva; may all things prosper with them as they and true virtue deserve!

I have the honour to be, &c. &c.

William Pitt.

MR. HENRY GRENVILLE, AMBASSADOR IN TURKEY TO THE EARL OF HALIFAX.

(*Extract.*)

Constantinople, August 1. 1765.

Things grow more and more serious in Georgia, but yet not enough to rouse the Grand Seignor from his present supineness, though his jealousy and suspicions of Russia increase every hour. The Porte has very lately demanded from the Russian Minister here explanation upon three questions, one after another. The first, what is the destination of those troops which are in march in Russia? This probably is nothing more than the camp forming in the neighbourhood of Petersburg. The second, what are these forts which the Muscovites are building at Cabarta, in Circassia? The Russian Minister gave for answer that they were not forts, but lines drawn against the incursions of those independent Tartars which that country swarms with. And here I will tell your Lordship, by-the-by, that such is the ignorance of the Porte with respect to their own frontiers, that they secretly sent a person of confidence to me to be informed where that Cabarta is situated! They have since despatched an officer to Circassia to view and examine the works carrying on there, and to make a report of his observations. To the third question, what is that fort building by the Muscovites on the frontiers of Bessarabia, answer was made that is no fortress neither, but a lazaretto for the performance of quarantine. From hence one sees with how jealous and suspicious an eye the Porte views every proceeding of Russia, whose most innocent steps are construed into some bad design.

MR. HENRY GRENVILLE TO MR. SECRETARY CONWAY

(*Extract.*)

Constantinople, Sept. 2. 1765.

THE spirit of sedition now reigning within the very walls of Constantinople, and the universal discontent among all ranks and orders of people there, may very well find sufficient employment for the Grand Seignor, and leave him no leisure to turn his thoughts to any other object. Anonymous bills are dispersed up and down in the Mosques demanding the heads of several persons in distinguished posts. The Grand Seignor has already sacrificed to them a great favourite of his, a

Greek immensely rich, who has been hanged within these few days at his own door, and the Prince of Wallachia, a known creature of his, is just deposed. It is imagined that he of Moldavia will meet the same fate.

THE KING TO GENERAL CONWAY.

[Orig. Brit. Mus.]

Dec. 6. 1765.

LIEUT. GEN. CONWAY,

THE inclosed is the Memorial I received from Mr. Pitt. It is the copy of the one delivered to me by Lord Halifax, but I received this a day or two before that one.—I am more and more grieved at the accounts from America. Where this spirit will end is not to be said; it is undoubtedly the most serious matter that ever came before Parliament. It requires more deliberation, candour, and temper than I fear it will meet with.

GEORGE R.

MR. PITT TO THE COUNTESS STANHOPE.

Burton Pynsent, June 20. 1766.

MADAM,

THE honour of your Ladyship's letter was conveyed to me from Mr. Peel, as well as the drawings which Lord Mahon has been so very obliging to send me. The drawings are so well done, and in so good a manner, that coming from a hand unknown I should think myself fortunate to be possessed of them. I shall not then be sus pected of flattery when I assure Lord Mahon that, in my collection, these two pieces shall hold the foremost place, and I beg his Lordship will accept my very sincere acknowledgments for his kind and pleasing presents. All the Virtuosi here, great and small, join in one applause.

How shall I next express to Lady Stanhope my respectful sense of the great honour her Ladyship's most obliging letter does me? and be able to say, with what true pleasure their friends and servants at Burton Pynsent receive every repetition of kind remembrance from the two respectable inhabitants of Geneva? Poor Geneva! How unlike its former self, and how little deserving such guests! I cannot but lament such a fall from a happiness to be envied by greater states into faction, confusion, and French mediation; the consummation, in my sense, of all political misery. Your Ladyship sees how the old surly English leaven works still in a retired breast. Farming, grazing, haymaking, and all the *Lethe* of Somersetshire cannot obliterate the memory of days of activity. France is still the object of my mind whenever a thought calls me back to a public world, infatuated, bewitched; in a word, a riddle, too hard for Œdipus to solve. After this short description your Ladyship will not wonder that I am where I am; and that I do not attempt to explain further to you things to me unintelligible. Wherever or however situated, I beg to assure your Ladyship of the unalterable respect with which I am, &c. &c.

William Pitt.

MR. PITT TO THE DUKE OF GRAFTON.

Harley Street, past two o'clock, Sunday,
(July 27. 1766.)

My Lord,

All being entirely fixed with Mr. C. Townshend, who has accepted the office of Chancellor of the Exchequer, your Grace is desired to be at the Queen's House to-morrow at twelve. His Majesty's intention is that we should arrange things for kissing hands on Wednesday, which may very well be, if your Grace should be of that opinion. I think it imports the King's Government that this kind of Inter-Ministerium should not be protracted. I shall be to-morrow at the Queen's House, where I hope to have the honour of seeing the Duke of Grafton perfectly well, and perfectly satisfied with his Chancellor of the Exchequer.

I took my chance to-day at Lord Rockingham's door, but found his Lordship going out, so was not let in. I meant to make a visit of respect as a private man to Lord Rockingham, and, had I found his Lordship, to have told him as Pitt to Lord Rockingham what I understood to be the King's fixed intentions. I am ever, with respectful and warm attachment, &c.

William Pitt.

I saw Mr. Yorke yesterday; his behaviour and language very handsome; his final intentions he will himself explain to the King in his audience to-morrow.

EARL GOWER TO THE DUKE OF GRAFTON.

(*Extract.*)

Trentham, August 22. 1766.

Your Grace says that a fundamental principle on which the present administration have embarked is to conciliate and unite. It gives me infinite pleasure to hear that their intention is such, for it is the only principle which can give stability to administration or ease to the Crown; and that this was my opinion I had the honour to tell your Grace more than once last winter.

EARL OF CHATHAM TO THE DUKE OF GRAFTON.

North End (*Hampstead*),

My Lord, *Saturday*, 4 *o'clock* (*August* 23. 1766).

I have the honour to agree entirely with your Grace in the view of the declining of Lord Gower.* The issue is not what I expected. The fruit of the offer will be full of advantage; and if His Majesty shall be pleased

* He had been offered, through the Duke of Grafton, the first seat at the Admiralty Board.

to form an Admiralty with Sir Charles Saunders and Mr. Keppel (Sir Charles First Lord Commissioner), I have no doubt that the public in general, and the sea service in particular, will receive such an arrangement with satisfaction and applause; the fleet will be well filled and served, and harmony ensured at the Board. Confirmed in these views by your Grace's full concurrence, I have presumed to write to the King this day to submit most humbly this arrangement to His Majesty's wisdom. It is necessary for me to be to-morrow at St. James's, which will oblige me to defer the honour of receiving your Grace's commands as you pass. I trust to Heaven we shall have your Grace confirmed safe and well by Sunday. The next week we all hope to fill with important objects, — meetings upon East India affairs (the greatest of all objects according to my sense of great), as well as the whole outline of the ensuing Session. The Duke of Rutland has in the most handsome and noble manner, through Lord Granby, offered his office for the accommodation of the King's affairs. Lord Hertford has been spoke to by His Majesty upon the subject, of which his Lordship will more properly give your Grace an account. The answer from Berlin is anxiously expected. That our expectations of seeing the Duke of Grafton well may be answered to-morrow is the ardent wish of your Grace's

most devoted humble servant,
CHATHAM.

EARL OF CHATHAM TO THE DUKE OF GRAFTON.

Bath, October 19. 1766.

MY DEAR LORD,

IT is with much difficulty, and at the same time with peculiar pleasure, that I attempt a few lines to return your Grace my respectful and warm thanks for the honour of several most obliging letters. That of the 17th, just received, gives me great satisfaction, as it informs me of a very agreeable conclusion to a matter which, I confess, gave me much uneasiness.*

As to the phalanx your Grace mentions, I either am full of false spirits infused by Bath waters, or there is no such thing existing. The gentleman your Grace points out as a necessary recruit † I think a man of parts, and an ingenious speaker. As to his notions and maxims of trade, they can never be mine. Nothing can be more unsound or more repugnant to every first principle of manufacture and commerce than the rendering so noble a branch as the cottons dependent for the first materials upon the produce of French and Danish islands, instead of British. My engagement to Lord Lisburne for the next opening at the Board of Trade is already known to your Grace; nor is it a thing possible to waive for Mr. Burke. Mr. Hussey ‡, I believe, is in Cornwall. That gentleman's ability and weight are great indeed, and my esteem and honour for his character the highest imaginable. I flatter myself with some share of his regard; but as to his intentions my Lord Chancellor may possibly be more able to inform your Grace when you meet than I can promise to do. Mr. Nugent I have not yet seen, having missed him when he was so good as to call.

The enclosed draft §, which is submitted to the consideration of your Grace, the Secretaries of State, and the Chancellor of the Exchequer, has the approbation of Lord Camden and Lord Northington. If new matter should arise before the Meeting, the Speech will, to be sure, adapt itself to the event.

I have the most sensible joy in being able to acquaint your Grace that Lord Spencer has, with infinite goodness, listened favourably to my earnest entreaties, and will move the Address. Your Grace will be so good as to think of a Seconder. I think of going about Wednesday next for one day to Burton Pynsent, and hope to pay my respects to your Grace in town about the 4th of November.

* On that day the Earl of Cardigan was created Duke of Montagu.

† Edmund Burke.

‡ Richard Hussey, Attorney General to the Queen, and Counsel to the Admiralty.

§ Of the King's Speech for the opening of Parliament.

My hand recovers very slowly, but my general health is mended by the waters, and I trust that a second reprieve of ten days will help my hand.

I am, &c.
CHATHAM.

I hope the Special Commission will not be delayed.

EARL OF CHATHAM TO THE DUKE OF GRAFTON.

Wednesday (*November* 26. 1766).

MY DEAR LORD,

I BEG to return your Grace many thanks for the obliging trouble you are so good as to take, and to express at the same time my just sense of the friendly and kind intention of the correspondent whose note your Grace takes the trouble to inclose. As to the present crisis, I view it in its whole extent, but knowing *where there is firmness,* I cannot consider the journey to Woburn as matter of alarm.* I doubt much whether Mr. Rigby is even now, after yesterday's vote, admissible†; if he is, it is as much as can be said, and that only on condition of another conduct. Unions with whomsoever it be give me no terrors; I know my ground, and I leave them to indulge their own dreams. If they can conquer, I am ready to fall, but I shall never consent to take any premature step from the consideration of what Rigby's manœuvres may produce. I repeat again that I doubt whether the above-said gentleman can be admitted; the consideration of the Duke of Bedford and Lord Gower

* It appears from the Political Register that the Duke of Portland, Lords Scarborough, Monson, &c. had resigned on the 26th of November; this was a Wednesday, and serves to fix the date of Lord Chatham's letter. He sent for Lord Gower on the very evening of the resignations (Lord Orford's Memoirs, vol. ii. p. 396.), and offered places for his Lordship and others of the Duke of Bedford's friends. Lord Gower, in answer, said that he would go to Woburn and consult the Duke, which he did next day.

† Alderman Beckford's Resolution on East India Affairs, carried November 25. by 129 votes against 76.

alone can bring that about. To sum up all in two words: *Faction will not shake the Closet nor gain the public.* I wait the issue without the possibility of any change in my sentiments. Give me leave, my dear Lord, under these considerations to decline taking any step, but that of advising the King to fill up the offices as they shall become vacant by the most eligible who will accept them. I depend on the Duke of Bedford's rectitude and wisdom; and I have every good to expect from Lord Gower's knowledge of things, his discernment, and his excellent sound understanding. I fear your Grace may think me fool-hardy and presuming. Indeed, my Lord, the Closet is firm, and there is nothing to fear.

I am ever, &c.

CHATHAM.

EARL OF CHATHAM TO THE DUKE OF GRAFTON.

(*London*), *December* 7. 1766.

MY DEAR LORD,

I GRIEVE most heartily at the report of the meeting last night. If the inquiry* is to be contracted within the ideas of Mr. Chancellor of the Exchequer† and of Mr. Dyson, the whole becomes a farce and the Ministry a ridiculous phantom. Mr. Beckford will move his Questions (waiving for the present the Bonds and Transfers), and upon the issue of Tuesday must turn the decision of the present system, whether to stand or make way for another scene of political revolution. Mr. Dyson's behaviour cannot be acquiesced in. Mr. C. Townshend's fluctuations and incurable weaknesses cannot comport with his remaining in that critical office. Your Grace will not, I trust, wonder at the pain I feel for the King's service and personal ease, as well as for the redemption of a nation within reach of being saved at once by a kind of gift from Heaven; and all marred and thrown away by fatal weaknesses, co-operating with the most glaring

* On East India affairs. † Mr. Charles Townshend.

factions. What possible objection fit to be listened to can be made to the bringing the revenues in India before the House? I hope Mr. Beckford will walk out of the House, and leave the name of an inquiry to amuse the credulous in other hands, in case this question be not fully supported and carried. For my own part I shall wash my hands of the whole business after that event. Pardon the zeal, my Lord, of a man in earnest for the King and for the community, and believe me in all events with the utmost respect and attachment, &c.

CHATHAM.

EARL OF CHATHAM TO THE DUKE OF GRAFTON.

Bath, January 10. 1767.

MY DEAR LORD,

IT is with very real concern that I learn from the honour of your Grace's letter you had brought back from the country the indisposition which troubles you but too often, and I feel myself more particularly obliged to your Grace for having the goodness to write to me under so painful a circumstance. Though I trust this will find your Grace in perfect health, I will not detain you with a long letter, as I propose setting out for London in a day or two, and shall principally mean at present to express my best thanks to your Grace for the communications you have done me the honour to give me with regard to East India affairs. I wish, my dear Lord, I could see cause to express any thanks to the good Chairman and Deputy Chairman for their communication to your Grace. I will say but a few words upon their captious and preposterous paper. The points on which the Committee are of opinion it is requisite and necessary to treat entirely pass by the great objects of Parliamentary inquiry and national justice, and to render the disingenuity of the proceedings more gross all this is (according to the words of the reference) "in pursuance "of the resolution of the General Court!" On this self-evident state of the thing I am forced to declare I have no hopes from the transaction. My only hope centres in the justice of Parliament, where the question of right can alone be decided, and which cannot upon any colourable pretence be in the Company. The temper and turn of your Grace's answer upon this occasion may be more discreet than such a one as, I confess, I should have made in like circumstances, for I should have desired the gentlemen to dispense me from receiving a resolution of the Committee not admissible as the opening of a treaty, because taking no notice of the revenues in question.

I hope soon to be at your Grace's orders in town, though I see not the least use I can be of in this matter, possibly rather in the way of others from whom I have the misfortune to differ *toto cœlo* upon these matters. With regard to Mr. Ch. Price, I beg leave to defer that consideration till we meet, only suggesting to your Grace at present that whatever shall be resolved, the agreement had better be specific, and must have the King's approbation.

Allow me to beg the favour of your Grace to tell Mr. Townshend I apprehend my account will not have passed soon enough for his view; no time shall be lost.

I am ever, my dear Lord, &c.

CHATHAM.

EARL OF CHATHAM TO THE DUKE OF GRAFTON.

Bath, February 9.* 1767.

My dear Lord,

I have very many thanks to return your Grace for the honour of your obliging letter, accompanying the proposal from the Committee of the East India Directors. If my wishes to be, where I might be, of a little use, were not what they are, your Grace's kind exhortations, and those of the Lords you mention, would be effectual spurs to me to quicken my motions. I can venture to assure

* There is another letter to the Duke of Grafton printed in the Chatham Correspondence (vol. iii. p. 199.), from the rough draft to which the editor has from conjecture assigned the same date as this, February 9. 1767. But some circumstance unknown to me must have misled him. That letter, as derived from the original sent, is contained in the Grafton Memoirs, and bears the date of January 23. 1767, undoubtedly the true one.

your Grace that the same duty and devotion to the King which animated me to attempt, and *sperare contra spem*, still prompts me to struggle under bodily infirmities, and equally incurable disadvantages which certain infelicities of the age throw upon public business. As soon as I can recover strength enough I will set out, but I cannot imagine the least utility in my lying short by the way, or being confined to my bed the moment I reach London. In the mean time reports about my absence seem quite immaterial; those of my not being satisfied with certain notions, and with a conduct consequential to them, from the beginning of the East India inquiry to this hour, I should be sorry to remove; on the contrary, I would have this clearly understood, but instead of this dissatisfaction being a cause of prolonging my absence, it would most certainly accelerate my return. My present state will hardly allow me to hope I can be in town before the 18th, nor can can I see the importance of a week more or less.

I now come to the papers of the 6th of February from the Committee of Directors. I shall not enter into the merits of the proposal. Parliament is the only place where I will declare my final judgment upon the whole matter, if ever I have an opportunity to do it. As a servant of the Crown I have no right or authority to do more than simply to advise that the demands and the offers of the Company should be laid before Parliament; referring the whole determination to the wisdom of that place.

But though I abstain for the present from entering into the merits of the above paper I must take notice of the manner of this transaction. The paper begins by asserting that the Committee have already offered to the consideration of Administration several articles in which their commerce seems to require new regulations and present relief. This refers (most ingenuously) to a paper put into your Grace's hands upon your return to town, to show respect, and only for communication to your Grace, requiring no answer. Well then, to take these gentlemen at their word, and according to their own sense of the thing, these articles requiring regulation and present relief cannot possibly be withheld from Parliament, and must in due time be laid there. Next I come to the notable attempt to render the proposal relating to the revenues only an *idea*, and authorized by their constituents. The transaction too to be a secret. Was ever anything so puerile and ridiculous as this State artifice? Who can abet these gentlemen in so captious and offensive a proceeding? I cannot talk seriously upon such a farce of negotiation. I sum up all I have to offer upon this affair; I beg to acquit myself by submitting, as my clear opinion, that Parliament is entitled to be informed what steps have been taken by the Directors in consequence of the resolution of the General Court, and that the servants of the Crown are indispensably bound in duty, not to suppress any, but to lay them in due time, even uncalled for, before the House. Besides their general duty, it is become still more incumbent, if possible, from the proceedings of the Committee of Inquiry being stopped, with regard to printing the papers, by a formal declaration of an expected proposal. Thus much I think necessary to say with regard to the secrecy of this strange business. Now, my dear Lord, give me leave to beg your Grace's forgiveness for this diffuse, prolix letter; the matter fills my mind and heart; the manner of proceeding of the Committee is insidious; the proposal deserves no other observation than that it is enormous and unconscionable, even to effrontery.

Thus, my Lord, your Grace sees I can declare to the Duke of Grafton a direct opinion out of Parliament. As to the poor cunning of these pedlars in negotiation, I am much mistaken if they are not already taken in their own snare; for they have done enough to lead by-and-by to the *denouement* in Parliament with more advantage to the friends of the public against the advocates of the Alley.

I am ever, &c.
CHATHAM.

EARL OF CHATHAM TO THE DUKE OF GRAFTON.

Bond Street, Wednesday (*March* 4. 1767).

LORD Chatham has the honour to agree entirely with the Duke of Grafton and other servants of the Crown, that a meeting of Cabinet should be had upon the East India business, the capital object of the public upon which Lord Chatham will stand or fall. Report, not rumour, is unjust indeed if Mr. Townshend did not give up the inquiry yesterday, and clearly convey his opinion not to call for more lights, or at least not to lay open the whole. If this be so, the writer hereof and the Chancellor of the Exchequer aforesaid cannot remain in office together; or Mr. C. Townshend must amend his proceeding. Duty to the King and zeal for the salvation of the whole will not allow of any departure from this resolution.

If to-morrow night should be agreeable to the Duke of Grafton, Lord Chatham desires the favour of his Grace to appoint the meeting at his Grace's house at seven in the evening, being the house from which firmness, candour, and salvation is to be hoped, if anywhere, in these factious times.

TAXES LAID ON AMERICA, May, 1767.

[Extract from the Duke of Grafton's MS. Memoirs.]

The Act which prohibited the Governor, Council, and Assembly of New York from passing any Act until they had in every respect complied with the requisition of Parliament, on the quartering, &c. of the troops, was considered to be a temperate but dignified proceeding, and purposely avoiding all harsh and positive penalties. Had such a conduct been uniformly observed, every day would have increased and not have alienated the affections of the two countries from each other. Such were the genuine sentiments of the King's servants, when in an ill-fated hour, Mr. Townshend chose to boast in Parliament that he knew the mode by which a revenue might be drawn from America *without offence.* Mr. Grenville fixed him down directly to pledge himself on the declaration, which was received with such a welcome by the bulk of the House as dismayed Mr. Conway, who stood astonished at the unauthorized proceeding of his vain and imprudent cólleague. On being questioned by the Cabinet on the evening following, how he had ventured to depart on so essential a point from the profession of the whole Ministry, Mr. C. Townshend turned to Mr. Conway, appealing to him whether the House was not bent on obtaining a revenue of some sort from the Colonies. Mr. Conway acknowledged that such a disposition had been indicated by the House in a very decided manner, though I never understood that any symptom of such disposition appeared before Mr. Townshend had himself given to Mr. Grenville the ground on which with eagerness he set his foot. No one of the Ministry had authority sufficient to advise the dismission of Mr. Charles Townshend, and nothing less could have stopped the measure; Lord Chatham's absence being, in this instance, as well as others, much to be lamented.

To render the business as little offensive as possible, articles were thought of which came within the description of port duties. A Board of Customs was proposed to be erected in some central spot of the Colonies; and I was not aware of the mistrust and jealousy which this appointment would bring on, nor of the mischief of which it was the source, otherwise it should never have had my assent; and I must here confess my want of foresight in this instance. The novelty of the situation in which I was placed may perhaps afford some excuse for me, and for those who then acted with me. The right of the mother country to impose taxes on the Colonies was then so generally admitted, that rarely any one thought of questioning it, though a few years afterwards it was given up as indefensible by everybody.

EARL OF CHATHAM TO THE DUKE OF GRAFTON.

North End (*Hampstead*),
Saturday Evening. (*May* 30. 1767).

Lord Chatham presents his respects to the Duke of Grafton, and begs to have the honour of seeing his Grace to-morrow morning at North End at eleven. Unfit as he is for the favour of such an interview, he can only hope his Grace will attribute this liberty to the most real respect for his Grace's person, and to the truest zeal for His Majesty.

FRENCH PROJECTS OF INVASION.

Two *Memoires* on this subject were drawn up with the utmost secrecy, and under the directions of the Duke de Choiseul, the former dated 1767, and the latter 1768. By some means not stated, official copies, or possibly even the originals, of both were obtained by, or for, Lord Chatham, and are still remaining, with several others, among his private MSS.—An extract from each is here subjoined.

MEMOIRE MILITAIRE FAIT PAR ORDRE DU MINISTRE PAR M. GRANT DE BLAIRFINDY, COLONEL DES TROUPES LÉGÈRES.

(ANNEÉ 1767.)

C'est dans le comté de Kent où l'on pourra avec le plus de facilité debarquer des troupes pour envahir l'Angleterre.

Deal, ou Dole, est un endroit propre pour cela, situé à huit milles nord-est de Dover. Le pays y est plat; on peut approcher les gros vaisseaux assez près pour protéger le debarquement des troupes, et les petits batiments peuvent approcher jusqu'à la terre même.

Il y a sur cette côte trois mauvais châteaux qu'on prendrait d'emblée; l'un est le château de Deal, l'autre celui de Walmer, et le troisième s'appelle Sandown Castle, ou château de Sandown.

Ces trois châteaux, qui ont été batis par Honri VIII., ne sont que des simples plate-formes, où il y a 8 à 10 canons sur chacune.

C'est à Deal où Jules César, ayant été repoussé à

Dover, débarqua son armée quand il a conquis l'Angleterre.

Avec une armée de cinquante mille hommes la France se rendra maîtresse de l'Angleterre quand elle le voudra. Je suppose qu'elle est en état de fournir une flotte composée de vingt vaisseaux de ligne depuis 40 jusqu'à 60 canons, douze frégates, et quarante corvettes, avec un nombre assez considérable de bâtiments pour le transport des troupes, de l'artillerie, et de toutes les munitions de guerre et de bouche qui seront jugées nécessaires.

L'armée sera composée de quarante mille hommes d'infanterie, six mille dragons, et quatre mille de troupes légères, avec un détachement d'artillerie proportionné.

Les dragons s'embarqueront sans chevaux, mais ils se muniront de l'équipage du cheval que l'on laissera aux bagages ; ils feront le service des grénadiers à pied, et seront montés à mesure que l'on pénétrera dans le pays.

Les troupes légères s'embarqueront avec des chevaux ; il faut qu'ils en menent avec eux pour pouvoir pousser tout de suite des détachements dans le pays pour assembler sur le champ le nombre des chevaux, bœufs, chariots, &c. dont l'armée aurait besoin, et que l'on trouvera à Sheldon, Norburn, Upper Deal, Mongham, Ripple, Walmer, Sutton, Kings Would, Oxney, &c. Ces neuf villages sont bien peuplés, riches, bien fournis en chevaux, voitures, et de tout ce dont une armée peut avoir besoin, que l'on peut ramasser en cinq heures de temps.

. . . .

. . . .

Les Anglais ont pris tous nos vaisseaux avant que de nous déclarer la dernière guerre ; aller chez eux au milieu de la paix ne serait qu'user de représailles.

. . . .

Pour venir aux obstacles que les troupes auraient à vaincre : premièrement, de la part des habitans nous n'aurons rien à craindre ; c'est un peuple mou, qui ignore absolument l'usage des armes. Il est certain, selon ce qui m'a été dit par les gens du pays même, qu'il se soumettrait sans la moindre resistance ; et pour gagner ces habitans tout à fait, et les rendre parfaitement nos amis, on n'aurait qu'à publier un manifeste, qui garantirait que l'on ne veut pas de mal au peuple, qu'on veut se venger seulement d'un gouvernement tyrannique, et rendre à un peuple opprimé ses anciennes libertés et prerogatives dont il n'existe que le nom ; et qu'en conséquence, pour leur prouver la bonne foi des troupes de Sa Majesté Très Chrétienne, Elle a ordonné, et ordonne, que toutes les denrées livrées à son armée soient payées comptant, et de 5 pour 100 plus que le prix ordinaire. Par cet arrangement je réponds que notre armée ne manquerait de rien, et que tout le pays nous serait bientôt entièrement devoué.

Pour mieux parvenir à cette fin je croirais nécessaire de tâcher de faire agir encore une fois le Roi Charles Edouard qui est à Rome. J'aurai l'honneur de rendre compte de vive voix à M. le Duc de Choiseul de ce que je pourrai dire à ce sujet. Je n'ignore pas la politique qui a toujours fait échouer les entreprises de cette malheureuse maison; mais il est certain que lui rendant la couronne il y aurait des moyens de concilier les intérêts de deux nations, qui ensemble donneraient la loi à toute l'Europe et peut-être au monde entier.

. . . .

RECONNAISSANCE FAITE EN ANGLETERRE AUX MOIS DE SEPT[s] ET OCT[s] 1768, PAR M. DE BÉVILLE, LIEUT. COLONEL DE DRAGONS.

In this MS. are comprised most full and detailed and, so far as my local knowledge goes, most accurate reports of the southern counties chiefly open to invasion. Nor are these descriptions confined to the coast, as the following extract will plainly show.

ROUTE DE TUNBRIDGE À LONDRES.

Itineraire.	*Remarques Geographiques et Militaires.*
TUNBRIDGE. Tunbridge est une grande villasse du comté de Kent toute couverte, à la rive gauche de la Medway, qui	

forme cinq branches devant cette ville. On passe les quatre premières, qui traversent une espèce de faubourg, sur quatre petits ponts de pierre; la cinquième, qui est la plus considérable, est à l'entrée de la ville; on la traverse sur un bon pont de pierre, assez long, proche lequel on voit quelques barques de rivière. [a]

On monte peu en sortant de la ville. Le chemin serpente dans les houblonnières. [b] On descend et on passe un petit ruisseau sur un pont de pierre; après lequel on entre dans une très belle plaine bien cultivée; on y passe un petit ruisseau à gué; le pays est ensuite un peu montueux; le chemin toujours entre deux haies et souvent encaissé. A quatre milles environ on monte une côte assez raide [c], et le pays est alors très couvert. Il continue d'être montueux jusqu'à Sevenoke, et le chemin de même nature que le précedent.

SEVENOKE.

Sevenoke est une petite ville ouverte du comté de Kent, assez bien batie, et où il y a un fort bel hôpital.

On descend beaucoup en

[a] La Medway est beaucoup plus facile à passer dans cette partie qu'à Maidstone et Rochester, où ses rives sont très elevées, au lieu qu'à Tunbridge la gauche l'est peu, et c'est la droite qui commande la ville.

[b] Il y a un bon camp a prendre sur ce coteau faisant face à la plaine.

[c] Ce passage serait difficile si elle était occupèe.

sortant de la ville, la descente est large et très allongée ; on traverse une prairie, et on entre dans le petit village de Riverhead. On traverse encore en sortant une prairie, et on y passe sur un pont de pierre la petite rivière de Dart. (d) Le pays est ensuite un peu montueux ; le chemin bordé de haies est souvent encaissé. A deux milles de Riverhead on monte un coteau assez raide, et le pays est couvert. (e) Le chemin serpente beaucoup en descendant cette hauteur, dont la pente est fort douce ; on passe ensuite un pays montueux, coupé de petits vallons, que l'on traverse les uns après les autres. Il est bien cultivé et ouvert ; le chemin toujours bon, bordé de haies, et souvent encaissé. On trouve après un peu de plaine ; puis le pays redevient montueux ; on monte entre autres une côte assez raide pour entrer dans Bromley.

(d) Elle se jette dans la Tamise au dessous de Dartford.

(e) Ce serait une position avantageuse à l'ennemi.

BROMLEY.

Bromley est une petite ville ouverte du comté de Kent, sur un coteau assez élevé ; elle est jolie et bien batie.

En sortant de la ville on entre dans une plaine bien cultivée ; le chemin y est très beau. A un mille on descend, le chemin est large, mais encaissé par la gauche. On traverse le village de Beckenham, où il y a un château avec des pièces d'eau ; on cotoie par la gauche le ruisseau qui les forme, et on entre en plaine en sortant du village, le chemin étant bordé de closages de pâture. Il y a beaucoup de cabarets le long du chemin. On traverse ensuite Levisham, gros village très long, rempli de jolies maisons bourgeoises. En sortant du dit village on tourne à gauche, et on passe aussitôt la boue sur un pont de pierre. On monte ensuite un petit rideau d'où on decouvre la ville de Londres. (f) On gagne de là la barrière neuve où l'on entre dans le grand chemin qui vient de Douvres à cette capitale.

(f) Il y a un camp à prendre en arrivant sur Londres par ce côté, qui serait de porter sa droite aux murs du parc de Greenwich, et la gauche à Southend, mettant la boue devant soi.

AUTHORSHIP OF JUNIUS.

1769.

The following letter on so curious a subject of inquiry, and from so high an authority on any point of historical literature as Sir James Mackintosh, was kindly placed at the disposal of the author of this History by its publisher.

SIR JAMES MACKINTOSH TO JOHN MURRAY, ESQ.

London, November 28. 1824.

MY DEAR SIR,

I AM well pleased to have an opportunity of showing my sense of your obliging conduct towards me, and I therefore hasten to give you my opinion of the MS. which you have sent to me.

If it were to be published by you I should take the liberty to recommend much condensation and revision. The larger part of it is made up of extracts needlessly long from very common books. That it might be reduced one half with advantage is a very moderate estimate. The language is frequently very incorrect, a great fault where the subject is partly connected with the style of a very celebrated writer.

As I write to you frankly and confidentially I must say that the author of the MS. is by no means familiar with the period of history to which his discussion relates. One instance of his ignorance really astonished me; I never could have believed that any man who undertook such a discussion could have confounded the Duke of Cumberland who commanded at Culloden with the Duke who married Mrs. Horton; the writer of the MS. has however not only done so, but founded a long argument upon his own ignorance. (MSS. pp. 77—90.) The whole of that argument must be erased. The first Duke was dead six years before the date of Junius's letter to the second. Junius attacked the second Duke as the King's brother, and the Luttrells because Colonel Luttrell opposed Wilkes in Middlesex. Lord George's burst of anger against Temple Luttrell in 1777, in answer to a bitter invective against himself, and in a debate which involved him personally, needs no reference to previous hostility.

Another as striking piece of ignorance is his representing Alexander Murray, the brother of Lord Elibank, who so boldly defied the House of Commons on a question of privilege, as a brother of Lord Mansfield. He evidently means the supposed connection to be some explanation of Junius's animosity against Lord Mansfield.

What can he mean by his "proofs" that Junius was a Privy Councillor? They and other circumstances favour a supposition that he neither had a more than common knowledge of political business, nor was connected with those who had. Does this writer imagine that a Privy Councillor, as such, has necessarily any such knowledge? He confounds the Privy Council with the Cabinet!

The main argument of the MS. is, that the animosities of Junius are against those who must have been obnoxious to Lord George Sackville for their share in the proceedings against him.

The very contrary of this proposition I take to be the truth. The bitterest of all the animosities of Junius is that against King George the Third. That prince took no part against Lord George Sackville, but on the contrary, as this writer seems to have heard, received him so graciously on his accession as to displease his Ministers. It is notorious that to have been obnoxious to George the Second was a title to the favour of his successor. Where was there any ground for animosity on the part of Lord George against Lord Mansfield? The writer of the MS. indeed tells us that Lord Mansfield "drew up "all state prosecutions" at the time of Lord George's trial, and was then "Solicitor for the Crown." This language is unintelligible. Is the writer ignorant that Lord Mansfield was made Chief Justice of the King's Bench in 1756, four years before Lord George's trial? Instead of believing Lord Mansfield to have been Lord George's enemy, there is reason to suppose that he was eminently the reverse. Lord Orford tells us that Lord George was believed to have consulted with Lord Mansfield about his case; and in the Memoirs of January 1760, in speaking of Lord Holderness's letter to Lord George, expressly calls Lord Mansfield Lord George's friend. We know from Cumberland's Memoirs that, twenty-six years after, Lord George made a dying declaration in person to Lord Mansfield of gratitude "for kind protection during "the course of an unprosperous life." It is clear that he at least could not mean to omit his trial, certainly the most unprosperous event of his life. He at the same time, indeed, asked forgiveness for any offence which he might have been led into by the heat of party. This submission was quite sufficient, if it be understood as applied to warm speeches in Parliament. But if Lord George, conscious that he was the author of Junius, asked forgiveness so solemnly for such a venial offence, he was guilty of more useless baseness than ought to be imputed to any man without the strongest evidence.

Another object of Junius's animosity was the Scotch nation. The proof on which the MS. ascribes the same feeling to Lord George is truly curious. It consists in some letters written by Lord George in 1746, by which it appears that he, a man of fashion at the age of thirty, was tired of his winter quarters at Perth. Is the writer sure he would have been better pleased at Whitehaven? On the opposite side there is rather better proof. Lord Orford tells us that Lord George in the army was haughty and reserved to all but a few, most of whom were Scots, and that at his trial all the Scotch were his friends.

The fierce and rancorous enmity of Junius against the Dukes of Bedford and Grafton would, on the hypothesis of this MS., require some proof that both these noblemen had aimed mortal wounds at Lord George Sackville. How utterly frivolous and inadequate are the causes assigned! The Duke of Bedford was Lord Lieutenant of Ireland, and it is said (it is not worth while to inquire whether truly) that he accepted the Rangership of Phœnix Park, of which Lord George had previously been deprived. Some family coolness subsisted between the Bedfords and Lord George at the time of the trial. These are the supposed causes of such ferocious attacks as those of Junius on the Duke of Bedford. If this was the revenge of Lord George, I wonder why the writer should have been melted into such tenderness at the sight of his remains. The Duke of Grafton is supposed to have been odious to Junius because he was the brother of Colonel Fitzroy, who was the bearer of the order of Prince Ferdinand. How does the writer reconcile this strange supposition with the fact that Junius is never once betrayed into an allusion to Fitzroy himself? He seems to be ignorant that Lord George was restored in 1765 to the Privy Council by the Rockingham Administration, of which the Duke of Grafton was a member; so little reason had he for any peculiar enmity against that nobleman.

I pass over the case of Lord Barrington. Lord George could have had no resentment against him on account of the dismissal or trial. The Secretary at War in such cases only executes the orders of the Government. The resentment of Junius against Lord Barrington has always been justly thought to indicate some connection with the details of official business. Whatever the boasts of Junius were, he seems to have known more of the War Office than of the army.

But all these observations on the persons who were the objects of Junius's invectives are greatly strengthened by considering who were not so. The two principal witnesses against Lord George were Colonel Ligonier and Colonel Sloper. If they are believed, his defence was false. To neither of them does Junius make an allusion, and he once adverts rather kindly to Lord Ligonier, the Colonel's uncle. But if we suppose that this very ingenious and most merciless writer could find no unsuspicious opportunity of alluding to these two not very conspicuous officers, the same explanation cannot be given of his silence about the Duke of Richmond, a member of Prince Ferdinand's family, who served at Minden. If Lord George had written such letters as those of Junius, could he have forborne from lashing his great enemy Prince Ferdinand himself? He might have found abundant pretexts for introducing him connected with the common-places against Hanoverian influence and German mercenaries which were too long popular. Could Lord George have spared the memory of George the Second, who, as we see in Lord Orford, was the most formidable of his enemies in England? Next to the King was Mr. Pitt (Lord Chatham), who, as Lord Orford truly says, was no bitter enemy, but who from zeal for the success of the war supported Prince Ferdinand. Junius shows to him in the beginning as much political opposition as was occasioned by difference of opinion about America, but never any appearance of personal resentment, and in the end the utmost admiration and reverence. In short, the supposition of the MS. is, that Lord George spared all his known bitter and formidable enemies, and poured forth torrents of invective against men who had no share in his downfall; that he inveighed against

George the Third and Lord Mansfield, who were his friends, and spared George the Second and Mr. Pitt, who were among his destroyers.

If the passage in Junius, II. 491, ed. 1812, be the production of that writer, there is an end to the claim of Lord George. It is an allusion to something of a very *different nature from cowardice.* I am surprised that the writer should have overlooked two passages in the very well written panegyric of Mr. Cumberland on Lord George, published on his death, and preserved in the last edition of Collins's Peerage: "The early avocations of a "military life, and perhaps a want of taste and disposition for classical studies, prevented his advances in "literature, so that he was not so well read as people of "his rank generally are."—"In delivering his thoughts "he generally chose the plainest, commonest expressions."—Is this Junius?

A little complimentary language used by Lord George in 1774, when speaking of G. Grenville, is no proof of such a connection with that statesman as the real writer of Junius must have had; nor are a few words spoken by him on the Stamp Act, when he was about to take the American department, any satisfactory evidence of his real opinions on that measure at the time of its repeal.

The last public letter of Junius was three years and a half before Lord George's appointment to be Secretary of State. The cessation of the letters had no connection with the appointment.

The only specious argument in support of Lord George's claim is the old one founded on a private note of Junius to Woodfall, where he complains of the impudence of one Swinney, who, he says, went to Lord George, whom Swinney had never spoken to, to ask if he was the author of Junius. It is asked, if Lord George was not Junius, how did the latter know of Swinney's visit and inquiry? The answer seems to me very simple. If Lord George was not the writer it was quite natural that he should mention so impertinent an intrusion with astonishment to his friends, and that he should not conceal the aggravation of the impudence that Swinney was wholly unknown to him. The story would inevitably be spread abroad, and Junius, who heard other political rumours, would not be unconcerned in this. He or his friends might be for a moment disquieted by any appearance of inquiry, and in this manner the fact admits of the easiest explanation.

I have been betrayed into greater length than I expected by my wish to assign to you my reason for thinking that the author of the MS. has altogether failed in his object, and for doubting whether, at least in its present state, the publication would be worthy of you.

I am, &c.

J. MACKINTOSH.

There seems no doubt that the MS. referred to in this letter by Sir James Mackintosh was the "Critical Inquiry," by Mr. George Coventry, which having first received some corrections and improvements was published by Mr. William Phillips, in the ensuing year, 1825. That book extending to 382 octavo pages, bears on the first page an announcement as follows: "The public "are respectfully informed that this is the work an- "nounced for publication by Mr. Murray in November "last."

I have also been so fortunate as to obtain the kind consent of both parties concerned to publish the following letter addressed, since my first edition of this volume, by Mr. Macaulay to the son and successor of Sir James's correspondent. First, however, let me insert the passage in the Quarterly Review (No. clxxix) to which Mr. Macaulay's main observations are directed.

"We may remark that Junius does not seem to have "had that sort of minute official information which "Francis must certainly have been possessed of. In his "correspondence with Sir William Draper, Junius evi- "dently expecting to catch him *in flagrante delicto* writes "in his most emphatic manner: —

"'The last and most important question remains. When "'you receive your half-pay do you, or do you not, take "'a solemn oath, or sign a declaration upon honour to "'the following effect—*that you do not actually hold any*

"'*place of profit, civil or military, under His Majesty?*
"'The charge which this question plainly conveys against
"'you is of so shocking a complexion that I sincerely
"'wish you may be able to answer it well, not merely for
"'the colour of your reputation but for your own inward
"'peace of mind.'

"Contrary to the anticipation of Junius, Sir William
"Draper is able to make a triumphant reply:—

"'I have a very short answer for Junius's important
"'question: I do not either take an oath or declare upon
"'honour, that I have no place of profit, civil or military,
"'when I receive the half-pay as an Irish Colonel. My
"'most gracious Sovereign gives it me as a pension; he
"'was pleased to think I deserved it.'

"Had Junius been Francis, he must have known as
"first clerk in the War Office the exact facts of Sir Wil-
"liam's position; and of course would not have made an
"attack which could so easily be repelled."

RIGHT HON. T. B. MACAULAY TO JOHN MURRAY, ESQ.

Albany, January 3. 1852.

SIR,

I am much obliged to you for the new Number of the Quarterly Review: I cannot say that it has shaken my opinion. I wonder indeed that so ingenious a person as the Reviewer should think that his objections have made any impression on the vast mass of circumstantial evidence which proves Francis to have been Junius. That evidence, I think, differs not only in degree, but in kind, from any evidence which can be adduced for any other claimant.

It seems to me too that one half of the arguments of the Reviewer is answered by the other half. First, we are told that Francis did not write the letters, because it would have been singularly infamous in him to write them. Then, we are told that he did not write them because he did not own them. Surely this reasoning does not hang well together. Is it strange that a very proud man should not confess what would disgrace him? I have always believed that Francis kept silence because he was well known to have received great benefits from persons whom he had as *Junius* or as *Veteran* abused with great malignity.

It is odd that the Reviewer should infer from the mistake about Draper's half-pay that Junius could not have been in the War Office. I talked that matter over more than ten years ago, when I was Secretary-at-War, with two of the ablest and best informed gentlemen in the department; and we all three came to a conclusion the very opposite of that at which the Reviewer has arrived. Francis was chief clerk in the English War Office. Everybody who drew half-pay through that office made the declaration which Junius mentions. But Draper's half-pay was on the Irish establishment; and of him the declaration was not required. Now, to me and to those whom I consulted, it seemed the most natural thing in the world that Francis, relying on his official knowledge, and not considering that there might be a difference between the practice at Dublin and the practice at Westminster, should put that unlucky question which gave Draper so great an advantage. I have repeatedly pointed out this circumstance to men who are excellent judges of evidence, and I never found one who did not agree with me.

It is not necessary for me to say anything about the new theory which the Reviewer has constructed. Lord Lyttleton's claims are better than those of Burke or Barré, and quite as good as those of Lord George Sackville or Single-speech Hamilton. But the case against Francis, or, if you please, in favour of Francis, rests on grounds of a very different kind, and on coincidences such as would be sufficient to convict a murderer.

There is, however, one strong objection to the theory of the Reviewer which strikes me at the first glance. Junius, whoever he was, wrote a long letter to George Grenville, which was preserved at Stowe many years, and of which I have seen a copy in Lord Mahon's possession. The letter contains no decisive indications of the writer's situation. But, on the whole, it seems to be written by a man not very high in rank or fortune. The tone, though not by any means abject, is that of an inferior. The author declares himself to be the writer of a squib, then famous, called "The Grand Council." He says, that Grenville must soon be Prime Minister. "Till then I wish to remain concealed even from you; "then I will make myself known, and explain what I "wish you to do for me." I quote from memory; but this is the substance. The original I have not seen: but I am told that it is the handwriting of Junius's letters.

Now this circumstance seems to me decisive against Lord Lyttleton. He was George Grenville's cousin. The connection between the Stowe family and the Hagley family had, during two generations, been extremely close. Is it probable that George Grenville would not have known Lyttleton's hand? Is it possible that a letter written by Lyttleton should have lain at Stowe eighty years, and that none of the Cousinhood should have been struck by the writing?

But in truth the strongest arguments against the Reviewer's theory are, the arguments which in my opinion prove that Francis was the author of the letters.

I have the honour to be, Sir,
Your faithful servant,
T. B. MACAULAY.

In addition to these valuable remarks of Mr. Macaulay I will venture here somewhat further to elucidate the brief statement on two or three other points in my text.

First as to the hand-writing. In the fourth volume of the Chatham Correspondence will be found fac-similes of some words from Junius ranged in alphabetical order, and side by side with the same, or nearly the same, words from the acknowledged writings of Sir Philip Francis. It may there be seen on close comparison that the difference is only as between an upright and a slanting hand; the formation of the capital letters being in each case, and in all respects, the very same. There is also in both the same habit of combining by a line some of the shorter words. From other passages admitting of more extended observation Mr. Taylor has been able to deduce that both writers appear equally unwilling to break a word at the end of a line, preferring instead of it to leave a great space; often with them filled up by a flourish of the pen, as is usual in law-writings, but not usual in any other. Both are very careful of punctuation, not neglecting even the commas when required, to a degree very seldom to be found in MSS. Both agree in some minute peculiarities of spelling ; as " endeavor," for " endeavour," " inhance " for " enhance," and "risque" for "risk."

Secondly as to Lord Holland. That nobleman, considering his line of politics, was one of the most obvious marks for Junius to assail. Few men of that time were more open to attack. Few men had less of popular favour to shield them. Yet by a most remarkable anomaly in Junius's career, Lord Holland was on all occasions designedly spared by that writer. In one of his private letters to Woodfall he goes so far as to say: " I wish Lord Holland may " acquit himself with honour." * And when he believed Lord Holland's son to have written against him anonymously in the newspapers, he does not strike blow for blow (as who could more readily ?), but merely, under another name, throws out this public warning : " Whether " Lord Holland be invulnerable or whether Junius should " be wantonly provoked, are questions worthy the *Black* " *Boy's* (Charles Fox's) consideration." † No theories then as to the authorship of Junius can be complete or satisfactory which do not supply some adequate explanation of this remarkable anomaly. In very few of these theories is any such explanation even attempted. In none is it so clear and plain as in the case of Sir Philip Francis, Lord Holland having been the early patron both of his father and himself.

Next as to Lord Chatham's speeches.—It appears from Junius's own statement that he was in the habit of attending the debates in Parliament. In one letter he says that he had himself heard Lord Camden's famous expression on " a forty days' tyranny ; " in another letter that he had often heard the Duke of Grafton ; in a third that he was present in the House of Commons at the opening of the Session in November 1770.‡ But further still, Junius, it appears, sometimes made reports of the more important speeches. Thus on one occasion he sent to Mr. Woodfall a full report of one of Burke's orations,

* To Mr. Woodfall, July 21. 1769.

† Letter in the Public Advertiser, October 16. 1771.

‡ Letters of Philo-Junius, Oct. 15. 1771 ; of Junius, Dec. 7. 1770 ; of Testis, Nov. 19. 1770.

in which report Mr. Woodfall requested and obtained permission to make " changes in certain expressions." * Thus again Junius in a note of his Preface to the collected letters introduces as follows an extract of an oration not as yet made known to the public. " The fol-" lowing quotation from a speech delivered by Lord " Chatham on the 11th of December 1770, is taken with " exactness." †

Let us now see how far Sir Philip Francis was connected with any of Lord Chatham's speeches in 1770.—Omitting for the sake of brevity the points connected with the earlier publications in contemporary newspapers, or in Almon's Anecdotes, it may here be sufficient to state that in the volume of the Parliamentary History which appeared in 1813 a full account of the first day of the Session in the Lords, January 9. 1770, is introduced by a note as follows: " This very important debate was taken " by a gentleman who afterwards made a distinguished " figure in the House of Commons, and by him it has " been obligingly revised for this work." ‡ On application to the publishers before the appearance of Mr. Taylor's book, and before his theory had been in any manner made known, they at once admitted that the gentleman referred to was Sir Philip Francis.

Here then, by a most striking coincidence at least, and such as no other theory of Junius supplies, we can show both the writer of the Letters and the object of the theory, each separately in the course of the same year, engaged upon reports of Lord Chatham's speeches. But the case does not end even here. Mr. Taylor has devoted a whole chapter of his able work mainly to a minute examination of the earliest of these reports, tending to show from various slight peculiarities of diction or turns of phrase, either that Chatham or Junius were one and the same person, or that the reporter of the speeches must also have been the writer of the Letters. §

* See in Woodfall's edition the letter to the Public Advertiser of Dec. 5. 1767, with the editor's explanatory note.

† Woodfall's Junius, vol. i. p. 28.

‡ Parl. Hist. vol. xvi. p. 647.

§ Junius Identified, p. 257—314.

With respect to Lady Francis it has been said to diminish the force of her testimony as published by Lord Campbell, that the vanity which was the ruling principle of Sir Philip's mind might easily induce him to accredit, though not expressly to affirm, the rumour of his being the "Great Unknown." But let the reader weigh the following statement. Lady Francis says of her husband, "His first gift after our marriage was an edition of Ju-"nius, which he bid me take to my room and not let it "be seen or speak on the subject, and his posthumous "present which his son found in his bureau was 'Junius "'Identified' (as Sir Philip Francis), sealed up and "directed to me." The marriage gift might pass on the score of vanity; but the "posthumous present" is not to be so lightly dismissed. To suppose that Sir Philip bequeathed such a book under such circumstances, he not being in truth the author of Junius, is to heap a most heavy imputation on his memory. It is to accuse him of imparting a falsehood, as it were, from beyond the grave.

Such is a part, and only a part, of the "vast mass of "circumstantial evidence," as Mr. Macaulay in his letter truly terms it, "which proves Francis to have been "Junius." It is no doubt far more gratifying for any writers on this question to set forth each for himself a new and striking theory, than merely, without the smallest claim of original discovery or any hope of honour thence arising, to follow as I have done in the footsteps of another. But I will presume to assert, with all possible respect for those who have arrived at a different conclusion, that this "vast mass of evidence," is not to be shaken, far less subverted, by passing over its main features in silence, and by only seeking (as with more or less success is in general attempted) to trace here and there scattered analogies and points of vague resemblance between Junius and some other person of his time.

M.

June, 1853.

MINUTE OF THE CABINET, MAY 1. 1769.

[Extract from the Duke of Grafton's MS. Memoirs.]

At a Meeting of the King's Servants at Lord Weymouth's Office, 1st May 1769.

Present,

Lord Chancellor.	Lord President.
Duke of Grafton.	Lord Granby.
Lord Rochford.	Lord Weymouth.
Lord North.	General Conway.
	Lord Hillsborough.

It is the unanimous opinion of the Lords present to submit to His Majesty, as their advice, that no measure should be taken which can any way derogate from the legislative authority of Great Britain over the Colonies; but that the Secretary of State, in his correspondence and conversation, be permitted to state it as the opinion of the King's Servants, that it is by no means the intention of administration, nor do they think it expedient for the interest of Great Britain or America, to propose or consent to the laying any further taxes upon America for the purpose of raising a revenue; and that it is at present their intention to propose in the next Session of Parliament to take off the duties upon paper, glass, and colours imported into America, upon consideration of such duties having been laid contrary to the true principles of commerce.

The Duke of Grafton, who inserts this Minute in his Memoirs, observes that it was not the original draft, which Lord Hillsborough had drawn up, but afterwards unfortunately mislaid; and he complains that his Lordship should have introduced the word "unanimous," notwithstanding the close division at this Cabinet (5 against 4) on the article of Teas.

LAST AUDIENCE OF LORD CHATHAM.

[Extract from the Duke of Grafton's MS. Memoirs.]

July 1769.

On the 24th of June 1769 I married Elizabeth, third daughter of Sir Richard and Lady Mary Wrottesley, whose merit as a wife, tenderness and affection as mother of a numerous family, and exemplary conduct through life need not be related to you.* In a week or ten days after I went from Woburn, accompanied by the Duke of Bedford, to the installation at Cambridge, where in the preceding year, on the death of the Duke of Newcastle, the University had done me the honour of electing me as Chancellor to succeed to his Grace. That ceremony being over, I returned to London, where I first heard that Lord Chatham was so well recovered as to be expected to attend the King's next Levee. Lord Camden had seen him, and I think the day before his appearing mentioned to me Lord Chatham's intention. Lord Camden informed me that he was far from being well pleased, but did not enter into particulars, except that he considered my marriage to be quite political, and it was without effect that Lord Camden laboured to assure him that it was otherwise, and that he could answer that I was as desirous as ever of seeing his Lordship again taking the lead in the King's administration. This neglect on the part of Lord Chatham piqued me much; I had surely a claim to some notice on his recovery, when at his earnest solicitation I embarked in an arduous post when he was incapable of business of any sort; and if Lord Chatham had wished to receive the state of political matters, I hope that it is not saying too much that he ought to have requested it of me. He chose the contrary, and even in the King's outer room, where we met before the Levee, when I went up to him with civility and ease, he received me with cold politeness, and from St. James's called and left his name at my door.

On my returning home I took down a Minute of this

* These Memoirs are addressed to the Duke's eldest son, who afterwards succeeded him in the title.

occurrence of the day which I have preserved.* It runs thus:

"July 7. 1769. Lord Chatham waited on the King for the first time since his long confinement, was graciously received at the Levee, and was desired to stay after it was over, when the King sent for him into the Closet. His Majesty took the opportunity of assuring him how much he was concerned that the ill state of his health had been the occasion of his quitting the King's service. His Lordship answered that His Majesty must feel that in his infirm state he must have stood under the most embarrassing difficulties holding an office of such consequence, and unable to give his approbation to measures that he thought salutary, or his dissent to those which appeared to him to have another tendency; that he was unwilling to go into particulars, yet he could not think that one especially † had been managed in the manner it might have been, for if it had been despised thoroughly at the outset, it never could have been attended with the disagreeable consequences which have happened, but that it was now too late to look back.

"The Indian transaction was also found fault with. His Lordship, besides, observed that their General Courts were got upon the worst of footings, exercising the conduct of little Parliaments; that he wondered that the Inspectors were not sent to three different places. There were also other observations on the head of India.

"His Lordship added that he doubted whether his health would ever again allow him to attend Parliament, but if it did, and if he should give his dissent to any measure, that His Majesty would be indulgent enough to believe that it would not arise from any personal consideration, for he protested to His Majesty, as Lord Chatham he had not a tittle to find fault with in the conduct of any one individual; and that His Majesty might be assured that it could not arise from ambition, as he felt so strongly the weak state from which he was re-

* It is clear that the Duke must have derived this Minute from His Majesty's own mouth.

† An allusion to Wilkes's case.

covering, and which might daily threaten him, that office therefore of any sort could no longer be desirable to him."

From this time until the meeting of Parliament I saw no more of Lord Chatham. His suspicions of me were probably too firmly rooted to be removed by Lord Camden's assurances that they were groundless. His Lordship desired no further interview; and I had such a sense of the unkindness and injustice of such a treatment, where I thought that I had a claim to the most friendly, that I was not disposed to seek any explanation.

EARL OF CHATHAM TO EARL STANHOPE.

Chevening, July 25. 1769.

My dear Lord,

Though I have long forgot how to write, my hand, not quite out of flannel, will not refuse my long impatience to express a word of the warmest acknowledgment to Lord and Lady Stanhope for their kind goodness to us. We are here in the most delightful abode, where, with all due respect to the charms of the Lake of Geneva, we envy those fair regions nothing but what they detain from Chevening. The place is in high beauty, and the plenty of the year more than smiles about us; the fields, according to the sacred poet, laugh and sing. To retire from scenes without — the feast of the eye — to the noble feast of the mind within — your Lordship's admirable library, I have the pleasure to tell you that the books appear in perfect preservation, and speak the commendation of the care which has been taken of that valuable charge. Pitt was struck with admiration and some fear at the sight of so much learning; but I have relieved his apprehensions by assuring him that he may be the most learned gentleman in England, except Lord Stanhope, if he will read and remember the tenth of the books he sees there. Your Lordship will pardon a papa, I know, for talking of his boy, whose faculties to learn give me much comfort; amongst other things, he has aptness enough towards mathematics, and likes them well; the exercises of the body also (amongst which cricket is not forgot) he is not bad at. I trust he will follow, as well as he can, Lord Mahon in the career of letters, arts, and manly exercises, and I am sure I need not wish more for him. My poor William is still ailing, but, thank God, is much better, insomuch that we can venture to leave him without too great anxiety for a visit to Stowe, where we propose to go Thursday next, and to stay about a week.

I am ever, &c.

CHATHAM.

MR. JOHNSON, AGENT FOR CONNECTICUT, TO GOVERNOR TRUMBULL.

(*Extract.*)

London, March 6. 1770.

THIS letter has been already published by Mr. Jared Sparks, in a note to his edition of the works of Franklin (vol. vii. p. 467.). But it is here reproduced, since the whole topic of America is omitted in the meagre and imperfect report of Lord Chatham's speech of March 2. 1770, the celebrated speech against secret influence, as given in the "London Museum," and the "Parliamentary History."

Lord Chatham said in debate three nights before:

I have been thought to be, perhaps, too much the friend of America. I own I am a friend to that country. I love the Americans because they love liberty, and I love them for the noble efforts they made in the last war. But I must own I find fault with them in many things; I think they carry matters too far; they have been wrong in many respects. I think the idea of drawing money from them by taxes was ill-judged. Trade is your object with them, and they should be encouraged. But (I wish every sensible American, both here and in that country, heard what I say,) if they carry their notions of liberty too far, as I fear they do, if they will not be subject to the laws of this country, especially if they would disengage themselves from the laws of trade and navigation, of which I see too many symptoms, as much of an American as I am, they have not a more determined opposer than they will find in me. They must be subordinate. In all laws relating to trade and navigation especially this is the mother country, they are the children; they must obey, and we prescribe. It is necessary; for in these cases between two countries so circumstanced as these two are, there must be something more than connection, there must be subordination, there must be obedience, there must be dependence. And if you do not make laws for them, let me tell you, my Lords, they do, they will, they must make laws for you.

EARL OF CHATHAM TO EARL STANHOPE.

Hayes, July 9. 1770.

My dear Lord,

The thoughts of your Lordship's friends at Hayes are certainly often in motion towards Geneva. We trust you found Lady Stanhope and Lord Mahon in perfect health; and we figure you all rejoicing in the long interrupted re-union, happy in yourselves, and in pain only for our country. The dangers of it seem to be growing, and to keep pace with the incapacity and iniquity of administration. If the perils increase, on all sides, thank God, the spirit of the City does not sink under the pressure of our late irreparable loss there.* The contemptuous rejection of the tools of the Court, and the honest and wise choice of the friends of the Constitution, promise such a stand for liberty as neither intimidation nor corruption will baffle. Liberty will not, I think, succumb; but the honour and greatness of England must, I fear, sink in the hands of such pilots as ours. How we are viewed abroad, your Lordship's situation gives you

* The death of the Lord Mayor (Alderman Beckford), June 21. 1770.

to see and hear abundantly; and for imbecility at home, I can pretty well answer for that. The late doctrines from the Bench, concerning the rights of juries to judge of *Law* and *Fact*, have spread universal alarm, and raised the justest indignation. This is laying the axe to the root with a vengeance! Jurors who may not judge, electors who may not elect, and suffering subjects who *ought not* to petition for relief, will compose a pretty system of English Government. The Father of Orleans would blush to own it. David Hume may, perhaps, apologize for it. But why all this to my Noble friend? whose mind forestalls the picture, and whose heart glows for redress. That day will, I doubt not, come, though *pede claudo*.

. . . .

I am ever, with the truest esteem,
your most devoted friend and kinsman,
CHATHAM.

EARL OF ROCHFORD TO MR. MURRAY, AMBASSADOR AT CONSTANTINOPLE.

St. James's, July 24. 1772.

SIR,

YOUR letters to No. 11. have been received and laid before the King.

I am sorry not to be able to convey to your Excellency that approbation which you wish to obtain on the late step you have taken towards the Porte, but, on the contrary, to have the disagreeable task of acquainting you that His Majesty and his Ministers could not but consider as an extraordinary misapprehension of your duty the advice you have, on your own speculation upon the intended dismemberment of Poland, taken upon you to give to the Porte, tending directly to retard the conclusion of that pacification which it has been His Majesty's constant wish to accelerate as much as possible. The King is disposed for his own part, in consideration of your long and faithful services, to overlook this error; but if it should be made a ground of complaint against you by the Court of Petersburg, as is too probable, it will be difficult to find a vindication of so unfriendly a conduct in his Ambassador. As to the extraordinary and unexpected event of a partition of Poland by three Powers who appeared some time since very unlikely to combine together for that object, I am to inform you that, although such a change suggests not improbable apprehensions that the trade of Europe may hereafter be affected by it, neither His Majesty nor the other Commercial Powers have thought it of such present importance as to make a direct opposition to it, or enter into action (as your Excellency supposes necessary) to prevent it. The King is still less inclined to try the indirect method of encouraging the continuance of a Turkish war, which, exclusive of the evils it carries with it of interruption of commerce, devastation, and pestilence, could by no means answer the end in a manner desirable to Great Britain. For if carried on successfully by Russia, the Porte must be more and more unable to interfere in regard to the independence of Poland, and if unsuccessfully, it must greatly weaken an empire which, although there has not been lately shown on their part that openness and confidence in His Majesty which he justly deserves, he cannot but look upon, nevertheless, as the natural ally of his Crown, and with which he is likely sooner or later to be closely connected.

. . . .

I am, &c.

ROCHFORD.

THE EMPRESS MARIA THERESA TO HER PRIME MINISTER PRINCE KAUNITZ ON THE SCHEME FOR THE PARTITION OF POLAND, 1772.

THIS document, so honourable to the feelings of Maria Theresa, was first published in her own original bad German by Von Hormayr (Taschen-buch, 1831, p. 66.), and is re-produced by Preuss (Lebens-Geschichte, vol. iv. p. 38.). I have attempted to translate it as follows:

"When all my lands were invaded, and when I did not even know where I could in quiet give birth to my child, then I firmly relied on my own good right and on the help of God. But in this present affair, when the public right is clearly* against us, and when against us also are all justice and sound reason, I must own that never in my whole life before did I feel so anxious, and that I am ashamed to let myself be seen. Let the Prince (Kaunitz) consider what an example we shall be giving to the whole world, if for a wretched piece of Poland or of Wallachia we give up our honour and fair fame. I plainly perceive that I stand alone, and am no longer *en vigueur;* therefore I let things, but not without the greatest grief, go their own way.

M. TH."

When the scheme of partition was afterwards more formally, and as the draft of a treaty, laid before the Empress, she wrote with her own hand upon the margin:

"*Placet*, because so many great and learned men will have it so; but long after I am dead and gone, people will see what will happen from having thus broken through everything that has hitherto been held holy and just.

M. TH."

DR. PRICE TO THE EARL OF CHATHAM.

(*Extract.*)

Newington Green, March 11. 1773.

YOUR Lordship probably well knows that the body of Protestant Dissenting Ministers are applying again to Parliament. A Bill for tolerating them was last night read a second time in the House of Commons. The opposition to it there is so feeble that we doubt not but that it will pass. In the House of Lords, where probably we shall be in three weeks or a month, our prospect is

* The German word is much stronger, *himmel-schreyend,* "crying "out to Heaven" against us.

indeed dark and doubtful. But it would be less so could we entertain any hope of being again distinguished by your Lordship's attendance and support. This would again dignify our defeat, and go a great way towards reconciling us to our lot, but we all know that we cannot expect the repetition of such a favour. The honours done us, and the obligation conferred upon us, last year by your Lordship, will never be forgotten by us. The zeal your Lordship then expressed for our rights as men and Christians, or (to use your Lordship's striking language) for *Toleration, that sacred right of nature and bulwark of truth, and most interesting of all objects to fallible man*, will be always mentioned with admiration and gratitude among us. We have made a few alterations in this year's Bill, but there are none of particular consequence, except the following. Instead of repealing the subscription to the Articles, the present Bill continues it, and only enacts that if any scruple it they shall be entitled to the benefits of the Toleration Act, if (besides taking the Oaths of Allegiance and Supremacy and renouncing Popery) they shall subscribe a declaration, *that they are Christians and Protestants, and receive the revelation of the will of God contained in the Scriptures of the Old and New Testament as the rule of their faith and practice.* We have thought that offering this alternative would have the appearance of greater respect to the Articles, and also tend to conciliate the Bishops. We have determined to apply this Session, partly because the public attention to the subject is now fresh, but principally because we thought it would appear more respectful to Government to apply now rather than the next Session, and just at the eve of a General Election.

Your Lordship has, I suppose, heard of a petition against us which has been presented to the House of Commons, and has originated with a set of lay-preachers in and about London who don't belong to the body of Dissenting Ministers, and whom most of us never heard of before. It is signed by 1,012 persons, most of them Methodists and persons in the lowest stations. They were to have been heard by their Counsel yesterday, but Mr. Perrin, whom they had retained, having returned his brief and disappointed them, a motion was made for granting them farther time, which was rejected by a great majority.

They pray for relief, and the only relief they can want is that we may not be relieved.

EXTRACTS OF LETTERS FROM KING GEORGE THE THIRD TO LORD NORTH.

1770—1774.

THE original letters from King George the Third to Lord North as his Prime Minister were laid before Sir James Mackintosh, who extracting the most important passages transcribed them in a manuscript volume. This afterwards passed into the hands of Lord North's surviving daughter, Lady Charlotte Lindsay; and from her into those of Lord Brougham. Through the friendly regard of Lady Charlotte, and in the year 1847, I obtained the communication of that volume; Lady Charlotte at the same time giving me full permission to make any use of it I might deem proper. I have accordingly selected several passages for this and many more for my next volume. M.

January 23. 1770.

LORD Weymouth and Lord Gower will wait upon you this morning to press you in the strongest manner to accept the offer of First Lord Commissioner of the Treasury. My mind is more and more strengthened in the rightness of the measure, which would prevent every other desertion. You must easily see that if you do not accept I have no Peer at present that I would consent to place in the Duke of Grafton's employment.

February 1. 1770.

A MAJORITY of forty on the old ground, at least ten times before, is a very favourable auspice on your taking the lead in administration. A little spirit will soon restore order in my service. I am glad to find Sir Gilbert Elliot has again spoke.

February 21. 1771.

I HAVE very much considered the affair of the printers, and in the strongest manner recommend that every caution may be used to prevent its becoming a serious business. It is highly necessary that this strange and lawless method of publishing debates in the papers should be put a stop to. But is not the House of Lords the best Court to bring such miscreants before, as it can fine as well as imprison, and has broader shoulders to support the odium of so salutary a measure?

February 28. 1771.

THE gaining the Court of Sweden is no real object for this country. If after considerable expense that is effected, it will be impossible to keep her friendship without a subsidy, for that Power cannot subsist without foreign money. Besides, as there is no public mode of obtaining the money expended in that corruption, it must be taken from my Civil List, and consequently new debts incurred, and when I apply to Parliament for them an odium is cast upon me as if the money had been expended in bribing Parliament. I therefore think we ought only to feed the Opposition to France, to prevent that Crown from carrying material points.

March 17. 1771.

IF Lord Mayor and Oliver be not committed the authority of the House of Commons is annihilated. Send Jenkinson to Lord Mansfield for his opinion of the best way of enforcing the commitment, if these people continue to disobey. You know very well I was averse to meddling with the printers, but now there is no retreating. The honour of the Commons must be supported.

January 2. 1772.

MR. ALLEN is only an additional proof of that aversion to the English Government *, and of that avowed profligacy, that the gentlemen of that country seem to despise masking with the name of Conscience, and must sooner or later oblige this country seriously to consider whether the uniting to this Crown would not be the only means of making both islands flourish.

March 12. 1772.

UNLESS my impression of the absence of Colonel Burgoyne and Lieutenant Colonel Harcourt from yesterday's division had been corrected, I certainly should have thought myself obliged to have named a new Governor instead of the former, and to have removed the other from my Bedchamber.

March 14. 1772.

I WISH a list to be prepared of those that went away, and of those that deserted to the minority. That will be a rule for my conduct in the Drawing Room tomorrow.

* In Ireland.

THE END OF THE FIFTH VOLUME.

www.ingramcontent.com/pod-product-compliance
Lightning Source LLC
LaVergne TN
LVHW020116110826
845151LV00001B/169

* 9 7 8 1 4 2 5 5 4 2 9 5 5 *